ABOUT THE ARTIST

Born in 1936, Kazuo Umezu is Japan's most respected and influential horror manga artist. Umezu began his artistic career at the age of 18, creating stories for both *shôjo* (girls) and *shonen* (boys) manga magazines, and working in an amazingly diverse range of genres. In Japan he is most famous for the gag manga *Makoto-chan* (1971), but his most ambitious works are horror and science fiction, including *The Drifting Classroom* (1972-1974), *My Name is Shingo* (1982-1986), *The Left Hand of God, the Right Hand of the Devil* (1986-1989) and *Fourteen* (1990-1995). His works have been adapted into anime and live-action films.

THE DRIFTING CLASSROOM
Vol. 10

STORY AND ART BY KAZUO UMEZU

Translation/Yuji Oniki
Touch-up Art & Lettering/Kelle Han
Design/Izumi Evers
Editor/Jason Thompson

Editor in Chief, Books/Alvin Lu
Editor in Chief, Magazines/Marc Weidenbaum
VP of Publishing Licensing/Rika Inouye
VP of Sales/Gonzalo Ferreyra
Sr. VP of Marketing/Liza Coppola
Publisher/Hyoe Narita

Printed in the U.S.A.

Published by VIZ Media, LLC
P.O. Box 77010
San Francisco, CA 94107

10 9 8 7 6 5 4 3 2 1
First printing, February 2008

www.viz.com
store.viz.com

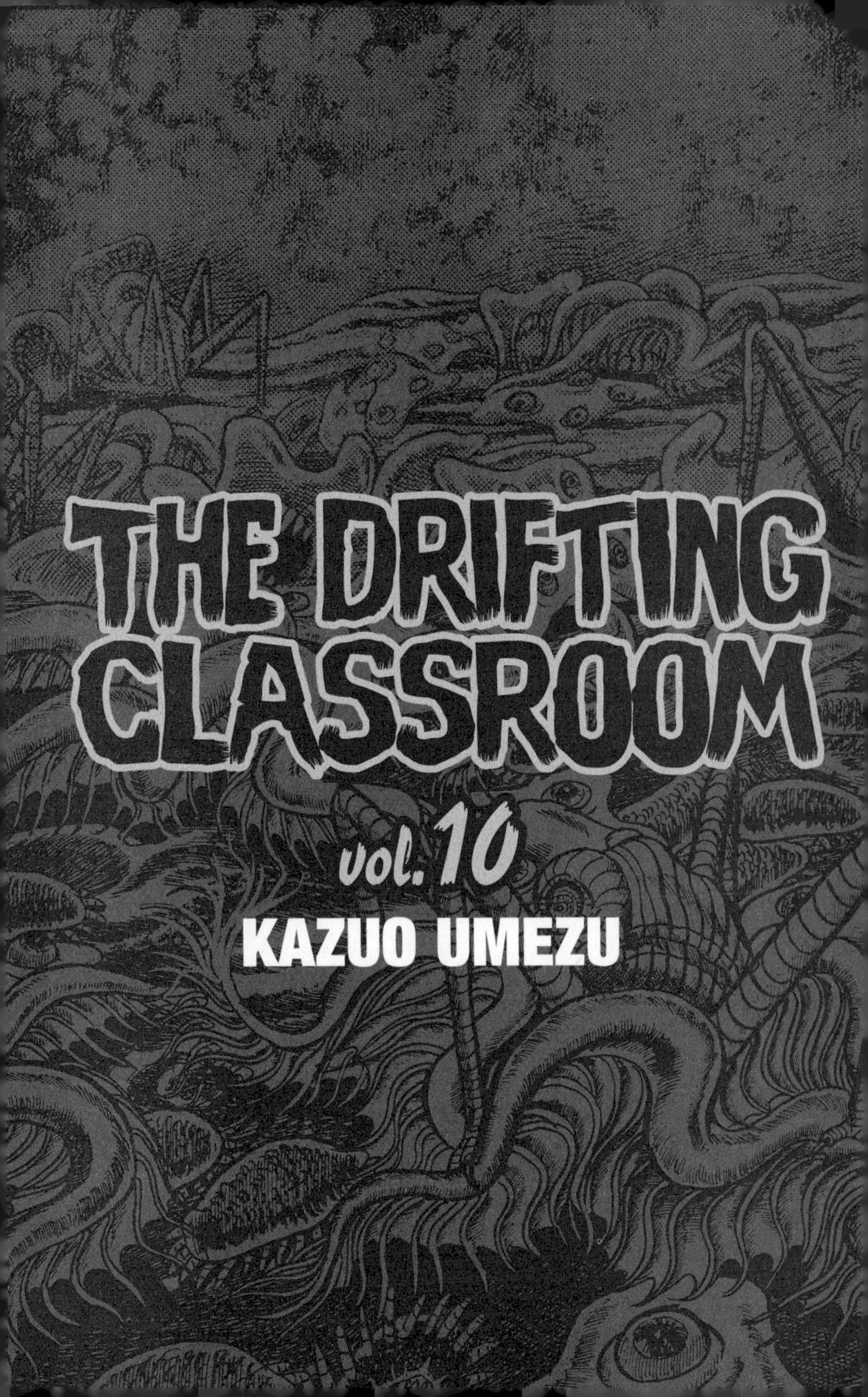

THE DRIFTING CLASSROOM

vol. 10

KAZUO UMEZU

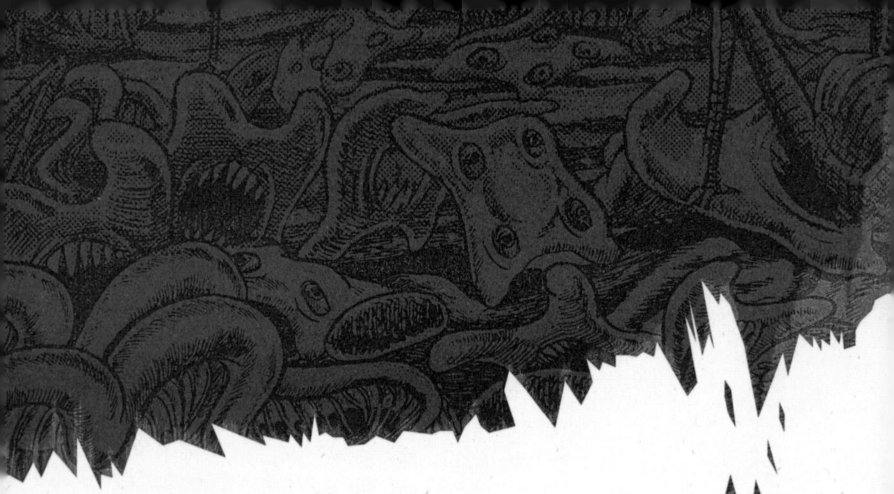

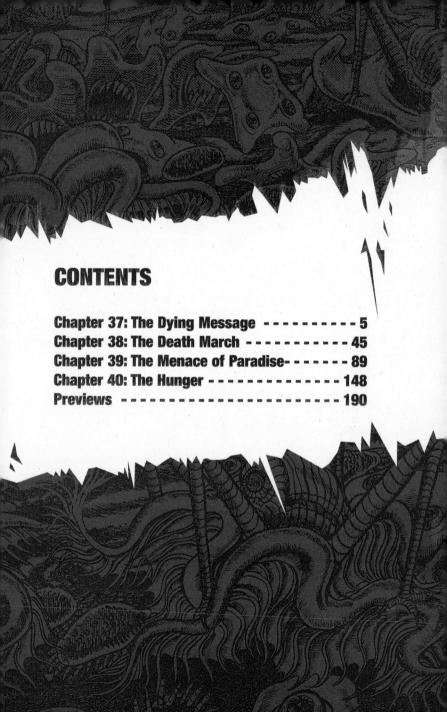

CONTENTS

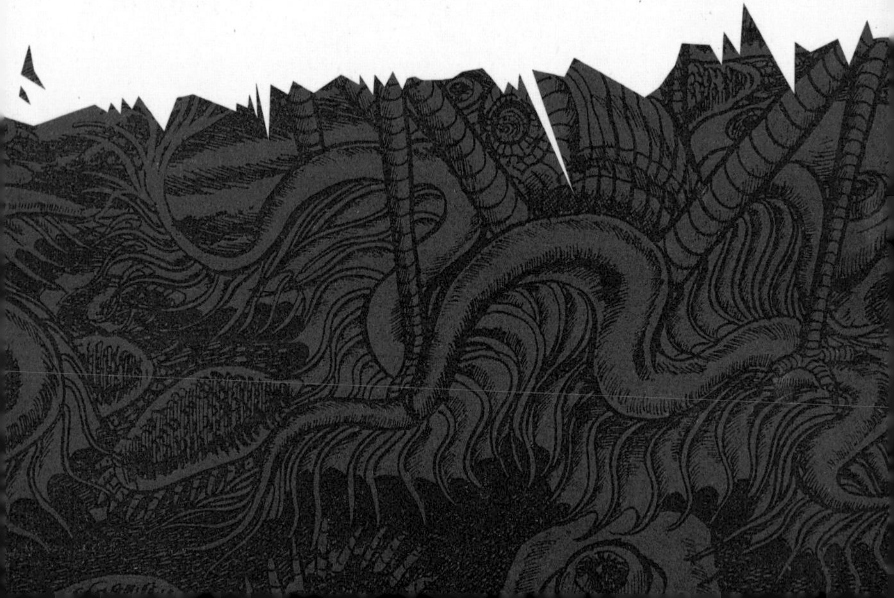

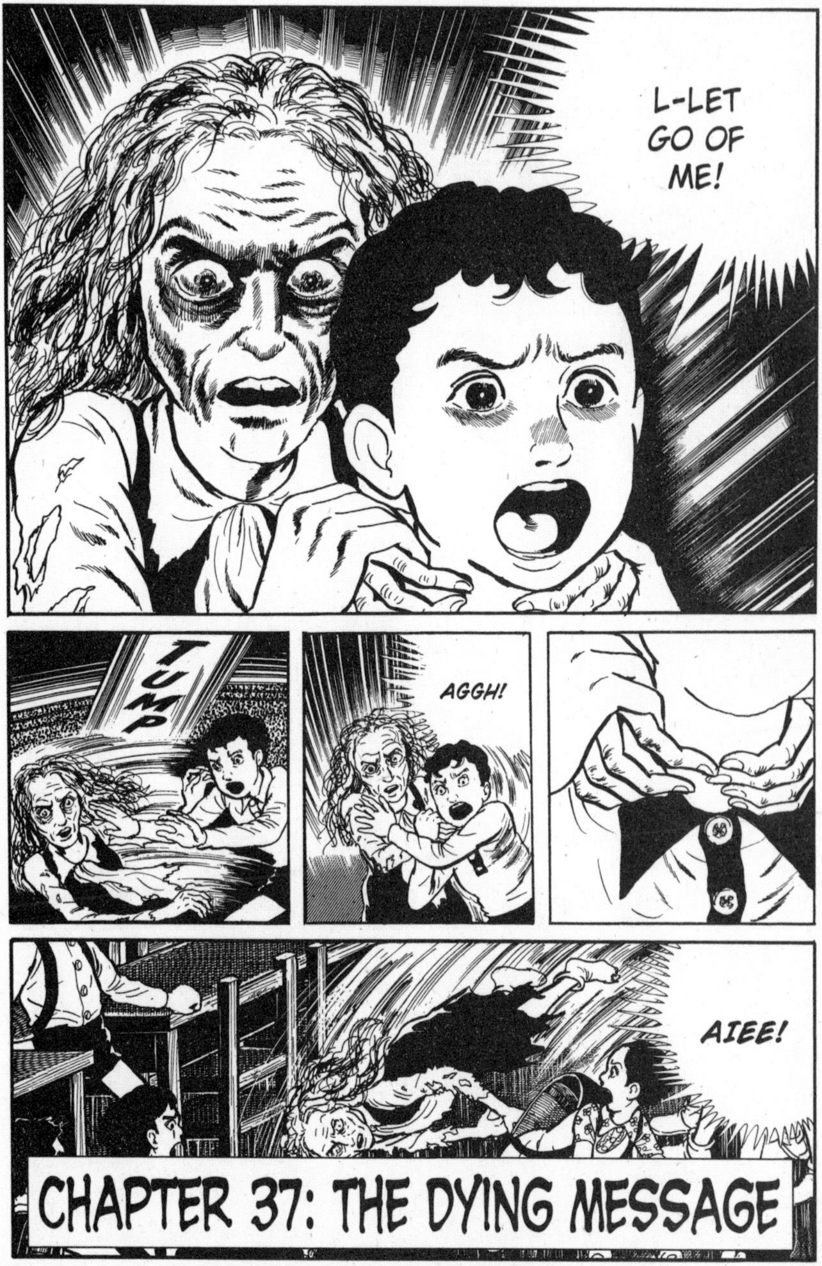
L-LET GO OF ME!
AGGH!
TUMP
AIEE!
CHAPTER 37: THE DYING MESSAGE

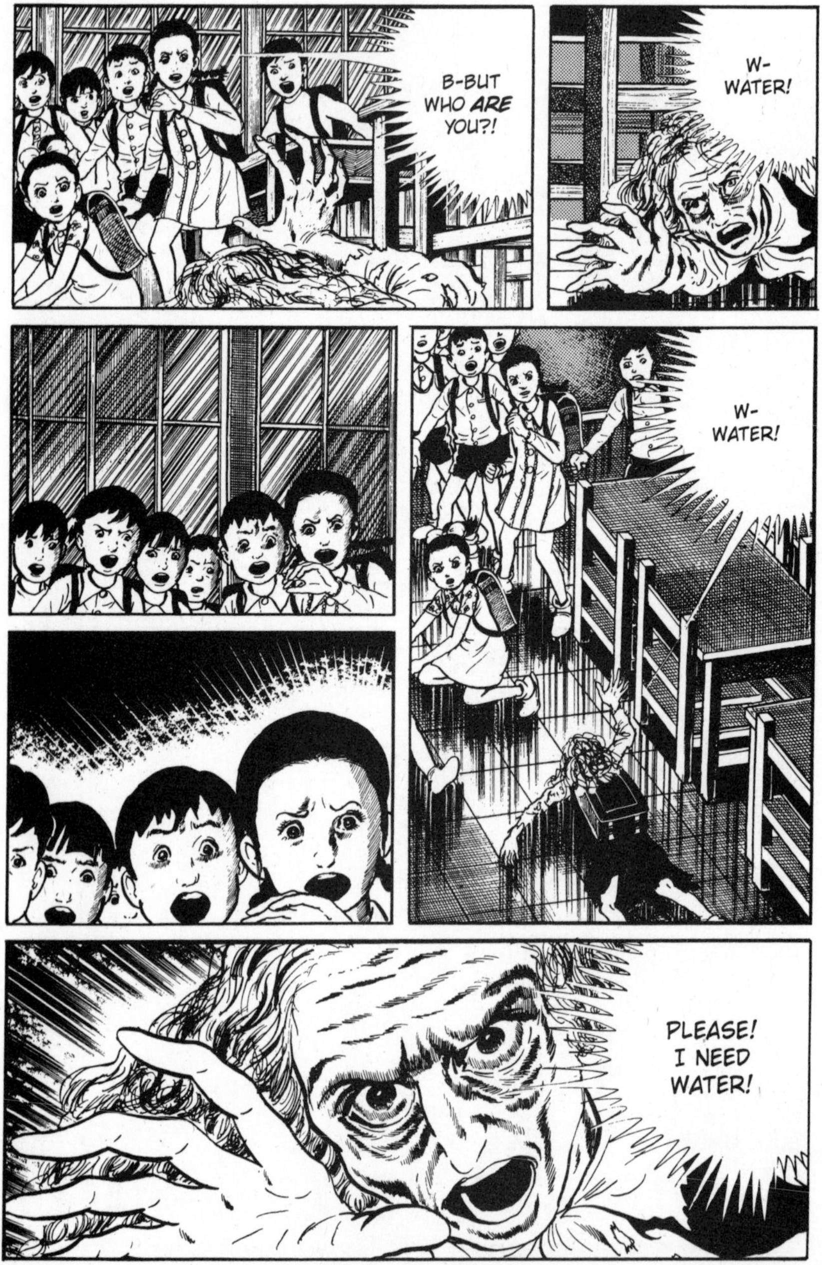
W- WATER!
B-BUT WHO ARE YOU?!
W- WATER!
PLEASE! I NEED WATER!

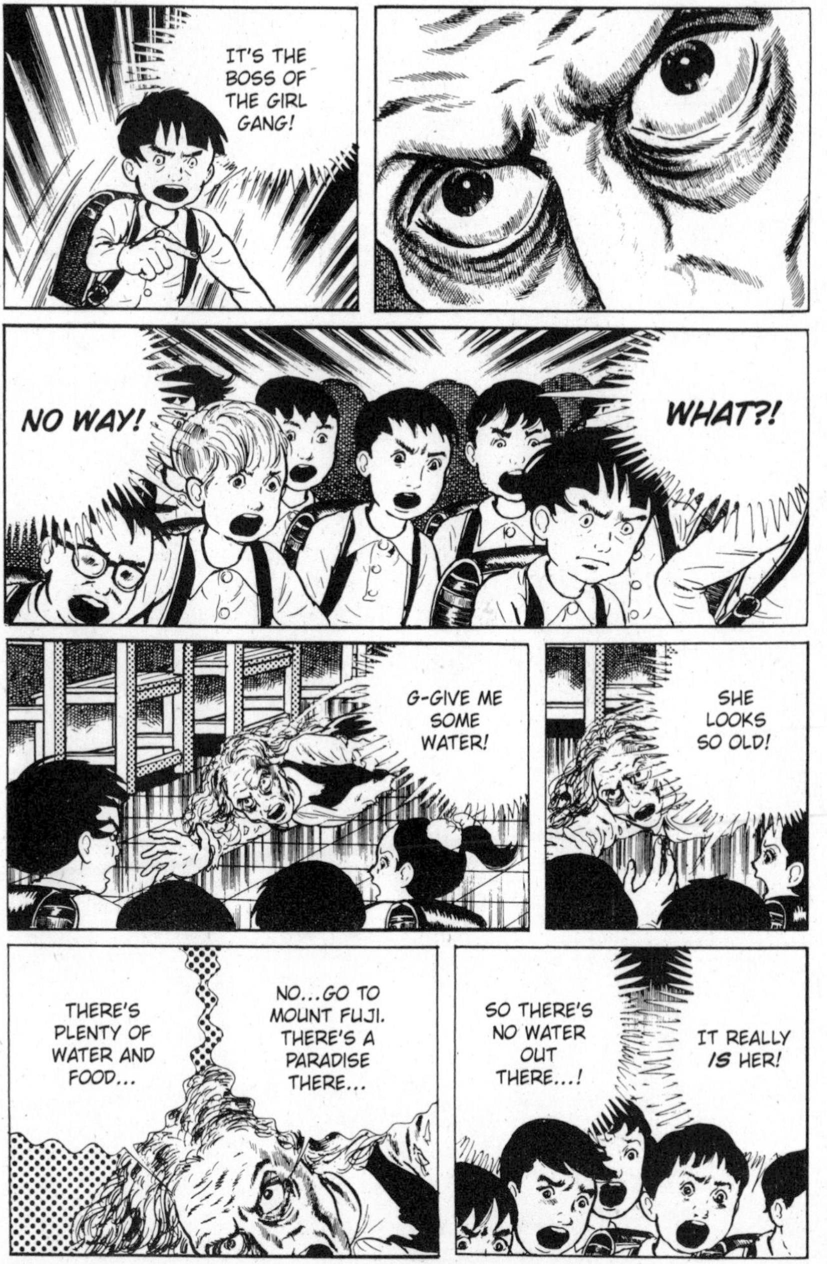
IT'S THE BOSS OF THE GIRL GANG!
WHAT?!
NO WAY!
SHE LOOKS SO OLD!
G-GIVE ME SOME WATER!
IT REALLY *IS* HER!
SO THERE'S NO WATER OUT THERE...!
NO...GO TO MOUNT FUJI. THERE'S A PARADISE THERE...
THERE'S PLENTY OF WATER AND FOOD...

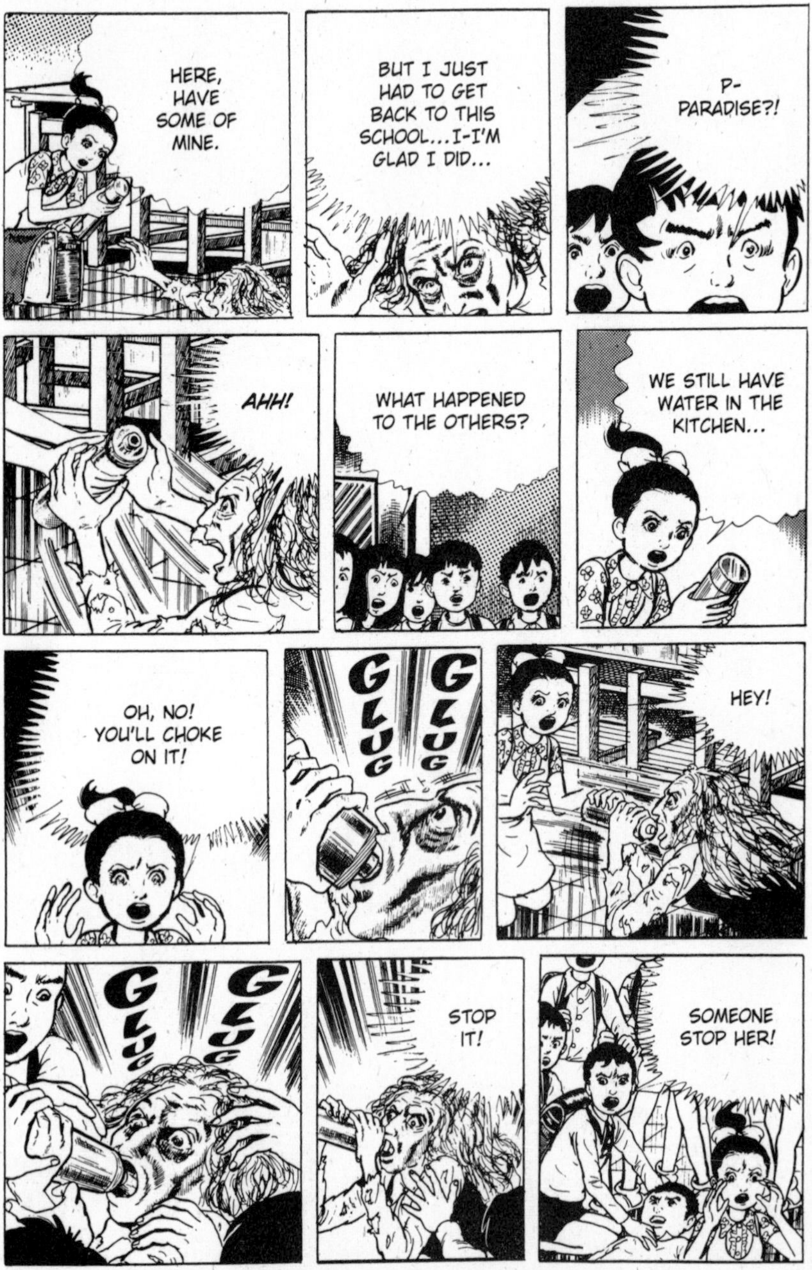
P-PARADISE?!
BUT I JUST HAD TO GET BACK TO THIS SCHOOL...I-I'M GLAD I DID...
HERE, HAVE SOME OF MINE.
WE STILL HAVE WATER IN THE KITCHEN...
WHAT HAPPENED TO THE OTHERS?
AHH!
HEY!
GLUG
GLUG
OH, NO! YOU'LL CHOKE ON IT!
SOMEONE STOP HER!
STOP IT!
GLUG
GLUG

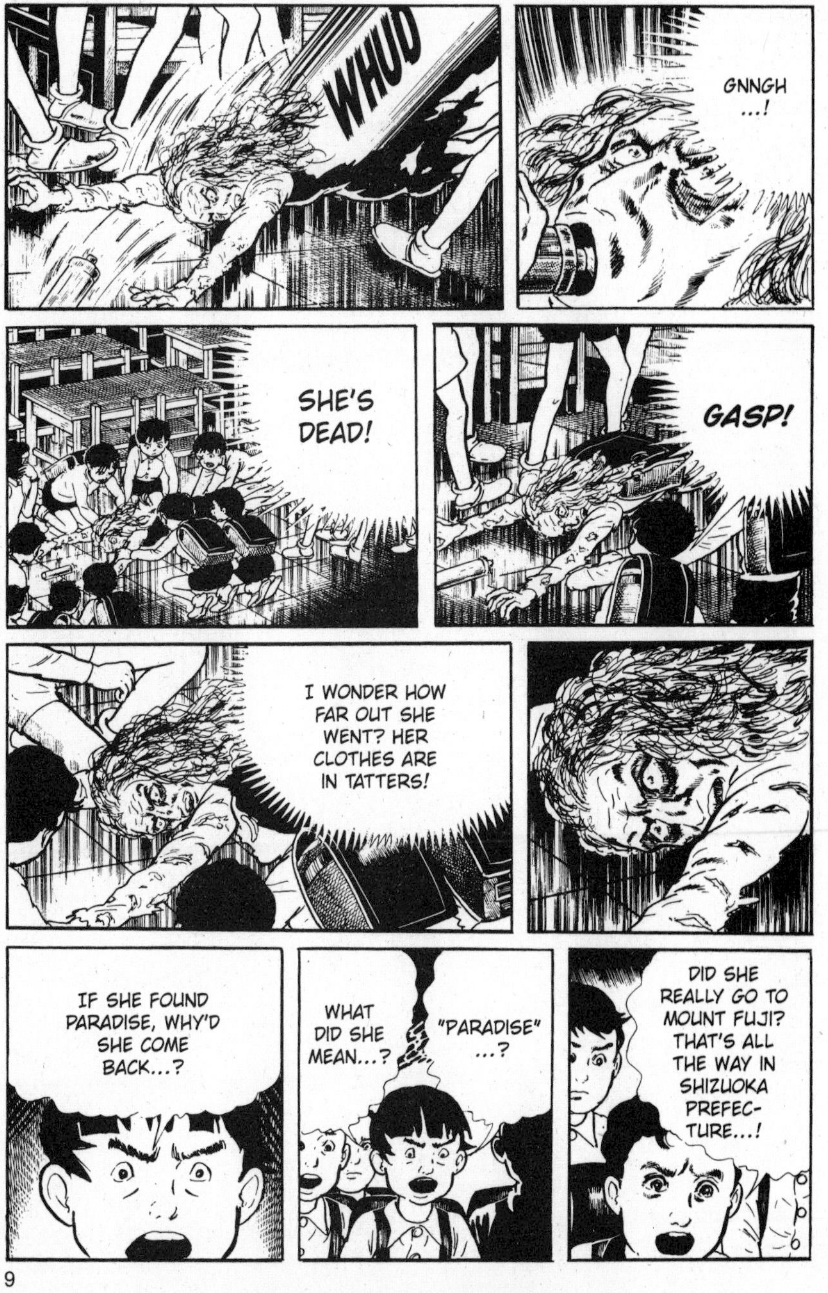
GNNGH ...!
WHUD
GASP!
SHE'S DEAD!
I WONDER HOW FAR OUT SHE WENT? HER CLOTHES ARE IN TATTERS!
DID SHE REALLY GO TO MOUNT FUJI? THAT'S ALL THE WAY IN SHIZUOKA PREFEC-TURE...!
"PARADISE" ...?
WHAT DID SHE MEAN...?
IF SHE FOUND PARADISE, WHY'D SHE COME BACK...?

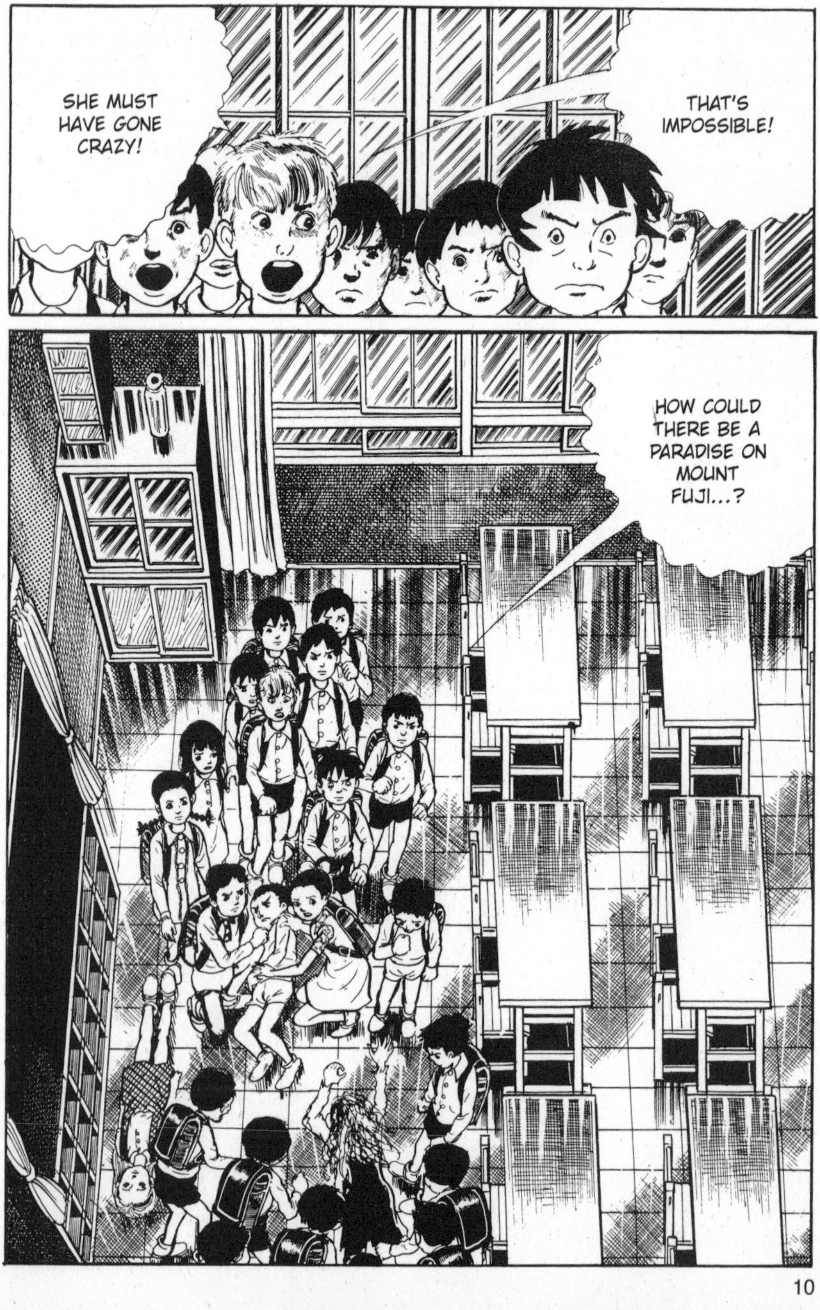
THAT'S IMPOSSIBLE!
SHE MUST HAVE GONE CRAZY!
HOW COULD THERE BE A PARADISE ON MOUNT FUJI...?

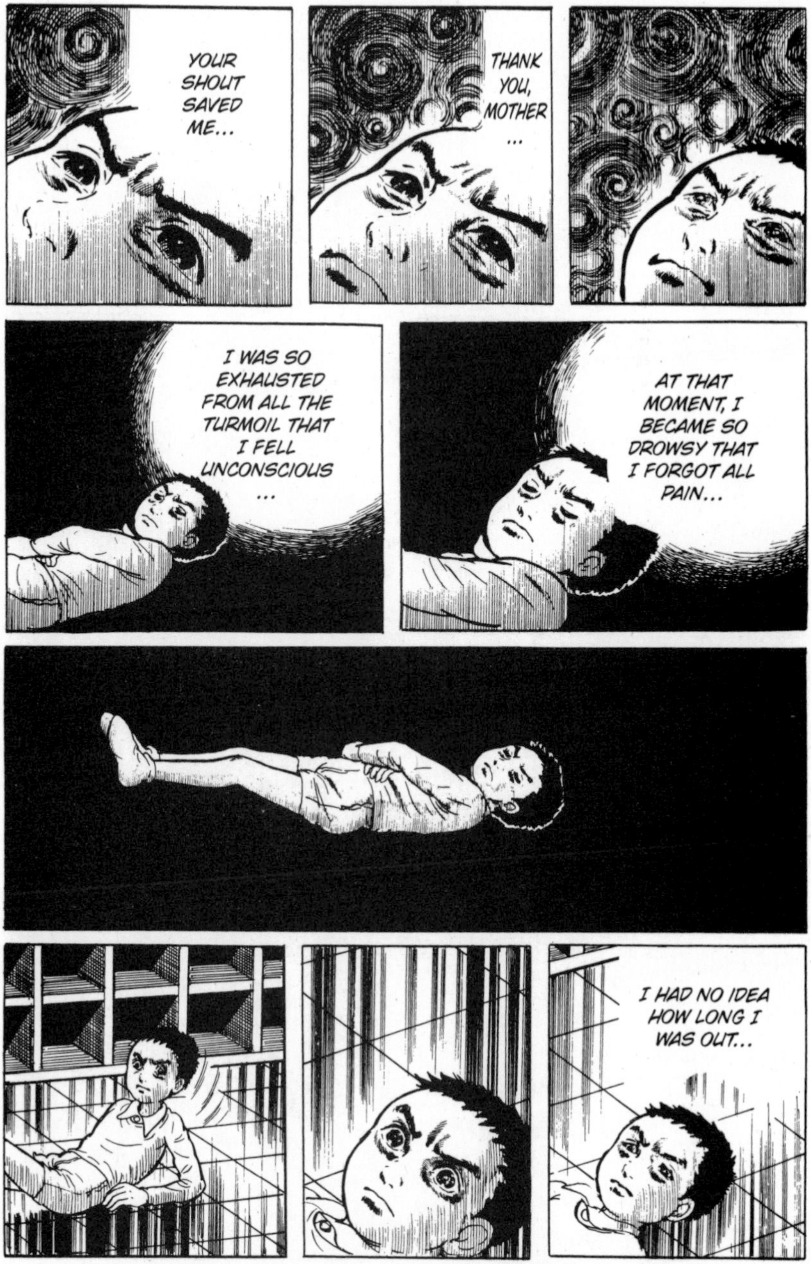
THANK YOU, MOTHER ...
YOUR SHOUT SAVED ME...
AT THAT MOMENT, I BECAME SO DROWSY THAT I FORGOT ALL PAIN...
I WAS SO EXHAUSTED FROM ALL THE TURMOIL THAT I FELL UNCONSCIOUS ...
I HAD NO IDEA HOW LONG I WAS OUT...

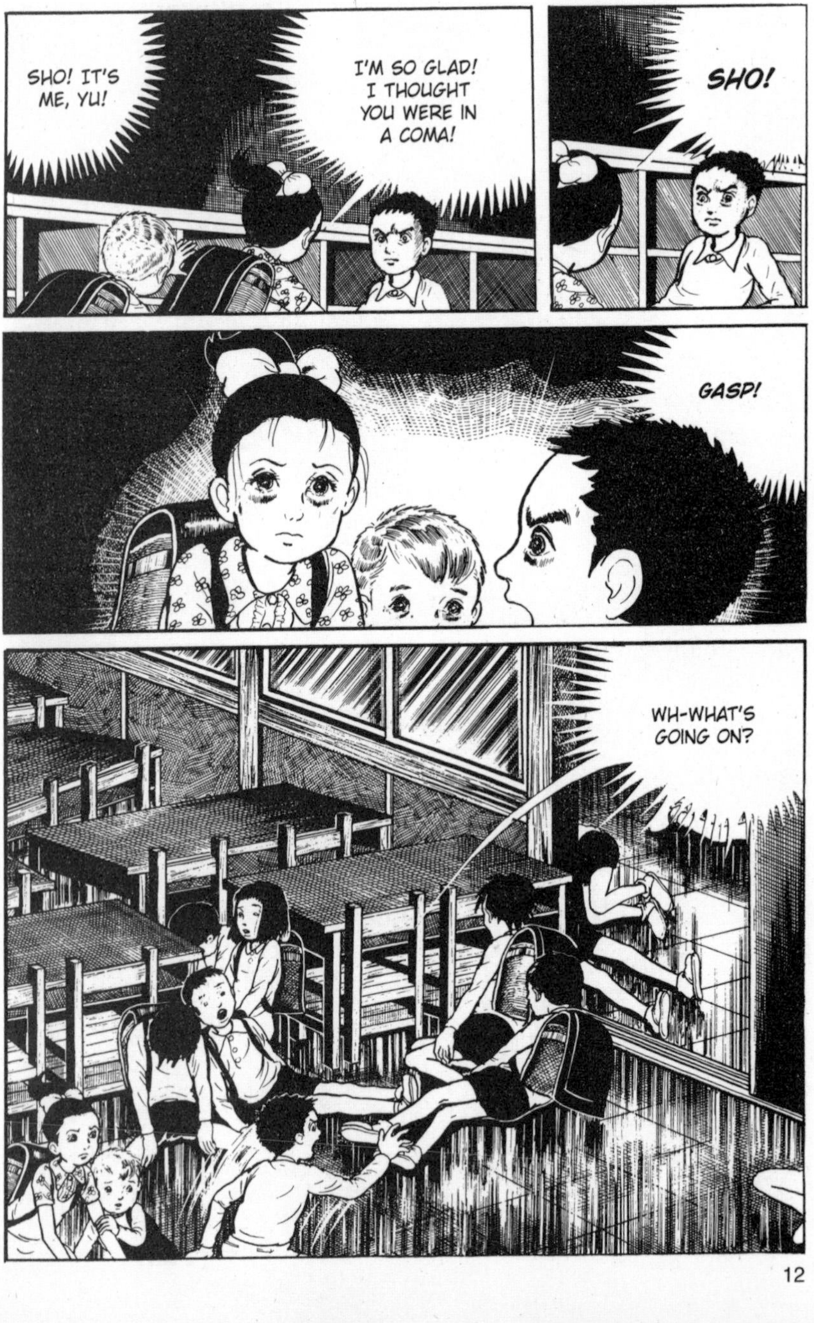
SHO!
I'M SO GLAD! I THOUGHT YOU WERE IN A COMA!
SHO! IT'S ME, YU!
GASP!
WH-WHAT'S GOING ON?

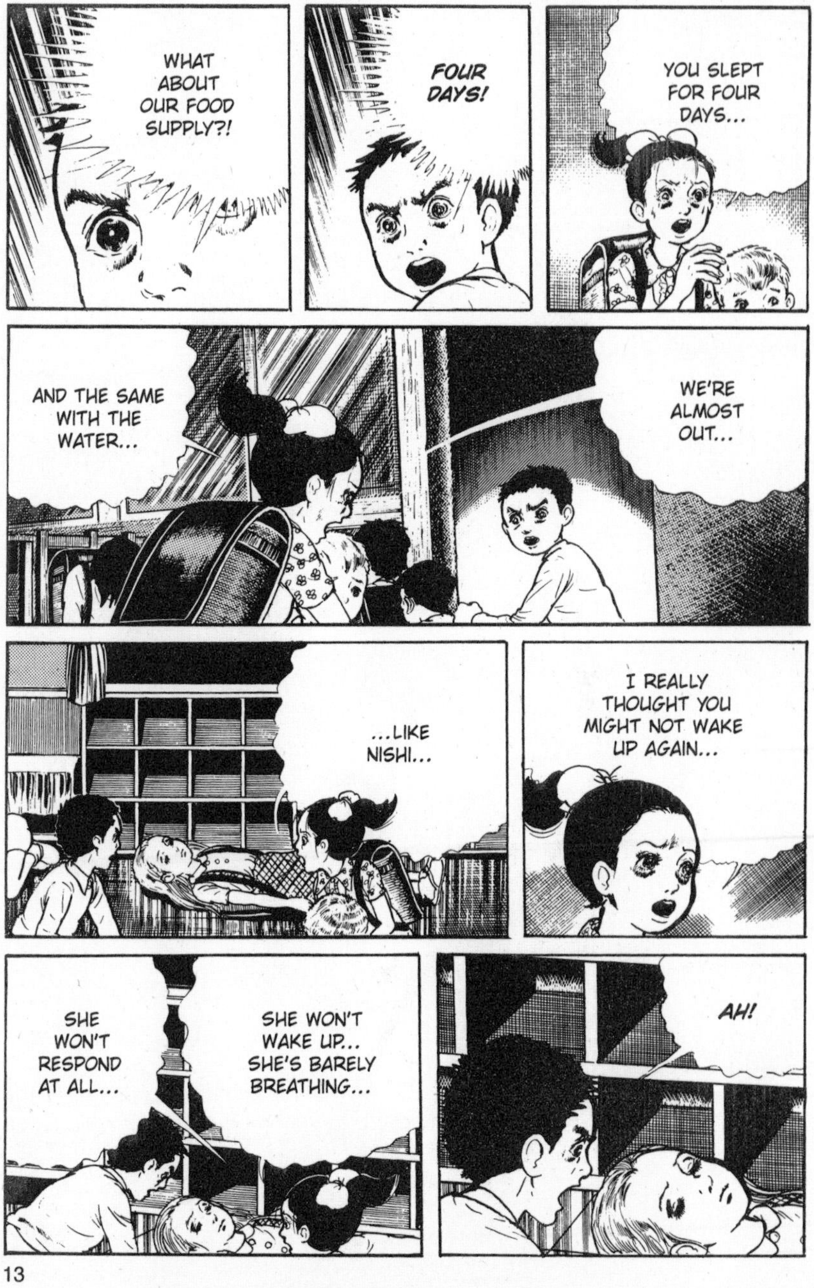
YOU SLEPT FOR FOUR DAYS...
FOUR DAYS!
WHAT ABOUT OUR FOOD SUPPLY?!
WE'RE ALMOST OUT...
AND THE SAME WITH THE WATER...
I REALLY THOUGHT YOU MIGHT NOT WAKE UP AGAIN...
...LIKE NISHI...
AH!
SHE WON'T WAKE UP... SHE'S BARELY BREATHING...
SHE WON'T RESPOND AT ALL...

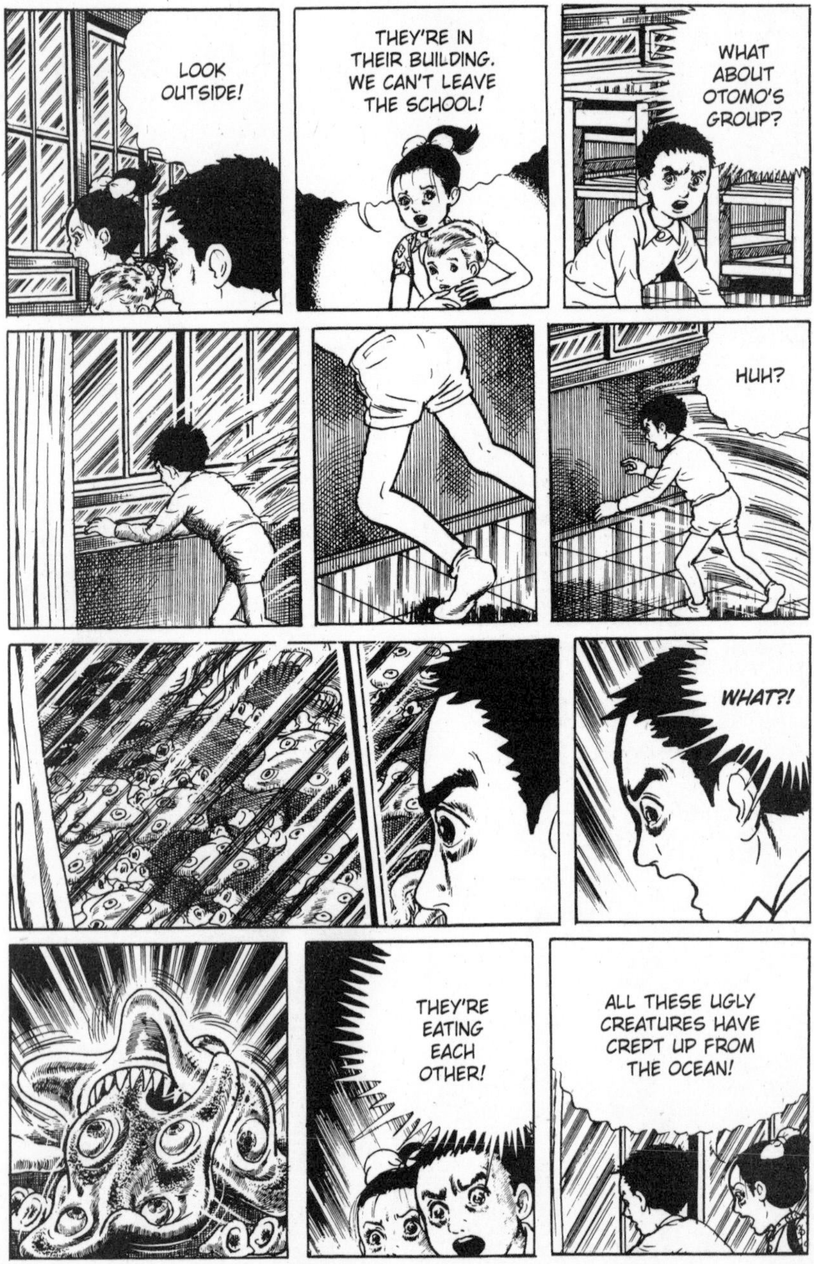
WHAT ABOUT OTOMO'S GROUP?
THEY'RE IN THEIR BUILDING. WE CAN'T LEAVE THE SCHOOL!
LOOK OUTSIDE!
HUH?
WHAT?!
ALL THESE UGLY CREATURES HAVE CREPT UP FROM THE OCEAN!
THEY'RE EATING EACH OTHER!

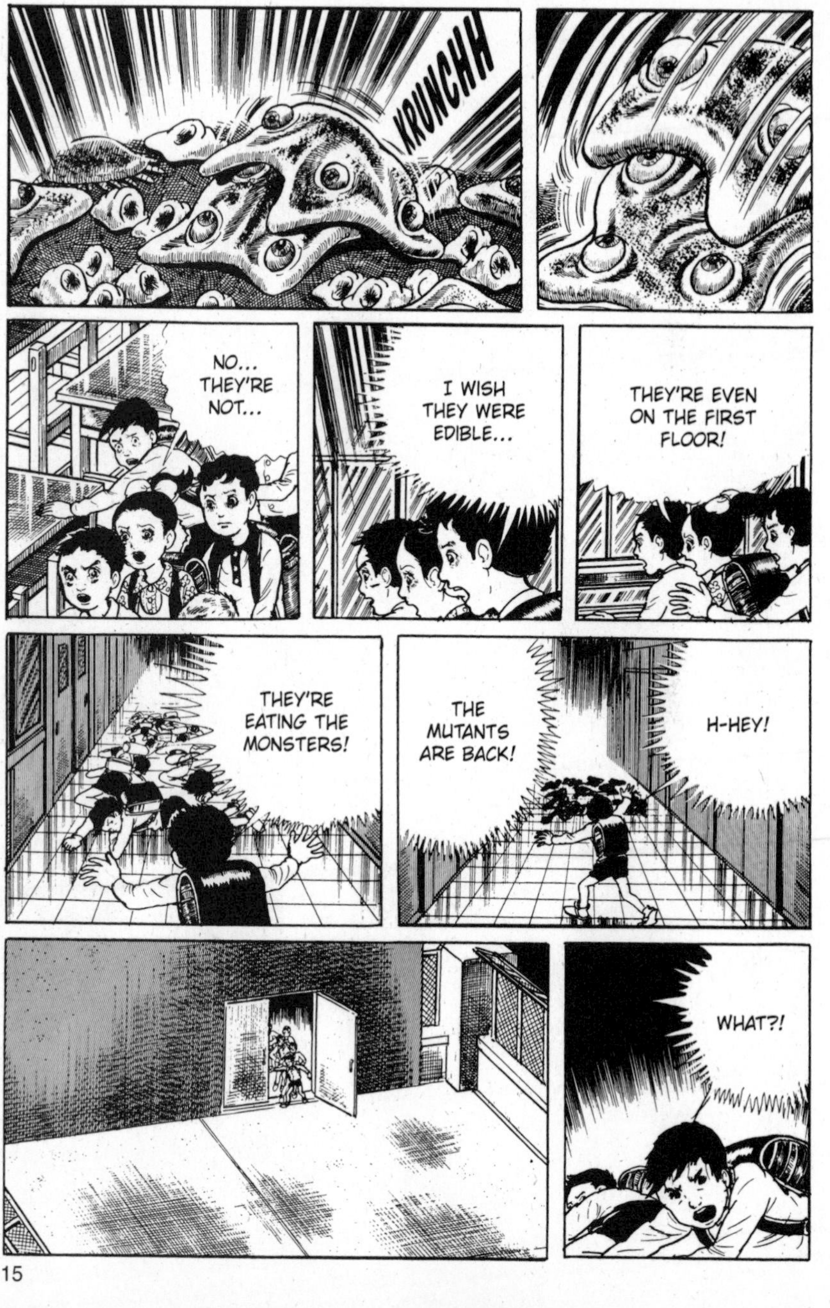
KRUNCHH
THEY'RE EVEN ON THE FIRST FLOOR!
I WISH THEY WERE EDIBLE...
NO... THEY'RE NOT...
H-HEY!
THE MUTANTS ARE BACK!
THEY'RE EATING THE MONSTERS!
WHAT?!

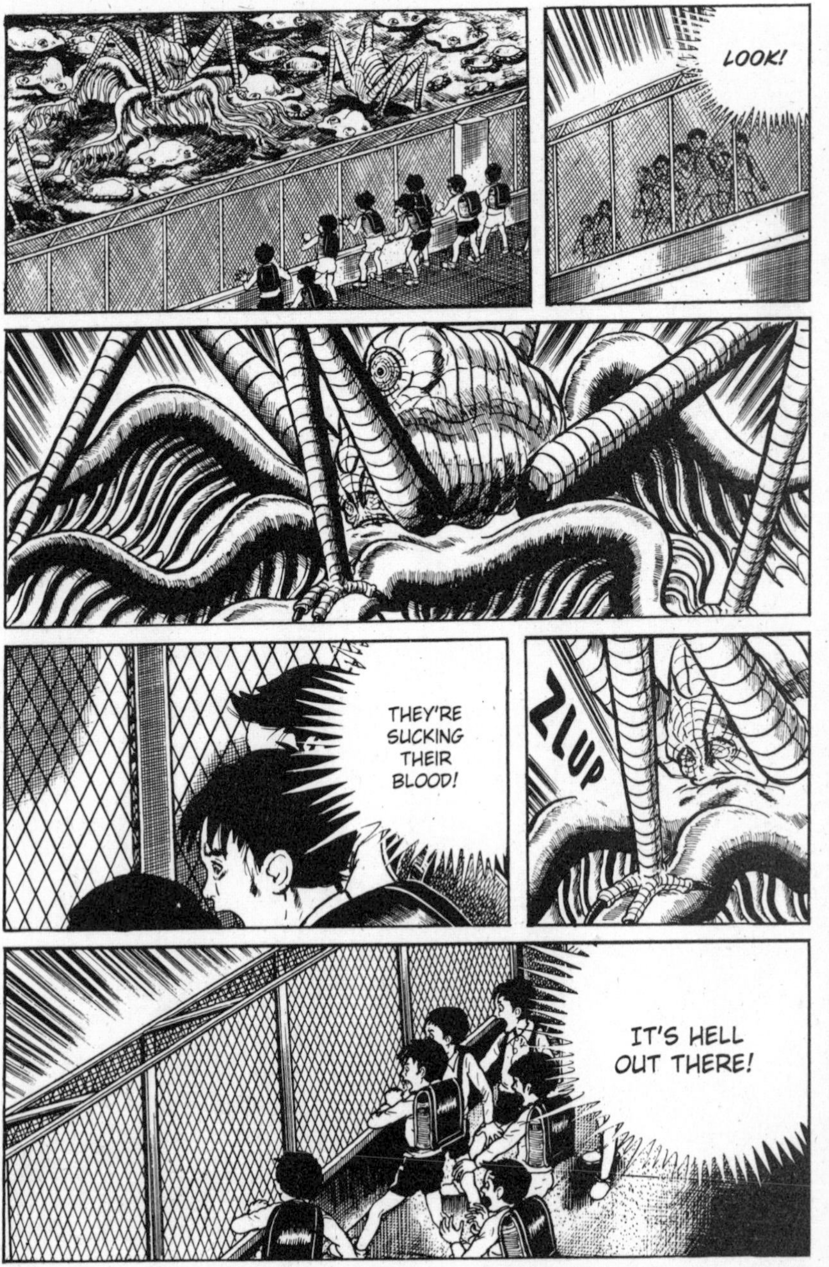
LOOK!
ZLUP
THEY'RE SUCKING THEIR BLOOD!
IT'S HELL OUT THERE!

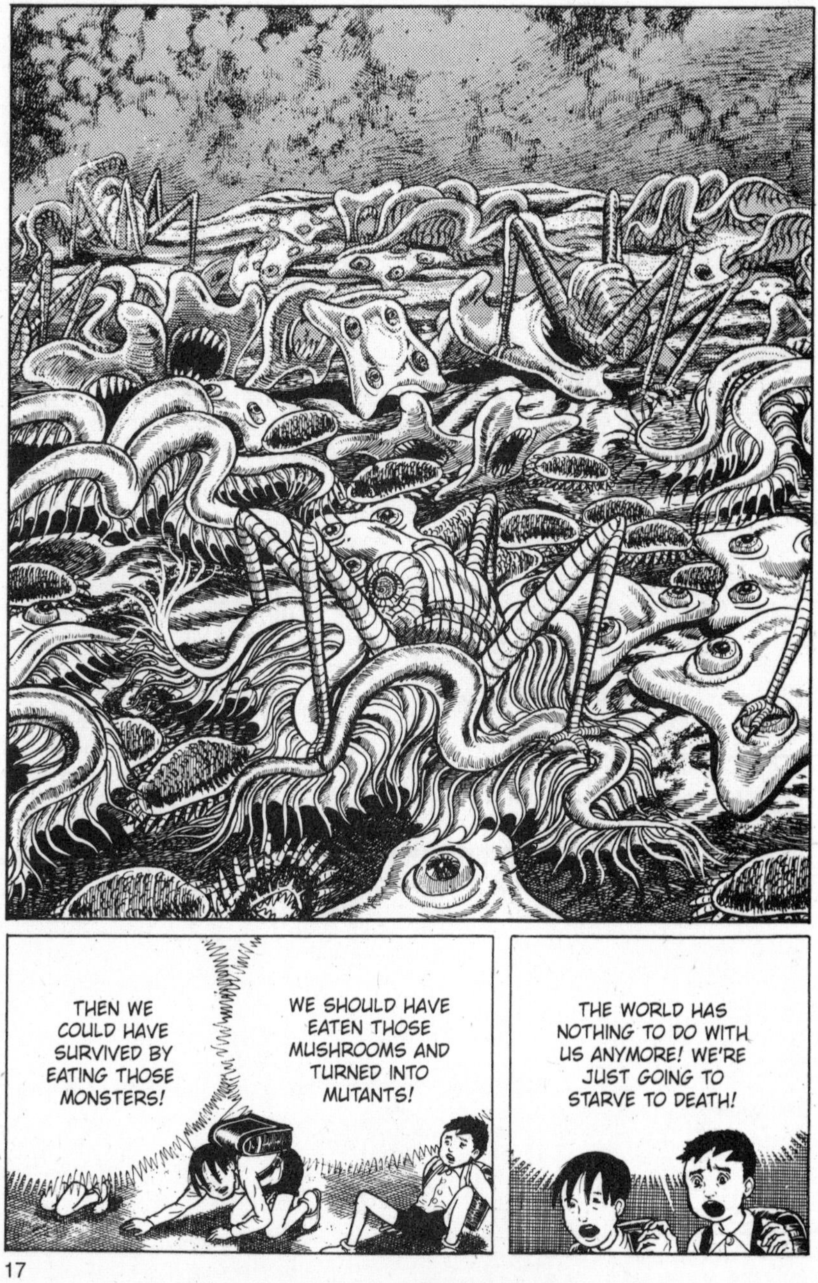
THE WORLD HAS NOTHING TO DO WITH US ANYMORE! WE'RE JUST GOING TO STARVE TO DEATH!
WE SHOULD HAVE EATEN THOSE MUSHROOMS AND TURNED INTO MUTANTS!
THEN WE COULD HAVE SURVIVED BY EATING THOSE MONSTERS!

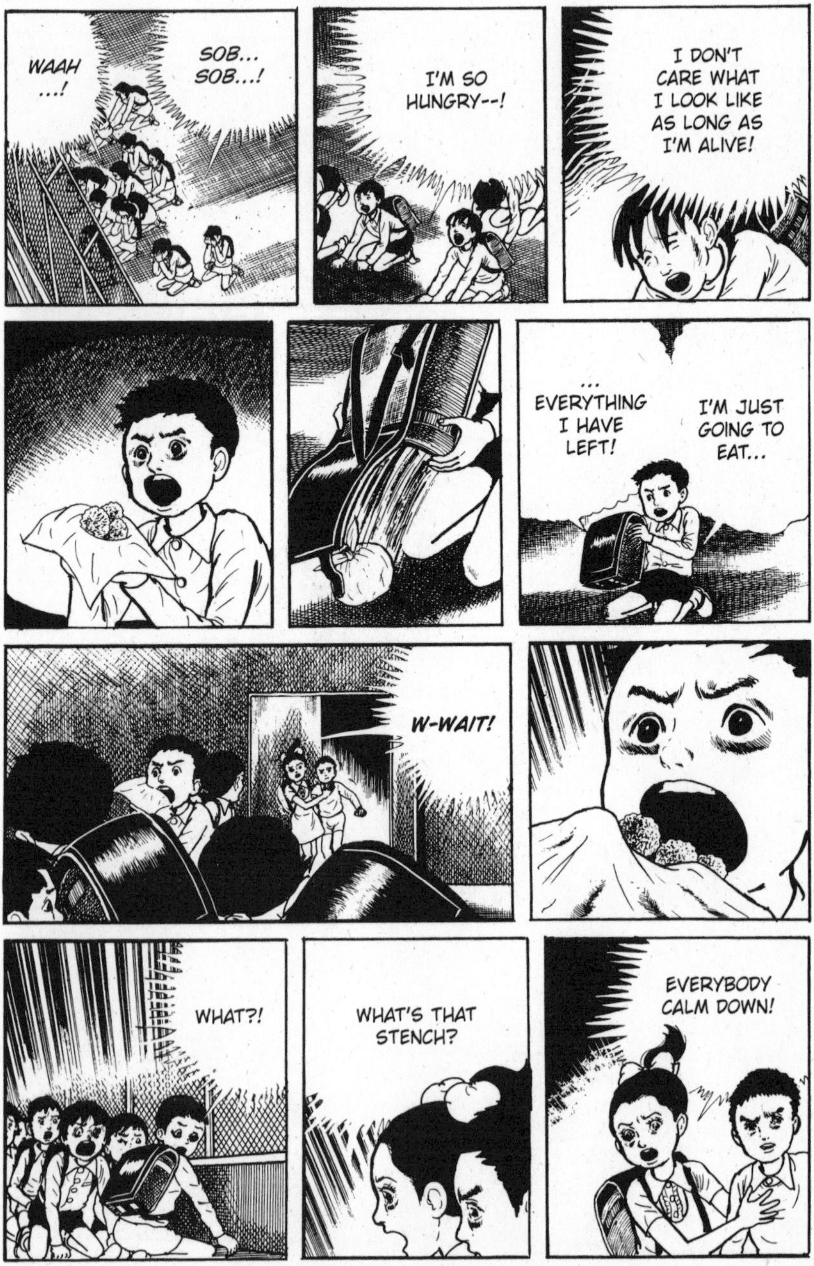
I DON'T CARE WHAT I LOOK LIKE AS LONG AS I'M ALIVE!
I'M SO HUNGRY--!
SOB... SOB...!
WAAH ...!
I'M JUST GOING TO EAT...
... EVERYTHING I HAVE LEFT!
W-WAIT!
EVERYBODY CALM DOWN!
WHAT'S THAT STENCH?
WHAT?!

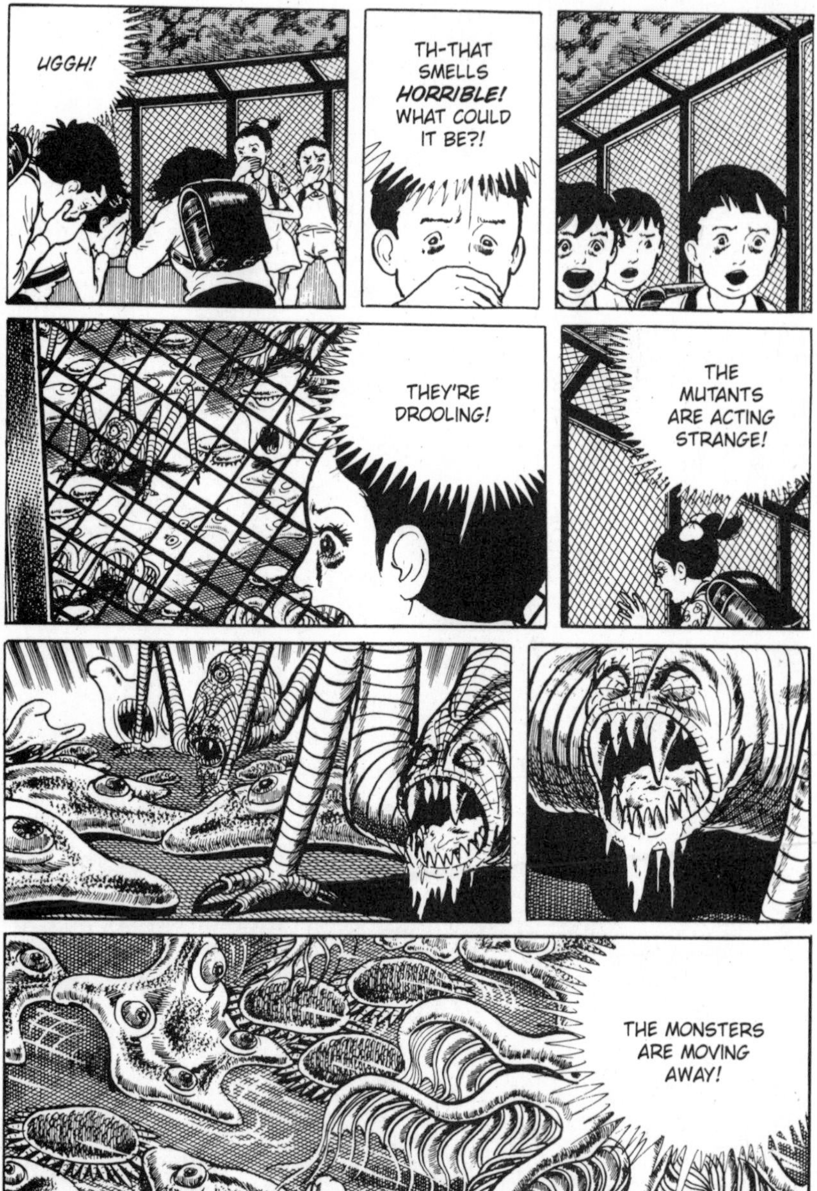
TH-THAT SMELLS *HORRIBLE!* WHAT COULD IT BE?!
UGGH!
THE MUTANTS ARE ACTING STRANGE!
THEY'RE DROOLING!
THE MONSTERS ARE MOVING AWAY!

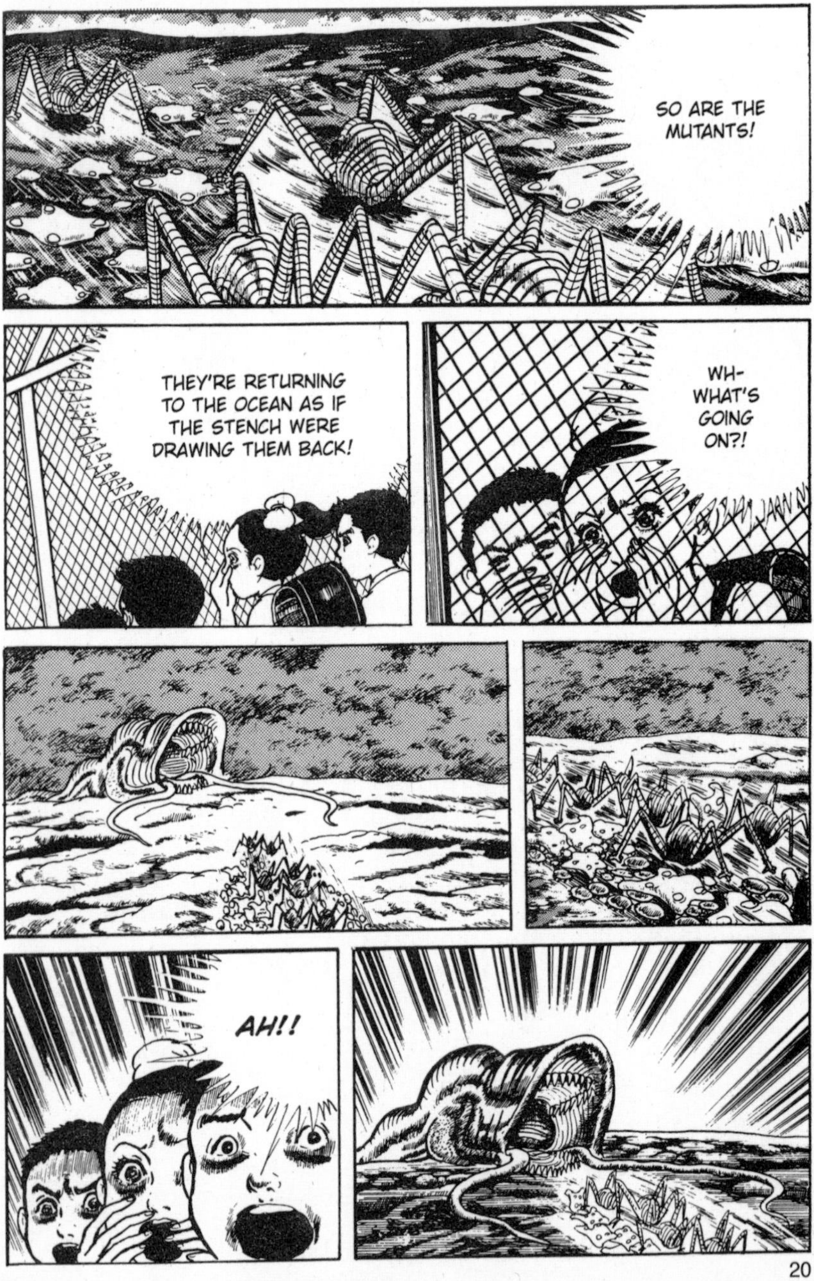
SO ARE THE MUTANTS!
WH- WHAT'S GOING ON?!
THEY'RE RETURNING TO THE OCEAN AS IF THE STENCH WERE DRAWING THEM BACK!
AH!!

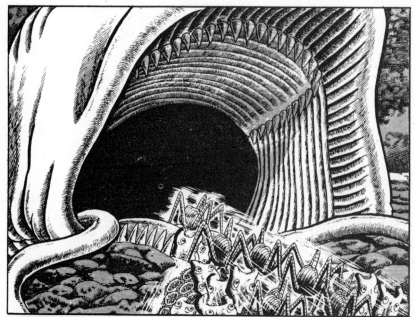

THEY'RE RUSHING INTO THAT THING'S MOUTH!

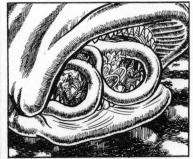

GYAAA!!
AAAGH!!

I-IT ATE
EVERYTHING
AND LEFT!

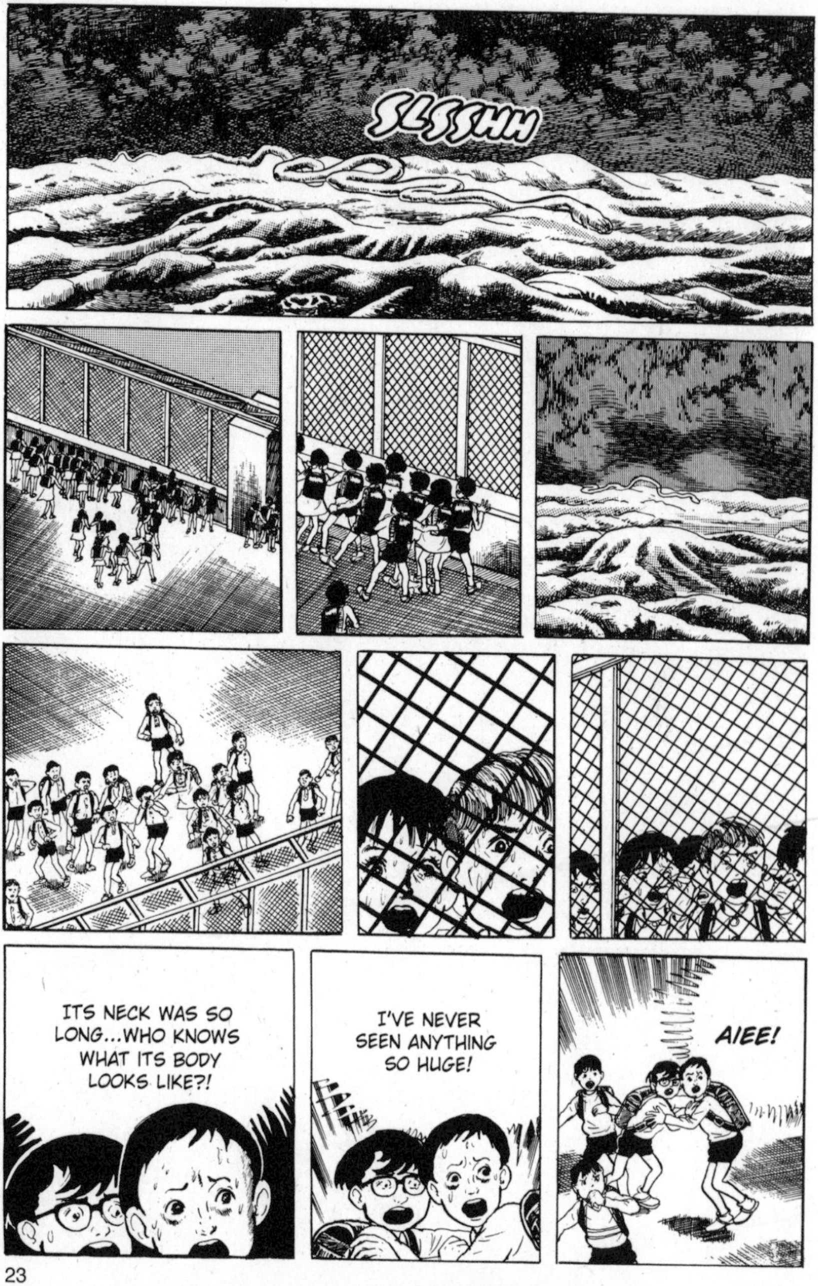
SLSSHH
AIEE!
I'VE NEVER SEEN ANYTHING SO HUGE!
ITS NECK WAS SO LONG...WHO KNOWS WHAT ITS BODY LOOKS LIKE?!

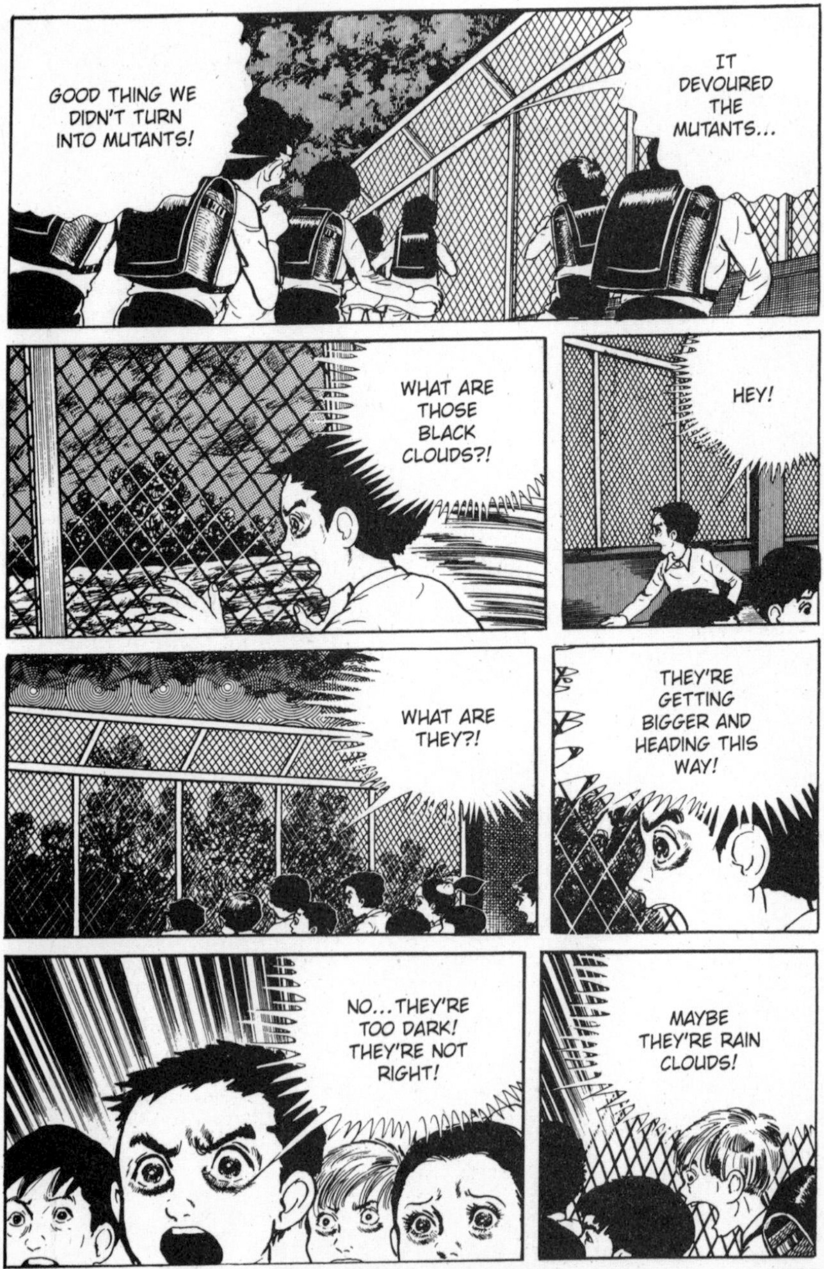
IT DEVOURED THE MUTANTS...
GOOD THING WE DIDN'T TURN INTO MUTANTS!
HEY!
WHAT ARE THOSE BLACK CLOUDS?!
THEY'RE GETTING BIGGER AND HEADING THIS WAY!
WHAT ARE THEY?!
MAYBE THEY'RE RAIN CLOUDS!
NO...THEY'RE TOO DARK! THEY'RE NOT RIGHT!

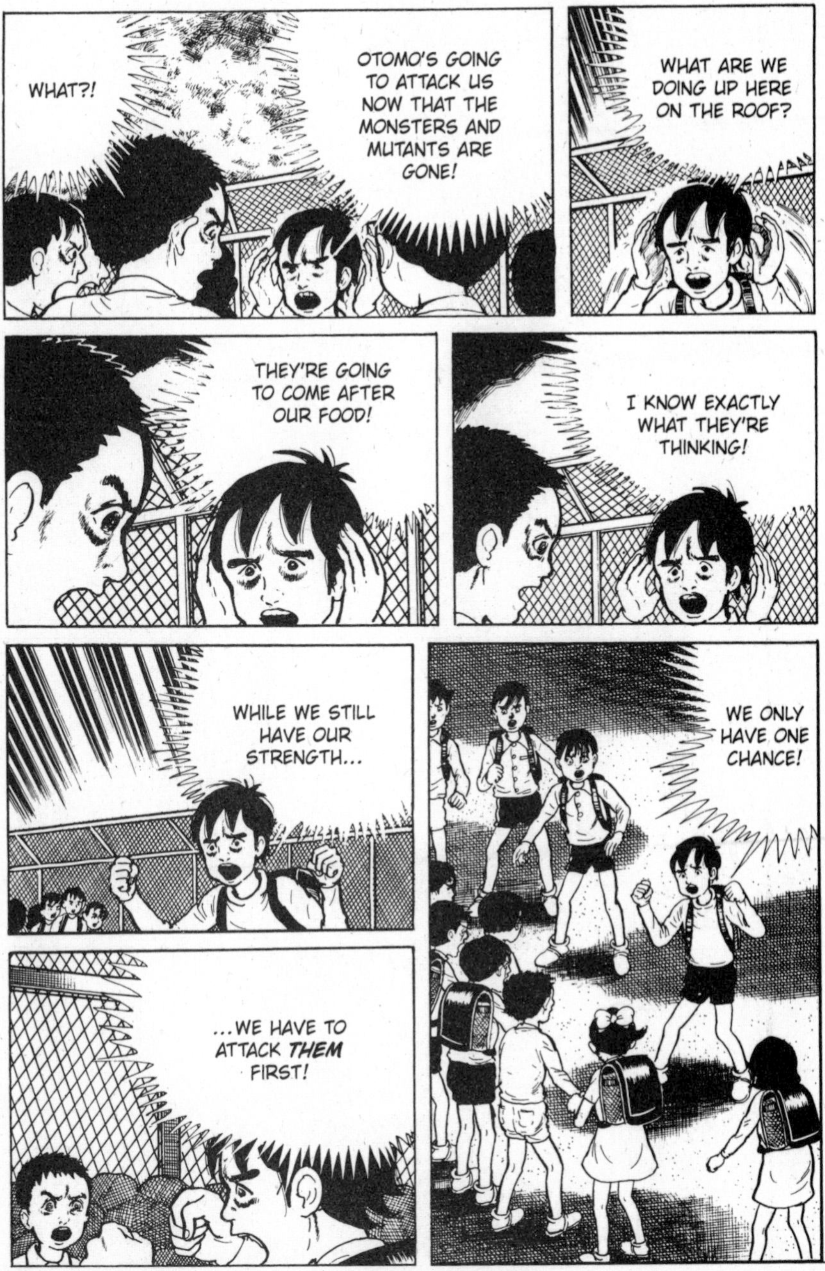
WHAT ARE WE DOING UP HERE ON THE ROOF?
OTOMO'S GOING TO ATTACK US NOW THAT THE MONSTERS AND MUTANTS ARE GONE!
WHAT?!
I KNOW EXACTLY WHAT THEY'RE THINKING!
THEY'RE GOING TO COME AFTER OUR FOOD!
WE ONLY HAVE ONE CHANCE!
WHILE WE STILL HAVE OUR STRENGTH...
...WE HAVE TO ATTACK *THEM* FIRST!

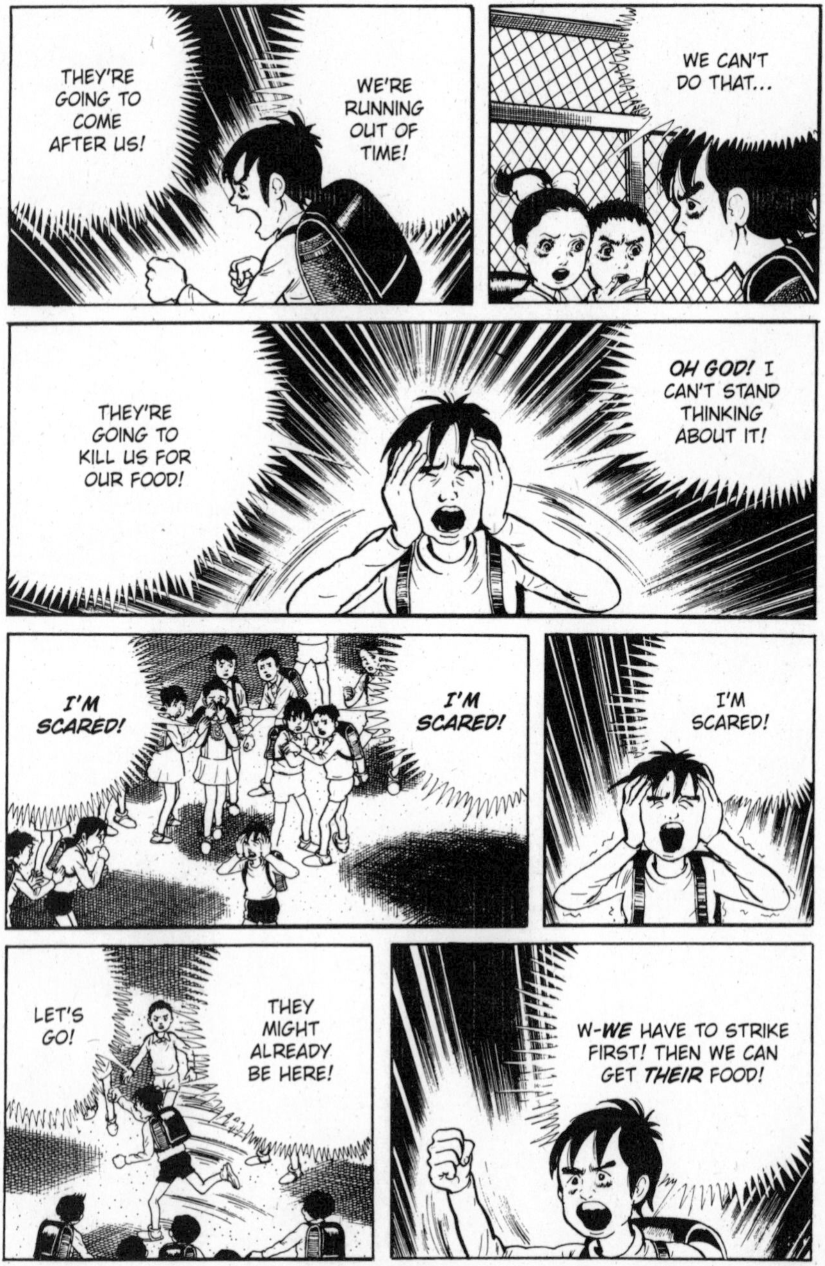
WE CAN'T DO THAT...
WE'RE RUNNING OUT OF TIME!
THEY'RE GOING TO COME AFTER US!
OH GOD! I CAN'T STAND THINKING ABOUT IT!
THEY'RE GOING TO KILL US FOR OUR FOOD!
I'M SCARED!
I'M SCARED!
I'M SCARED!
W-*WE* HAVE TO STRIKE FIRST! THEN WE CAN GET *THEIR* FOOD!
THEY MIGHT ALREADY BE HERE!
LET'S GO!

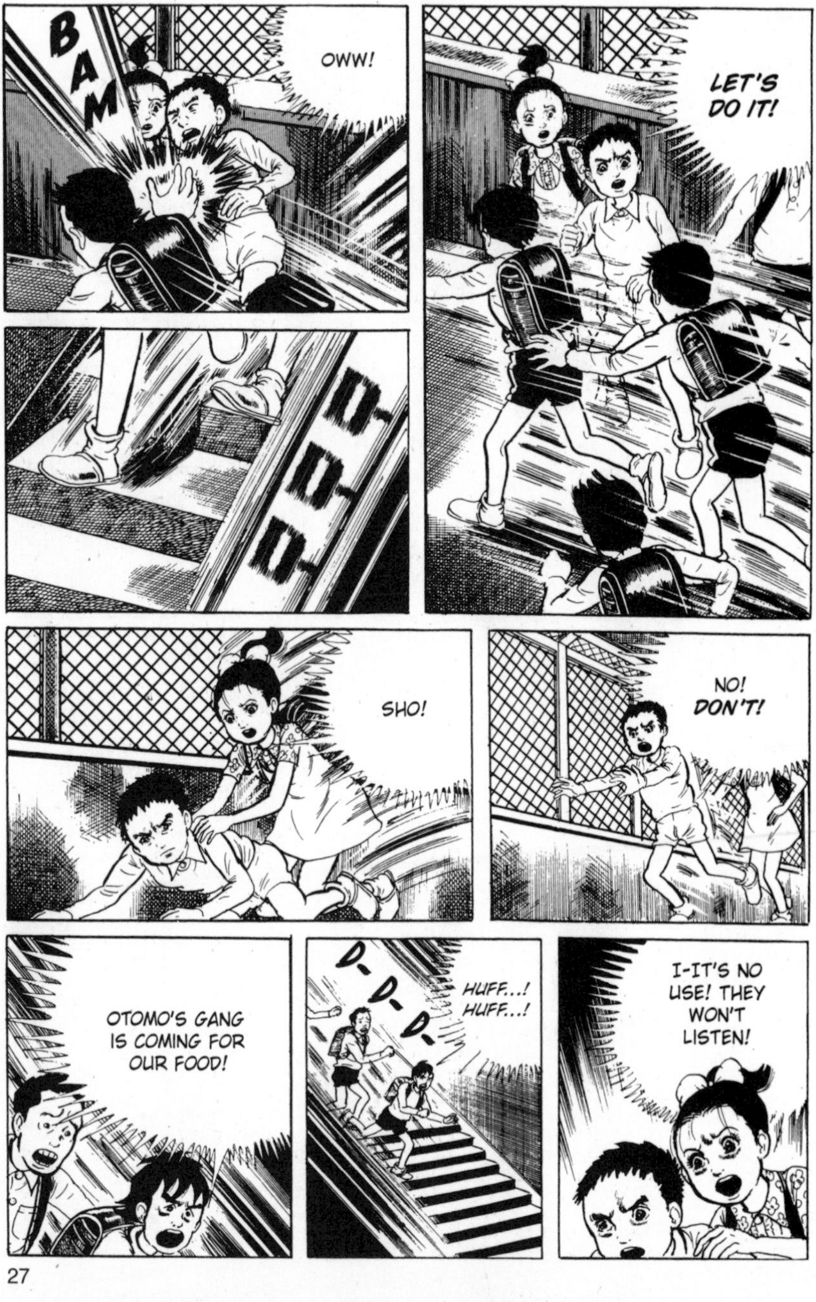
LET'S DO IT!
BAM
OWW!
D-D-D
NO! DON'T!
SHO!
I-IT'S NO USE! THEY WON'T LISTEN!
D- D- D-
HUFF...! HUFF...!
OTOMO'S GANG IS COMING FOR OUR FOOD!

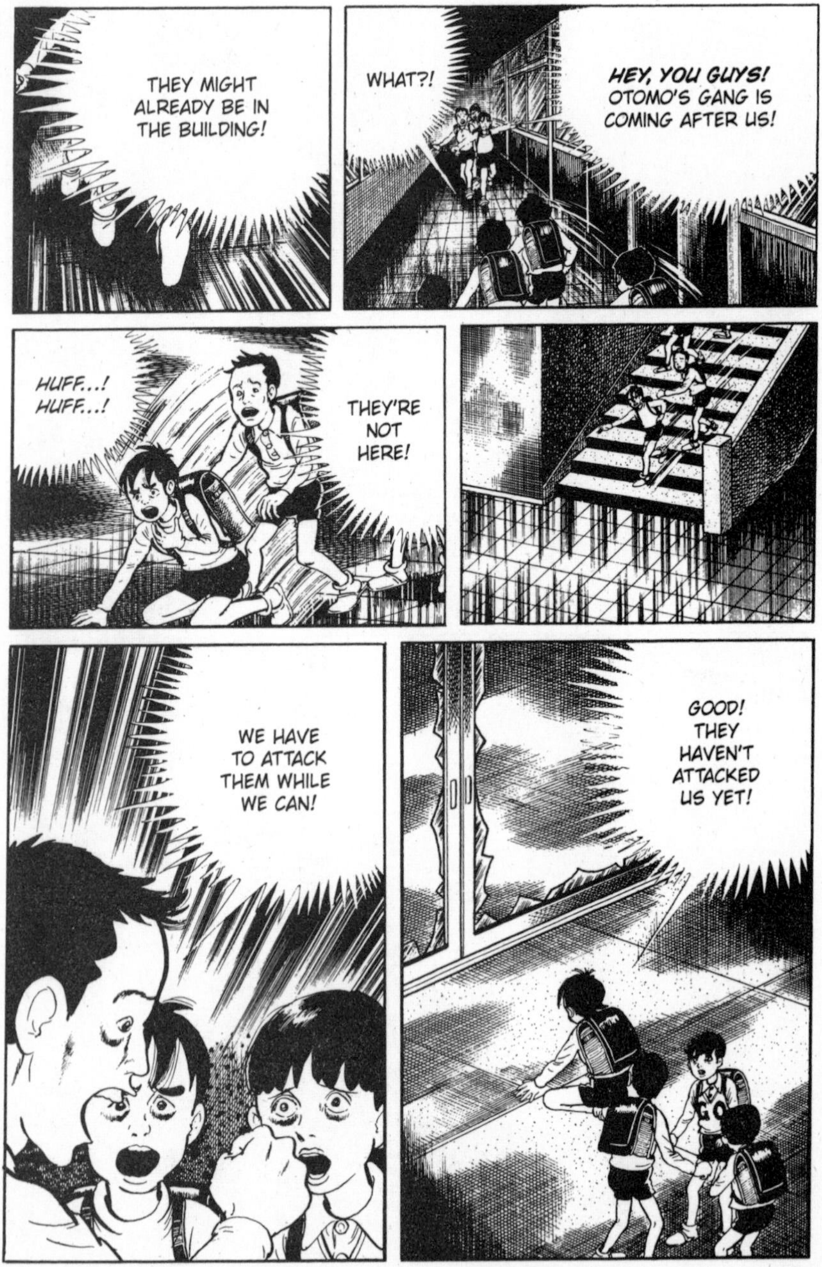
HEY, YOU GUYS! OTOMO'S GANG IS COMING AFTER US!
WHAT?!
THEY MIGHT ALREADY BE IN THE BUILDING!
THEY'RE NOT HERE!
HUFF...! HUFF...!
GOOD! THEY HAVEN'T ATTACKED US YET!
WE HAVE TO ATTACK THEM WHILE WE CAN!

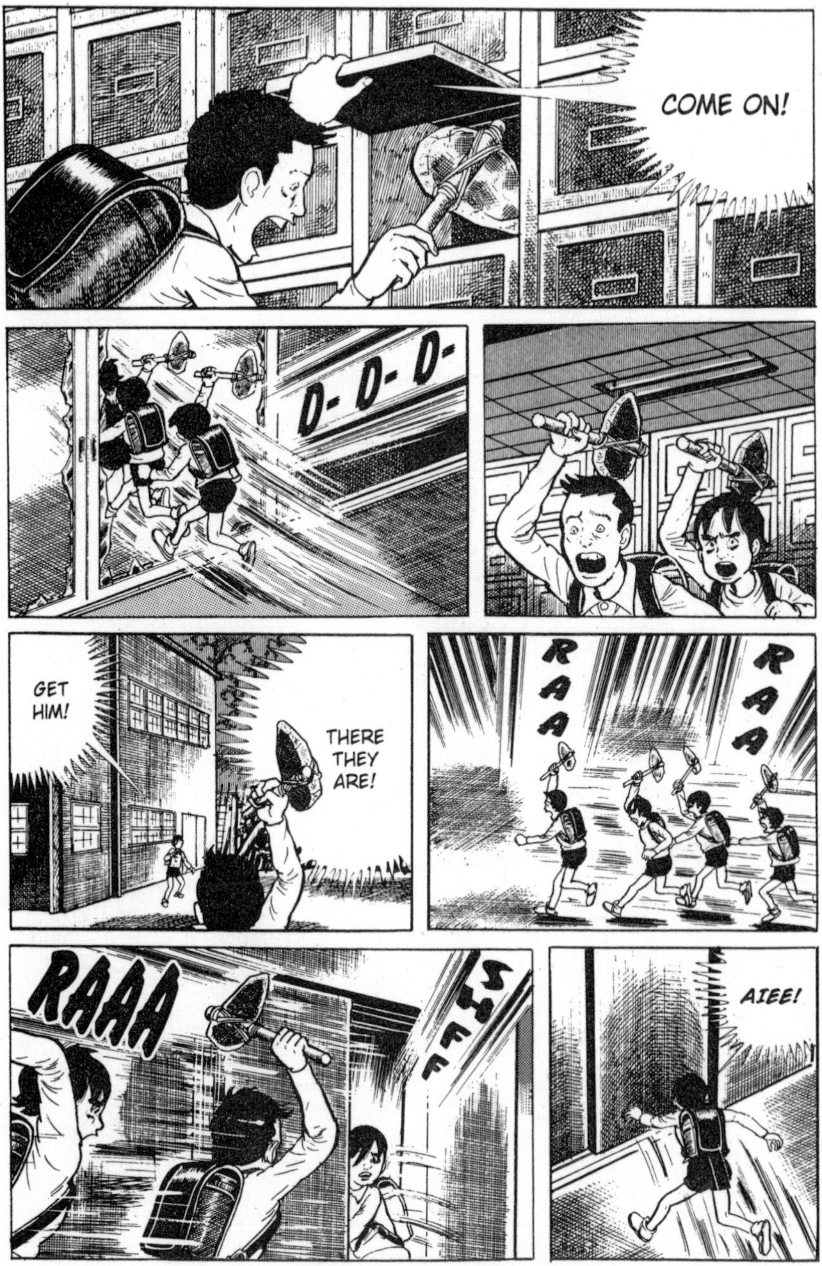
COME ON!
D- D- D-
RAAA
RAAA
THERE THEY ARE!
GET HIM!
AIEE!
SHFF
RAAA

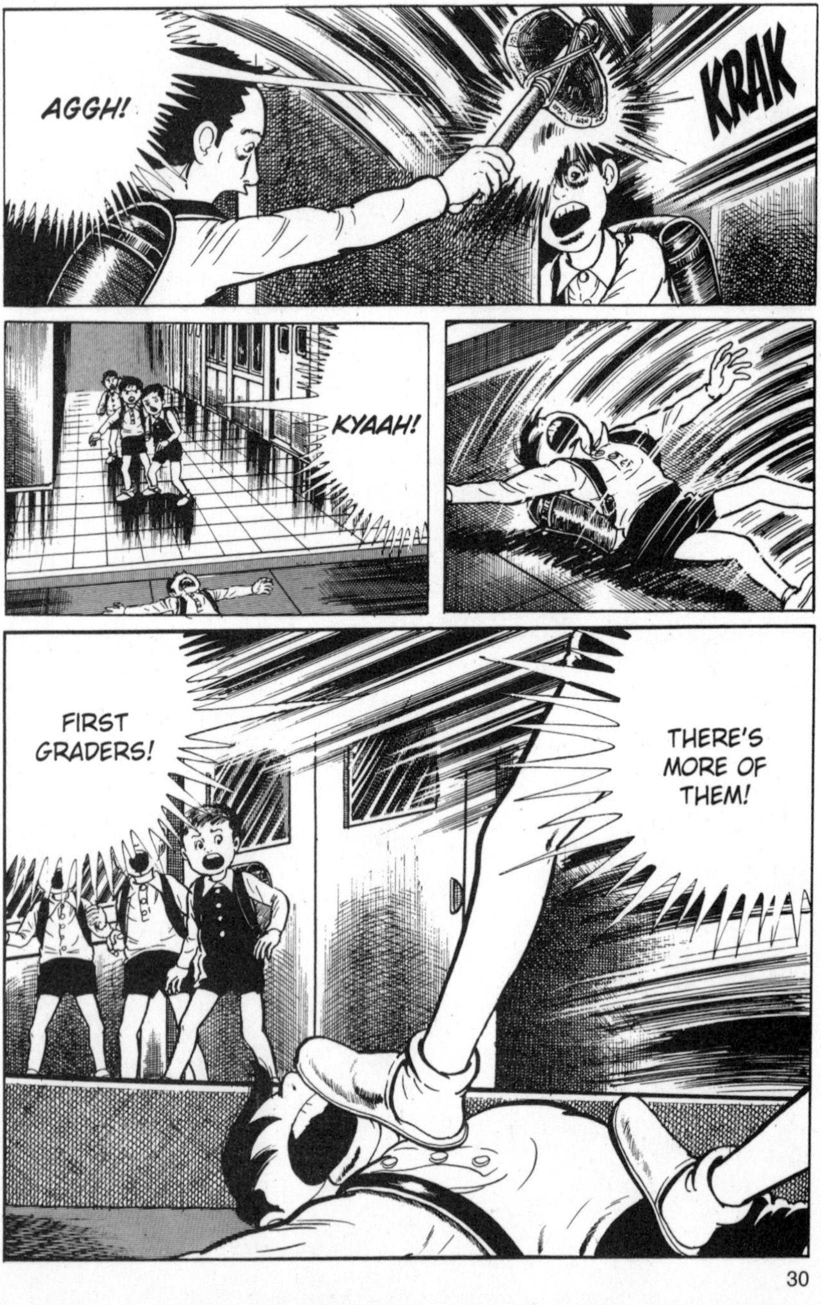
KRAK
AGGH!
KYAAH!
THERE'S MORE OF THEM!
FIRST GRADERS!

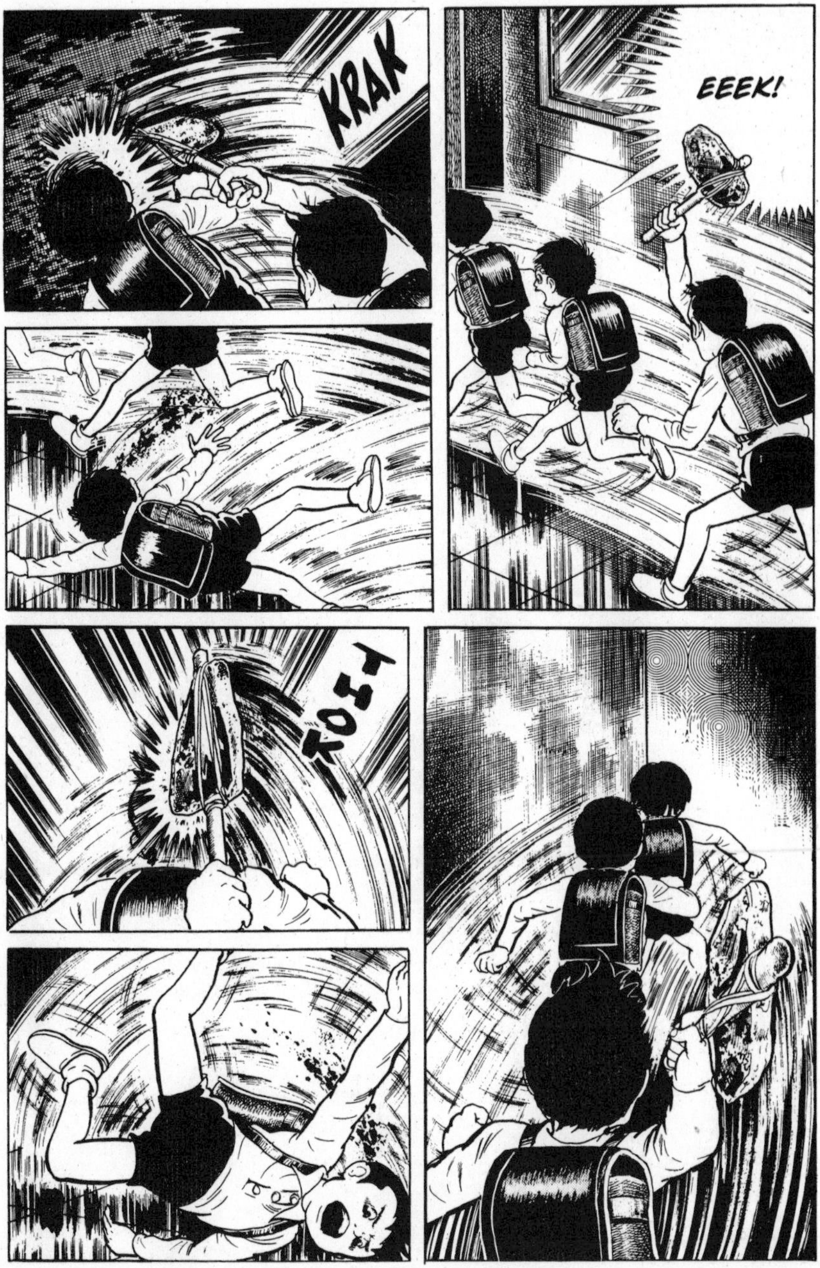
EEEK!
KRAK
THOK

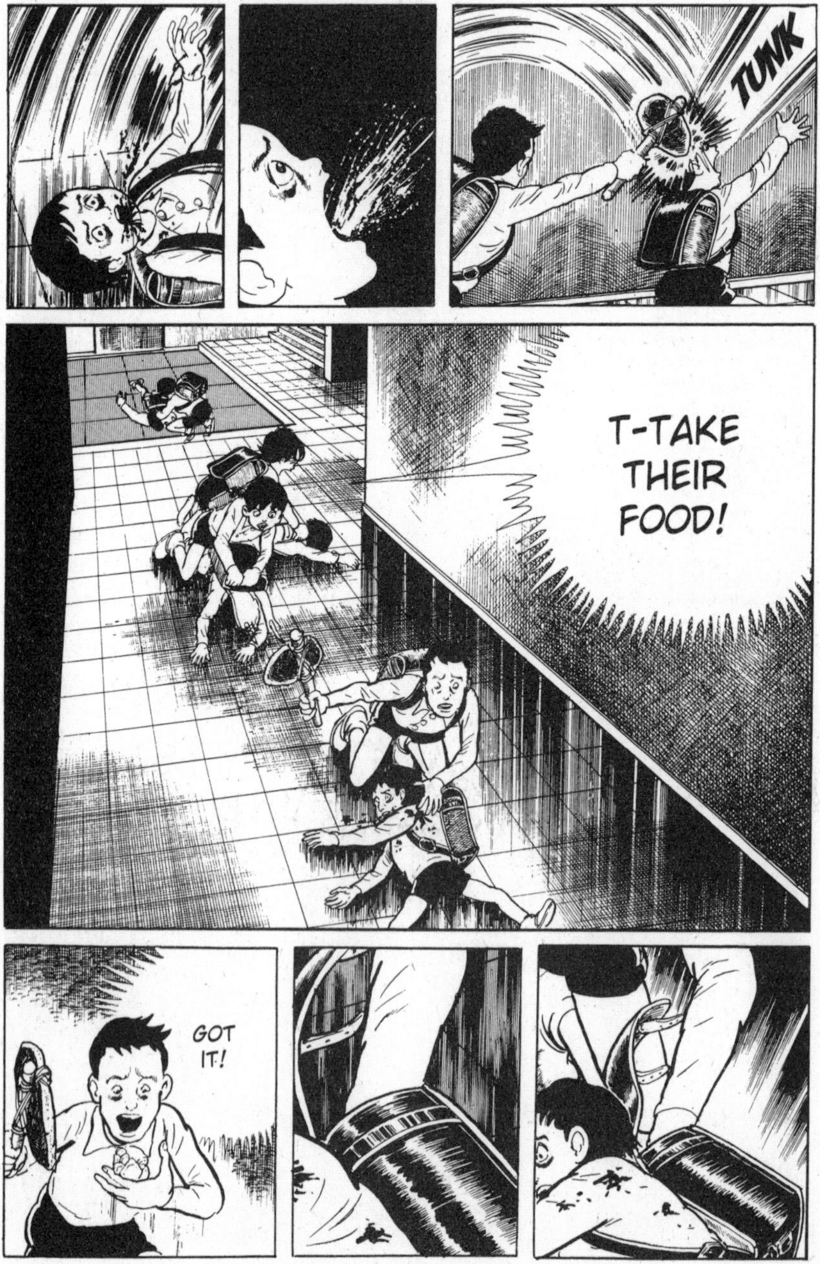
TUNK
T-TAKE THEIR FOOD!
GOT IT!

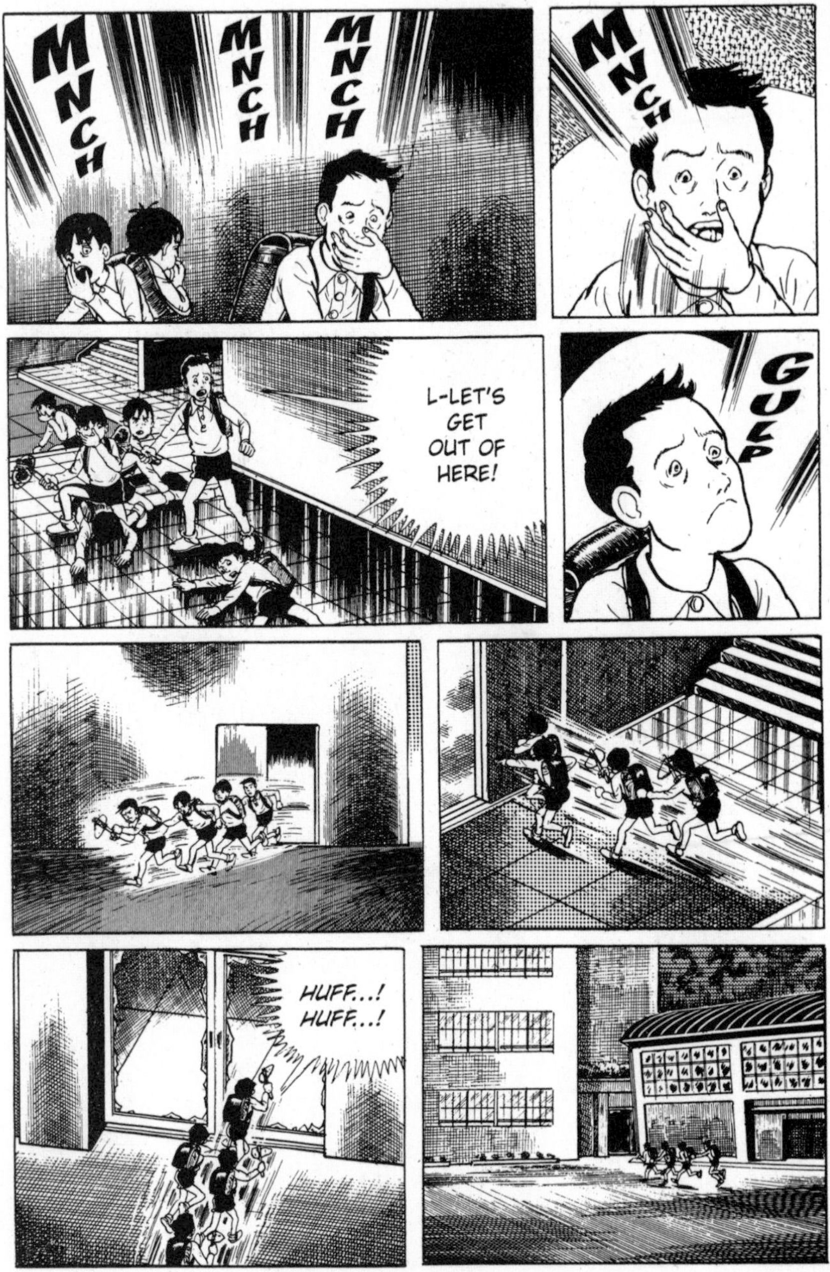
MNCH
MNCH
MNCH
MNCH
GULP
L-LET'S GET OUT OF HERE!
HUFF...! HUFF...!

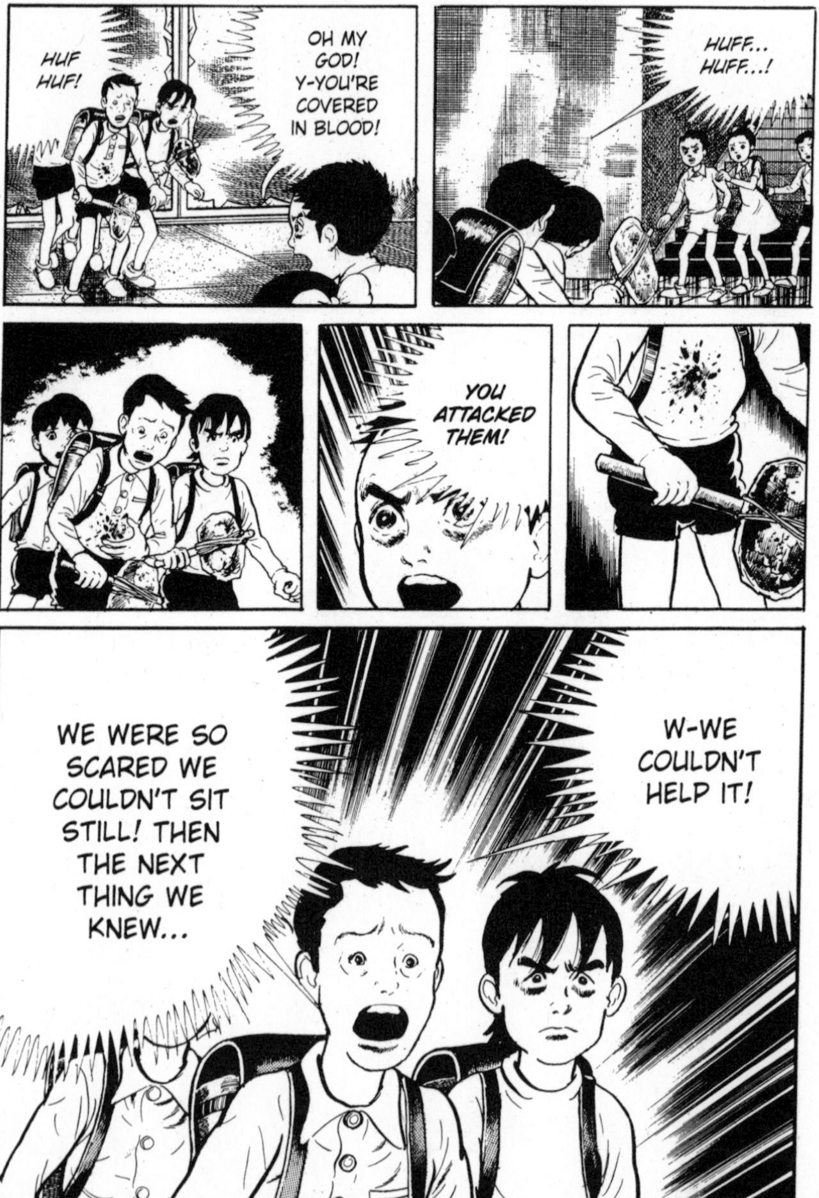
HUFF... HUFF...!
OH MY GOD! Y-YOU'RE COVERED IN BLOOD!
HUF HUF!
YOU ATTACKED THEM!
W-WE COULDN'T HELP IT!
WE WERE SO SCARED WE COULDN'T SIT STILL! THEN THE NEXT THING WE KNEW...

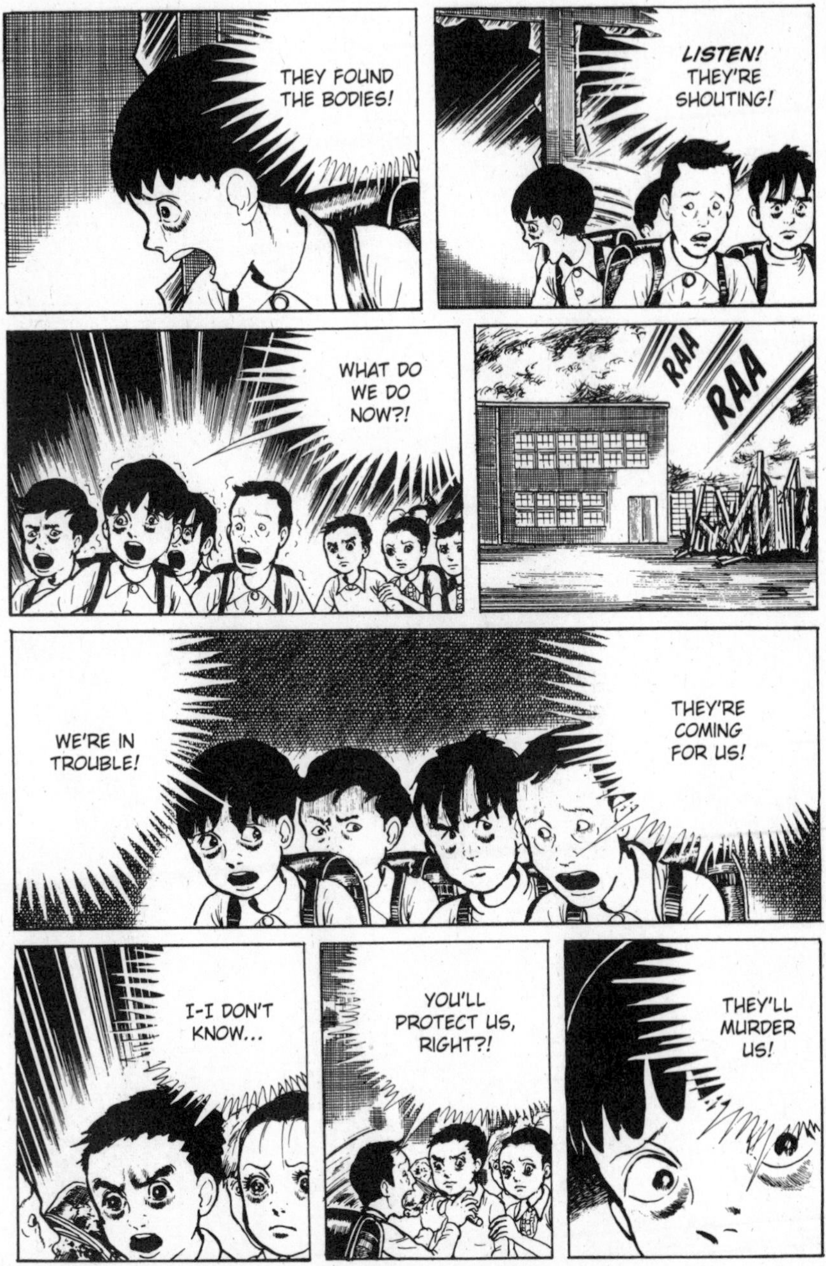

LISTEN! THEY'RE SHOUTING!
THEY FOUND THE BODIES!
RAA
RAA
WHAT DO WE DO NOW?!
THEY'RE COMING FOR US!
WE'RE IN TROUBLE!
THEY'LL MURDER US!
YOU'LL PROTECT US, RIGHT?!
I-I DON'T KNOW...

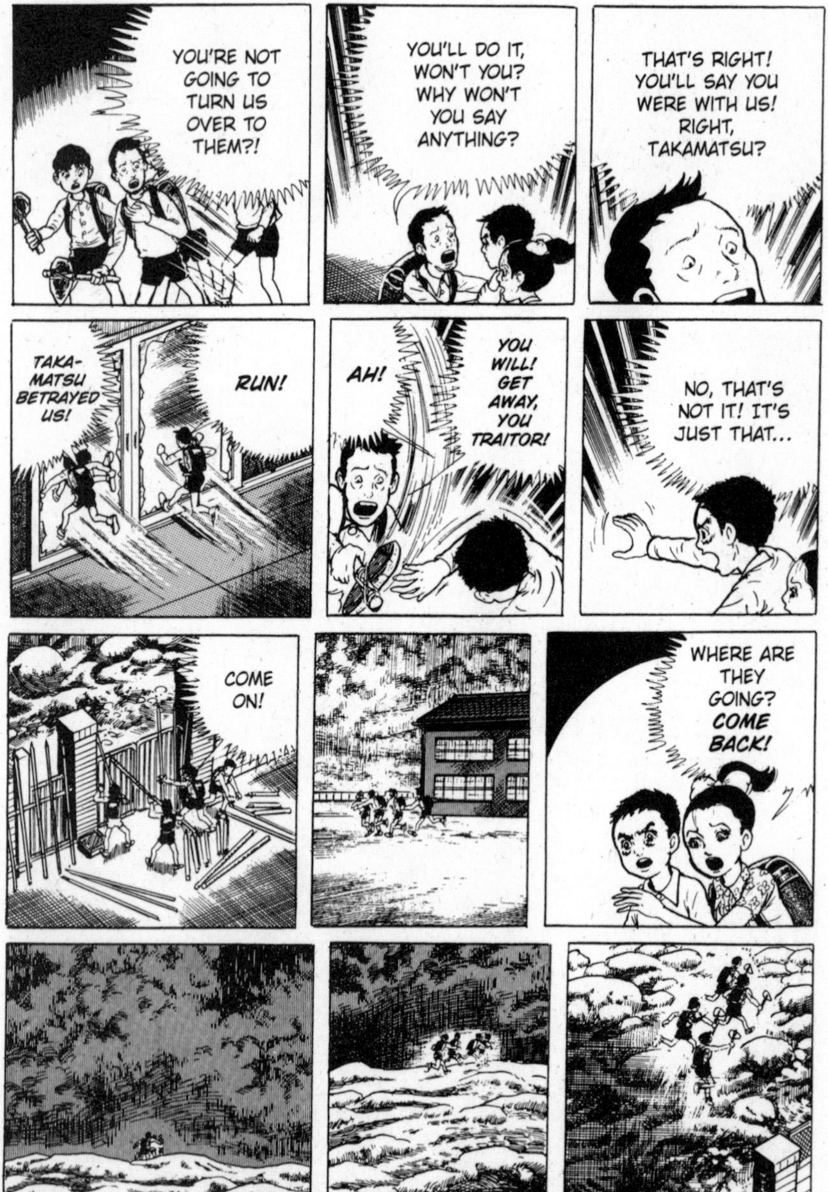
THAT'S RIGHT! YOU'LL SAY YOU WERE WITH US! RIGHT, TAKAMATSU?
YOU'LL DO IT, WON'T YOU? WHY WON'T YOU SAY ANYTHING?
YOU'RE NOT GOING TO TURN US OVER TO THEM?!
NO, THAT'S NOT IT! IT'S JUST THAT...
YOU WILL! GET AWAY, YOU TRAITOR!
AH!
RUN!
TAKA-MATSU BETRAYED US!
WHERE ARE THEY GOING? COME BACK!
COME ON!

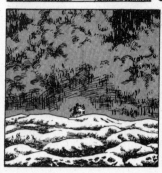

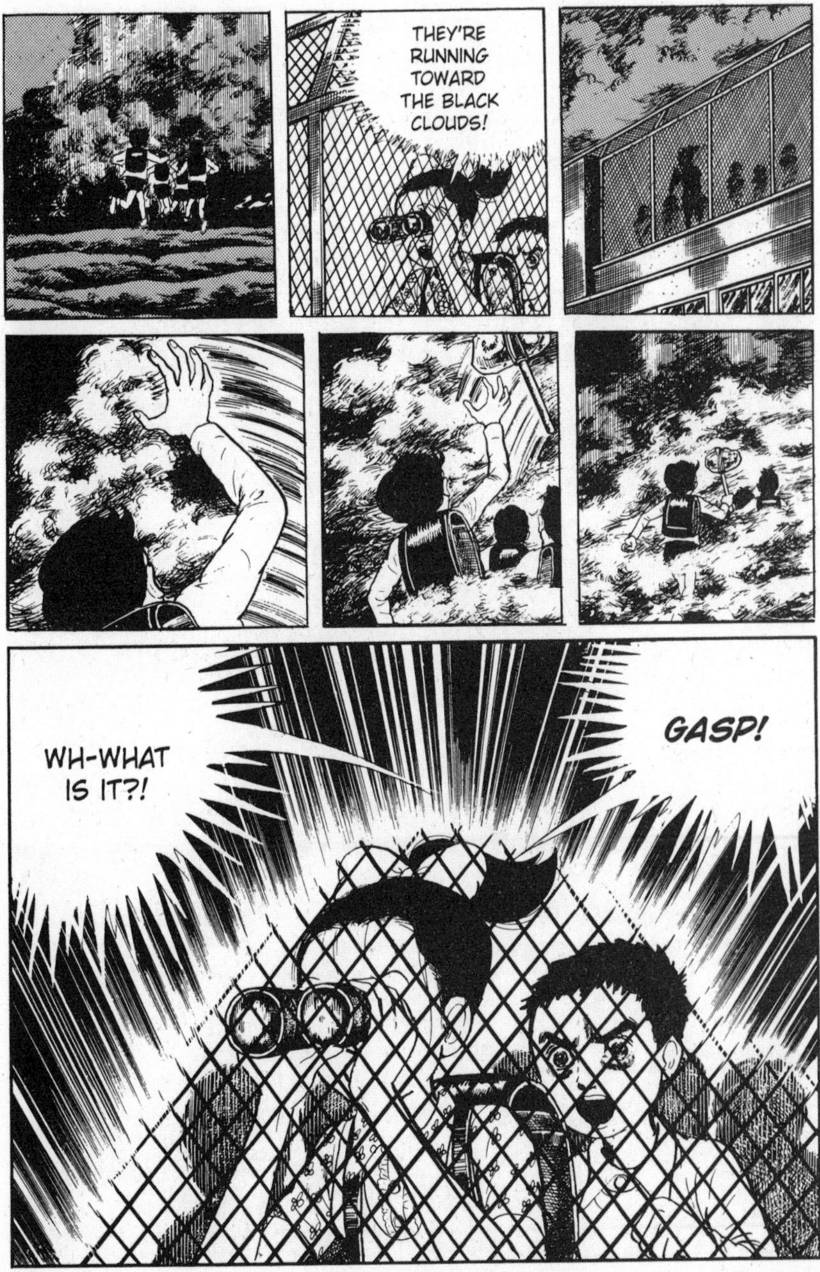
THEY'RE RUNNING TOWARD THE BLACK CLOUDS!
GASP!
WH-WHAT IS IT?!

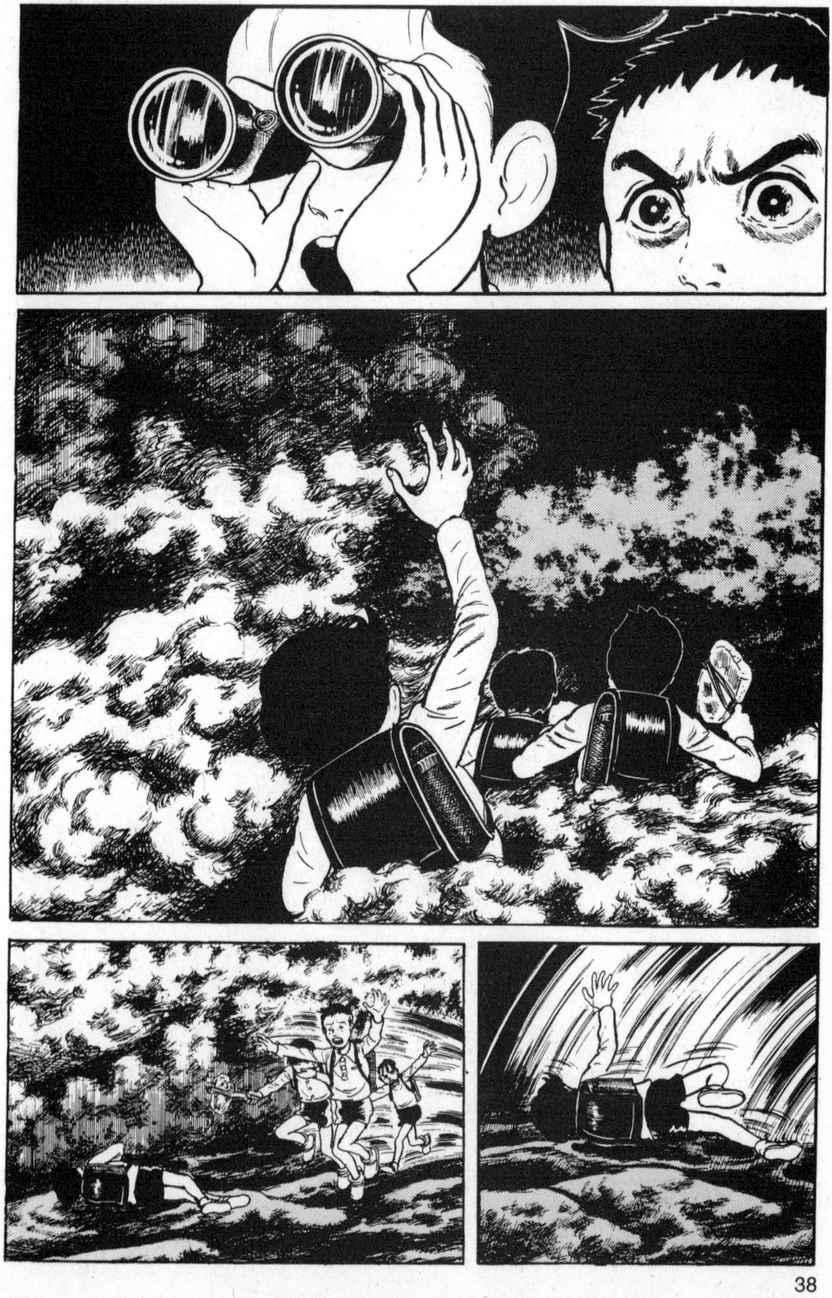

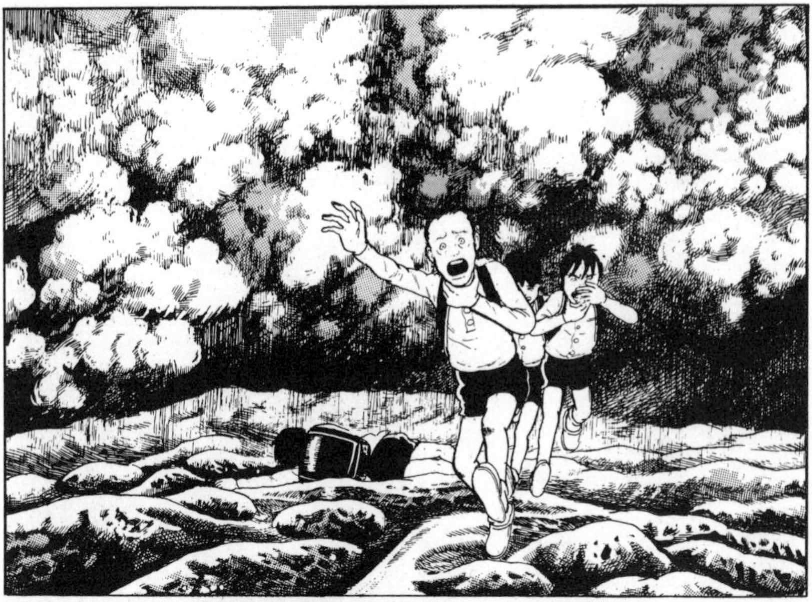

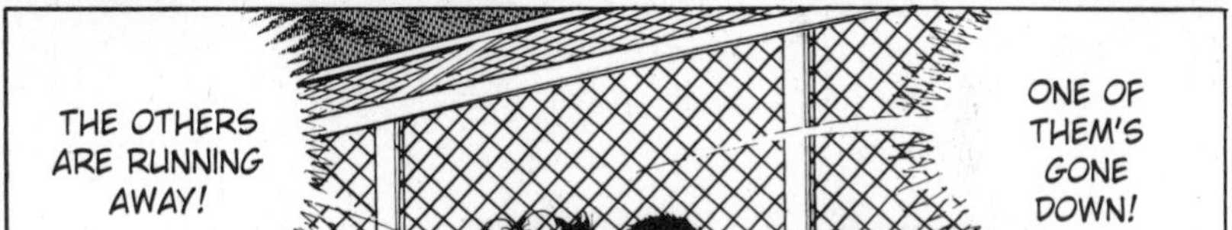
ONE OF THEM'S GONE DOWN!
THE OTHERS ARE RUNNING AWAY!

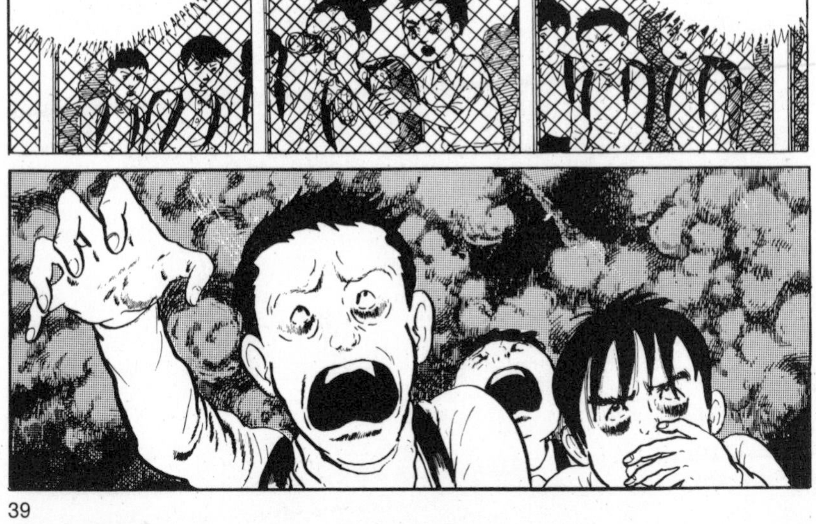

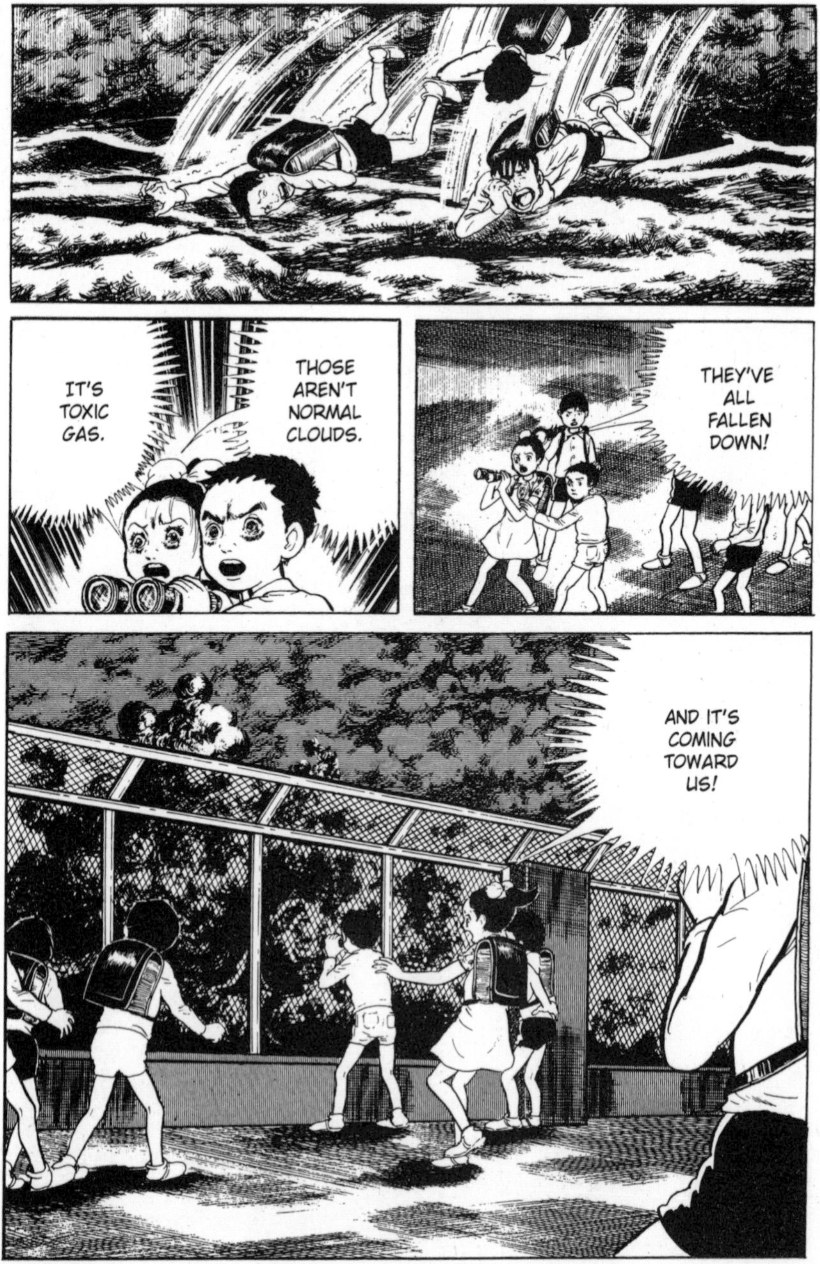
THEY'VE ALL FALLEN DOWN!
THOSE AREN'T NORMAL CLOUDS.
IT'S TOXIC GAS.
AND IT'S COMING TOWARD US!

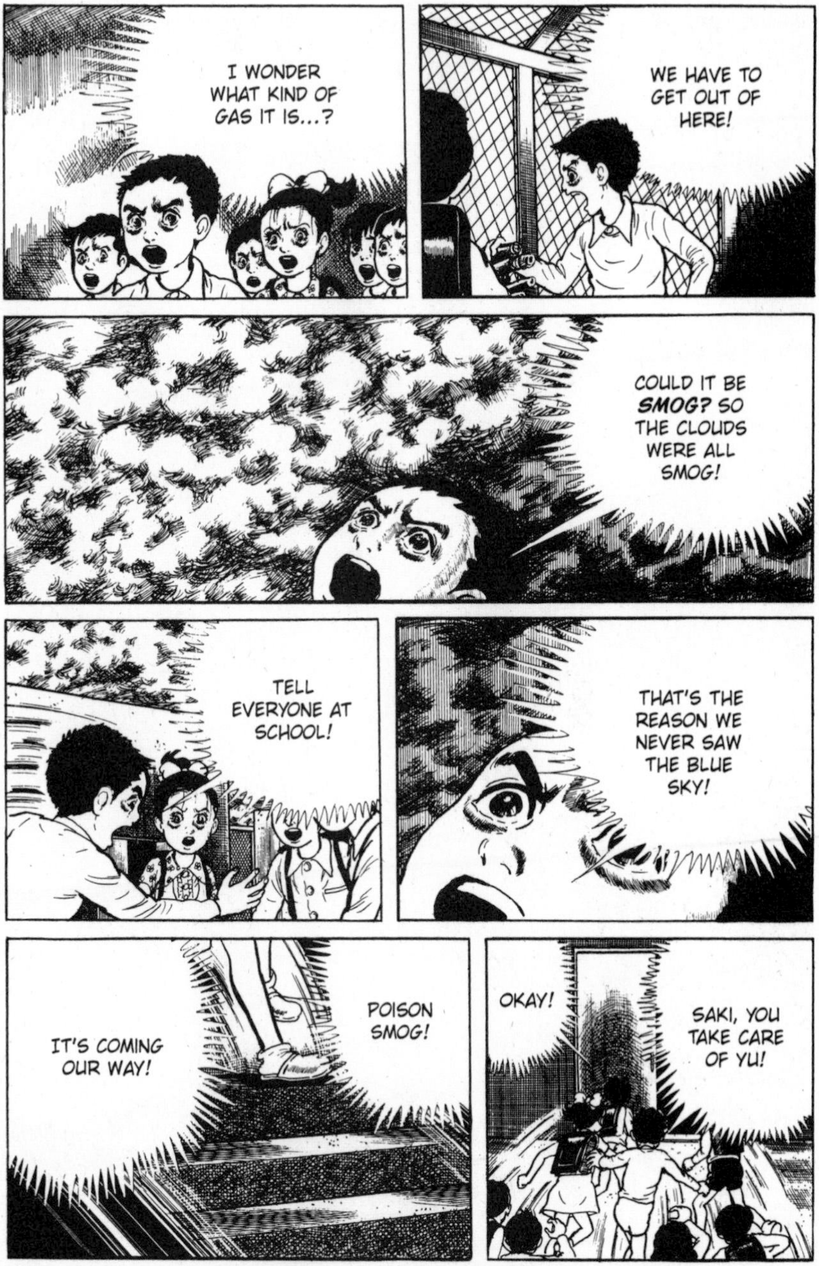
WE HAVE TO GET OUT OF HERE!
I WONDER WHAT KIND OF GAS IT IS...?
COULD IT BE **SMOG?** SO THE CLOUDS WERE ALL SMOG!
THAT'S THE REASON WE NEVER SAW THE BLUE SKY!
TELL EVERYONE AT SCHOOL!
SAKI, YOU TAKE CARE OF YU!
OKAY!
POISON SMOG!
IT'S COMING OUR WAY!

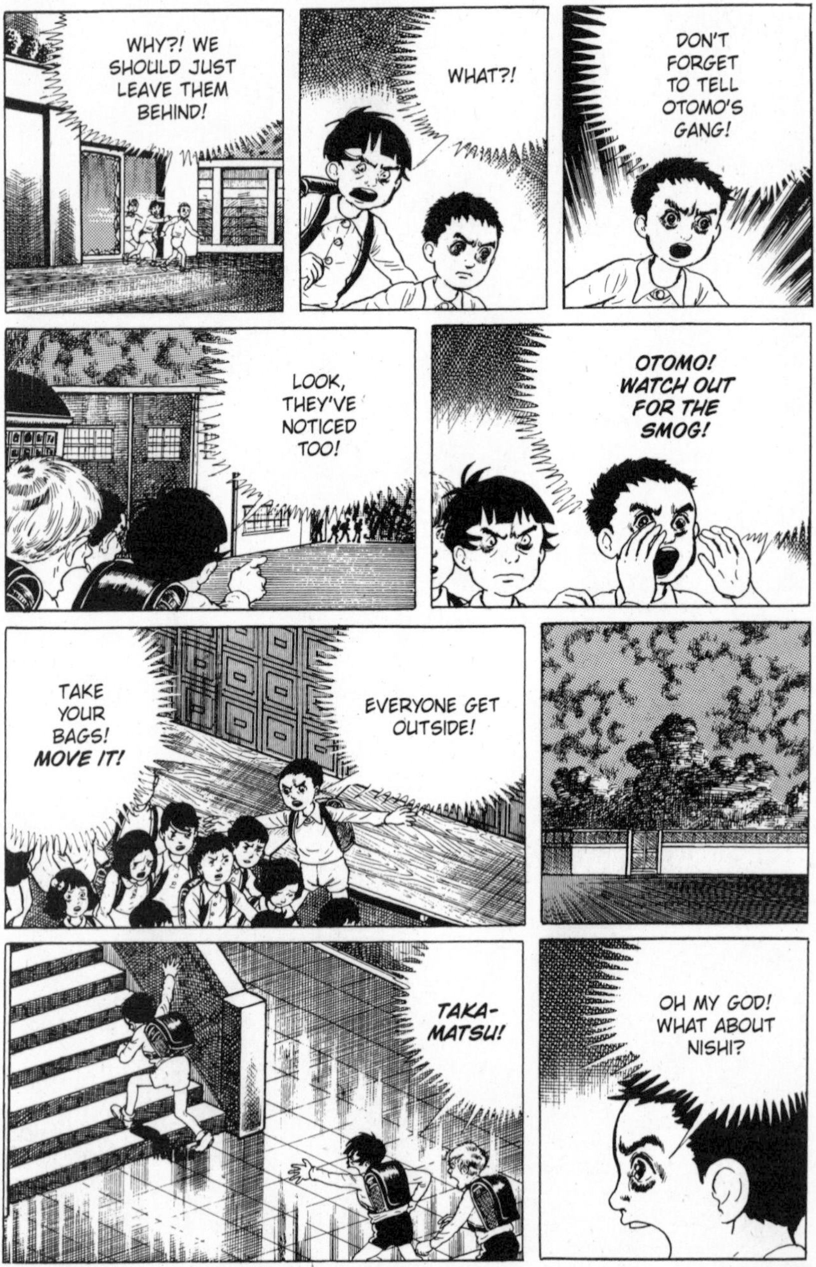
DON'T FORGET TO TELL OTOMO'S GANG!
WHAT?!
WHY?! WE SHOULD JUST LEAVE THEM BEHIND!
OTOMO! WATCH OUT FOR THE SMOG!
LOOK, THEY'VE NOTICED TOO!
EVERYONE GET OUTSIDE!
TAKE YOUR BAGS! MOVE IT!
OH MY GOD! WHAT ABOUT NISHI?
TAKA-MATSU!

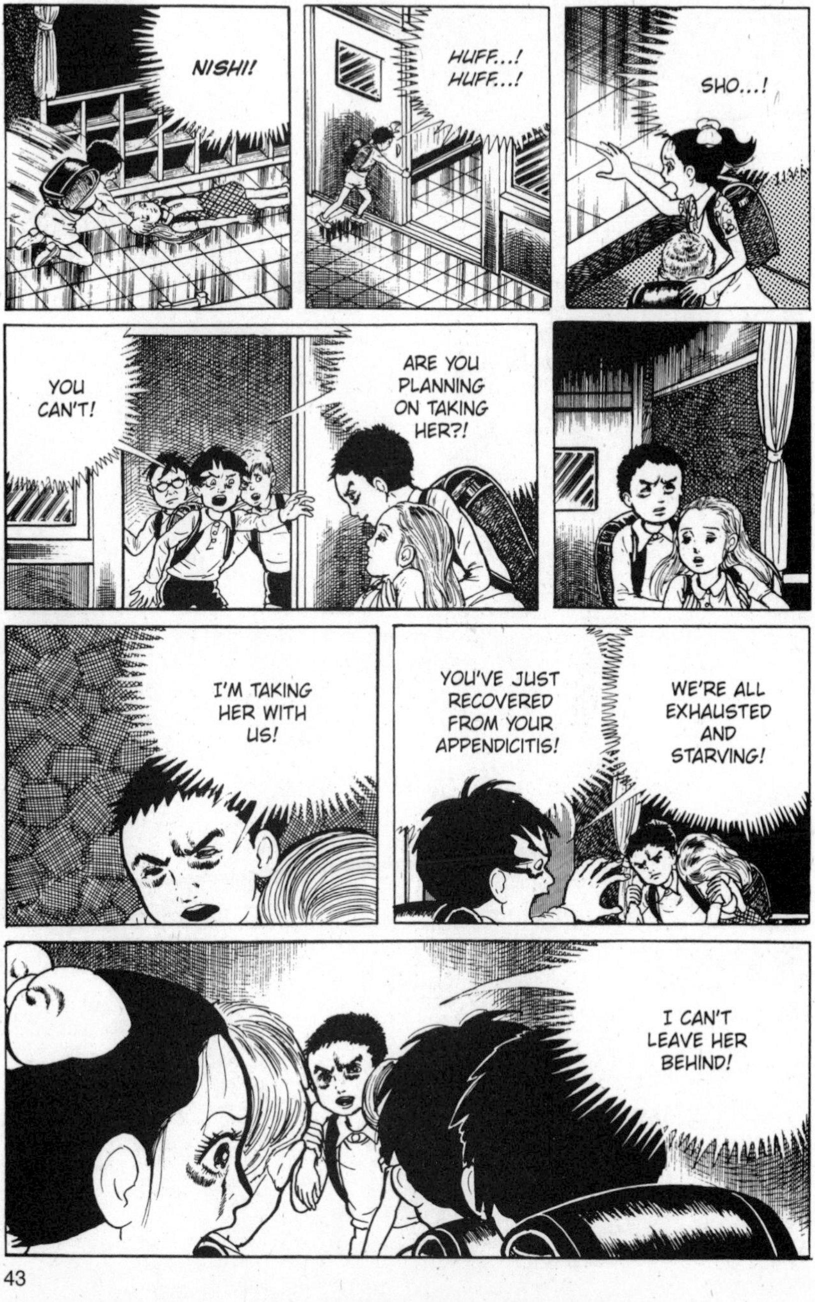
SHO...!
HUFF...! HUFF...!
NISHI!
ARE YOU PLANNING ON TAKING HER?!
YOU CAN'T!
WE'RE ALL EXHAUSTED AND STARVING!
YOU'VE JUST RECOVERED FROM YOUR APPENDICITIS!
I'M TAKING HER WITH US!
I CAN'T LEAVE HER BEHIND!

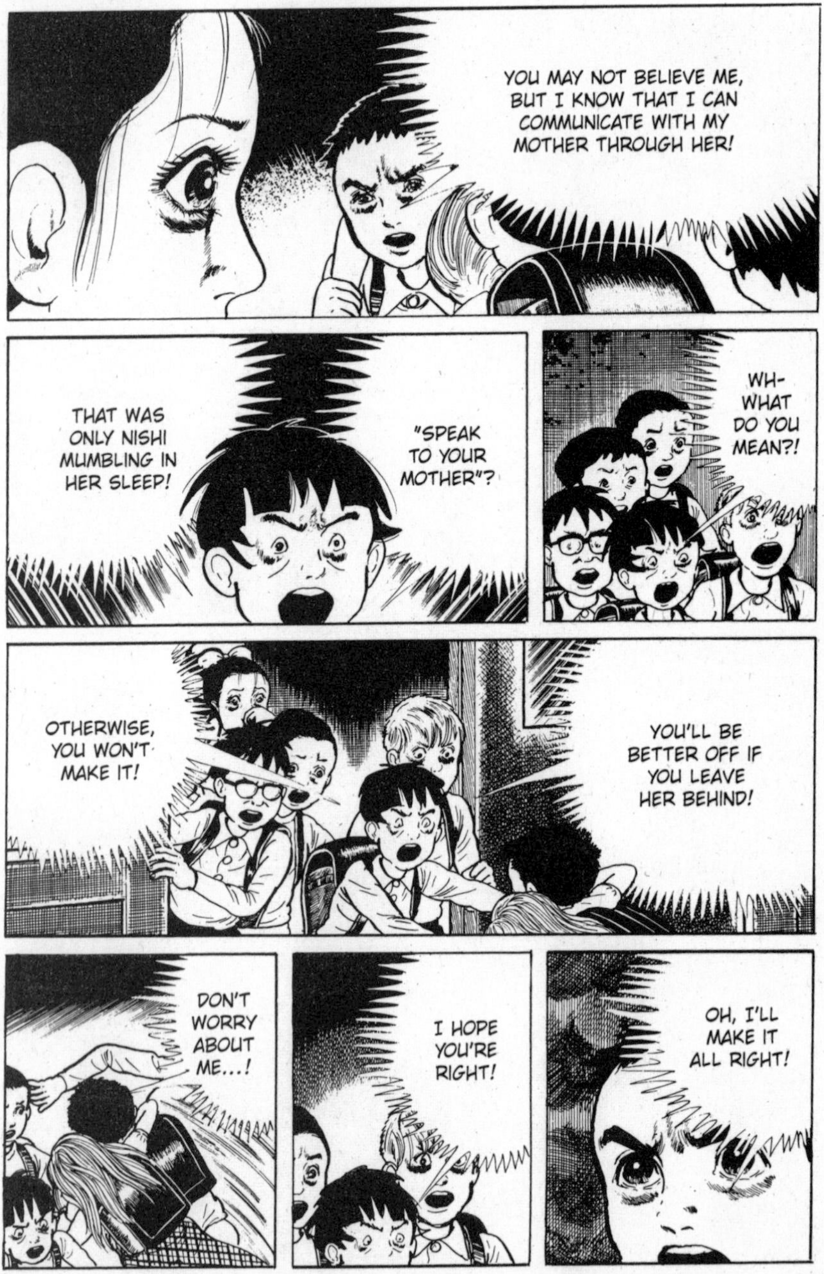
YOU MAY NOT BELIEVE ME, BUT I KNOW THAT I CAN COMMUNICATE WITH MY MOTHER THROUGH HER!
WH- WHAT DO YOU MEAN?!
"SPEAK TO YOUR MOTHER"?
THAT WAS ONLY NISHI MUMBLING IN HER SLEEP!
YOU'LL BE BETTER OFF IF YOU LEAVE HER BEHIND!
OTHERWISE, YOU WON'T MAKE IT!
OH, I'LL MAKE IT ALL RIGHT!
I HOPE YOU'RE RIGHT!
DON'T WORRY ABOUT ME...!

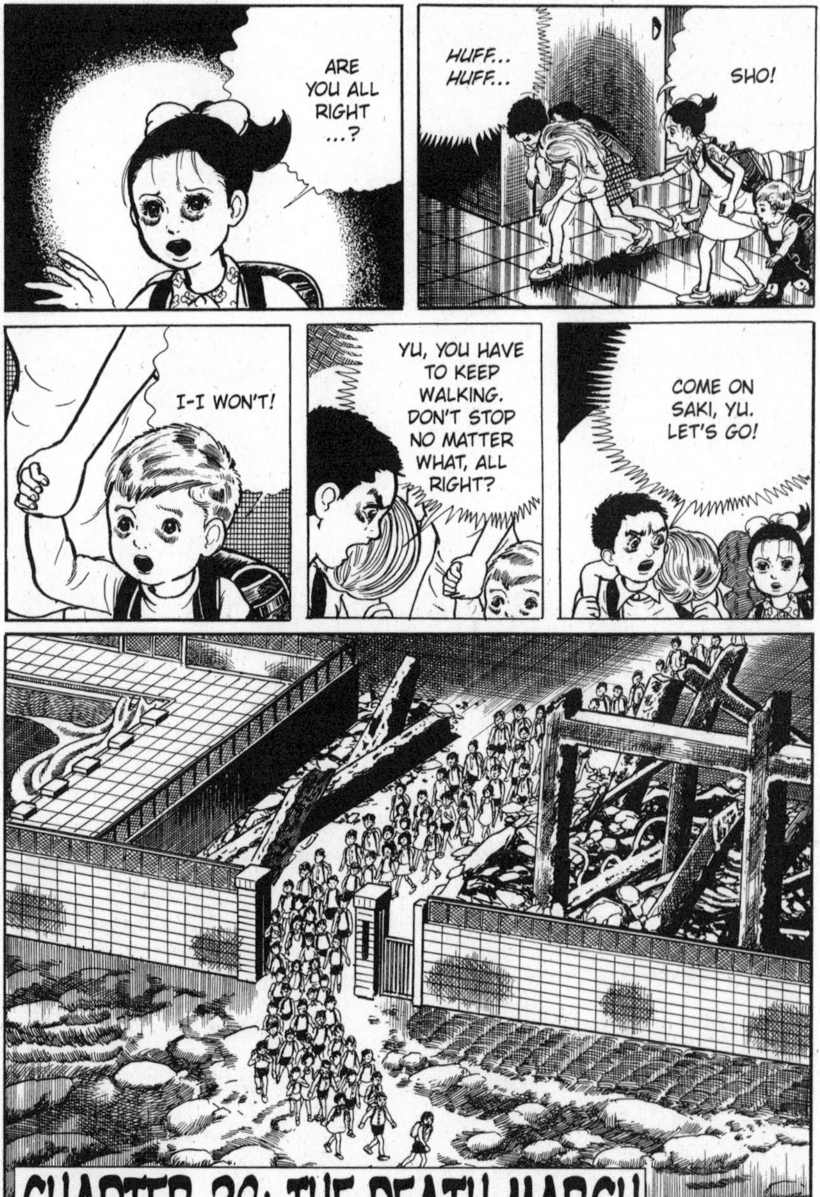
SHO!
HUFF... HUFF...
ARE YOU ALL RIGHT ...?
COME ON SAKI, YU. LET'S GO!
YU, YOU HAVE TO KEEP WALKING. DON'T STOP NO MATTER WHAT, ALL RIGHT?
I-I WON'T!
CHAPTER 38: THE DEATH MARCH

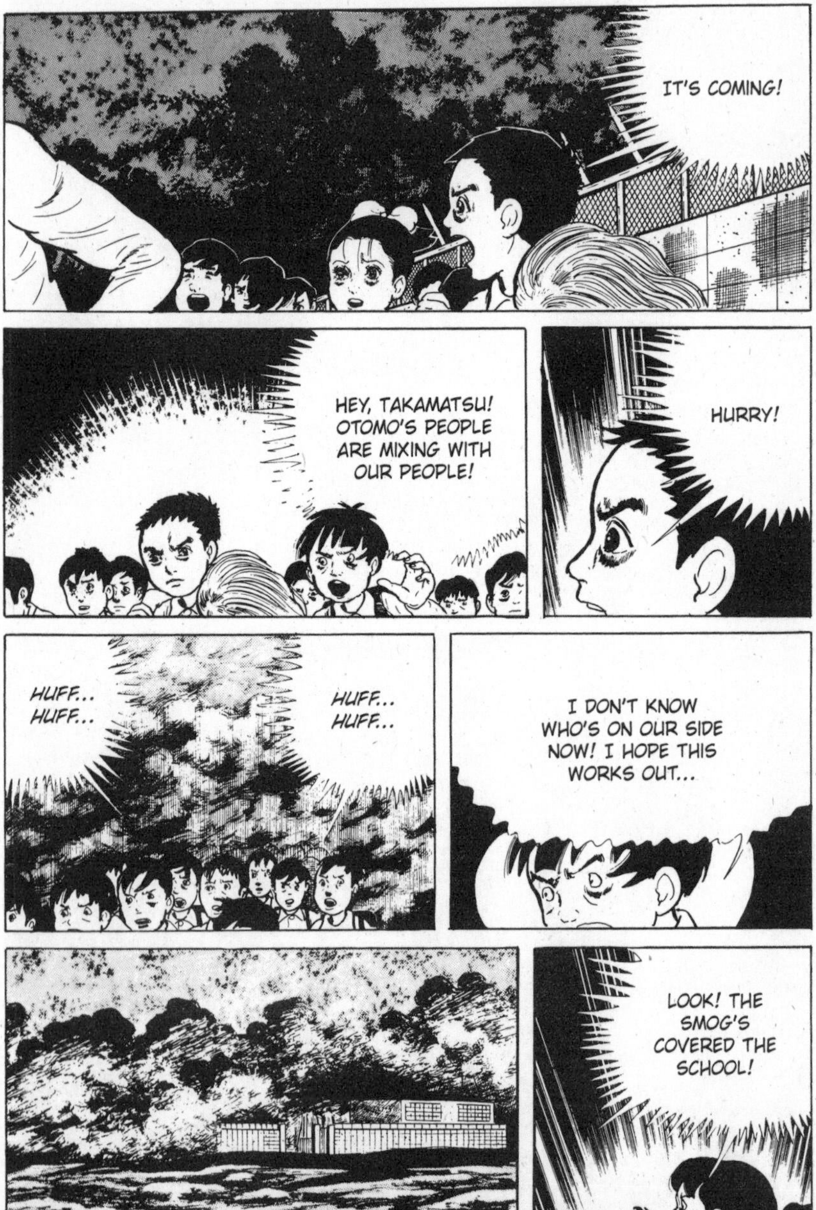
IT'S COMING!
HURRY!
HEY, TAKAMATSU! OTOMO'S PEOPLE ARE MIXING WITH OUR PEOPLE!
I DON'T KNOW WHO'S ON OUR SIDE NOW! I HOPE THIS WORKS OUT...
HUFF... HUFF...
HUFF... HUFF...
LOOK! THE SMOG'S COVERED THE SCHOOL!

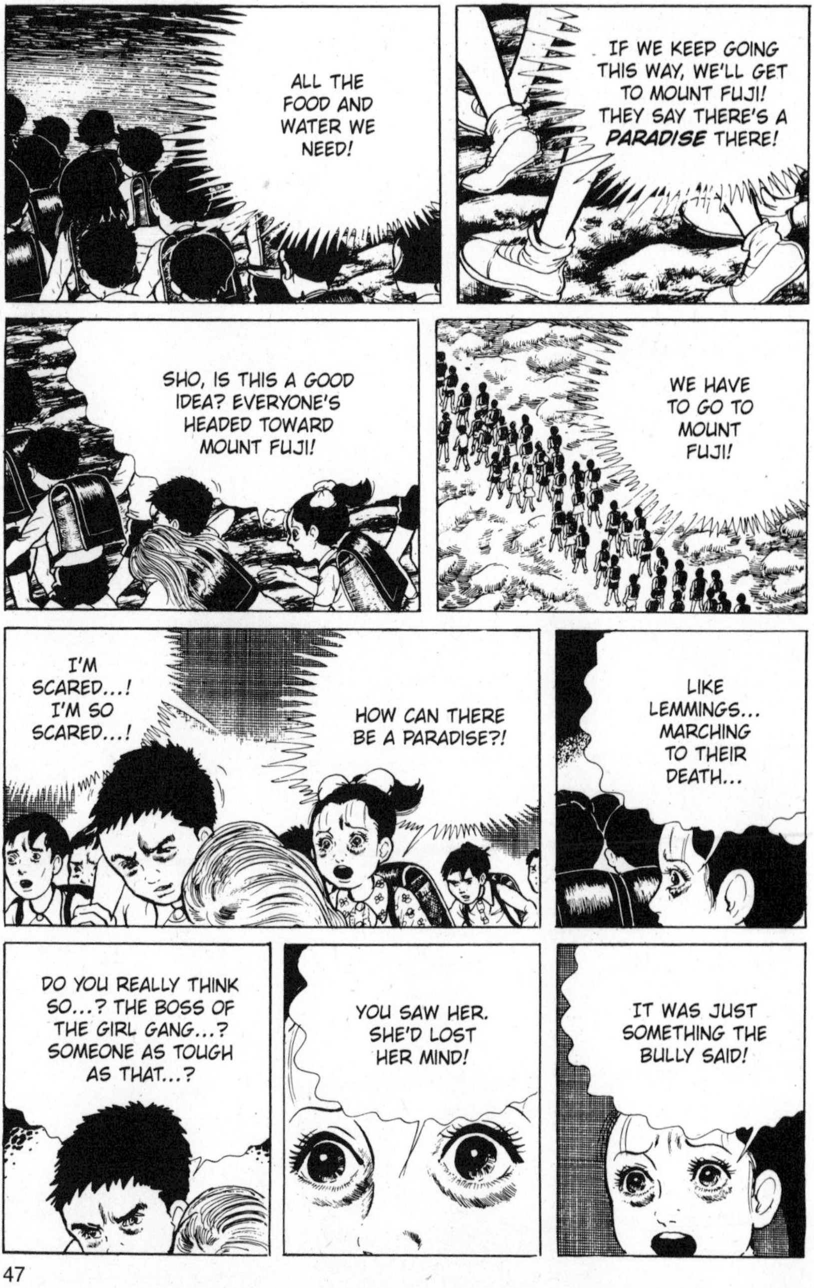
IF WE KEEP GOING THIS WAY, WE'LL GET TO MOUNT FUJI! THEY SAY THERE'S A *PARADISE* THERE!
ALL THE FOOD AND WATER WE NEED!
WE HAVE TO GO TO MOUNT FUJI!
SHO, IS THIS A GOOD IDEA? EVERYONE'S HEADED TOWARD MOUNT FUJI!
LIKE LEMMINGS... MARCHING TO THEIR DEATH...
HOW CAN THERE BE A PARADISE?!
I'M SCARED...! I'M SO SCARED...!
IT WAS JUST SOMETHING THE BULLY SAID!
YOU SAW HER. SHE'D LOST HER MIND!
DO YOU REALLY THINK SO...? THE BOSS OF THE GIRL GANG...? SOMEONE AS TOUGH AS THAT...?

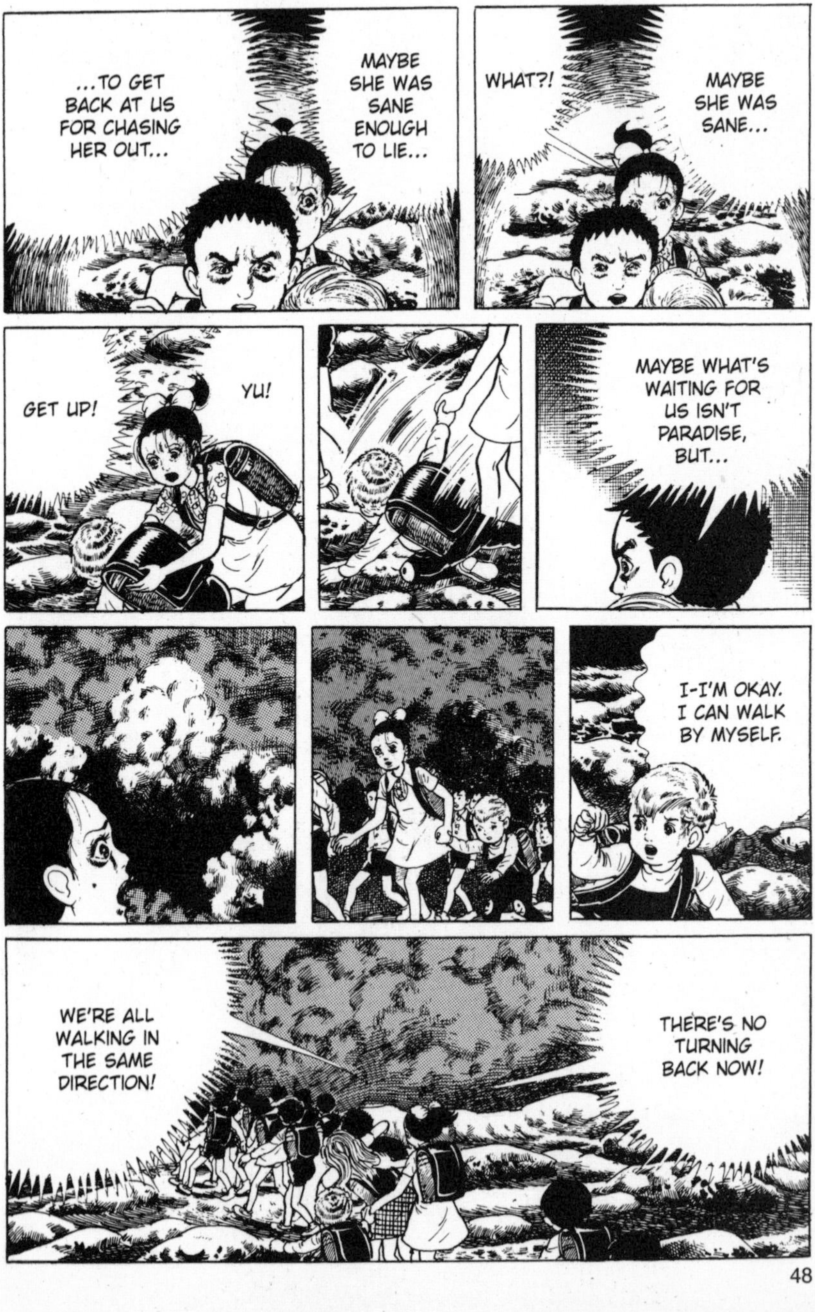
MAYBE SHE WAS SANE...
WHAT?!
MAYBE SHE WAS SANE ENOUGH TO LIE...
...TO GET BACK AT US FOR CHASING HER OUT...
MAYBE WHAT'S WAITING FOR US ISN'T PARADISE, BUT...
YU!
GET UP!
I-I'M OKAY. I CAN WALK BY MYSELF.
THERE'S NO TURNING BACK NOW!
WE'RE ALL WALKING IN THE SAME DIRECTION!

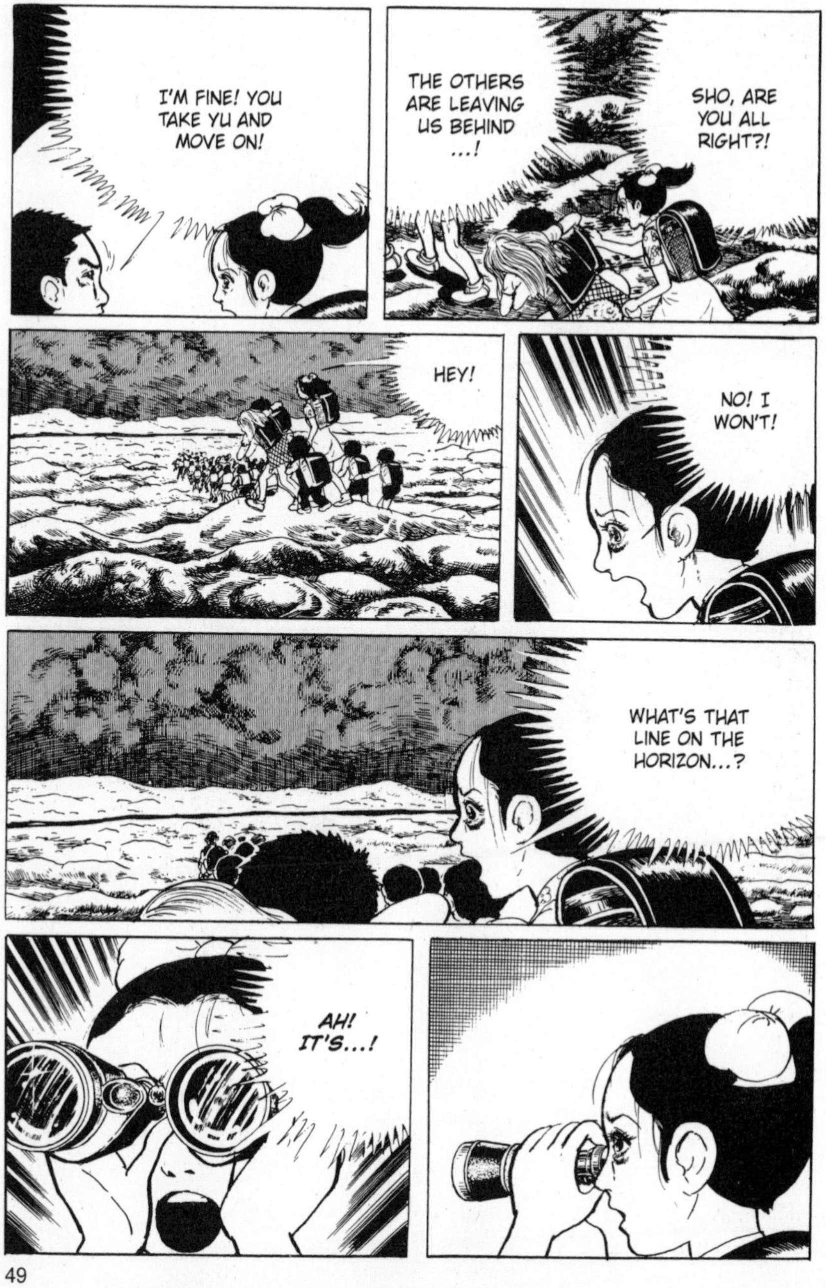
SHO, ARE YOU ALL RIGHT?!
THE OTHERS ARE LEAVING US BEHIND ...!
I'M FINE! YOU TAKE YU AND MOVE ON!
NO! I WON'T!
HEY!
WHAT'S THAT LINE ON THE HORIZON...?
AH! IT'S...!

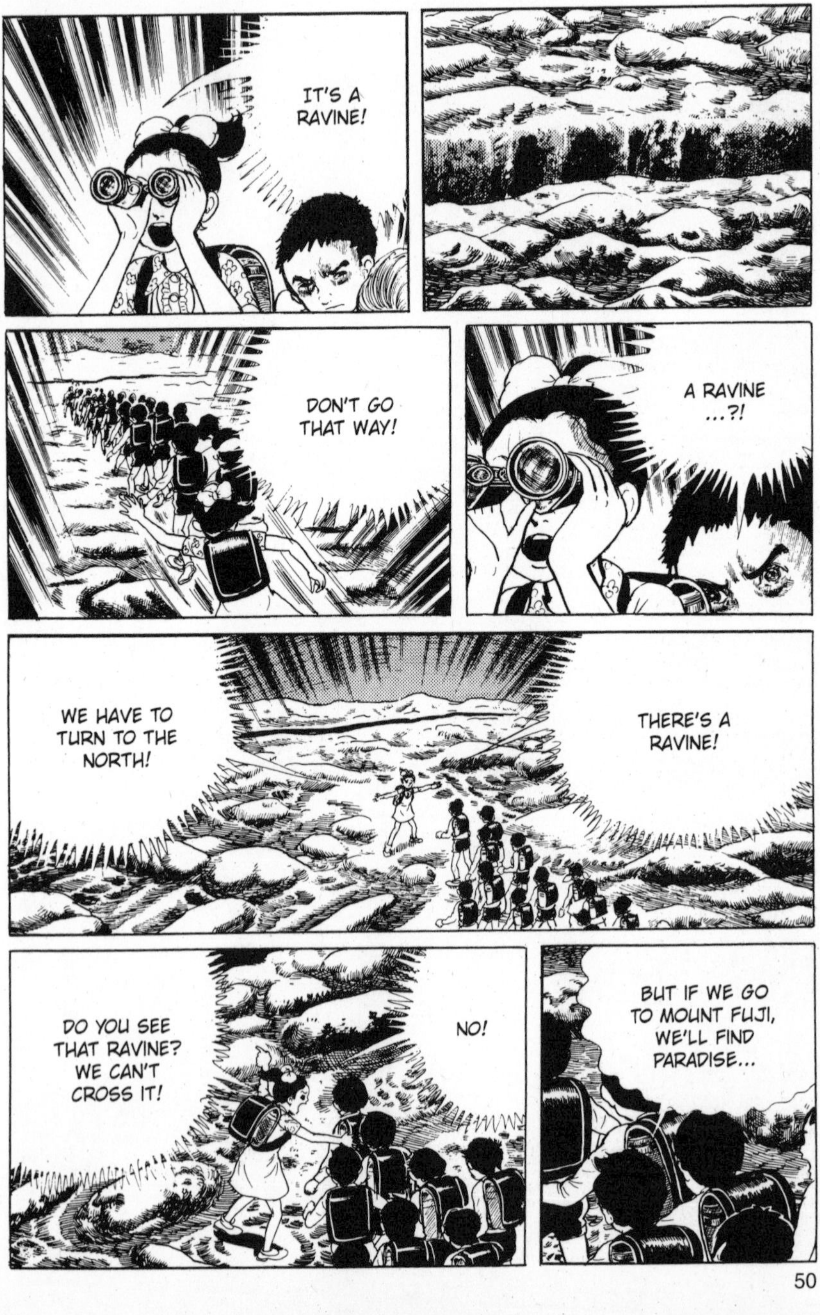
IT'S A RAVINE!
A RAVINE ...?!
DON'T GO THAT WAY!
THERE'S A RAVINE!
WE HAVE TO TURN TO THE NORTH!
BUT IF WE GO TO MOUNT FUJI, WE'LL FIND PARADISE...
NO!
DO YOU SEE THAT RAVINE? WE CAN'T CROSS IT!

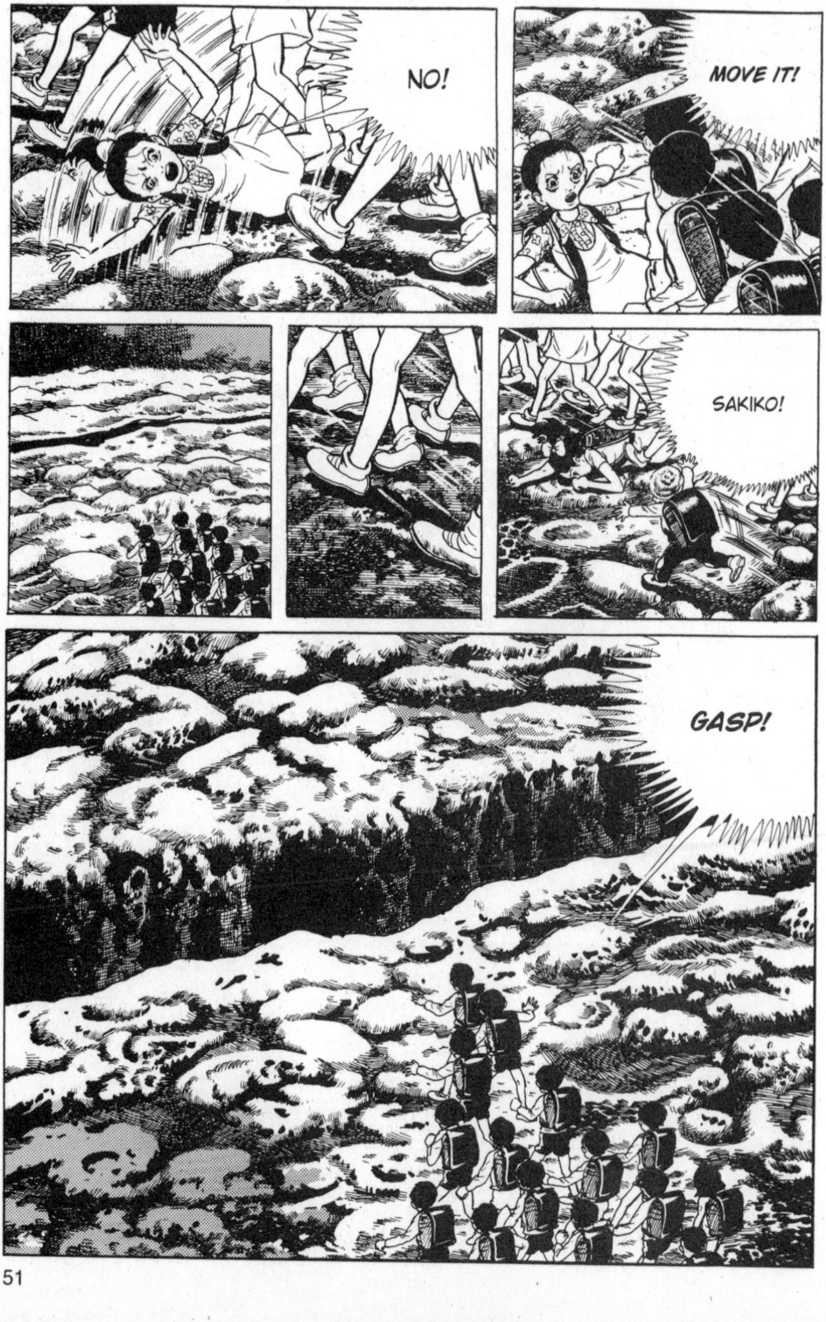
MOVE IT!
NO!
SAKIKO!
GASP!

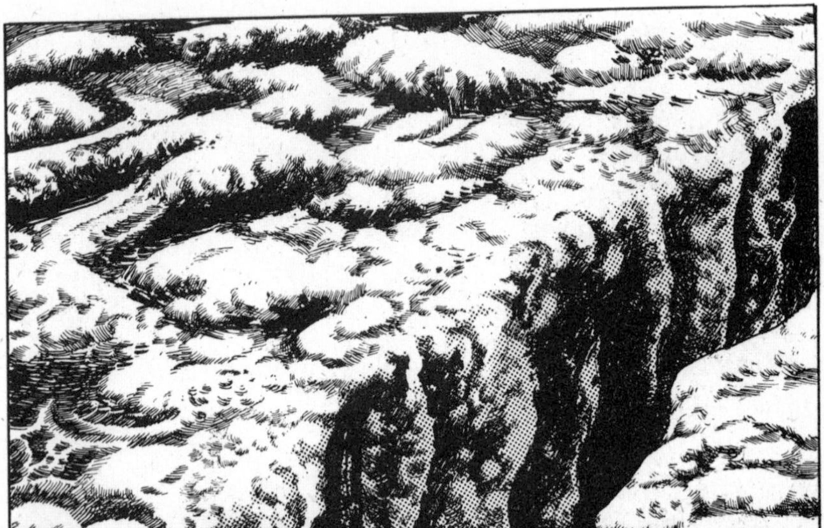

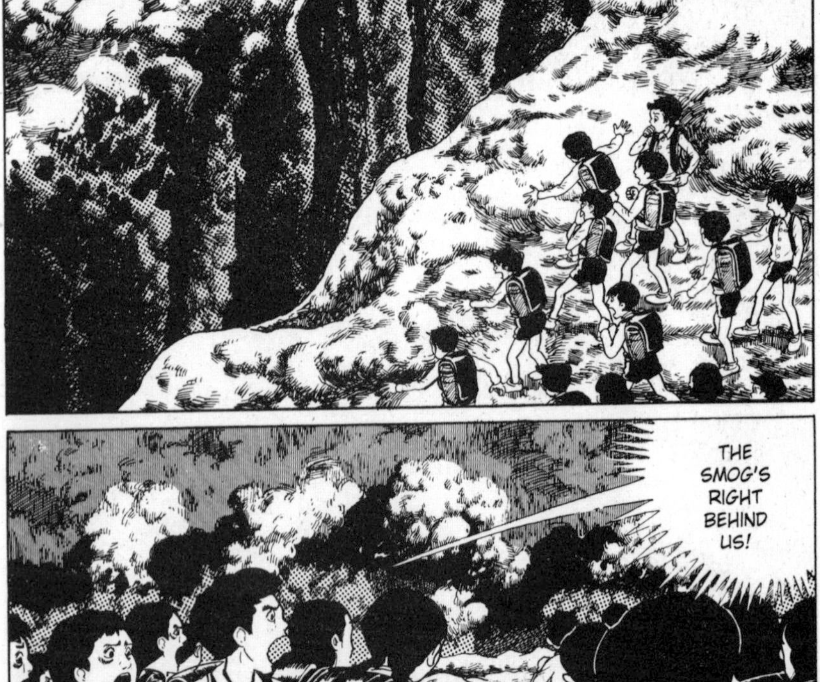
THE SMOG'S RIGHT BEHIND US!

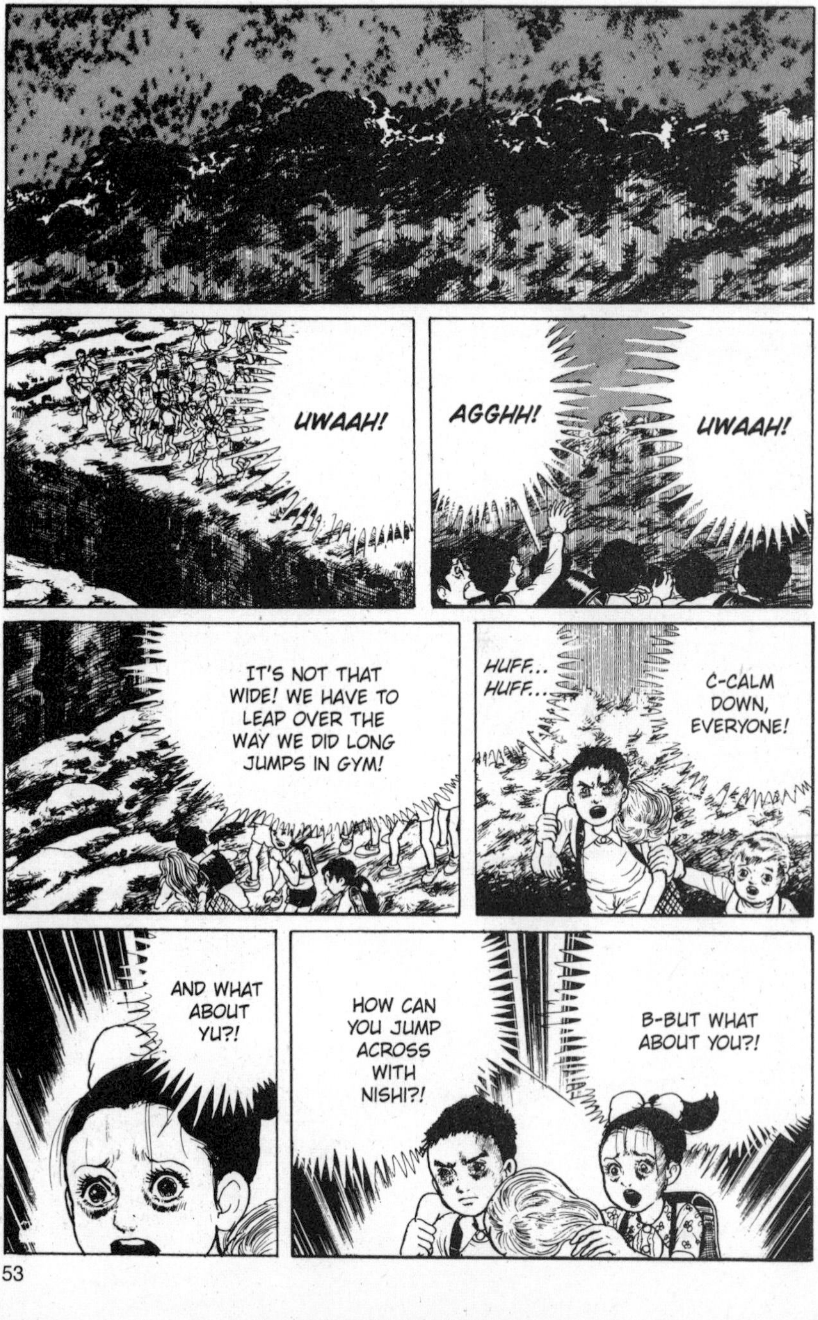
UWAAH!
AGGHH!
UWAAH!
C-CALM DOWN, EVERYONE!
HUFF... HUFF...
IT'S NOT THAT WIDE! WE HAVE TO LEAP OVER THE WAY WE DID LONG JUMPS IN GYM!
B-BUT WHAT ABOUT YOU?!
HOW CAN YOU JUMP ACROSS WITH NISHI?!
AND WHAT ABOUT YU?!

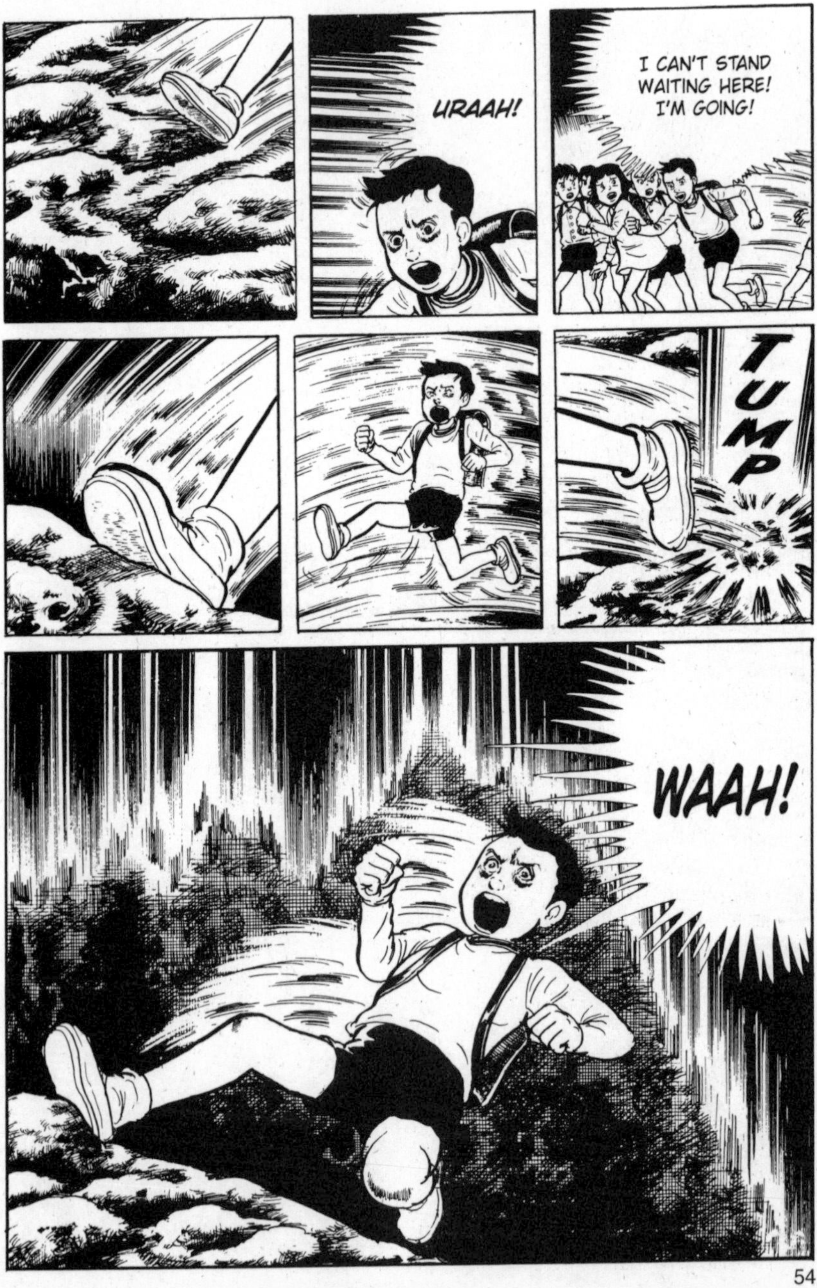
I CAN'T STAND WAITING HERE! I'M GOING!
URAAH!
TUMP
WAAH!

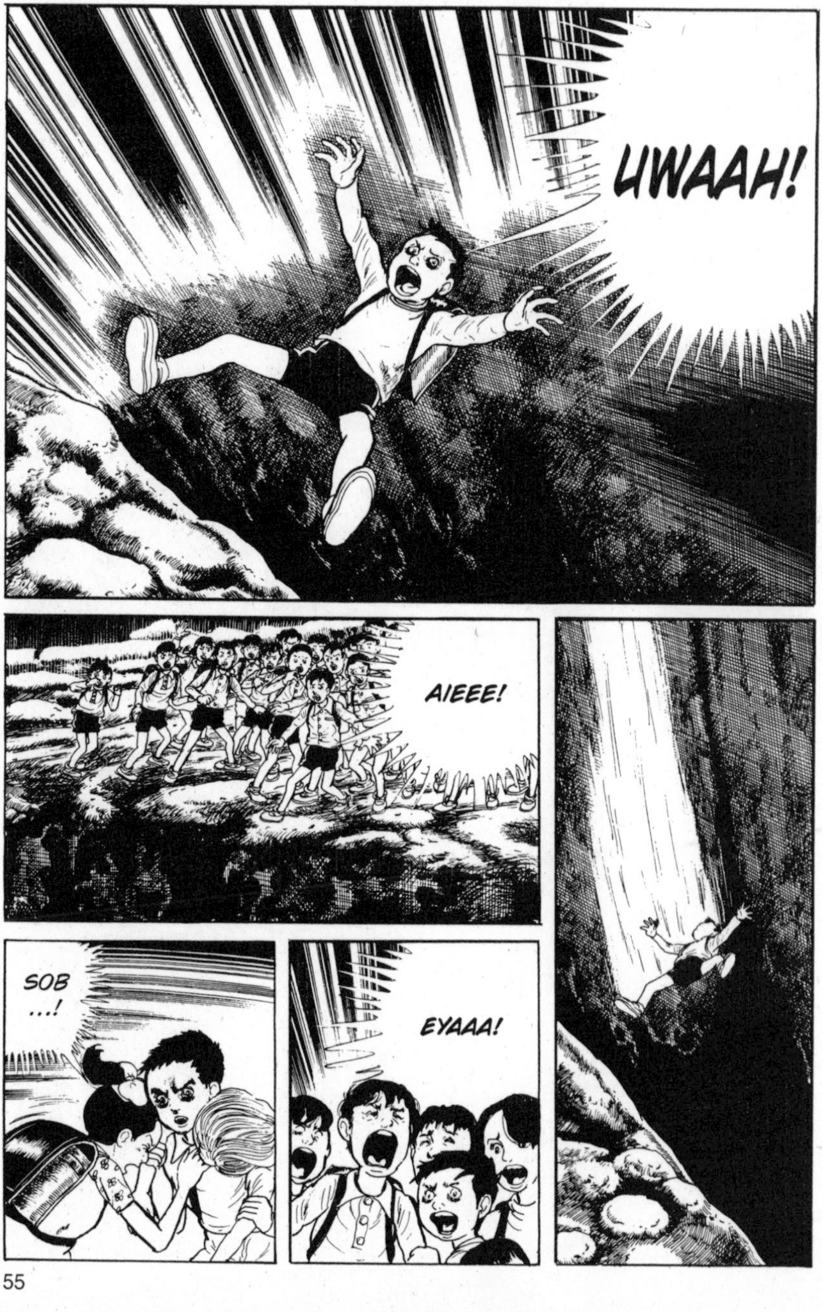
UWAAH!
AIEEE!
EYAAA!
SOB ...!

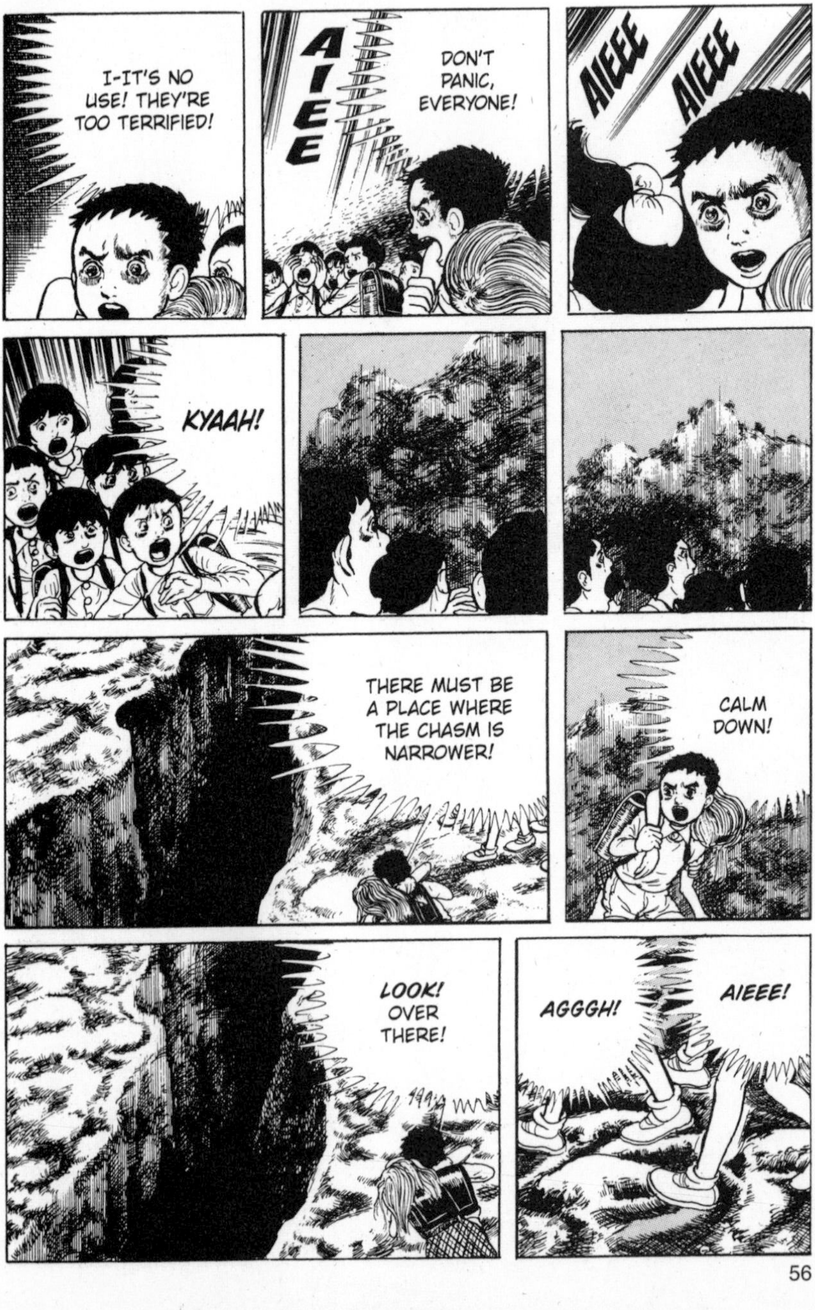
AIEEE
AIEEE
AIEE
DON'T PANIC, EVERYONE!
I-IT'S NO USE! THEY'RE TOO TERRIFIED!
KYAAH!
CALM DOWN!
THERE MUST BE A PLACE WHERE THE CHASM IS NARROWER!
AIEEE!
AGGGH!
LOOK! OVER THERE!

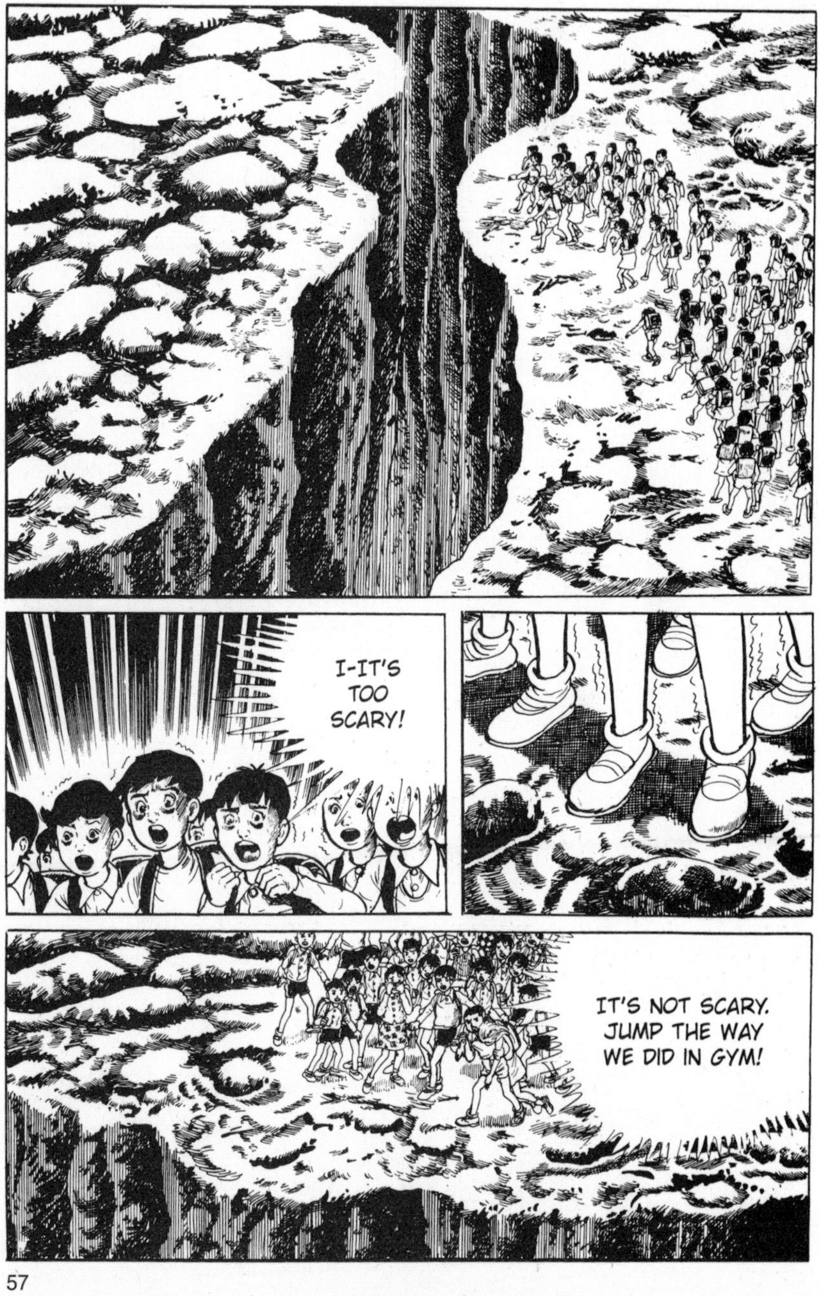
I-IT'S TOO SCARY!
IT'S NOT SCARY. JUMP THE WAY WE DID IN GYM!

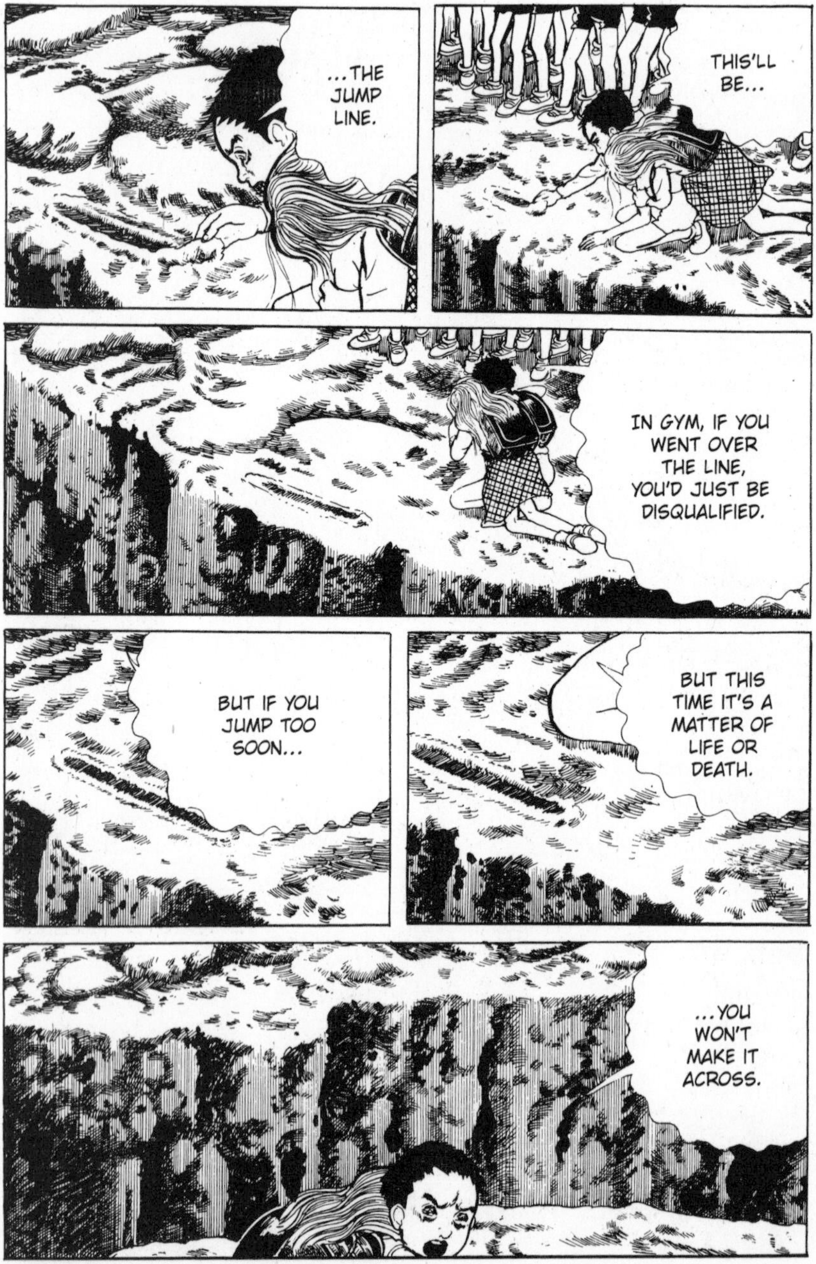
THIS'LL BE...
...THE JUMP LINE.
IN GYM, IF YOU WENT OVER THE LINE, YOU'D JUST BE DISQUALIFIED.
BUT THIS TIME IT'S A MATTER OF LIFE OR DEATH.
BUT IF YOU JUMP TOO SOON...
...YOU WON'T MAKE IT ACROSS.

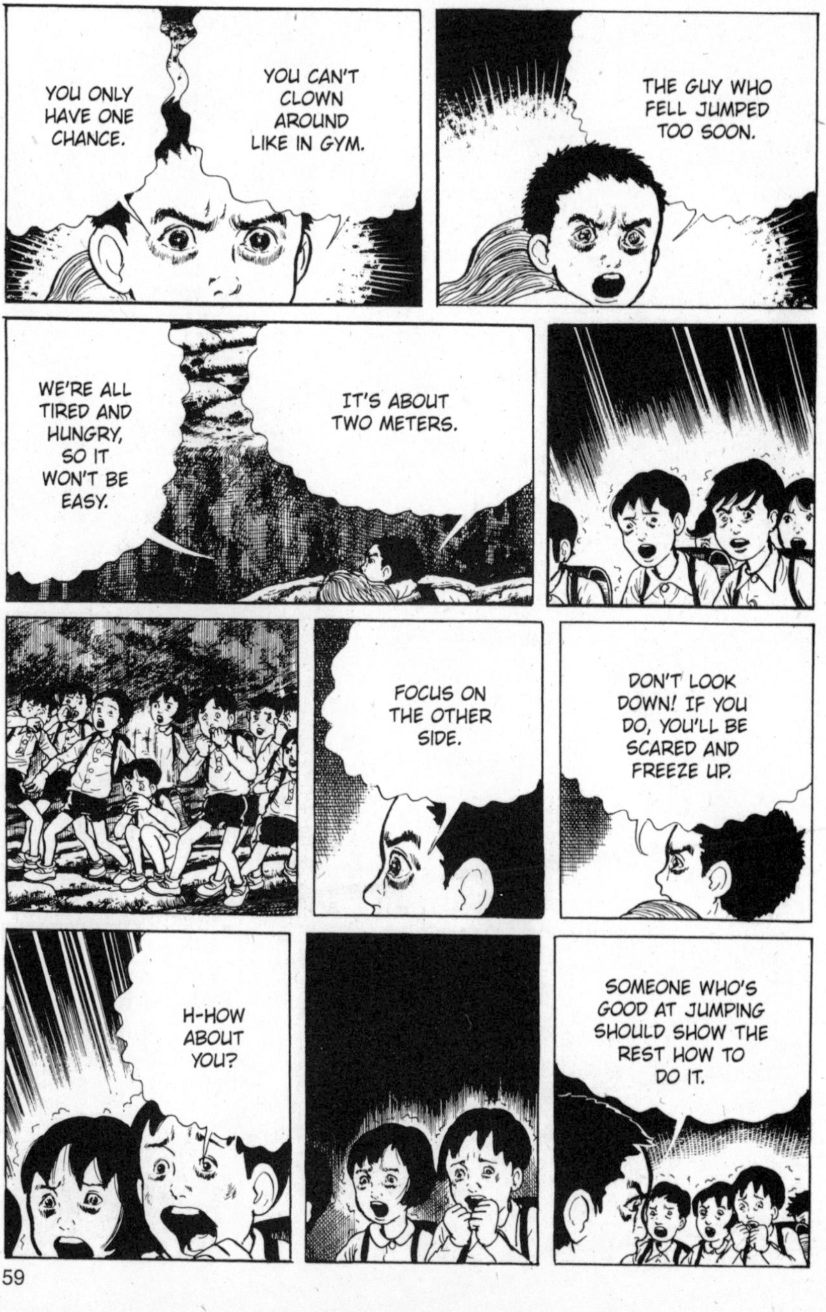
THE GUY WHO FELL JUMPED TOO SOON.
YOU CAN'T CLOWN AROUND LIKE IN GYM.
YOU ONLY HAVE ONE CHANCE.
IT'S ABOUT TWO METERS.
WE'RE ALL TIRED AND HUNGRY, SO IT WON'T BE EASY.
DON'T LOOK DOWN! IF YOU DO, YOU'LL BE SCARED AND FREEZE UP.
FOCUS ON THE OTHER SIDE.
SOMEONE WHO'S GOOD AT JUMPING SHOULD SHOW THE REST HOW TO DO IT.
H-HOW ABOUT YOU?

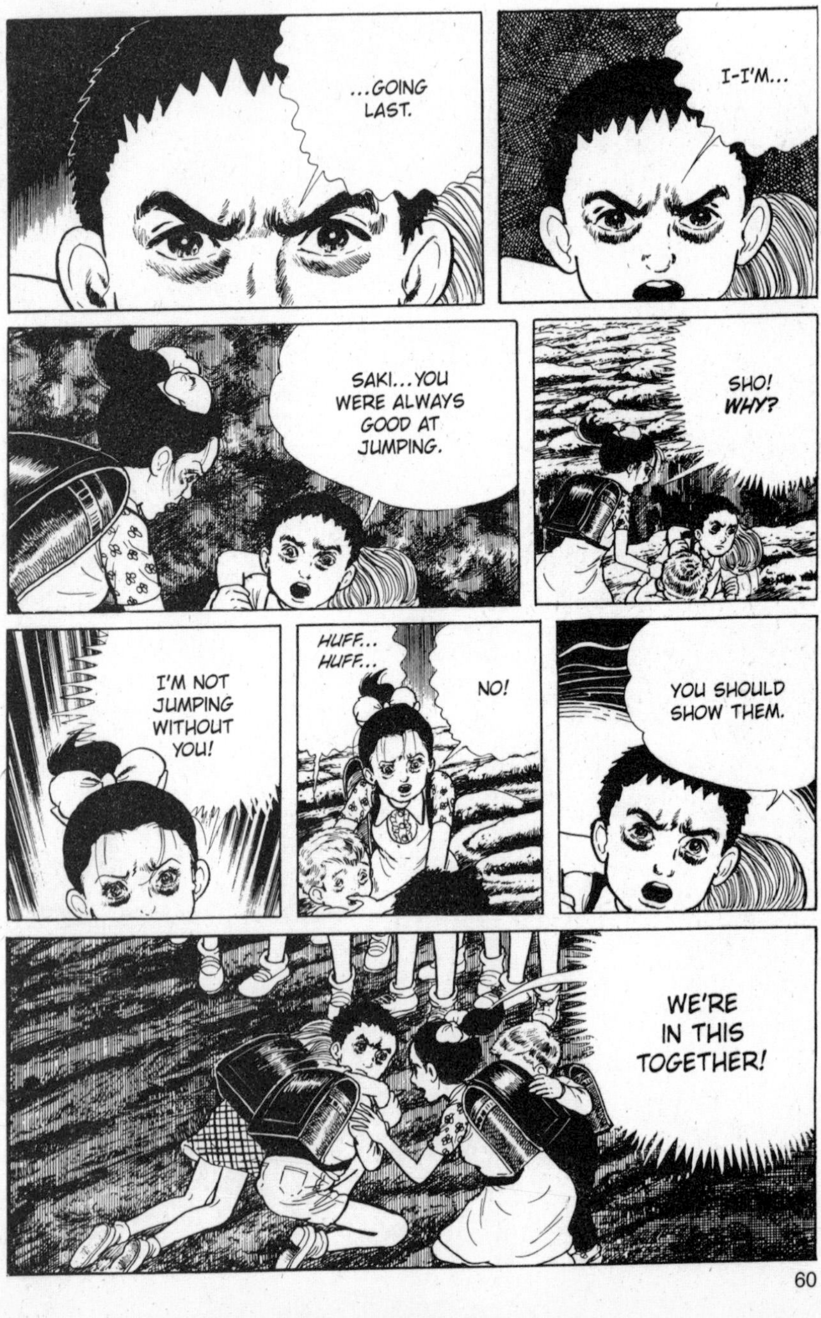
I-I'M...
...GOING LAST.
SHO! *WHY?*
SAKI...YOU WERE ALWAYS GOOD AT JUMPING.
YOU SHOULD SHOW THEM.
HUFF... HUFF...
NO!
I'M NOT JUMPING WITHOUT YOU!
WE'RE IN THIS TOGETHER!

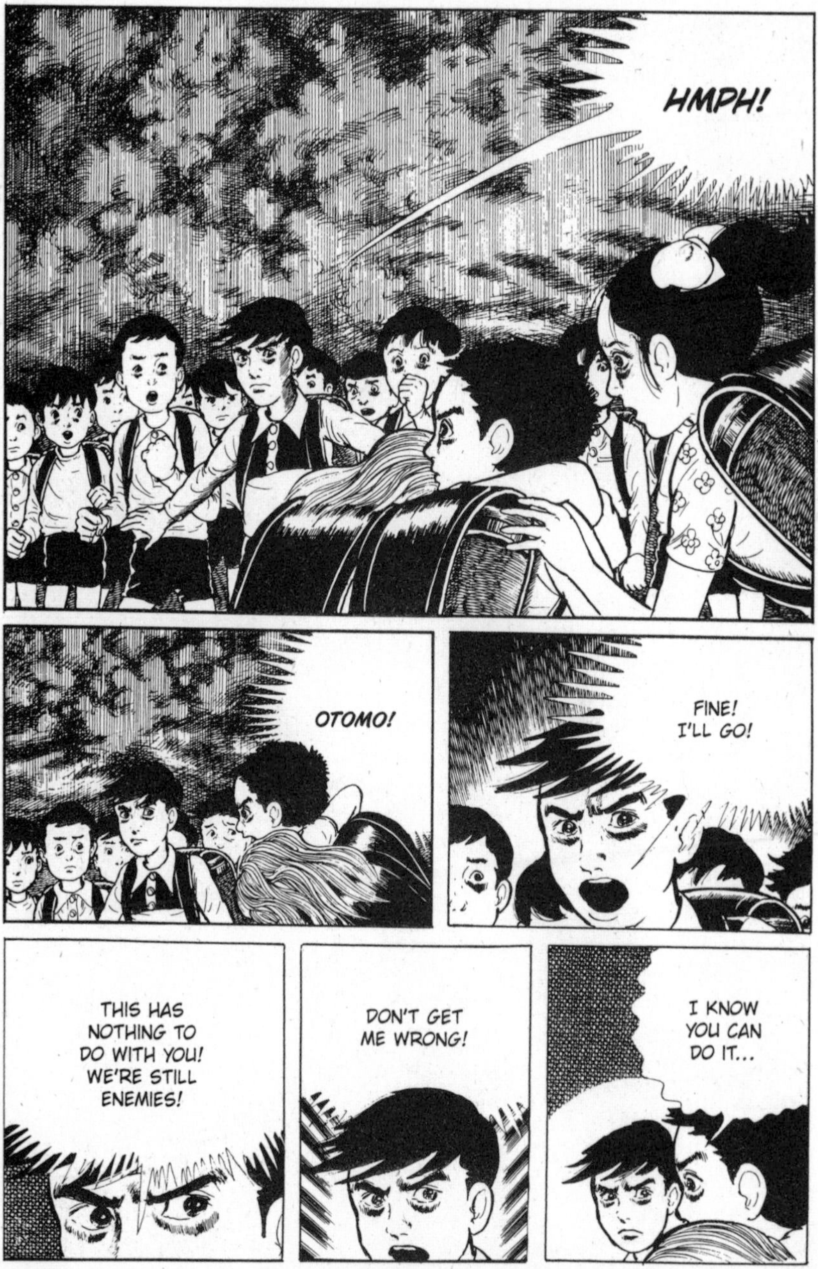
HMPH!
FINE! I'LL GO!
OTOMO!
I KNOW YOU CAN DO IT...
DON'T GET ME WRONG!
THIS HAS NOTHING TO DO WITH YOU! WE'RE STILL ENEMIES!

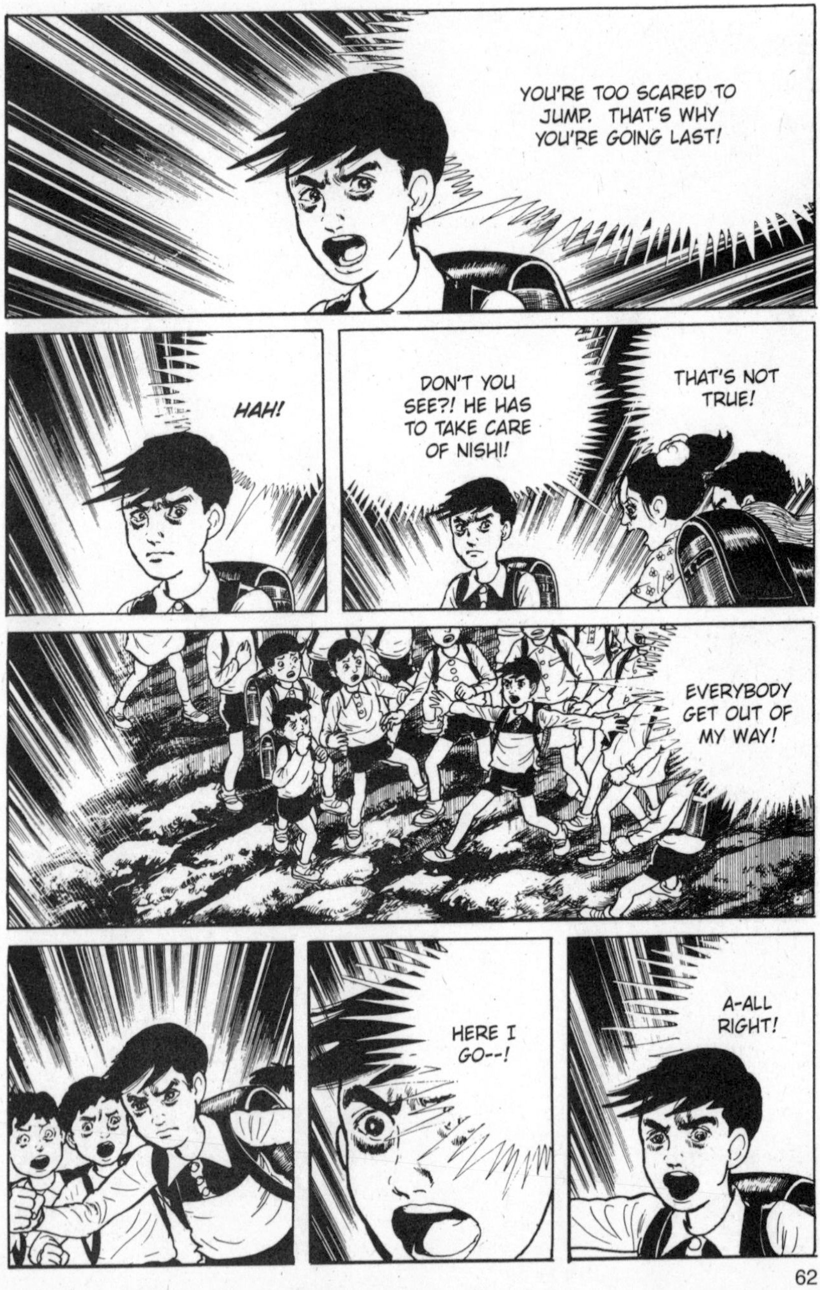
YOU'RE TOO SCARED TO JUMP. THAT'S WHY YOU'RE GOING LAST!
THAT'S NOT TRUE!
DON'T YOU SEE?! HE HAS TO TAKE CARE OF NISHI!
HAH!
EVERYBODY GET OUT OF MY WAY!
A-ALL RIGHT!
HERE I GO--!

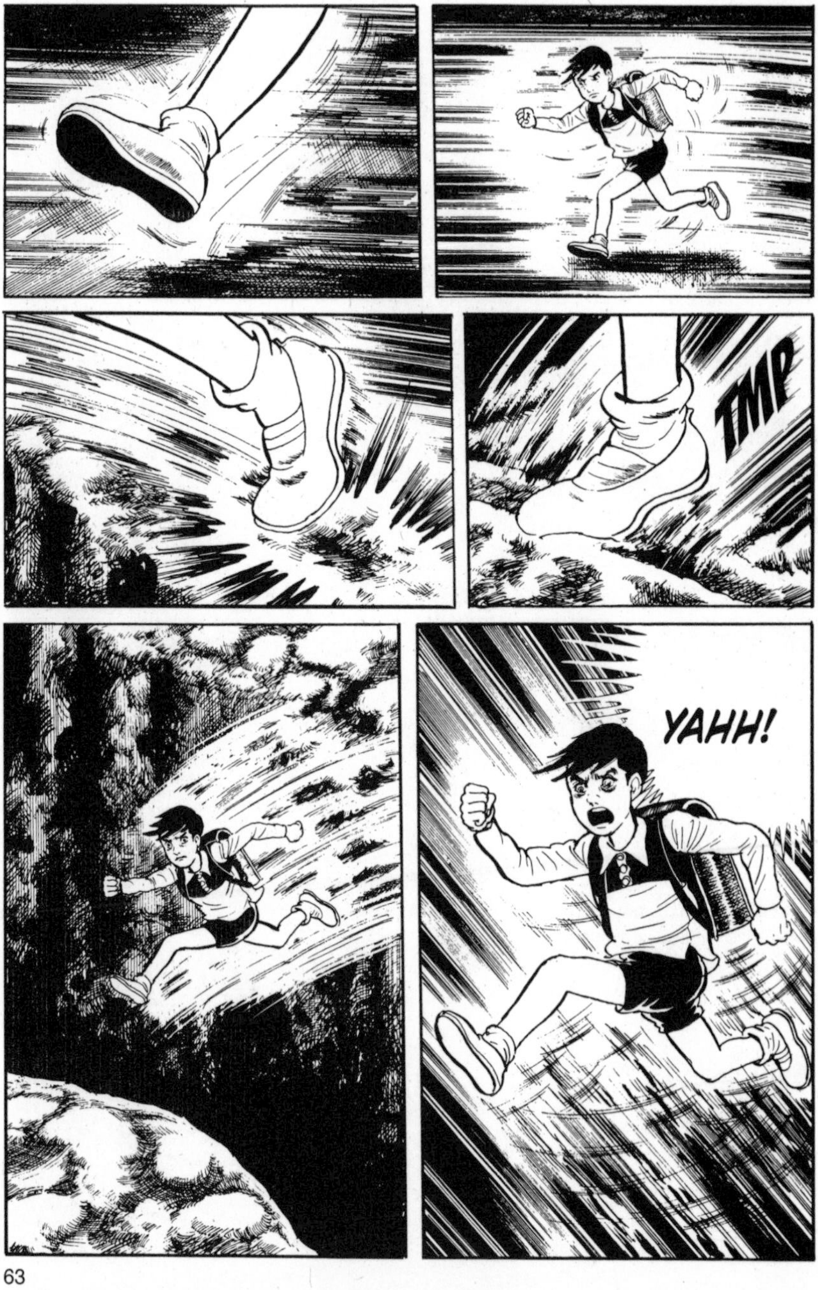
TMP
YAHH!

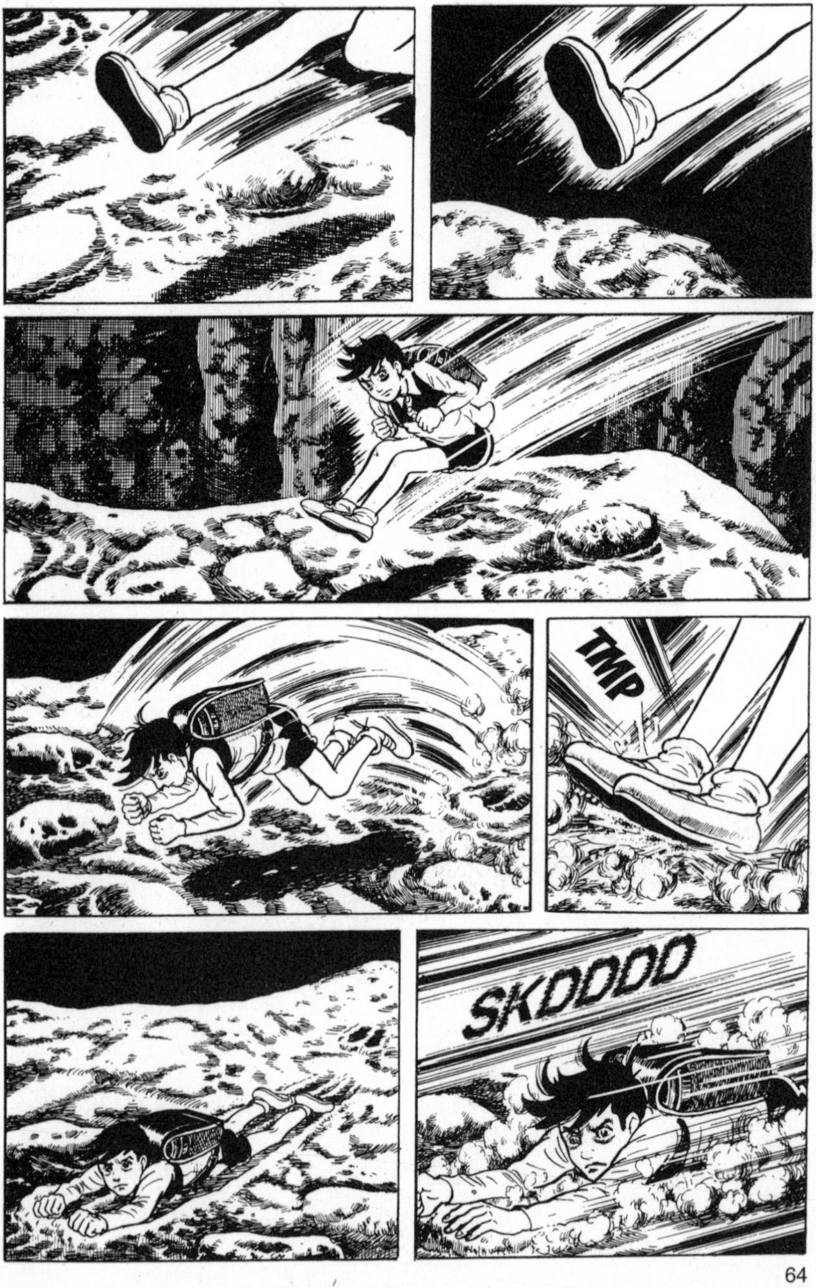
TMP
SKDDDD

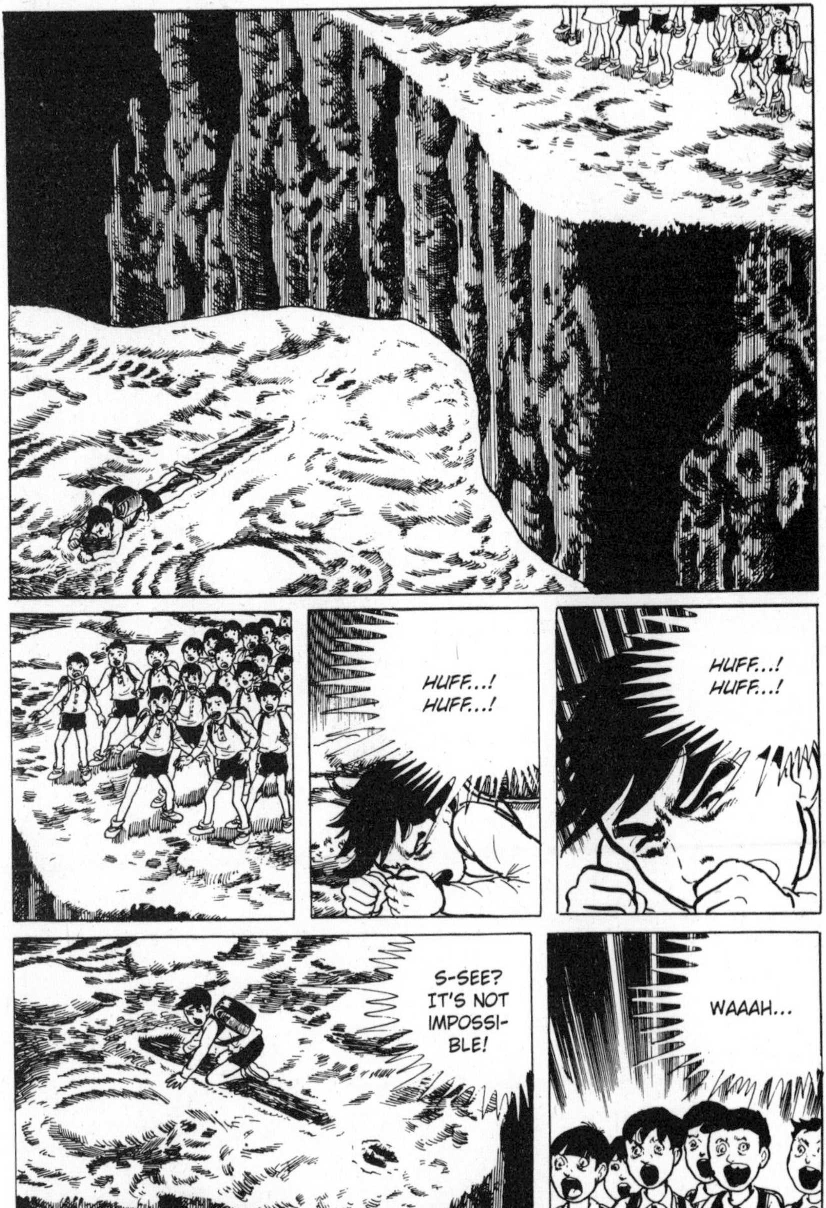
HUFF...! HUFF...!
HUFF...! HUFF...!
WAAAH...
S-SEE? IT'S NOT IMPOSSI-BLE!

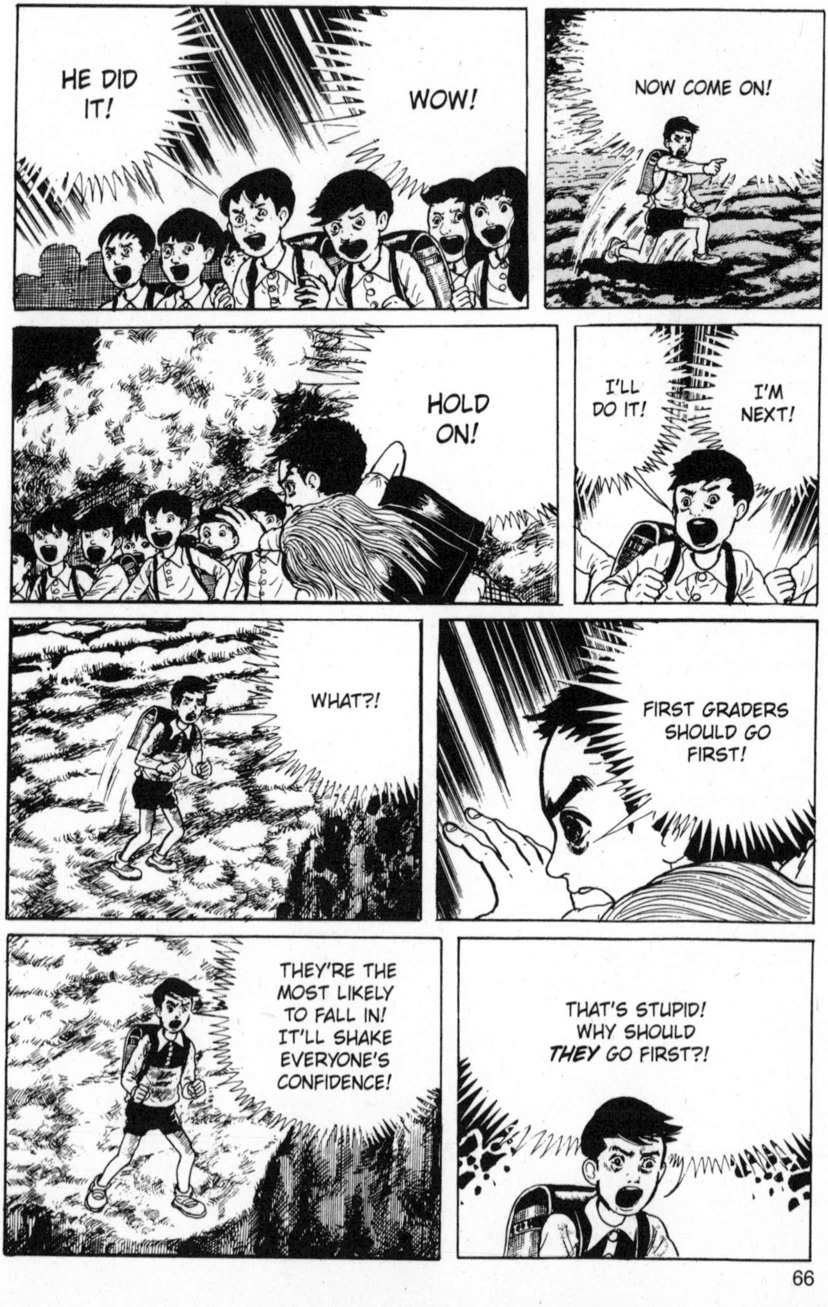
NOW COME ON!
WOW!
HE DID IT!
I'M NEXT!
I'LL DO IT!
HOLD ON!
FIRST GRADERS SHOULD GO FIRST!
WHAT?!
THAT'S STUPID! WHY SHOULD *THEY* GO FIRST?!
THEY'RE THE MOST LIKELY TO FALL IN! IT'LL SHAKE EVERYONE'S CONFIDENCE!

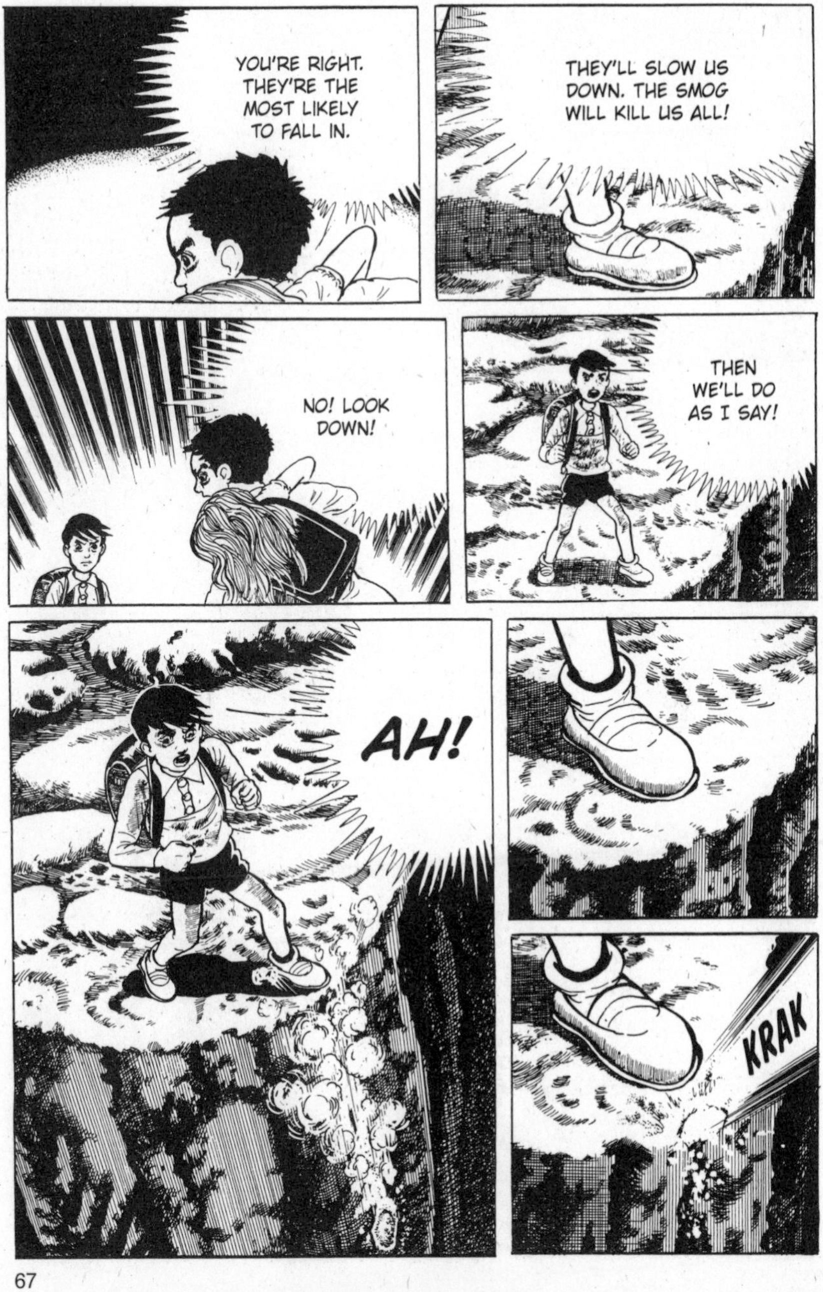
THEY'LL SLOW US DOWN. THE SMOG WILL KILL US ALL!
YOU'RE RIGHT. THEY'RE THE MOST LIKELY TO FALL IN.
THEN WE'LL DO AS I SAY!
NO! LOOK DOWN!
KRAK
AH!

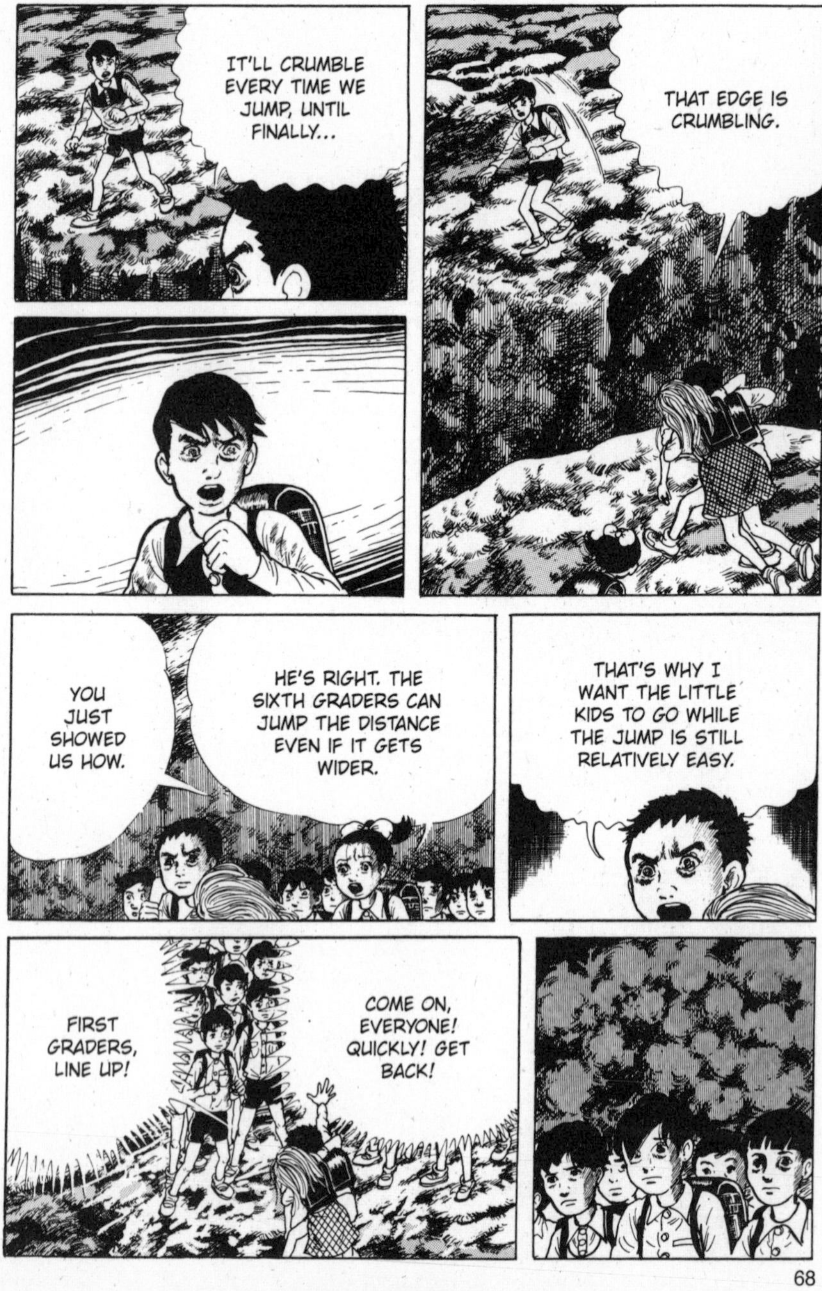
THAT EDGE IS CRUMBLING.
IT'LL CRUMBLE EVERY TIME WE JUMP, UNTIL FINALLY...
THAT'S WHY I WANT THE LITTLE KIDS TO GO WHILE THE JUMP IS STILL RELATIVELY EASY.
HE'S RIGHT. THE SIXTH GRADERS CAN JUMP THE DISTANCE EVEN IF IT GETS WIDER.
YOU JUST SHOWED US HOW.
COME ON, EVERYONE! QUICKLY! GET BACK!
FIRST GRADERS, LINE UP!

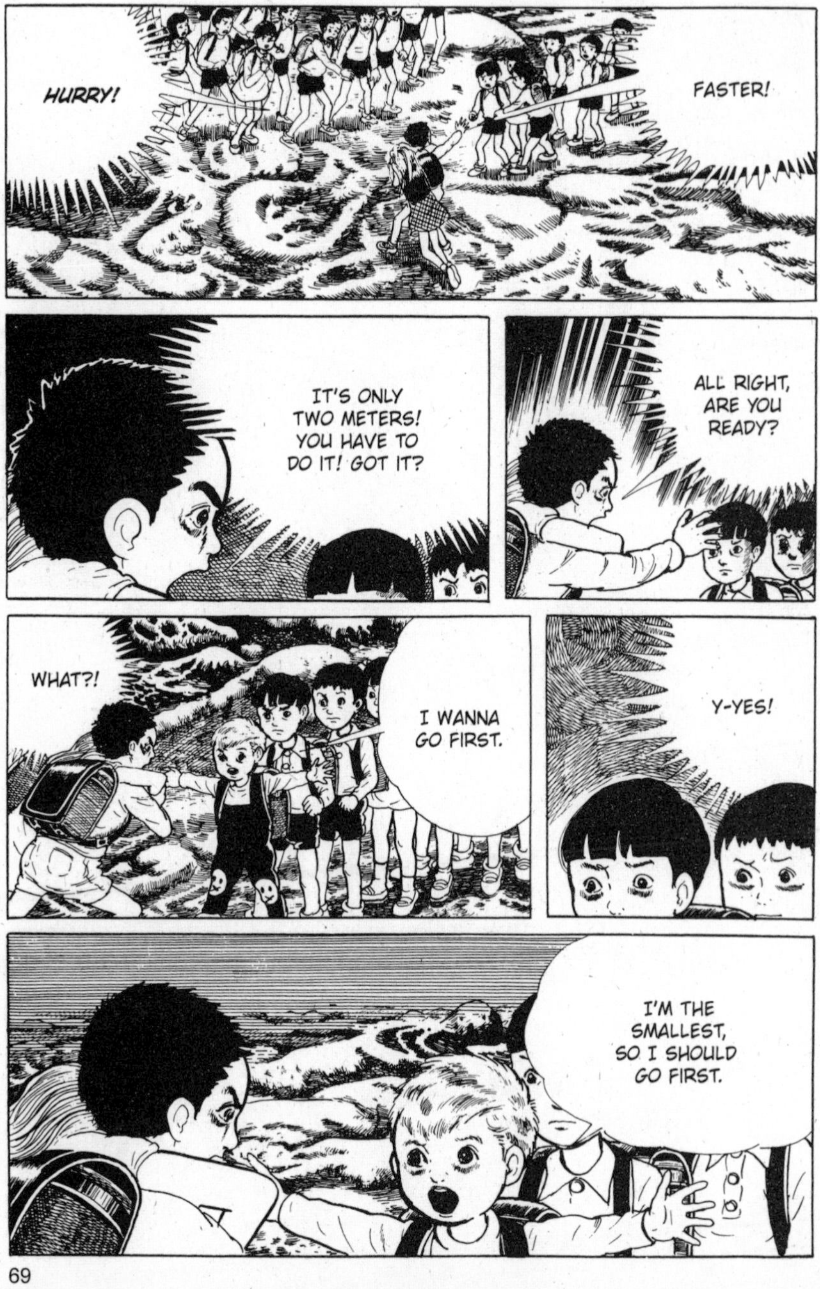
FASTER!
HURRY!
ALL RIGHT, ARE YOU READY?
IT'S ONLY TWO METERS! YOU HAVE TO DO IT! GOT IT?
Y-YES!
I WANNA GO FIRST.
WHAT?!
I'M THE SMALLEST, SO I SHOULD GO FIRST.

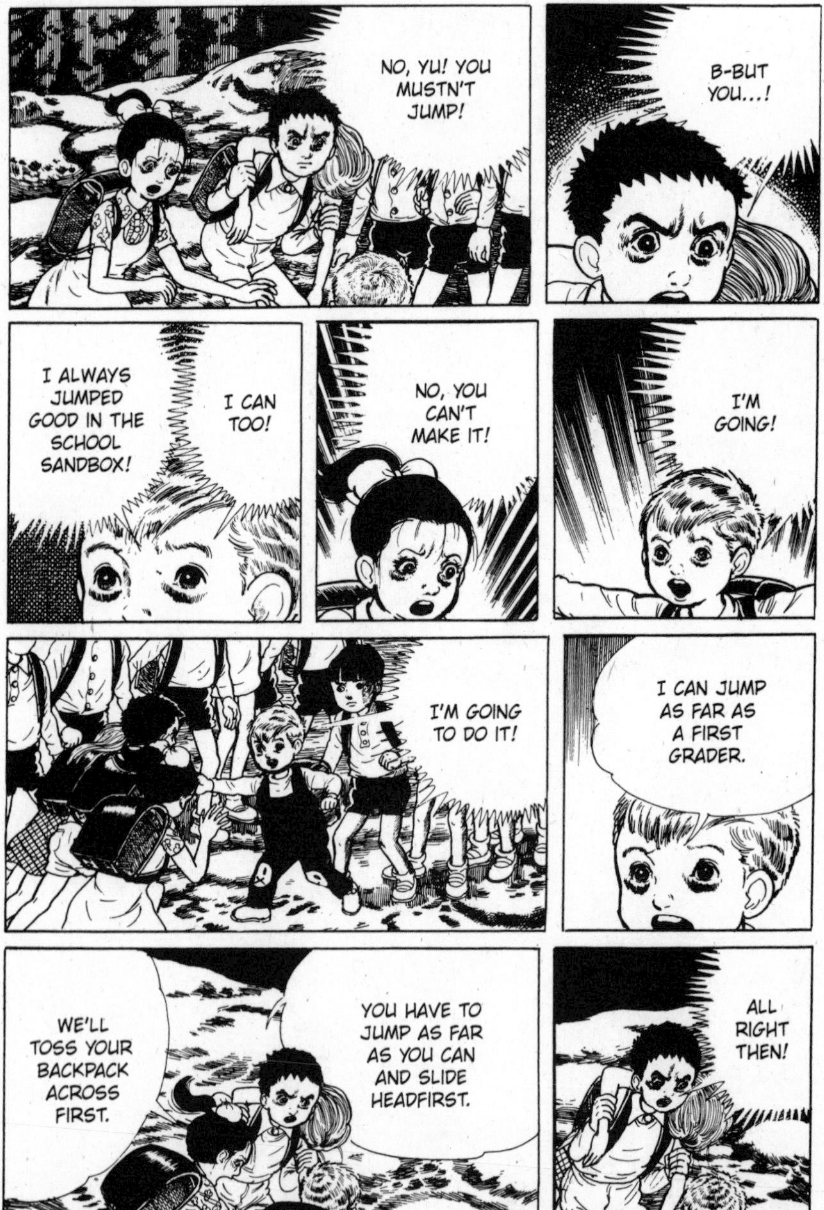
B-BUT YOU...!
NO, YU! YOU MUSTN'T JUMP!
I'M GOING!
NO, YOU CAN'T MAKE IT!
I CAN TOO!
I ALWAYS JUMPED GOOD IN THE SCHOOL SANDBOX!
I CAN JUMP AS FAR AS A FIRST GRADER.
I'M GOING TO DO IT!
ALL RIGHT THEN!
YOU HAVE TO JUMP AS FAR AS YOU CAN AND SLIDE HEADFIRST.
WE'LL TOSS YOUR BACKPACK ACROSS FIRST.

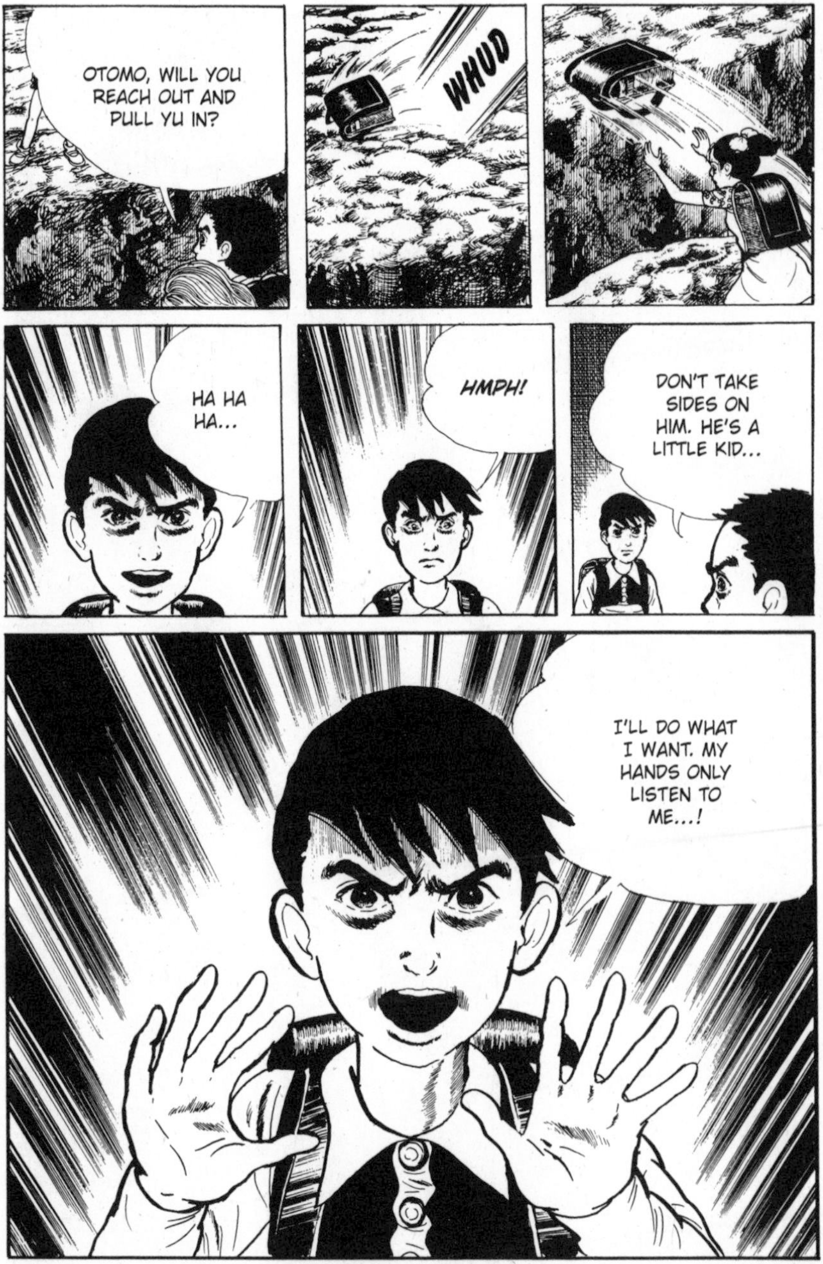
WHUD
OTOMO, WILL YOU REACH OUT AND PULL YU IN?
DON'T TAKE SIDES ON HIM. HE'S A LITTLE KID...
HMPH!
HA HA HA...
I'LL DO WHAT I WANT. MY HANDS ONLY LISTEN TO ME...!

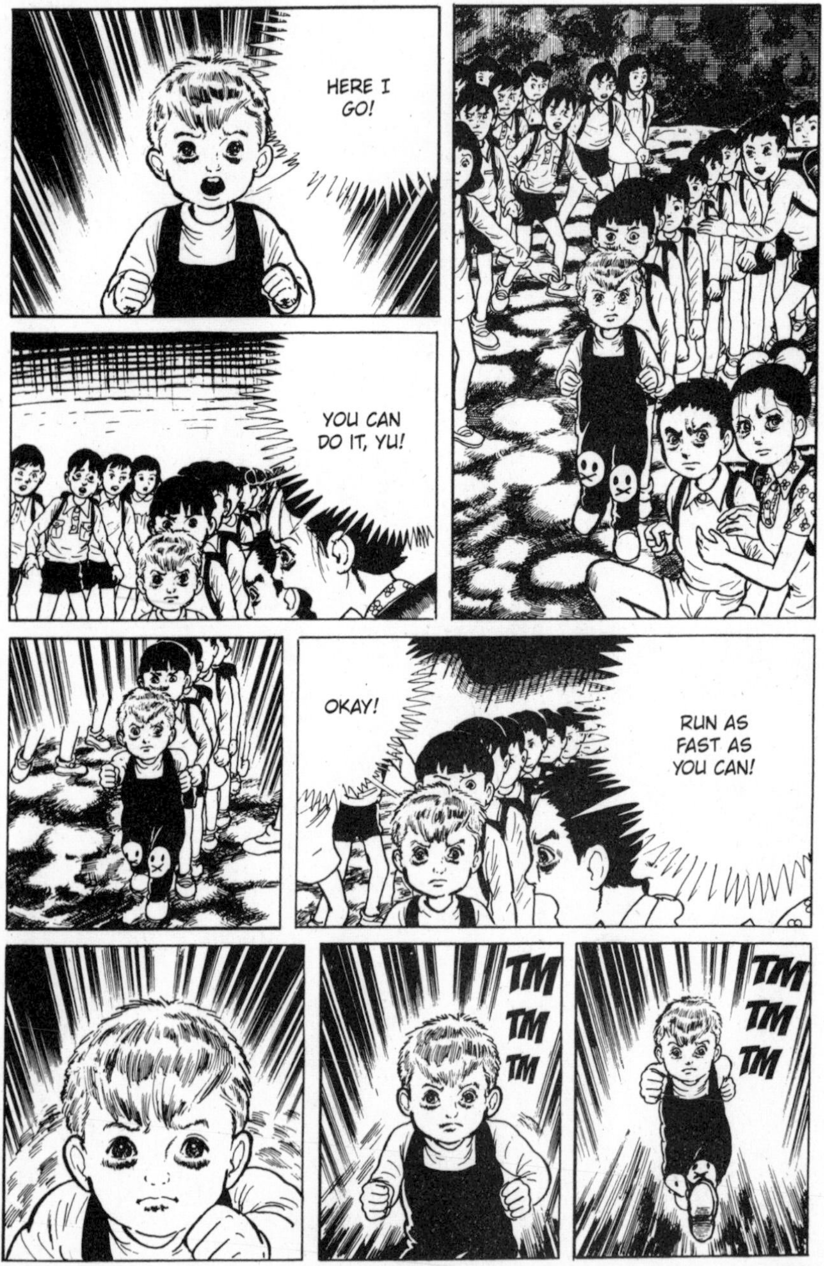
HERE I GO!
YOU CAN DO IT, YU!
RUN AS FAST AS YOU CAN!
OKAY!
TM TM TM
TM TM TM

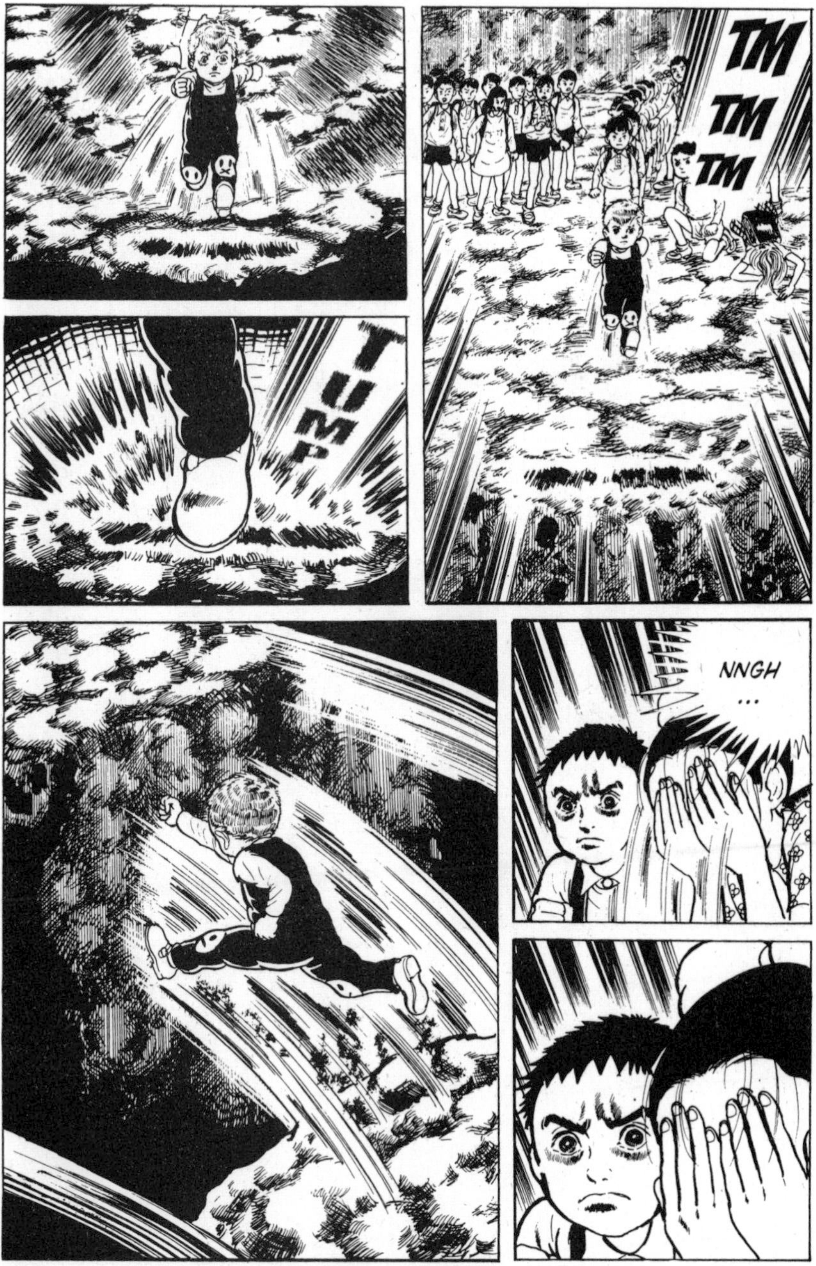
TM
TM
TM
TUMP
NNGH ...

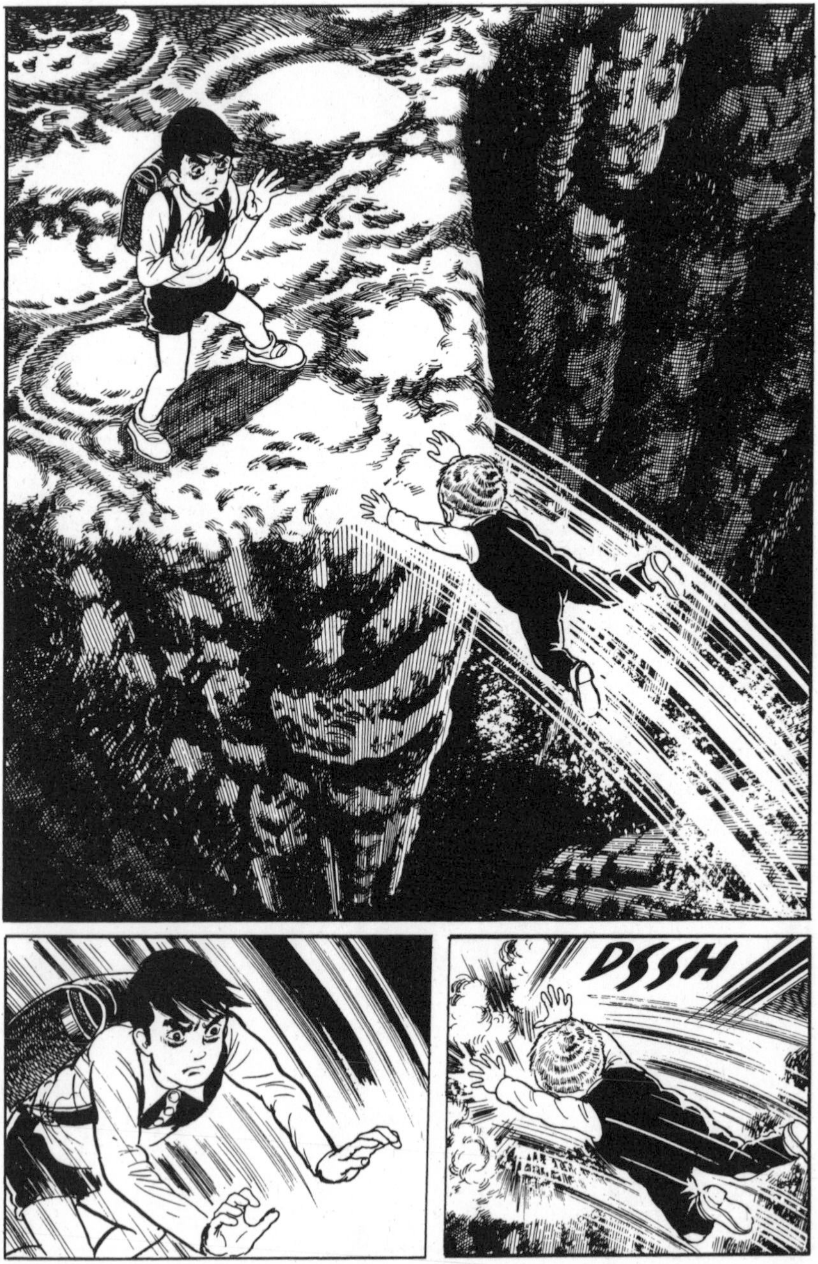
DSSH

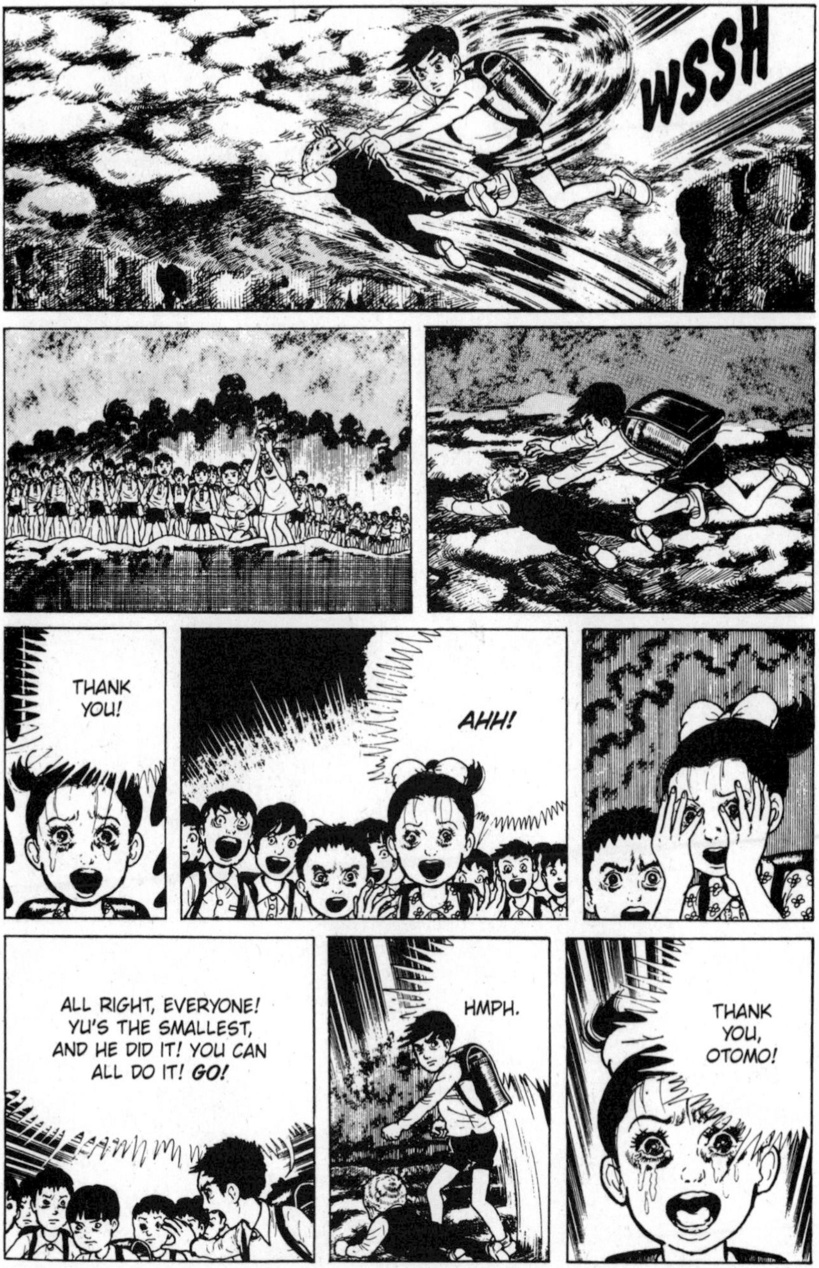
WSSH
AHH!
THANK YOU!
THANK YOU, OTOMO!
HMPH.
ALL RIGHT, EVERYONE! YU'S THE SMALLEST, AND HE DID IT! YOU CAN ALL DO IT! **GO!**

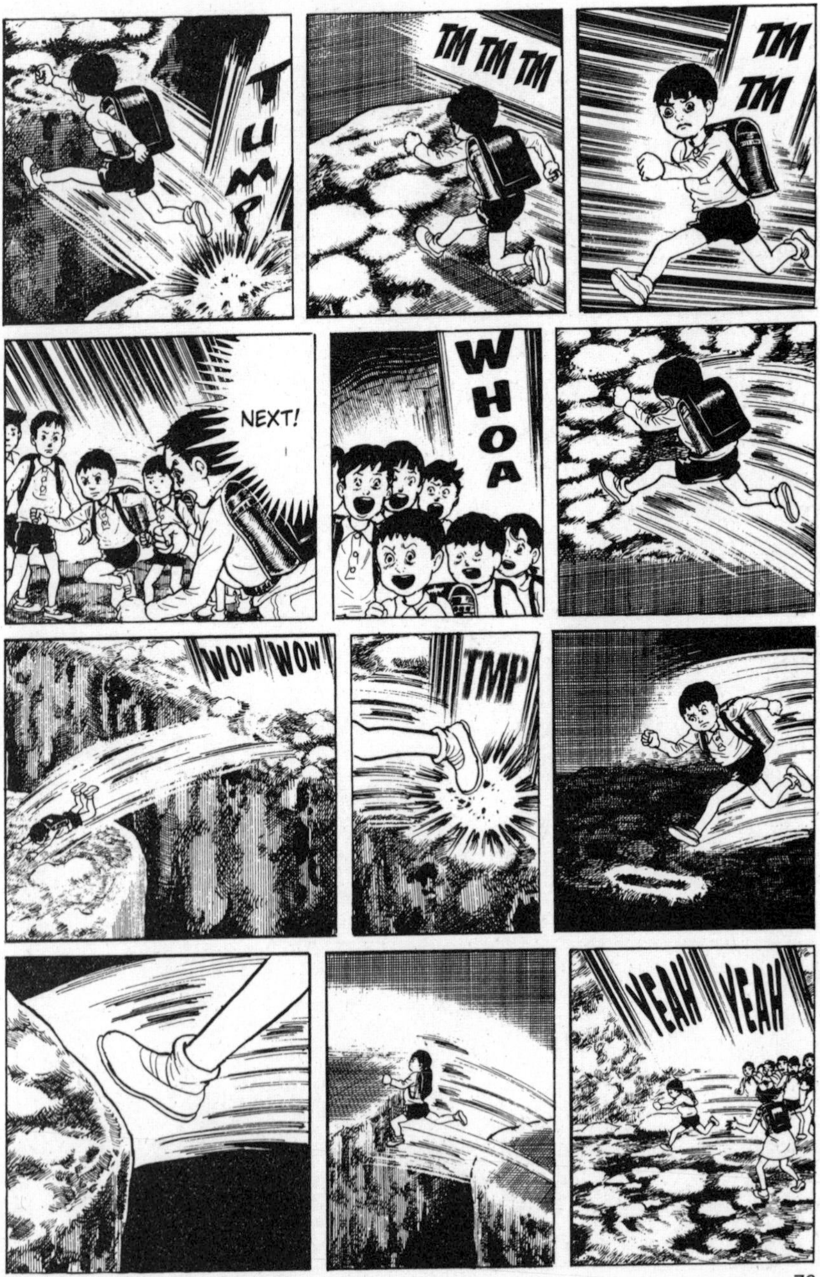
TM
TM
TM TM TM
TUMP
WHOA
NEXT!
TMP
WOW WOW
YEAH YEAH

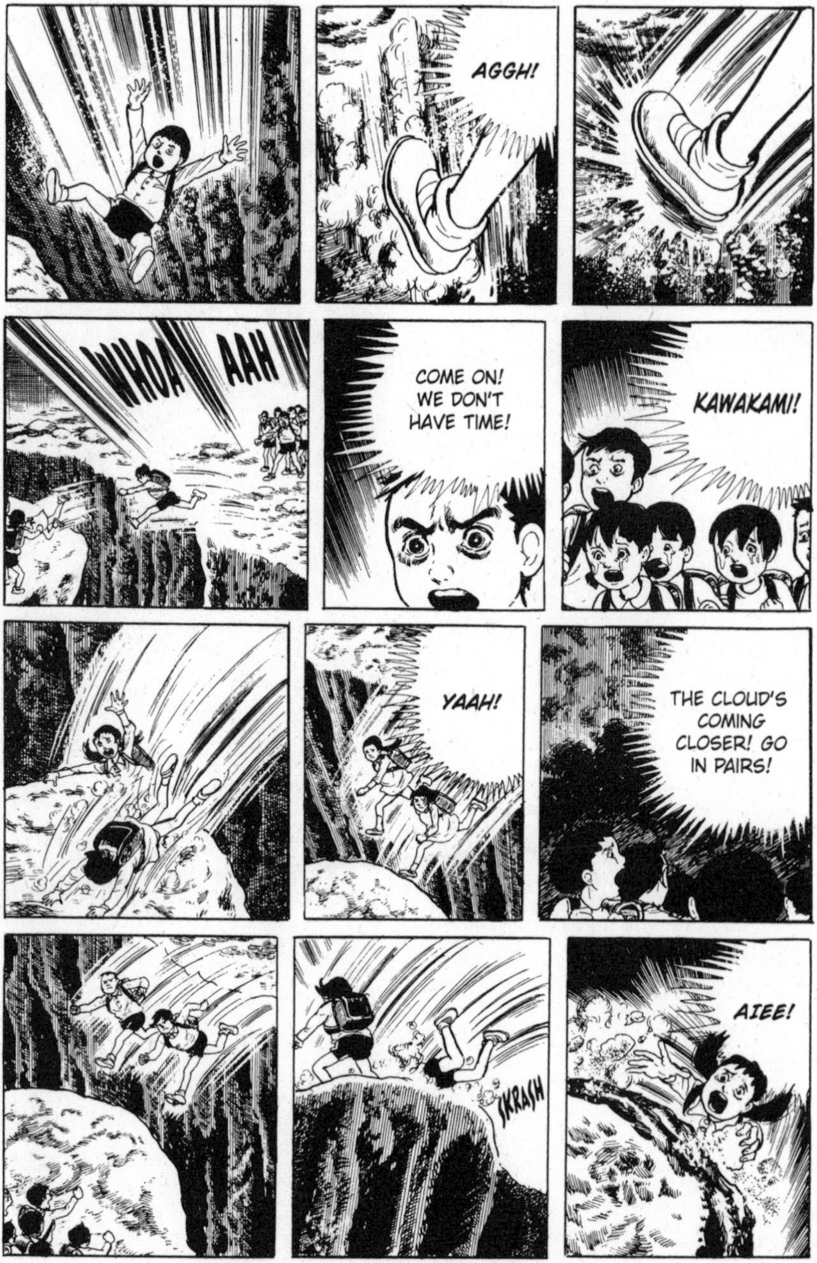
AGGH!
KAWAKAMI!
COME ON! WE DON'T HAVE TIME!
WHOA AAH
THE CLOUD'S COMING CLOSER! GO IN PAIRS!
YAAH!
AIEE!
SKRASH

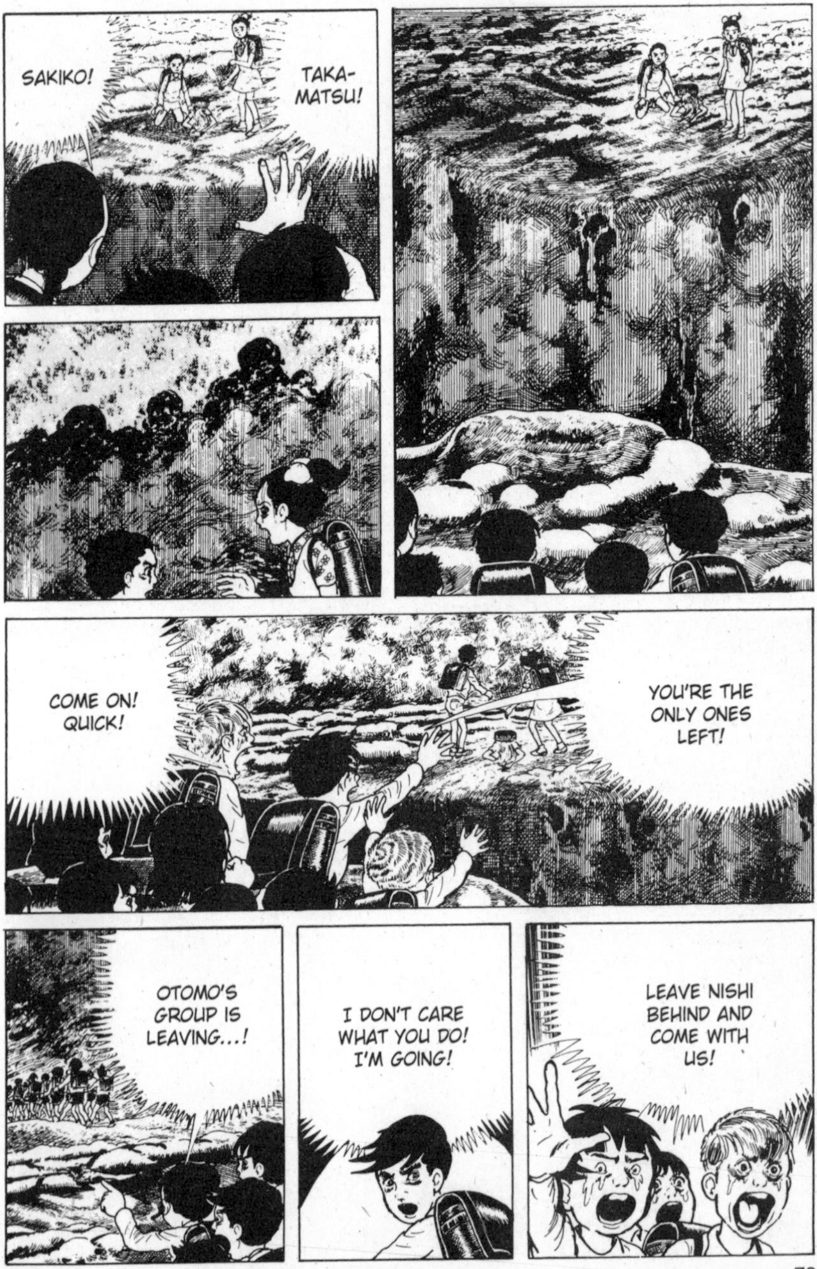
TAKA-MATSU!
SAKIKO!
YOU'RE THE ONLY ONES LEFT!
COME ON! QUICK!
LEAVE NISHI BEHIND AND COME WITH US!
I DON'T CARE WHAT YOU DO! I'M GOING!
OTOMO'S GROUP IS LEAVING...!

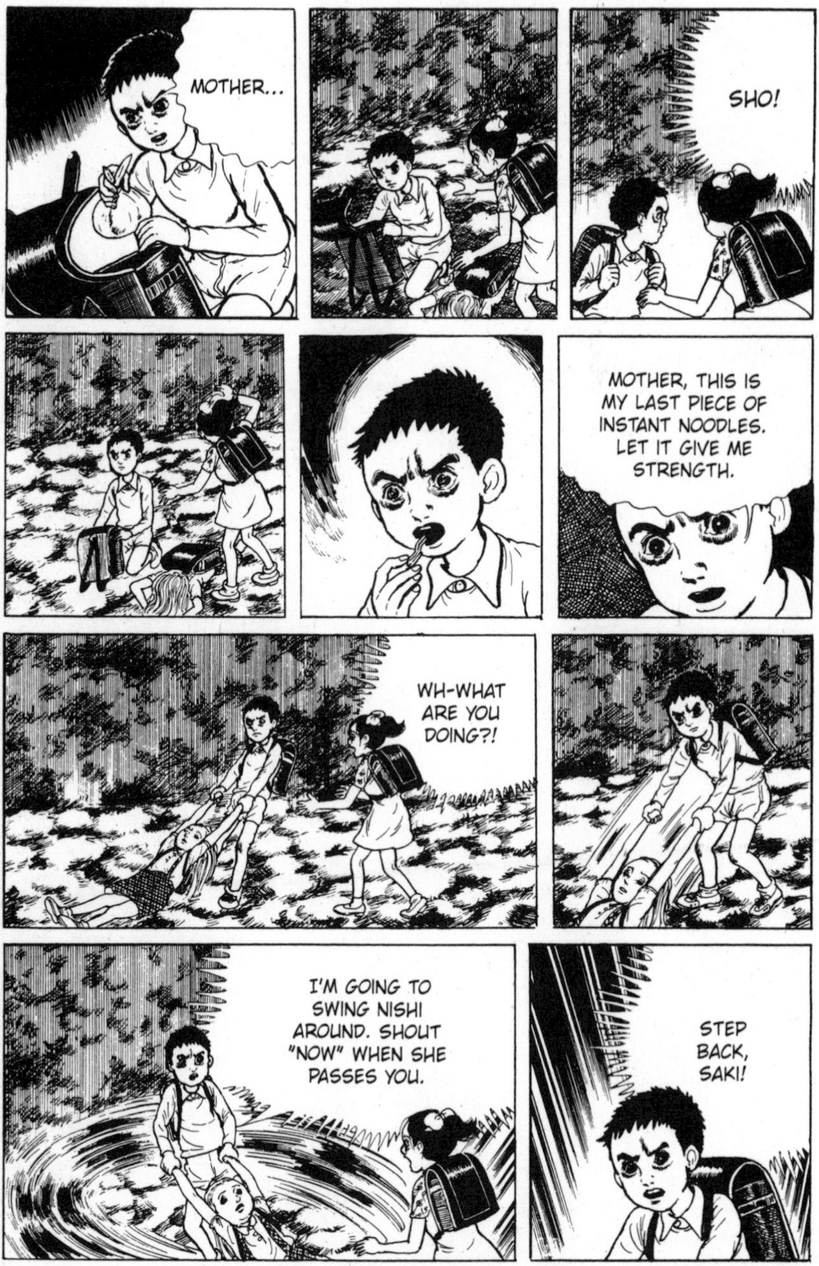
SHO!
MOTHER...
MOTHER, THIS IS MY LAST PIECE OF INSTANT NOODLES. LET IT GIVE ME STRENGTH.
WH-WHAT ARE YOU DOING?!
STEP BACK, SAKI!
I'M GOING TO SWING NISHI AROUND. SHOUT "NOW" WHEN SHE PASSES YOU.

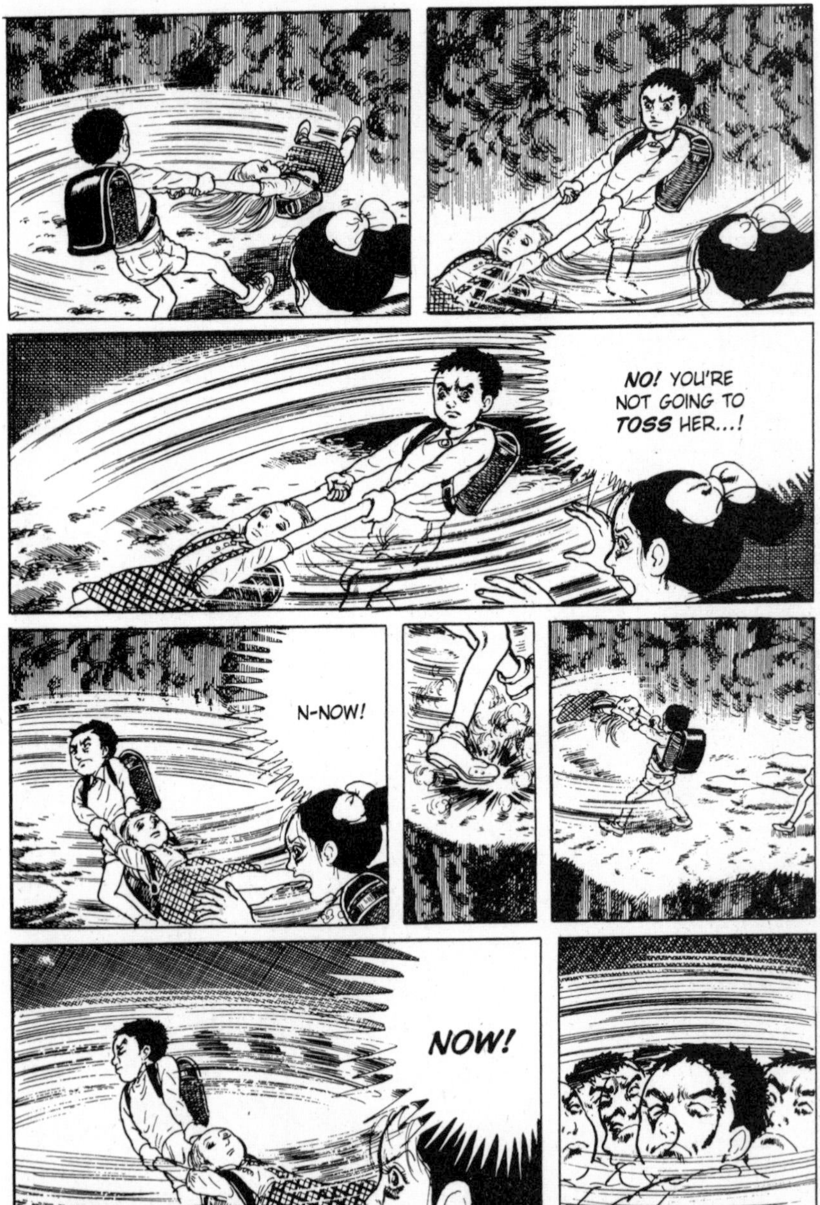
NO! YOU'RE NOT GOING TO TOSS HER...!
N-NOW!
NOW!

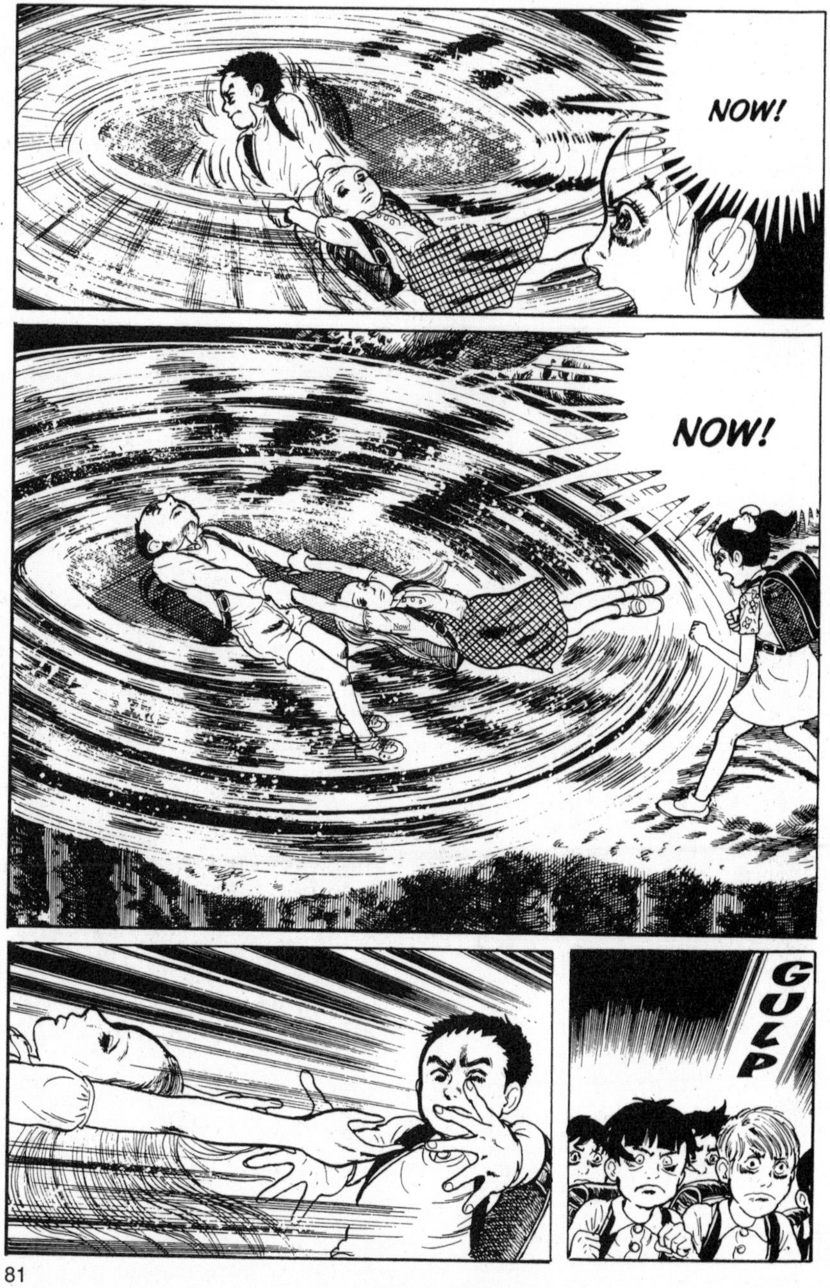
NOW!
NOW!
Now!
GULP

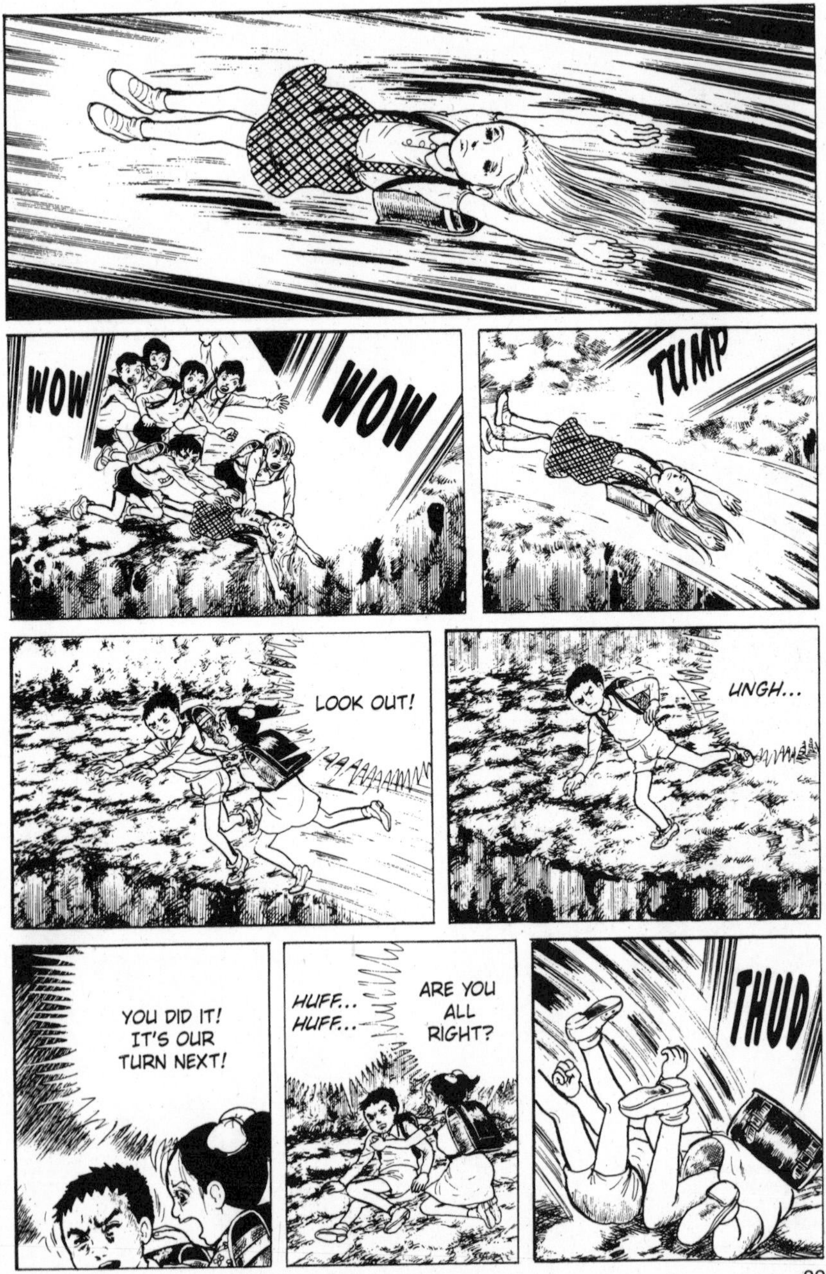
TUMP
WOW
WOW
UNGH...
LOOK OUT!
THUD
ARE YOU ALL RIGHT?
HUFF... HUFF...
YOU DID IT! IT'S OUR TURN NEXT!

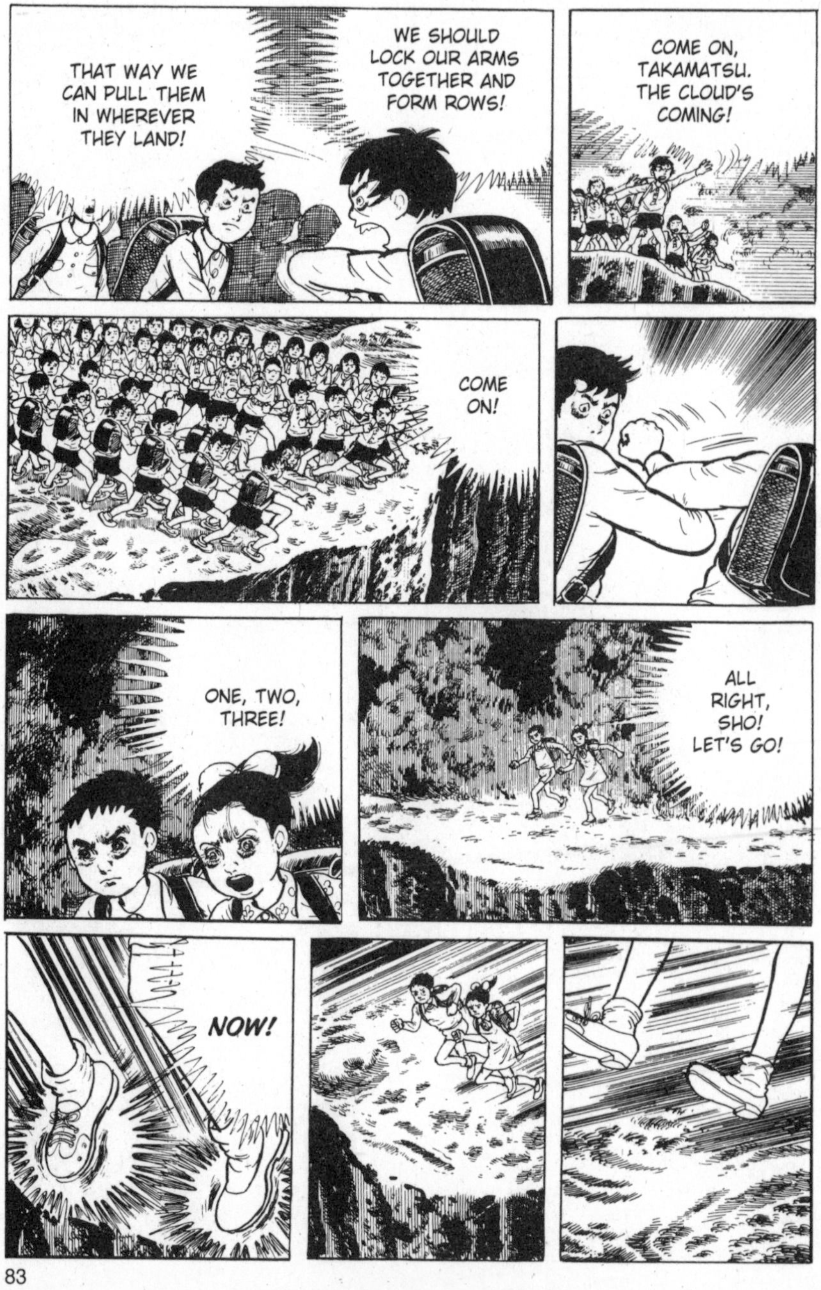
COME ON, TAKAMATSU. THE CLOUD'S COMING!
WE SHOULD LOCK OUR ARMS TOGETHER AND FORM ROWS!
THAT WAY WE CAN PULL THEM IN WHEREVER THEY LAND!
COME ON!
ALL RIGHT, SHO! LET'S GO!
ONE, TWO, THREE!
NOW!

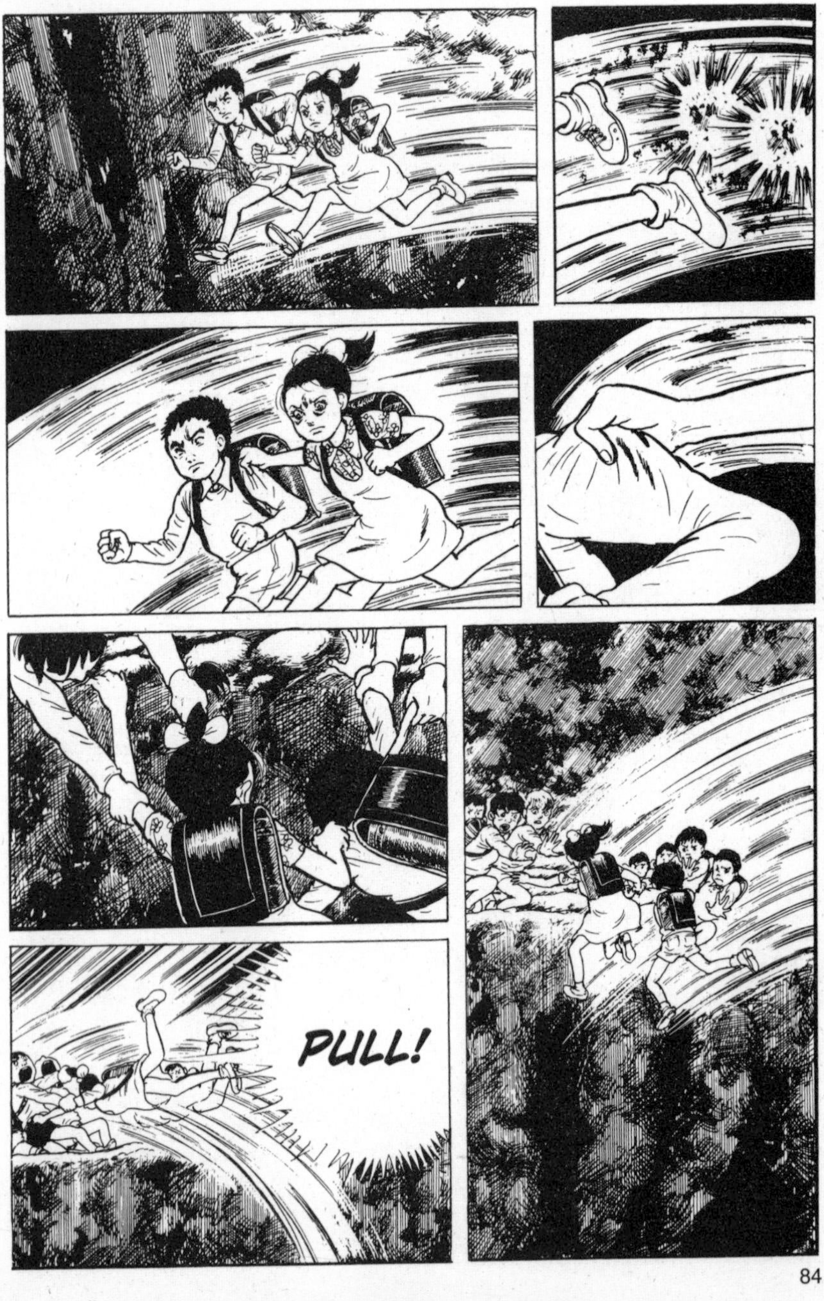
PULL!

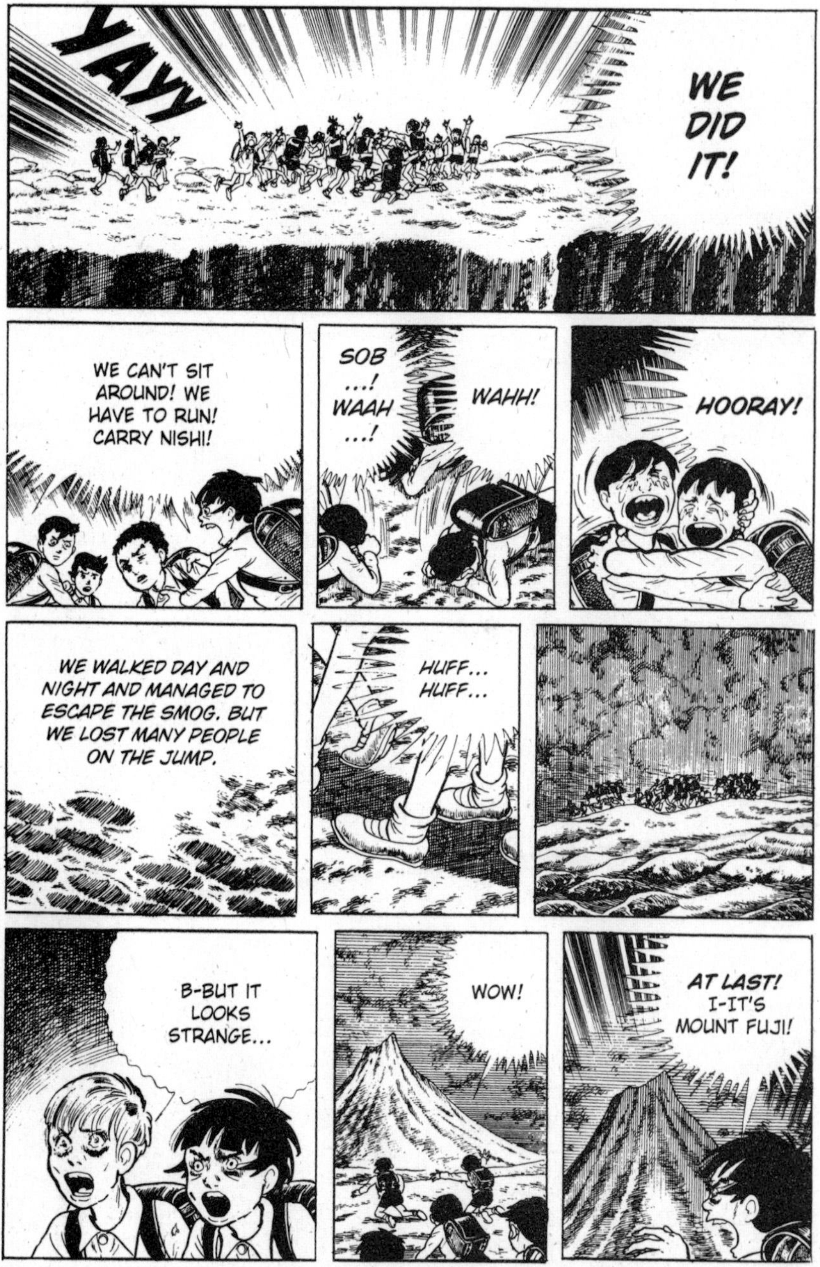
WE DID IT!
YAYY
HOORAY!
WAHH!
SOB ...! WAAH ...!
WE CAN'T SIT AROUND! WE HAVE TO RUN! CARRY NISHI!
HUFF... HUFF...
WE WALKED DAY AND NIGHT AND MANAGED TO ESCAPE THE SMOG. BUT WE LOST MANY PEOPLE ON THE JUMP.
AT LAST! I-IT'S MOUNT FUJI!
WOW!
B-BUT IT LOOKS STRANGE...

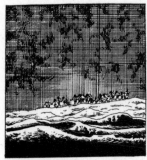

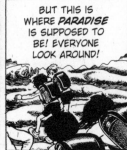

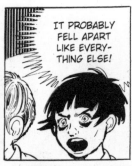

IT PROBABLY FELL APART LIKE EVERY-THING ELSE!
BUT THIS IS WHERE *PARADISE* IS SUPPOSED TO BE! EVERYONE LOOK AROUND!
THERE'S OTOMO'S GANG'S FOOT-PRINTS!
HEY!
WHAT'S THAT?!
A-A FLYING SAUCER!
WOWW!

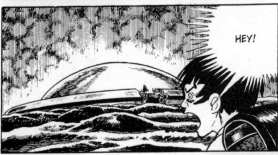

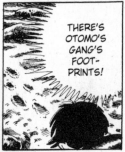

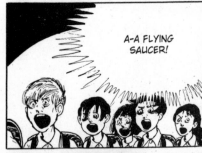

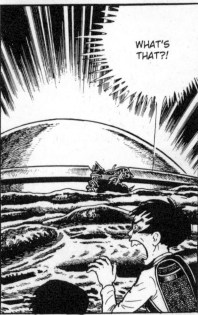

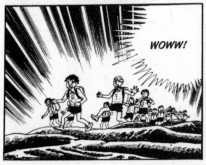

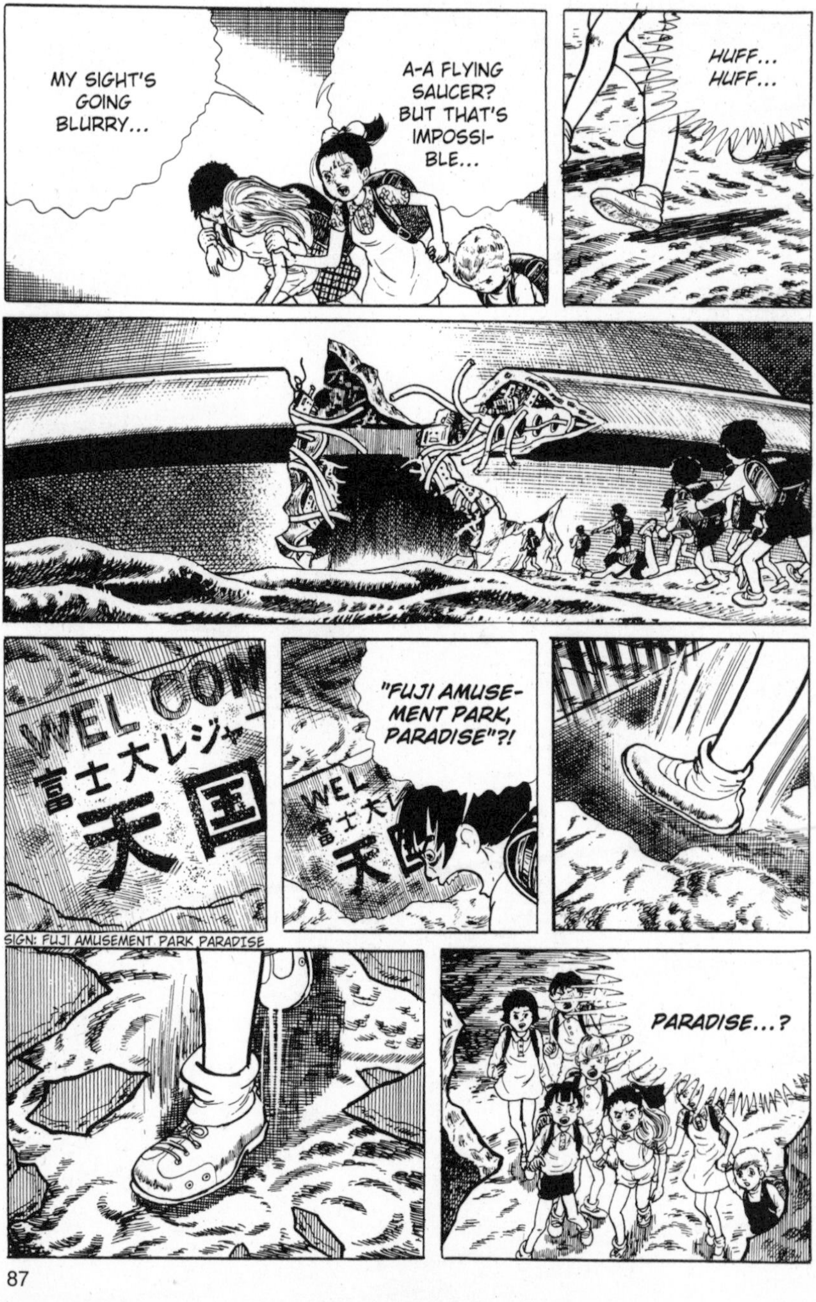
HUFF... HUFF...
A-A FLYING SAUCER? BUT THAT'S IMPOSSI-BLE...
MY SIGHT'S GOING BLURRY...
"FUJI AMUSE-MENT PARK, PARADISE"?!
WEL
富士大レ
天国
WEL COM
富士大レジャー
天国
SIGN: FUJI AMUSEMENT PARK PARADISE
PARADISE...?

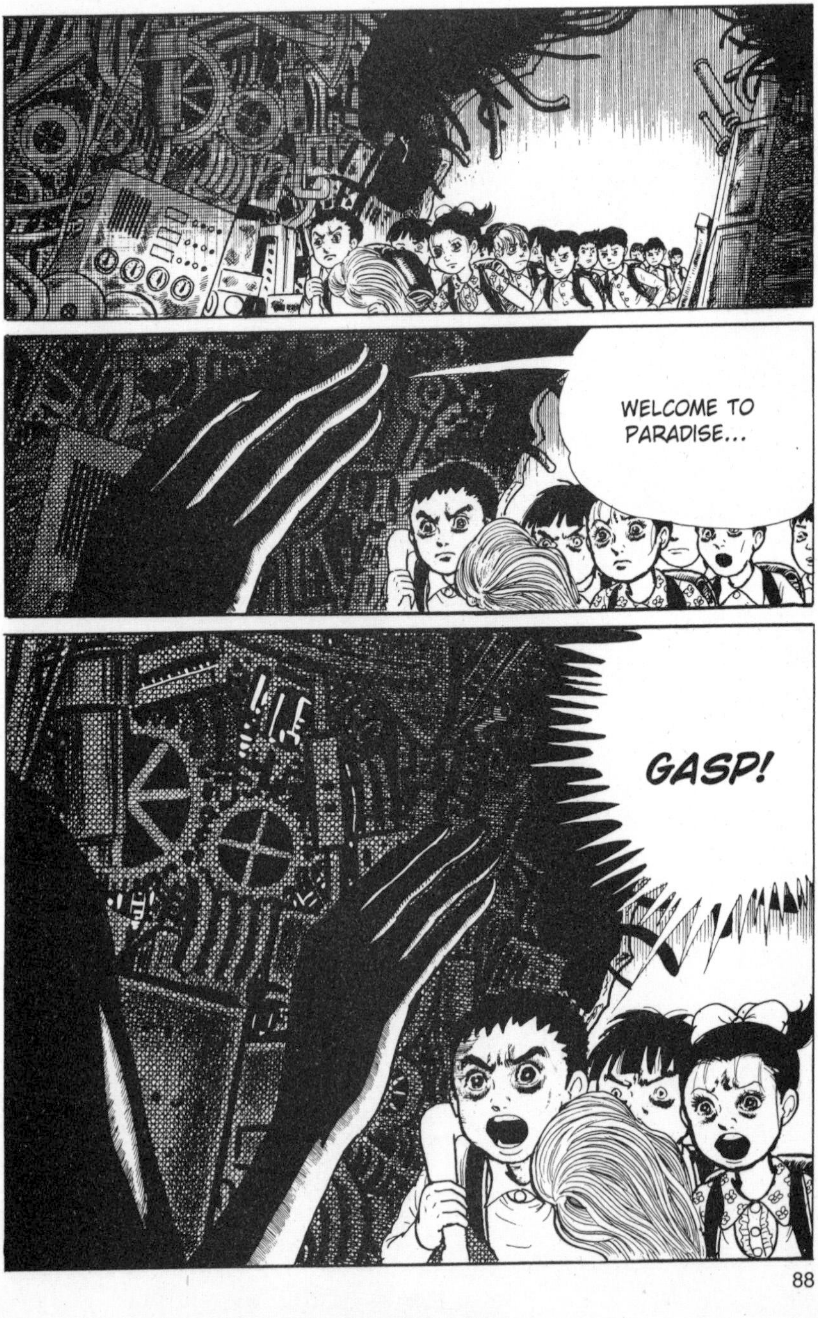
WELCOME TO PARADISE...
GASP!

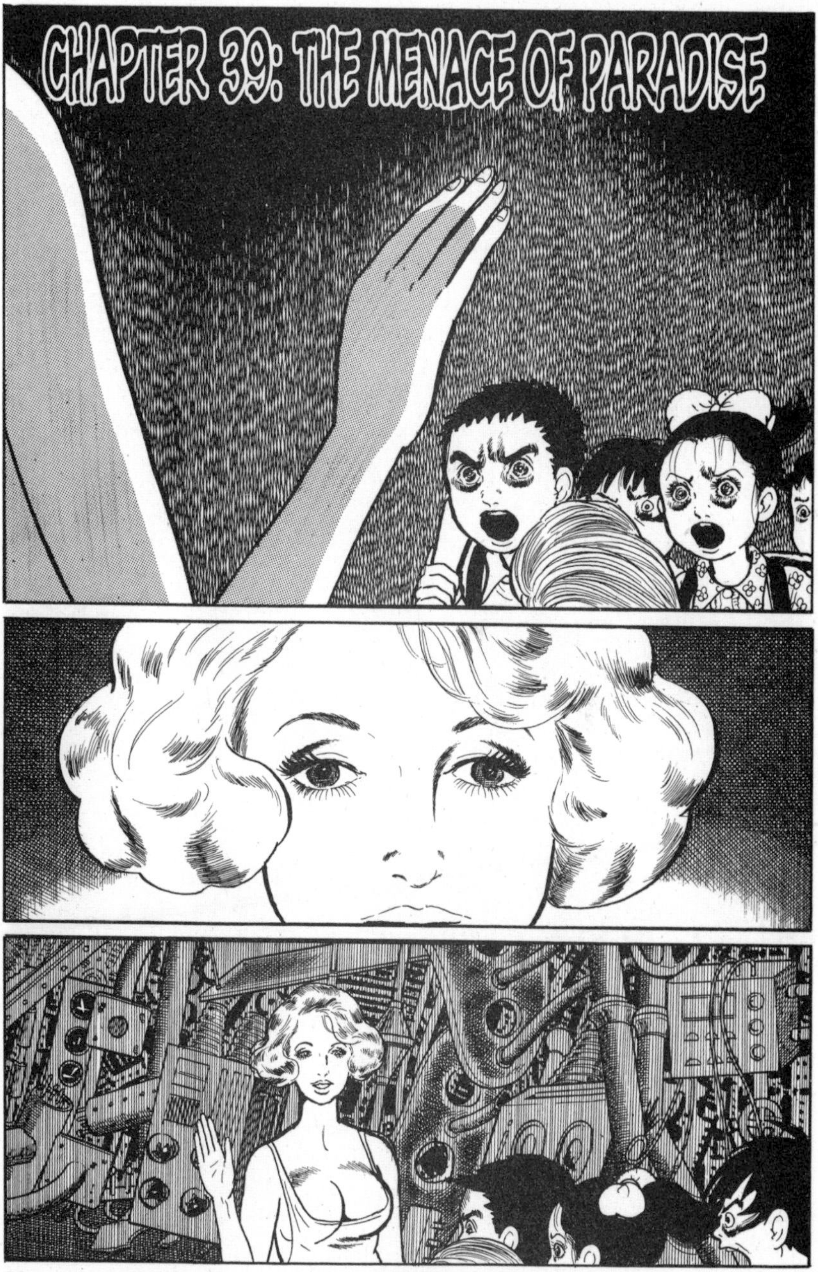
CHAPTER 39: THE MENACE OF PARADISE

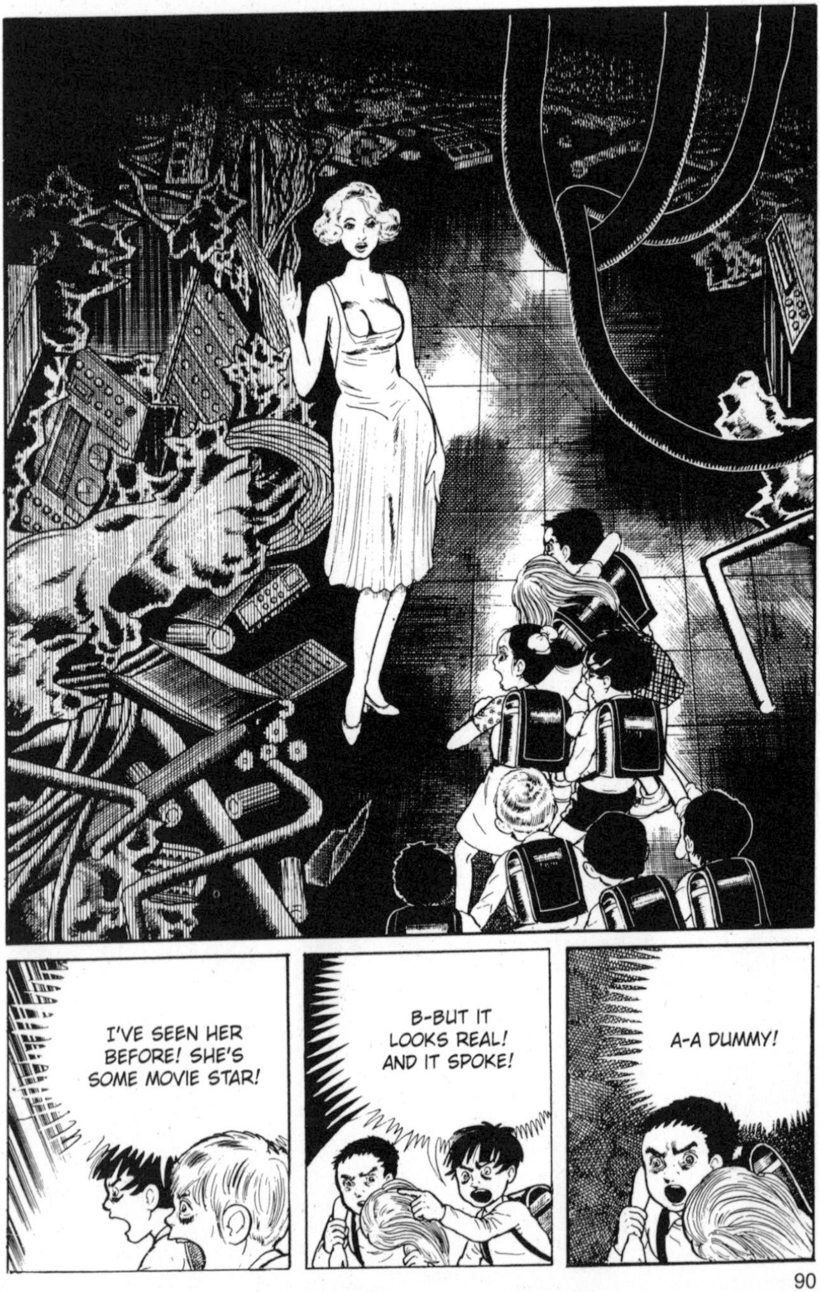
A-A DUMMY!
B-BUT IT LOOKS REAL! AND IT SPOKE!
I'VE SEEN HER BEFORE! SHE'S SOME MOVIE STAR!

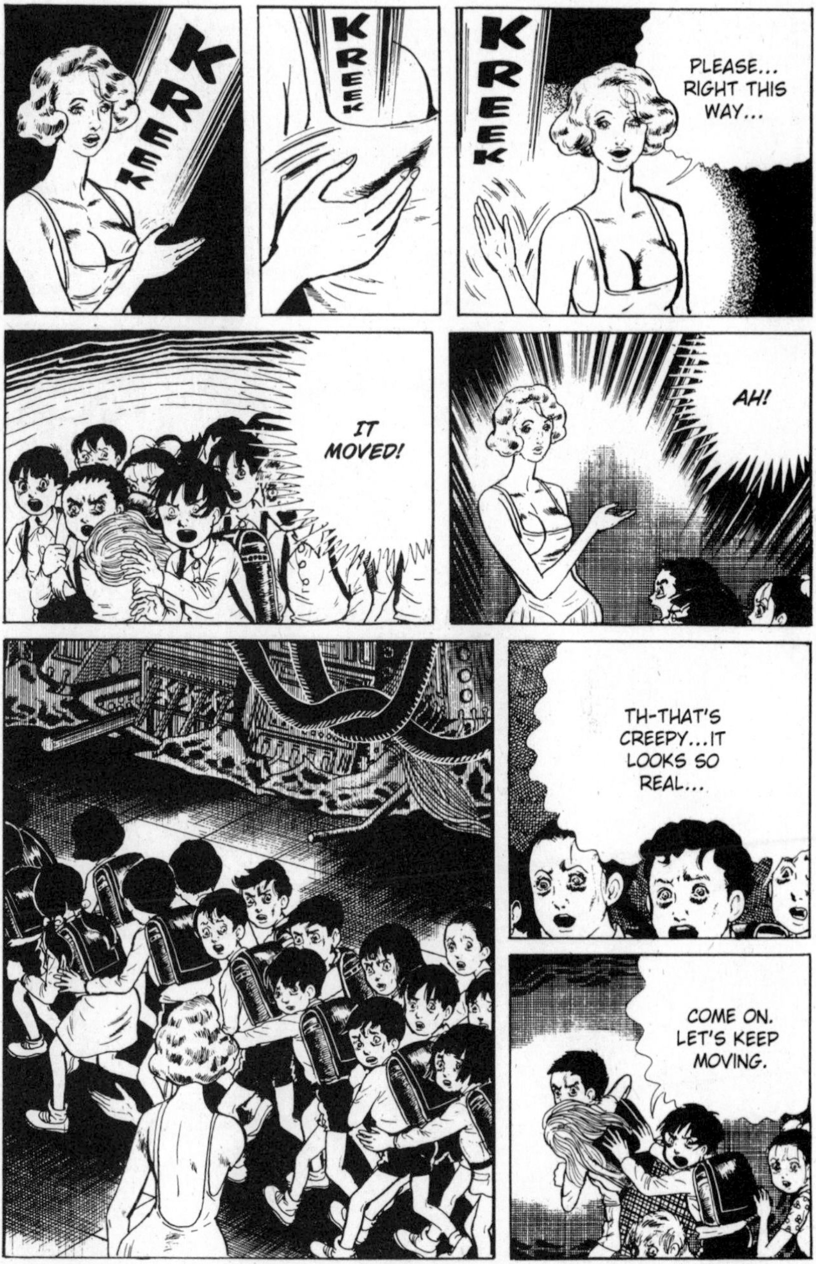
KREEK
PLEASE... RIGHT THIS WAY...
KREEK
KREEK
AH!
IT MOVED!
TH-THAT'S CREEPY...IT LOOKS SO REAL...
COME ON. LET'S KEEP MOVING.

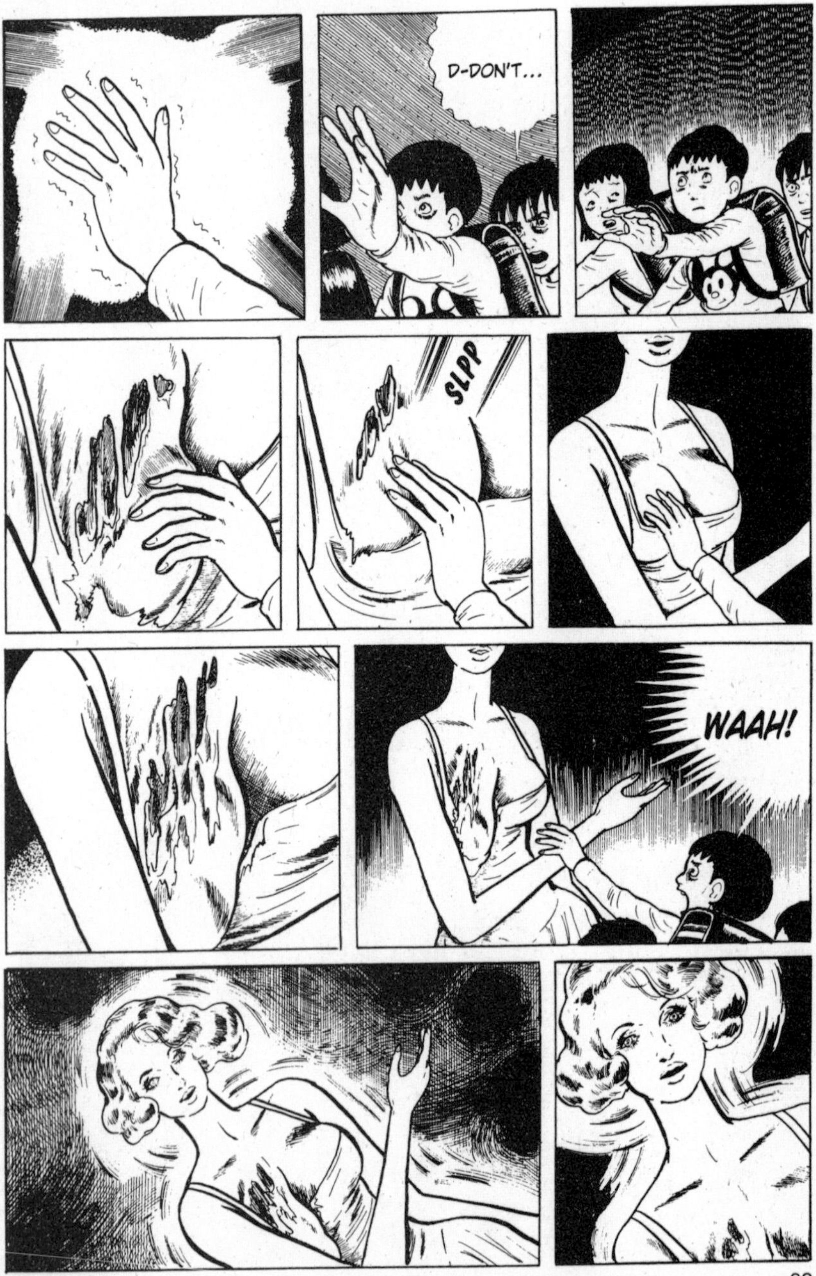
D-DON'T...
SLPP
WAAH!

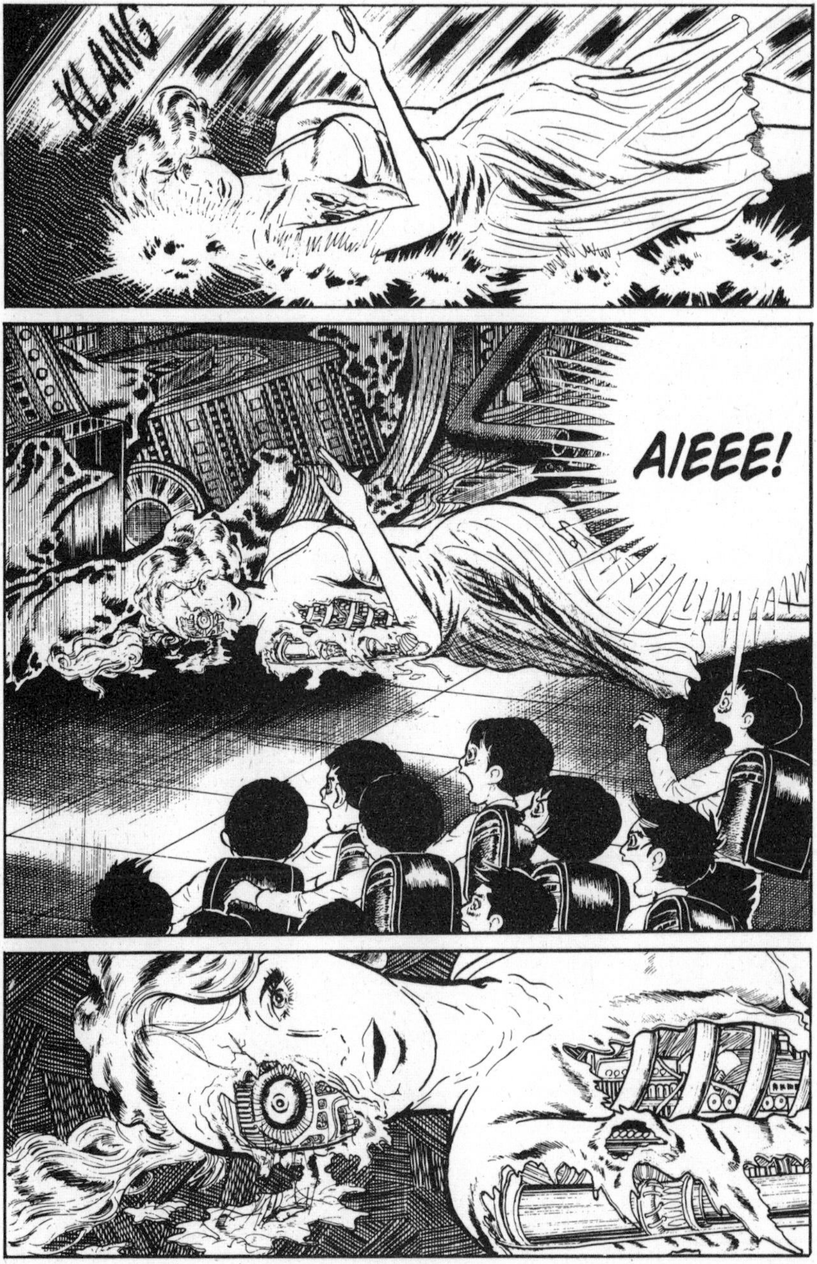
KLANG
AIEEE!

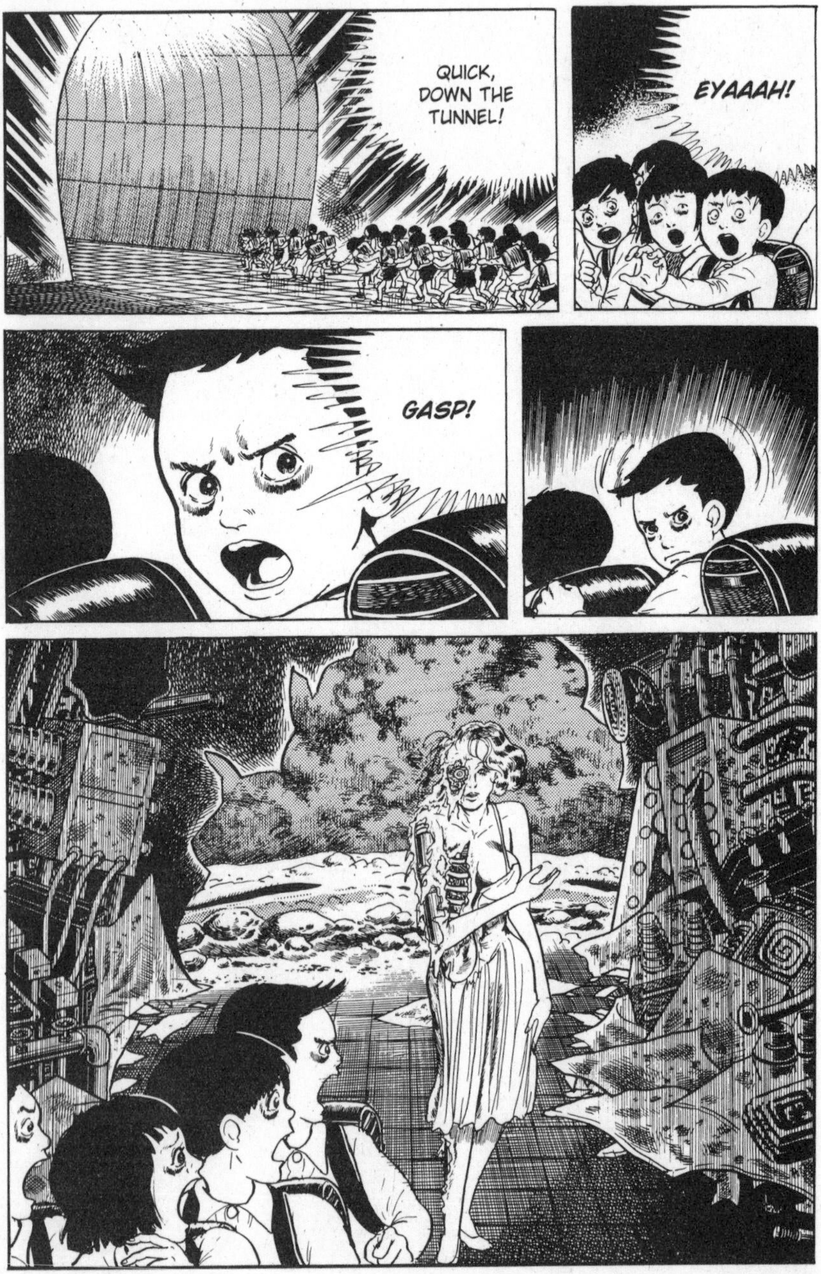
EYAAAH!
QUICK, DOWN THE TUNNEL!
GASP!

KREEK

KRIK KRIK

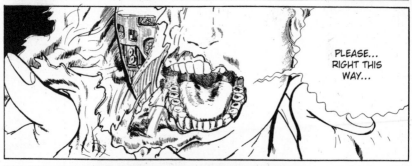

PLEASE...
RIGHT THIS
WAY...

EEYAAGH!!

PLEASE...
RIGHT THIS
WAY...

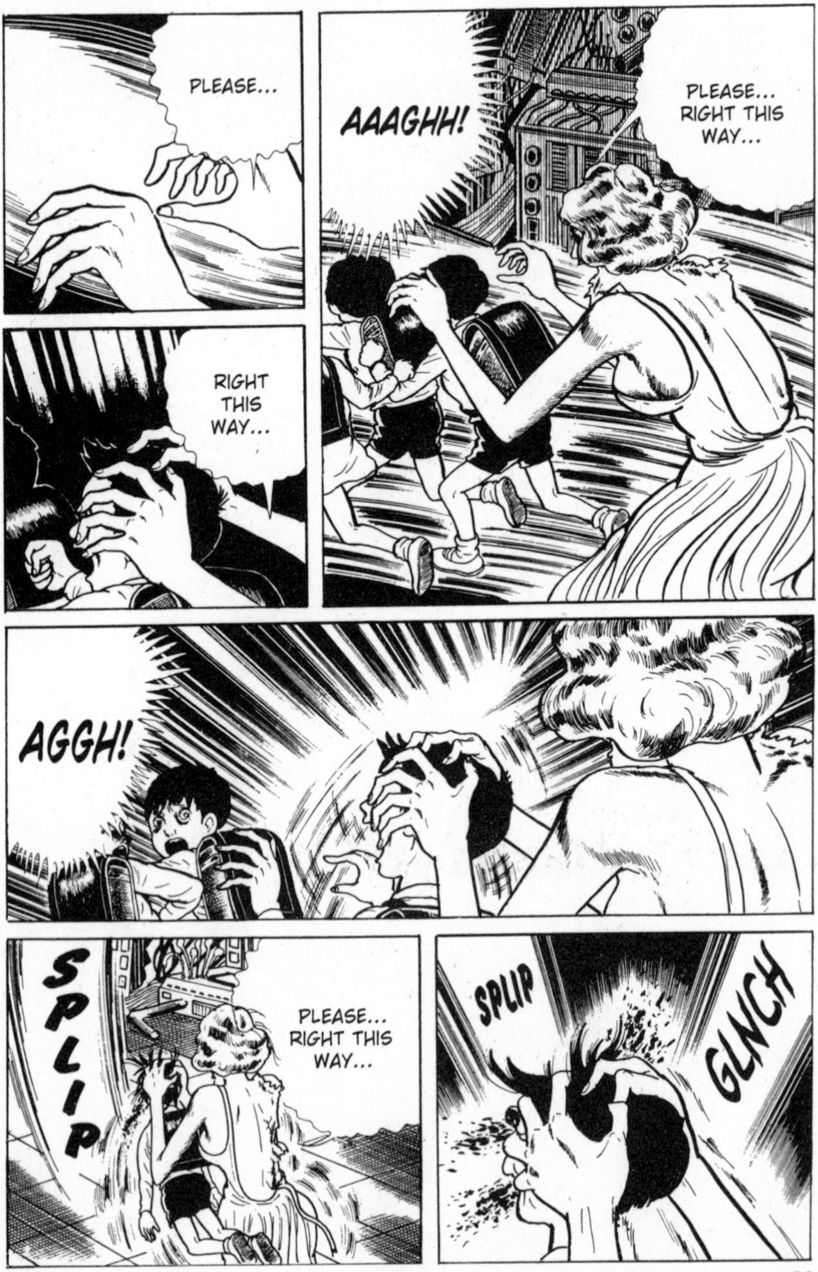
PLEASE... RIGHT THIS WAY...
AAAGHH!
PLEASE...
RIGHT THIS WAY...
AGGH!
GLNCH
SPLIP
PLEASE... RIGHT THIS WAY...
SPLIP

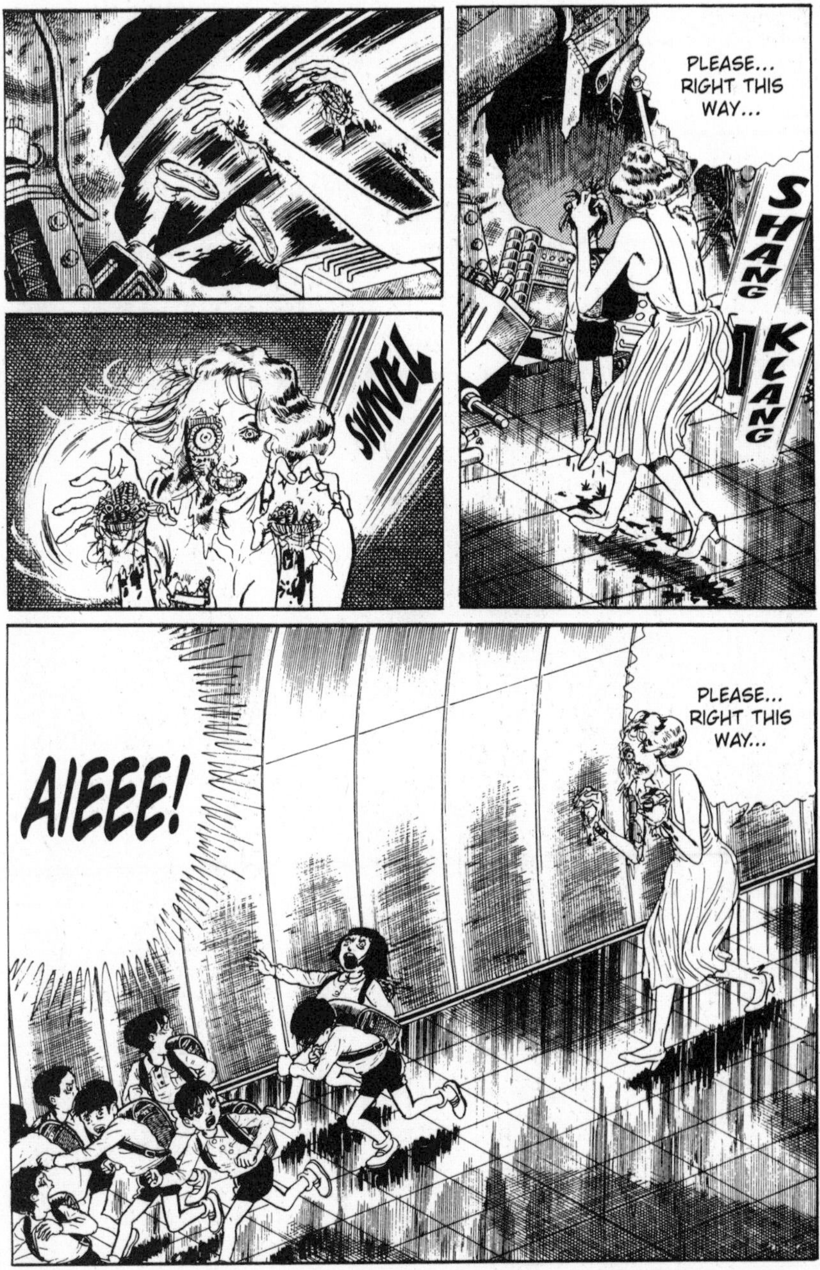
PLEASE... RIGHT THIS WAY...
SHANG
KLANG
SWIVEL
PLEASE... RIGHT THIS WAY...
AIEEE!

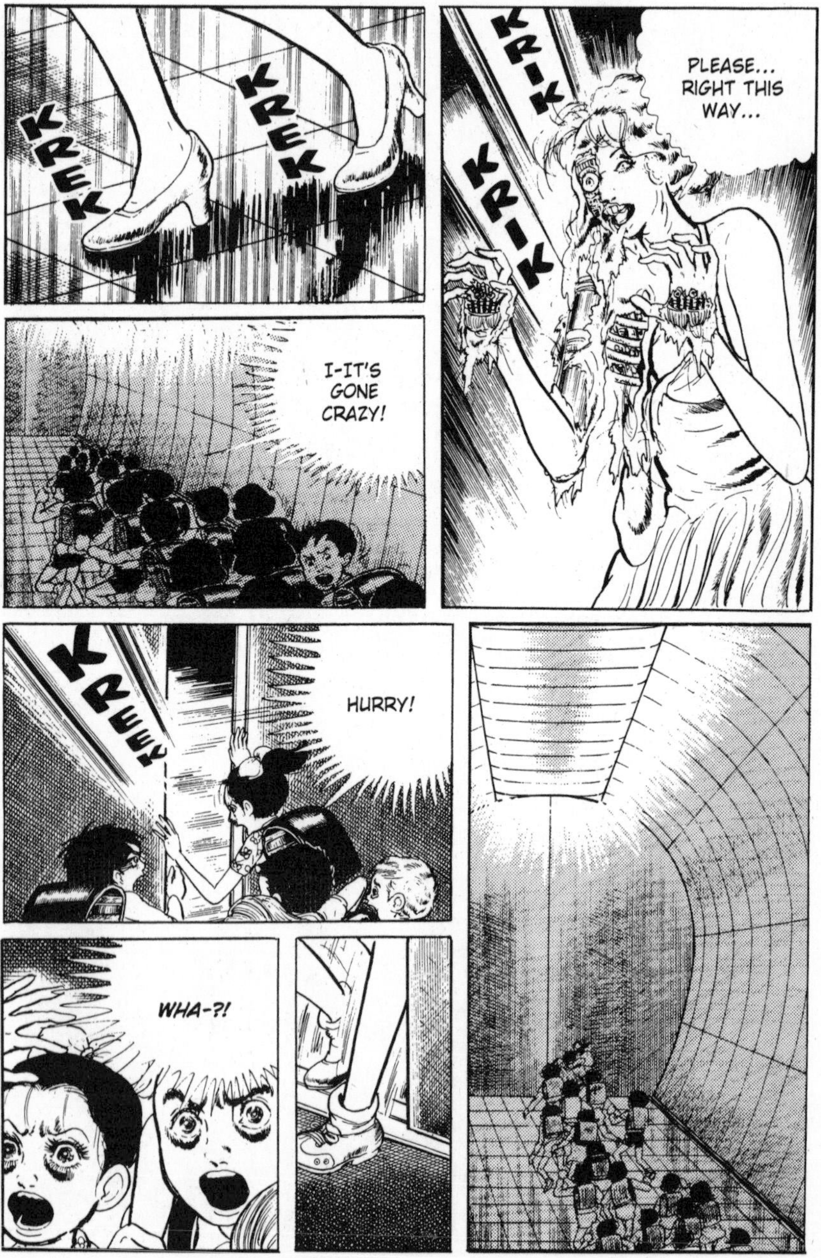
KRIK
KRIK
PLEASE... RIGHT THIS WAY...
KREK
KREK
I-IT'S GONE CRAZY!
KREEEK
HURRY!
WHA-?!

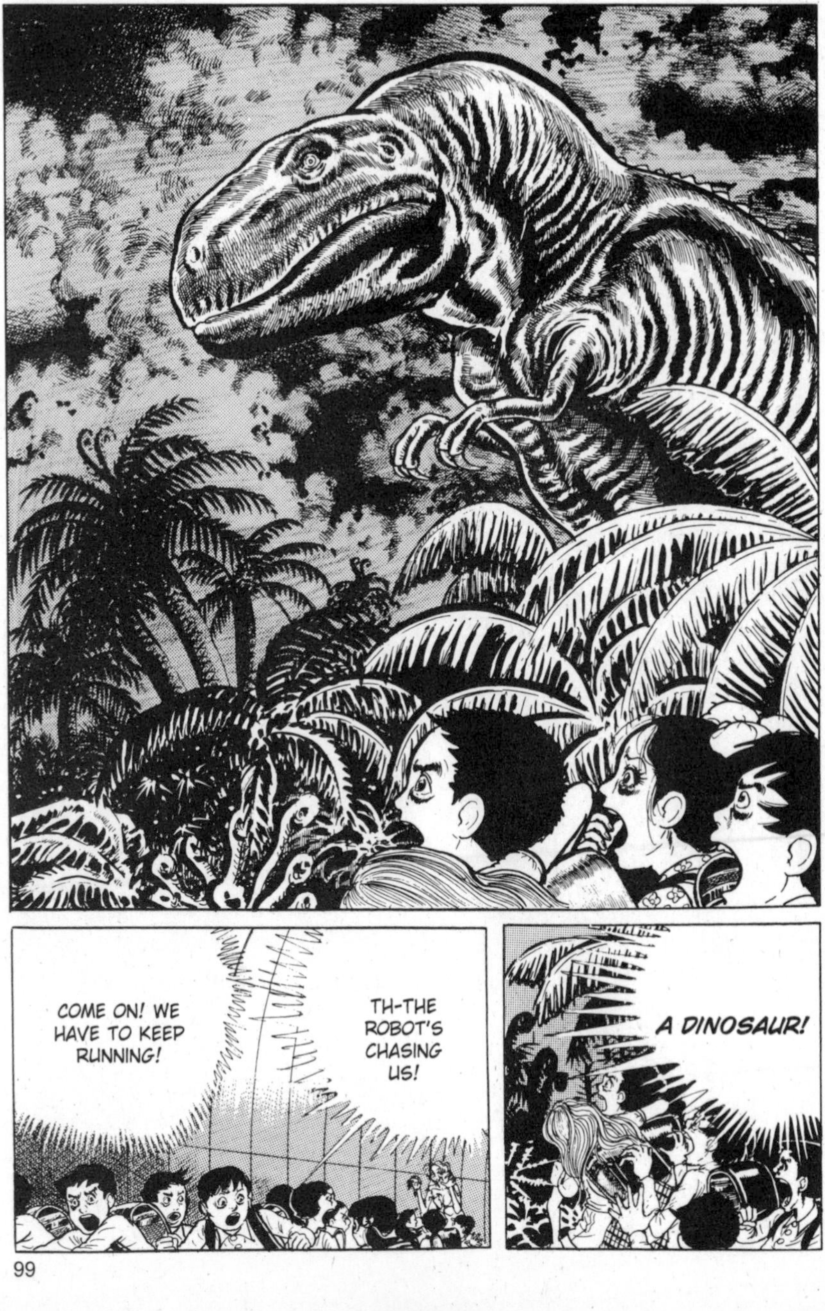
A DINOSAUR!
TH-THE ROBOT'S CHASING US!
COME ON! WE HAVE TO KEEP RUNNING!

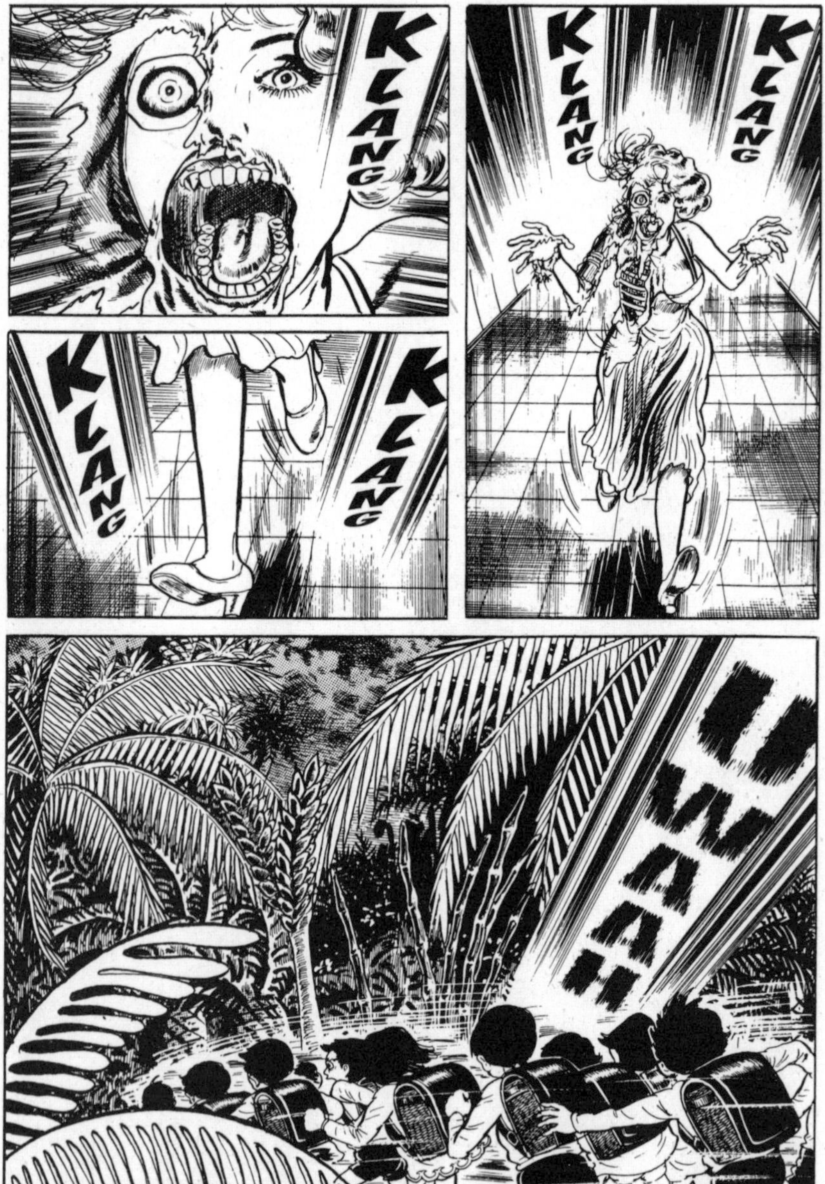
KLANG
KLANG
KLANG
KLANG
KLANG
UWAAH

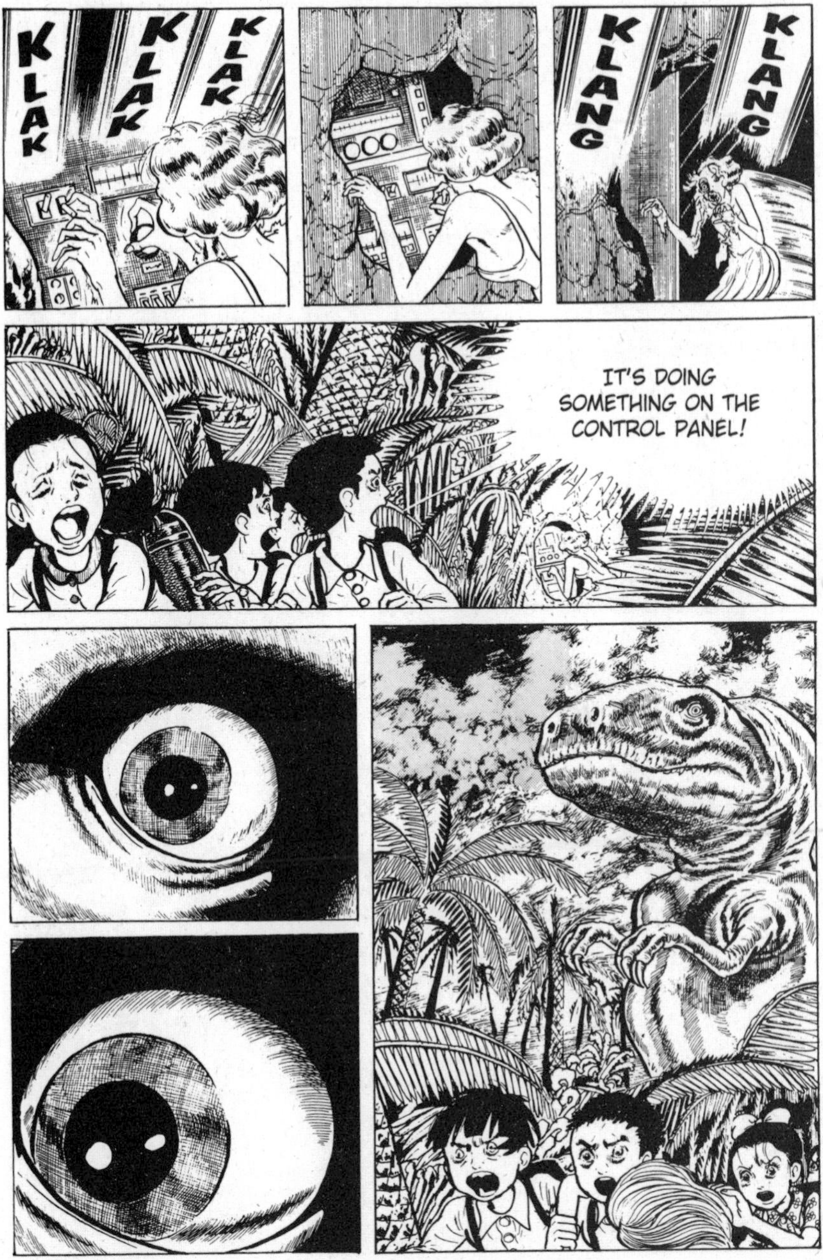
KLANG
KLANG
KLAK
KLAK
KLAK
IT'S DOING SOMETHING ON THE CONTROL PANEL!

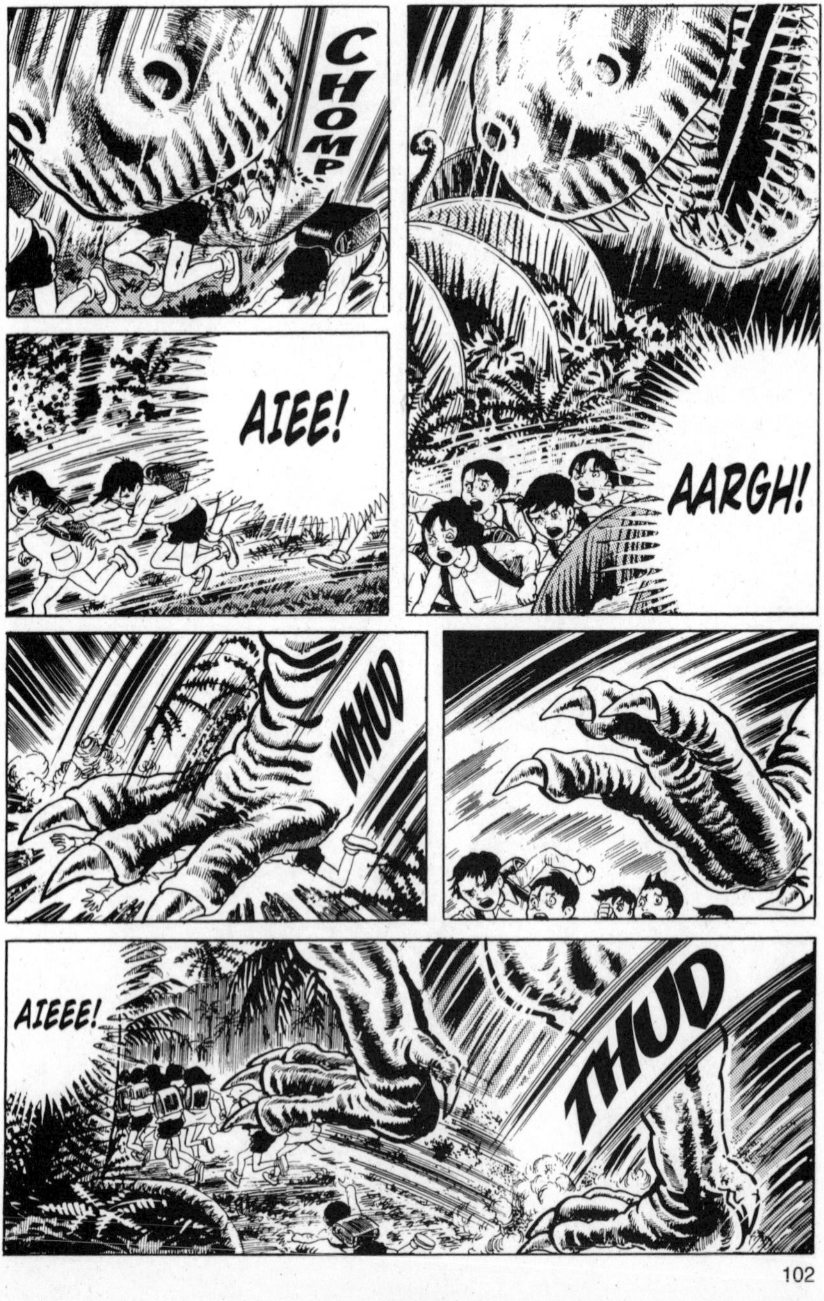
AARGH!
CHOMP
AIEE!
WHUD
THUD
AIEEE!

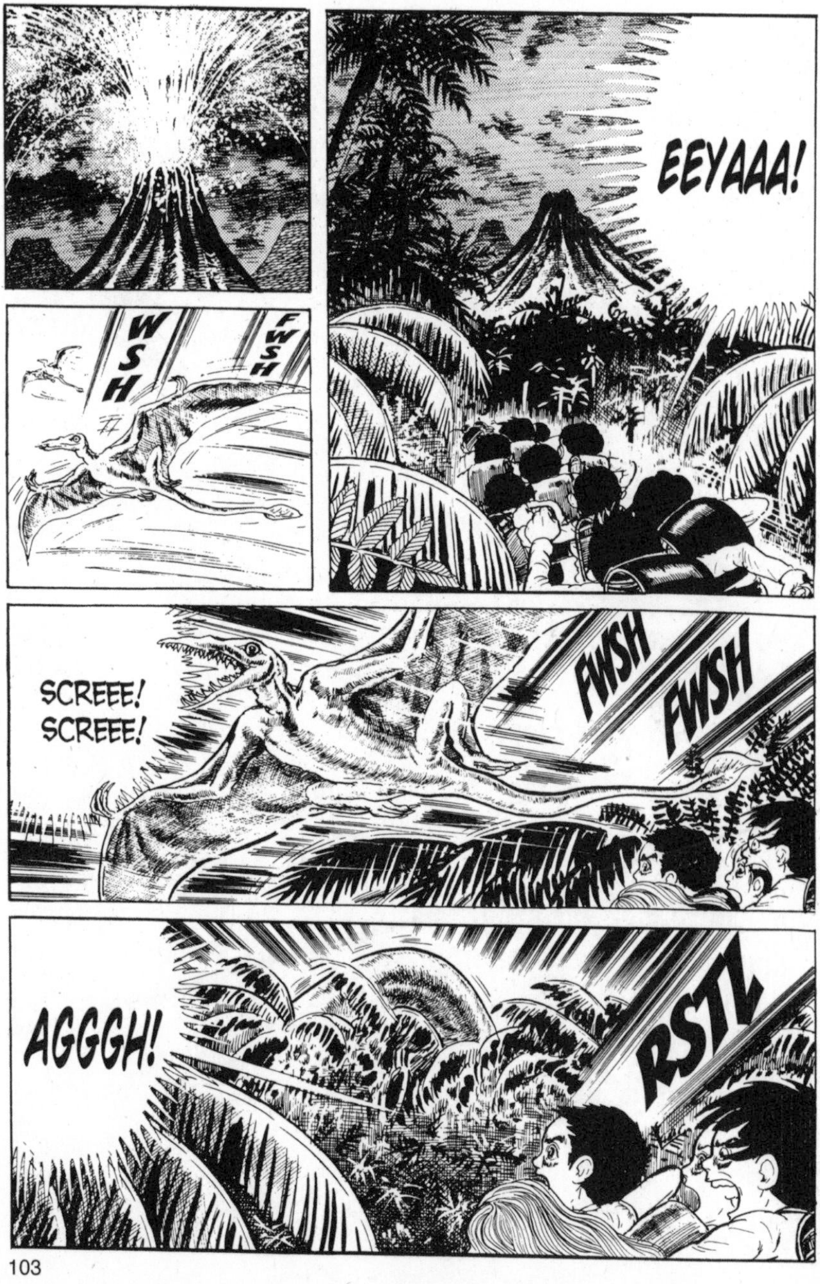
EEYAAA!
FWSH
WSH
FWSH
FWSH
SCREEE!
SCREEE!
RSTL
AGGGH!

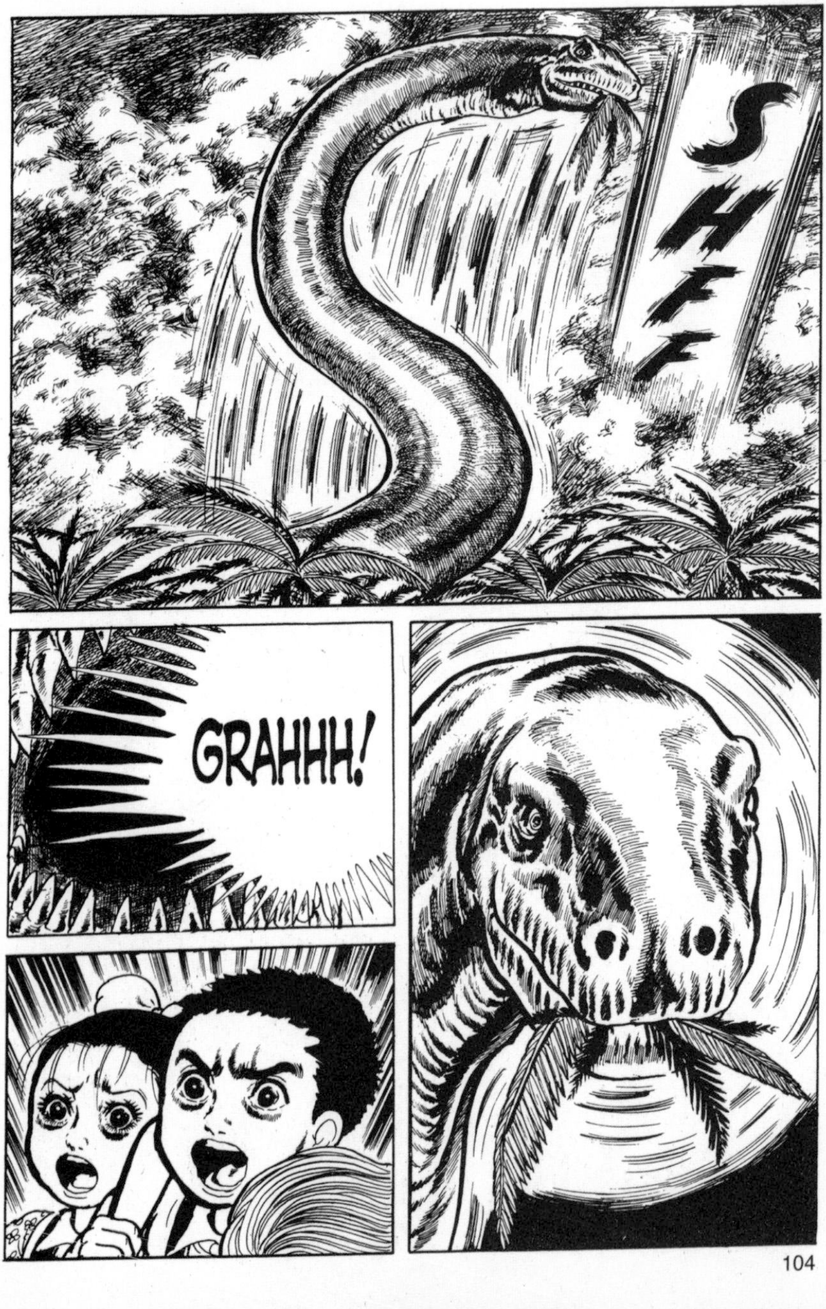
SHFFF
GRAHHH!

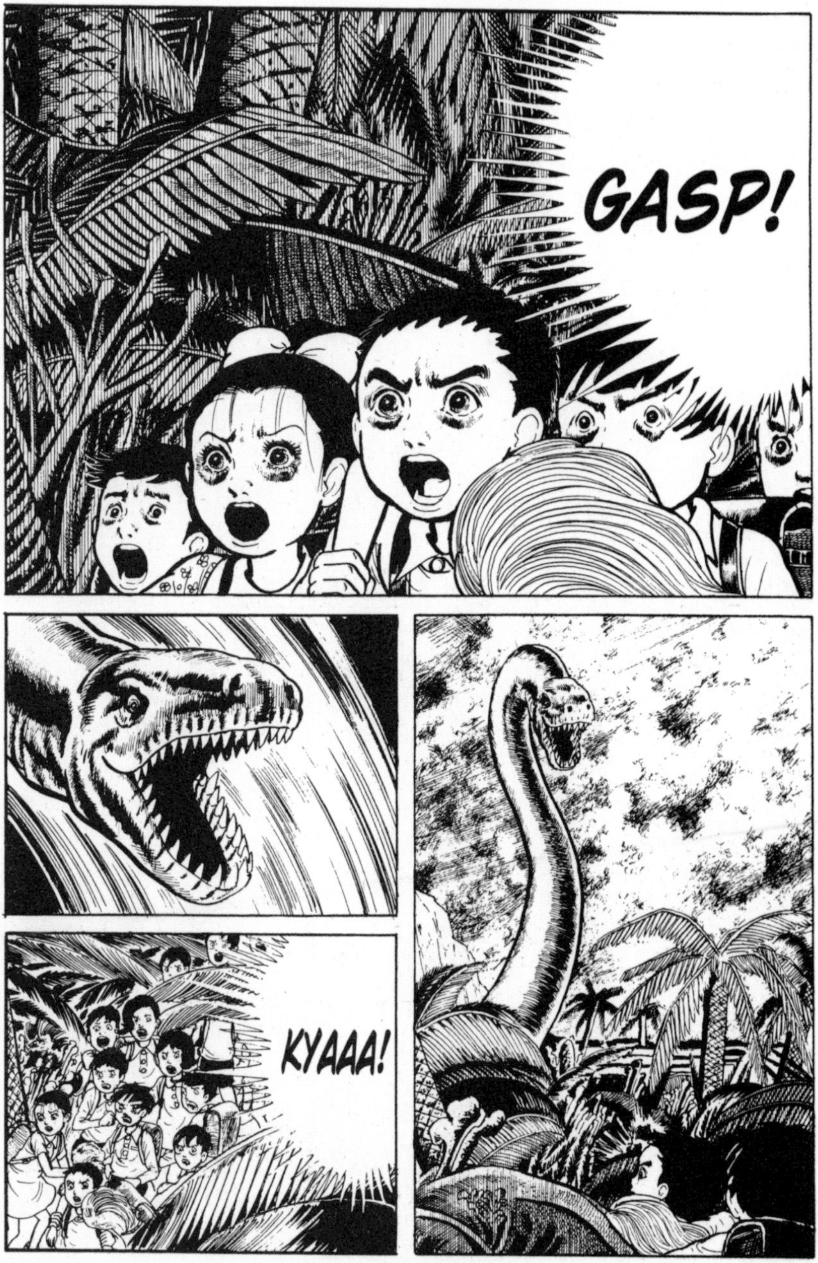
GASP!
KYAAA!

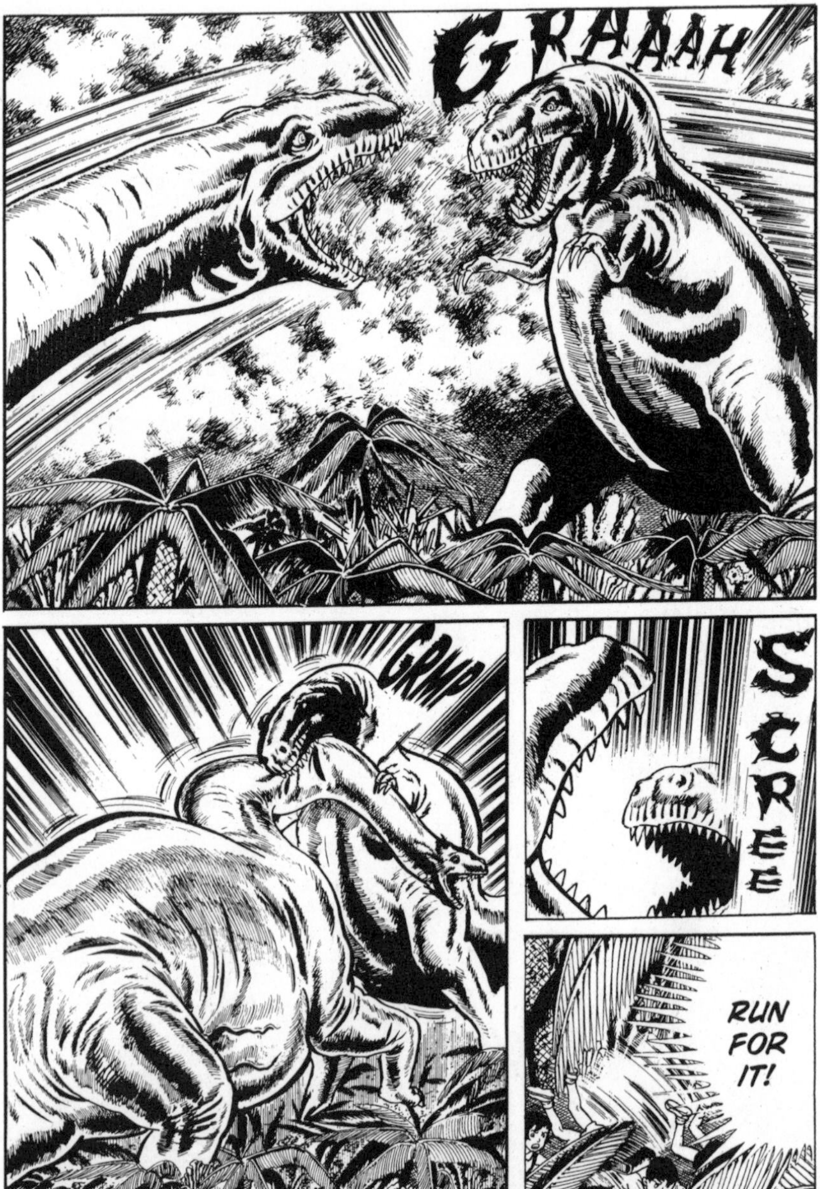
GRAAAH
SCREE
RUN FOR IT!
GRMP

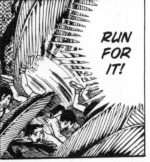

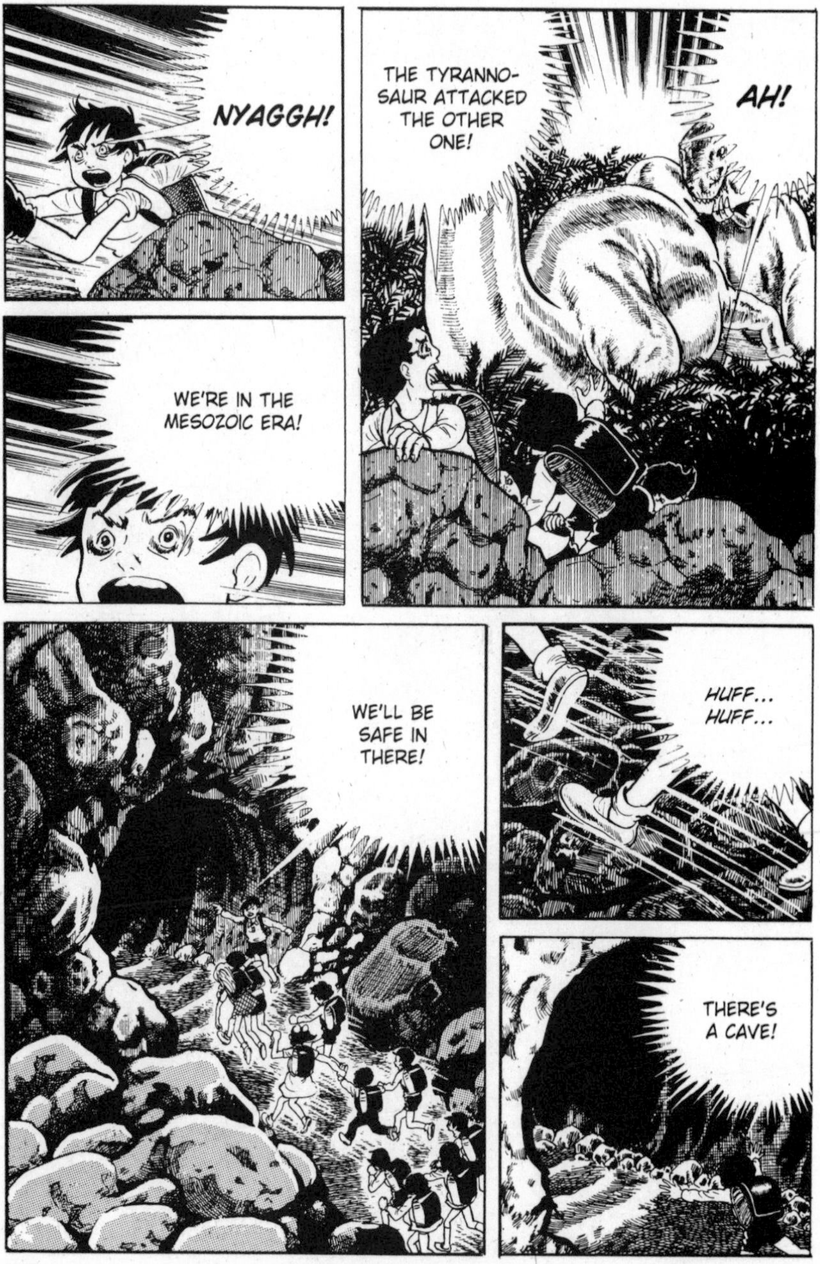
AH!
THE TYRANNO-SAUR ATTACKED THE OTHER ONE!
NYAGGH!
WE'RE IN THE MESOZOIC ERA!
HUFF... HUFF...
THERE'S A CAVE!
WE'LL BE SAFE IN THERE!

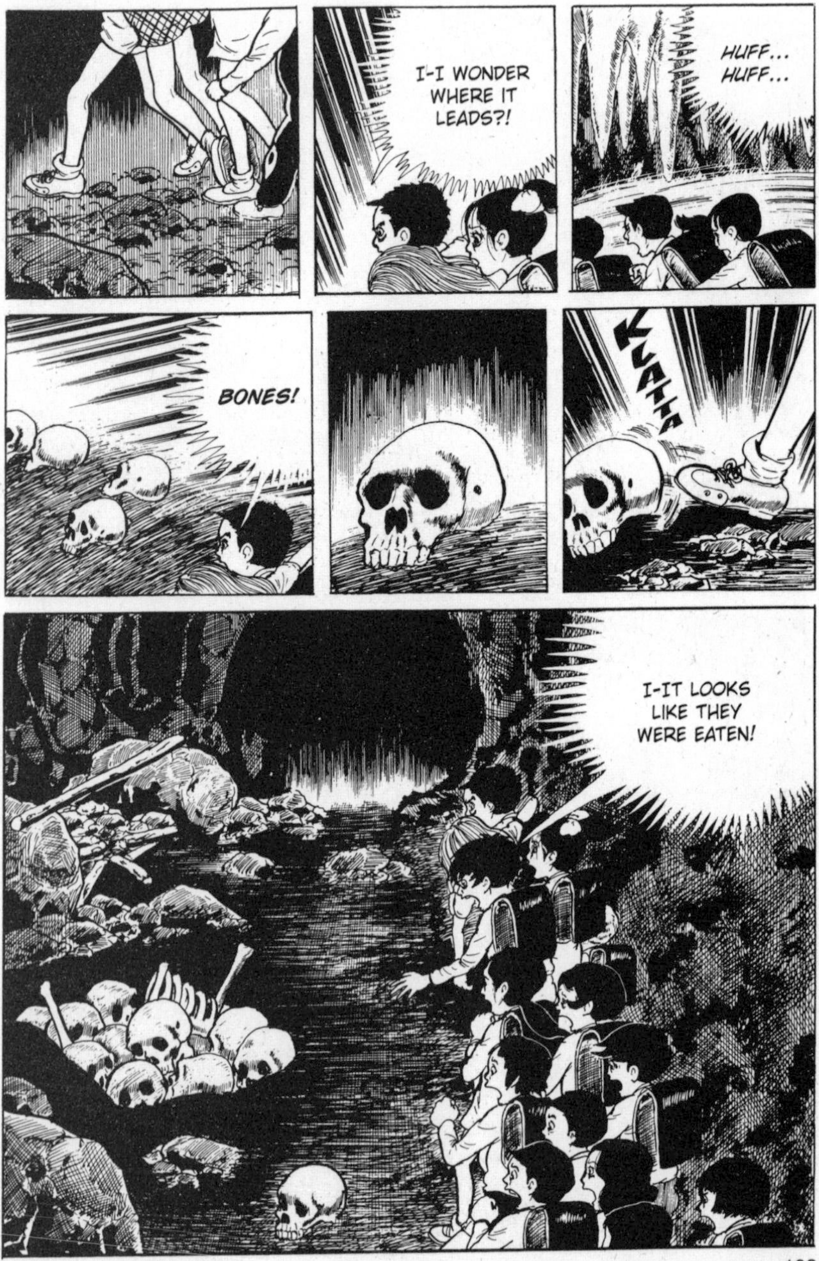
HUFF... HUFF...
I-I WONDER WHERE IT LEADS?!
KLATTA
BONES!
I-IT LOOKS LIKE THEY WERE EATEN!

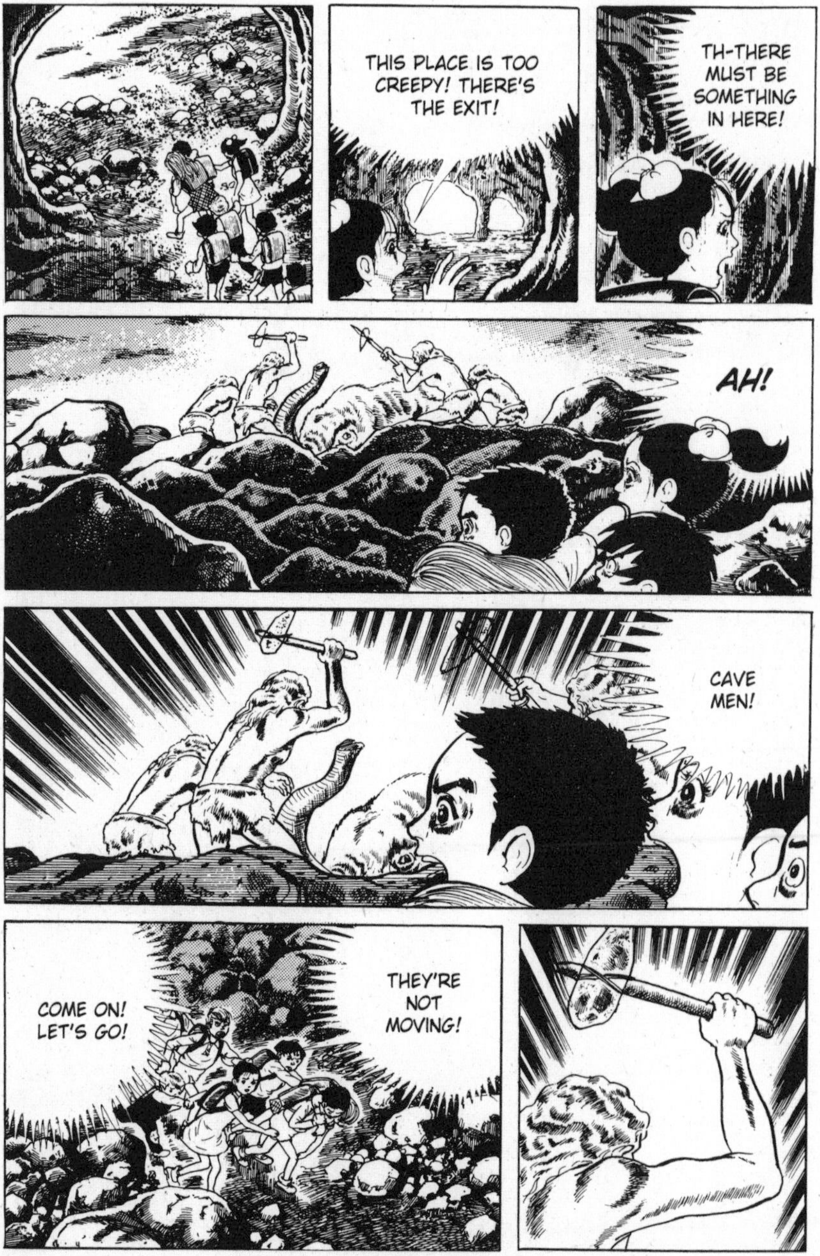
TH-THERE MUST BE SOMETHING IN HERE!
THIS PLACE IS TOO CREEPY! THERE'S THE EXIT!
AH!
CAVE MEN!
THEY'RE NOT MOVING!
COME ON! LET'S GO!

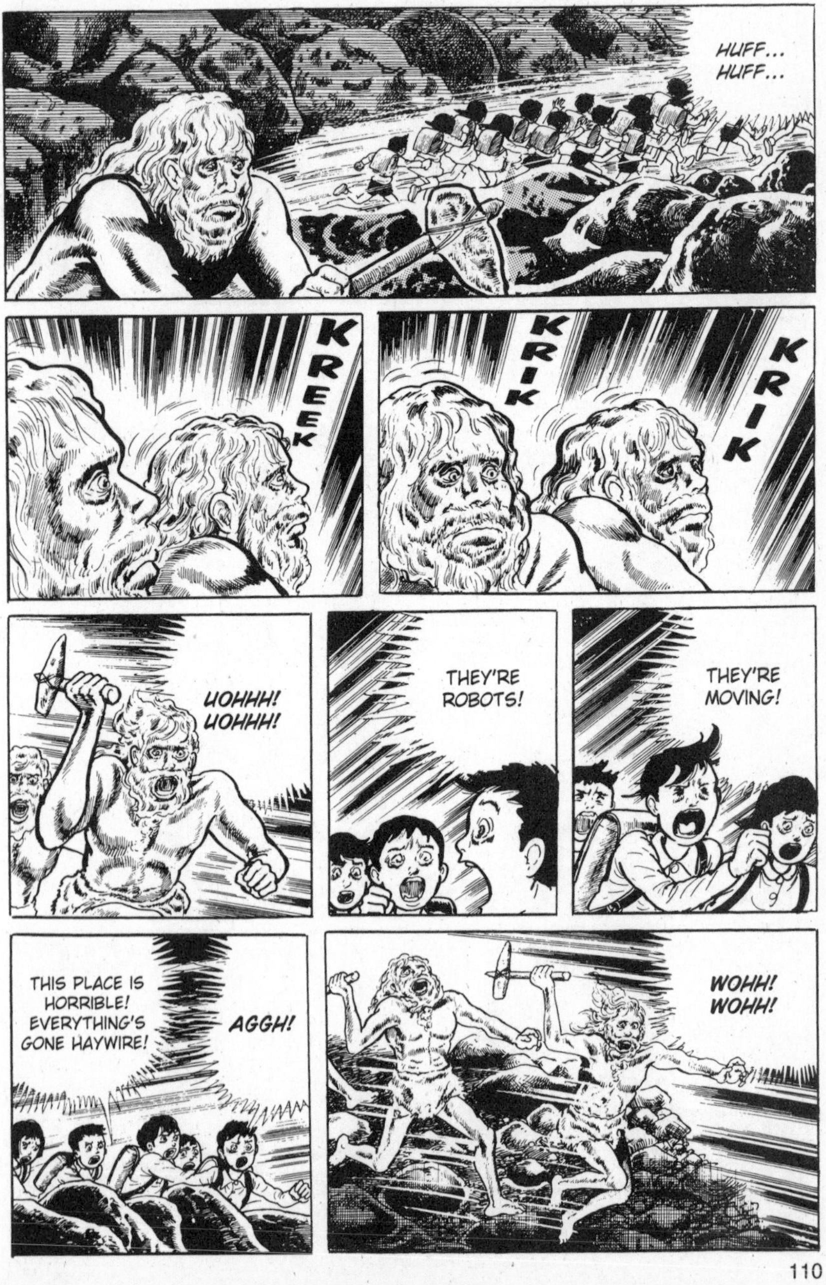
HUFF... HUFF...
KRIK
KRIK
KREEK
THEY'RE MOVING!
THEY'RE ROBOTS!
UOHHH! UOHHH!
WOHH! WOHH!
AGGH!
THIS PLACE IS HORRIBLE! EVERYTHING'S GONE HAYWIRE!

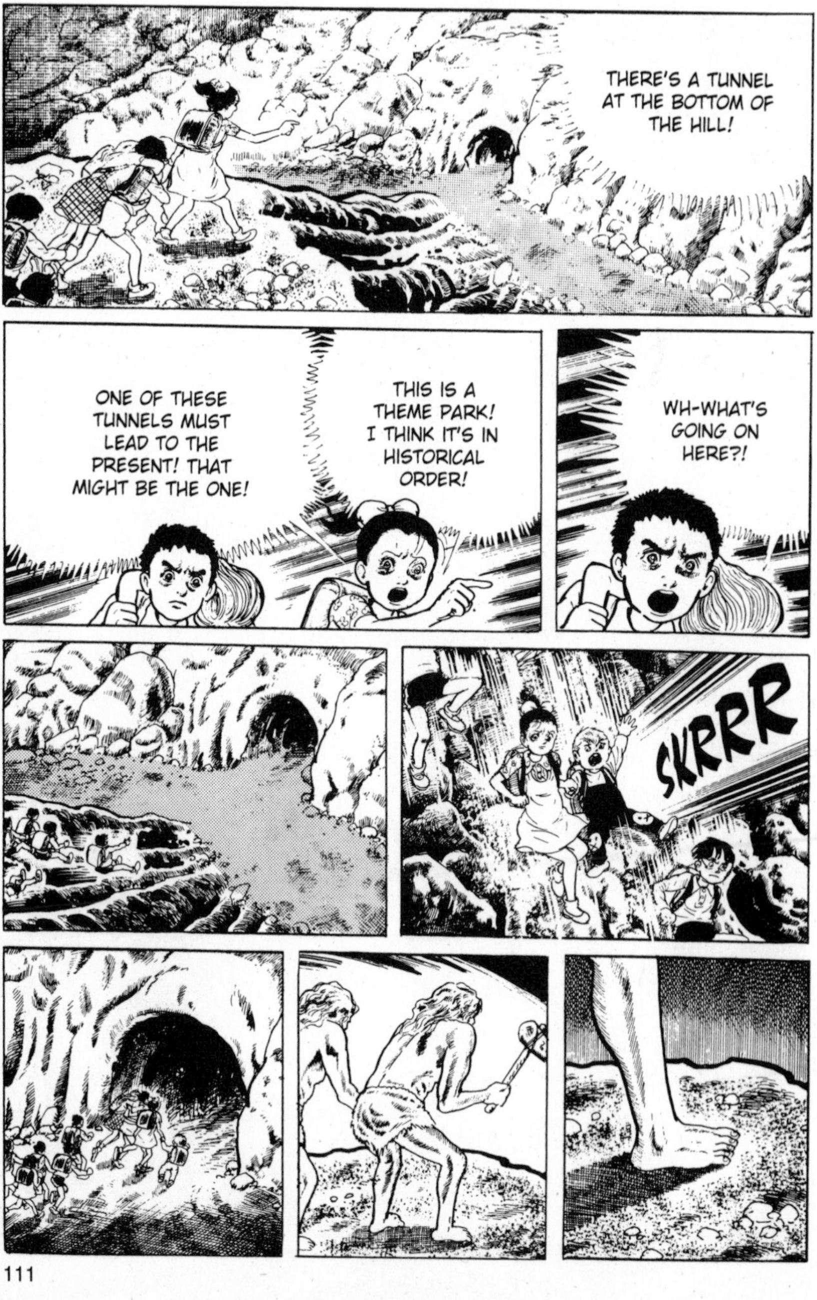

THERE'S A TUNNEL AT THE BOTTOM OF THE HILL!
WH-WHAT'S GOING ON HERE?!
THIS IS A THEME PARK! I THINK IT'S IN HISTORICAL ORDER!
ONE OF THESE TUNNELS MUST LEAD TO THE PRESENT! THAT MIGHT BE THE ONE!
SKRRR

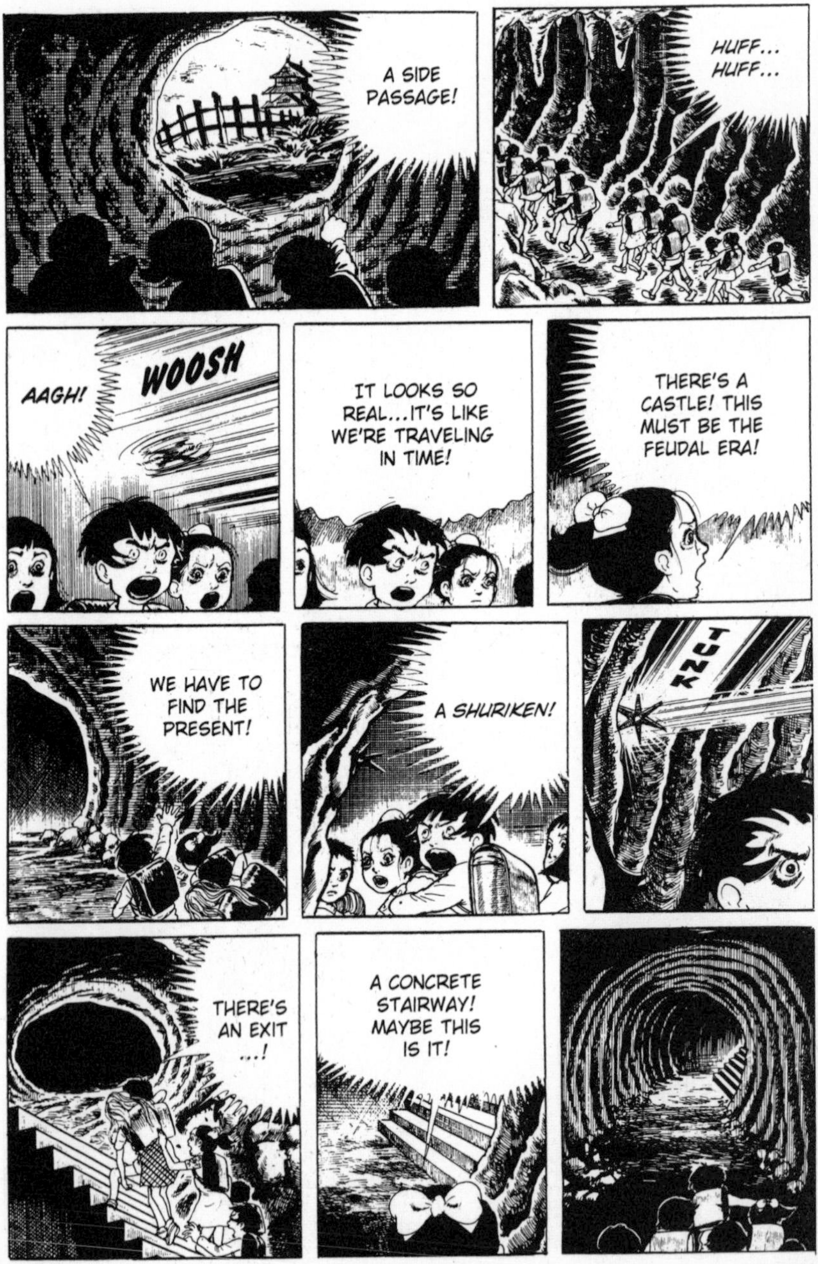
HUFF... HUFF...
A SIDE PASSAGE!
THERE'S A CASTLE! THIS MUST BE THE FEUDAL ERA!
IT LOOKS SO REAL...IT'S LIKE WE'RE TRAVELING IN TIME!
WOOSH
AAGH!
TUNK
A SHURIKEN!
WE HAVE TO FIND THE PRESENT!
A CONCRETE STAIRWAY! MAYBE THIS IS IT!
THERE'S AN EXIT ...!

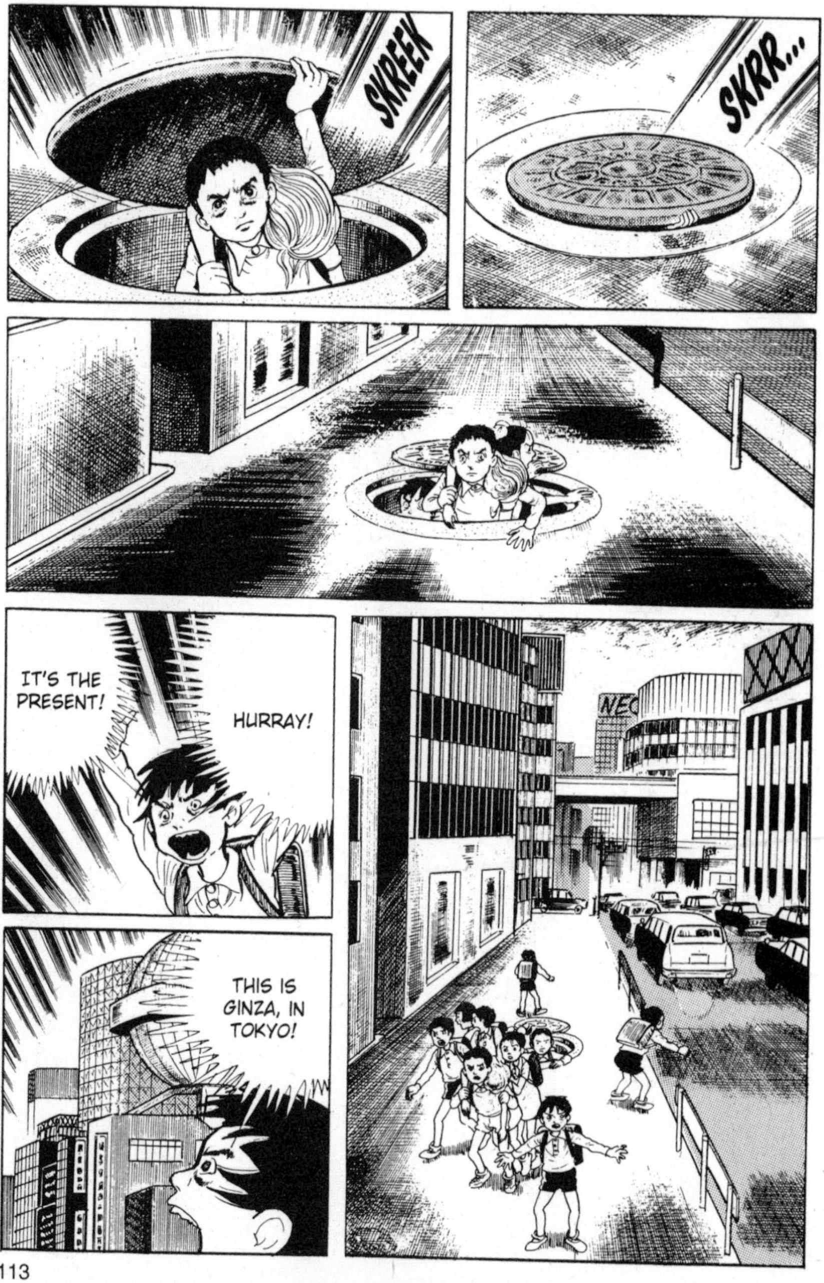
SKRR...
SKREEK
NEC
HURRAY!
IT'S THE PRESENT!
THIS IS GINZA, IN TOKYO!

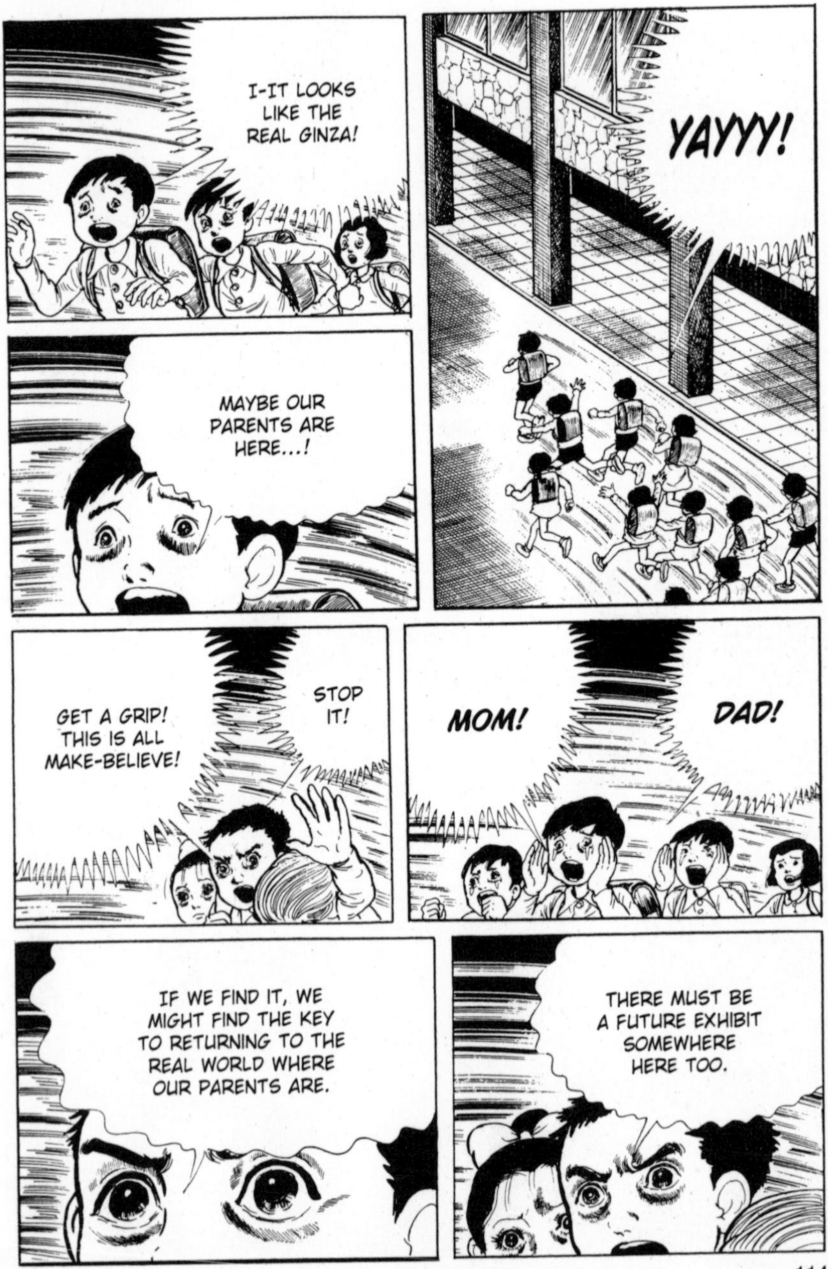
YAYYY!
I-IT LOOKS LIKE THE REAL GINZA!
MAYBE OUR PARENTS ARE HERE...!
DAD!
MOM!
STOP IT!
GET A GRIP! THIS IS ALL MAKE-BELIEVE!
THERE MUST BE A FUTURE EXHIBIT SOMEWHERE HERE TOO.
IF WE FIND IT, WE MIGHT FIND THE KEY TO RETURNING TO THE REAL WORLD WHERE OUR PARENTS ARE.

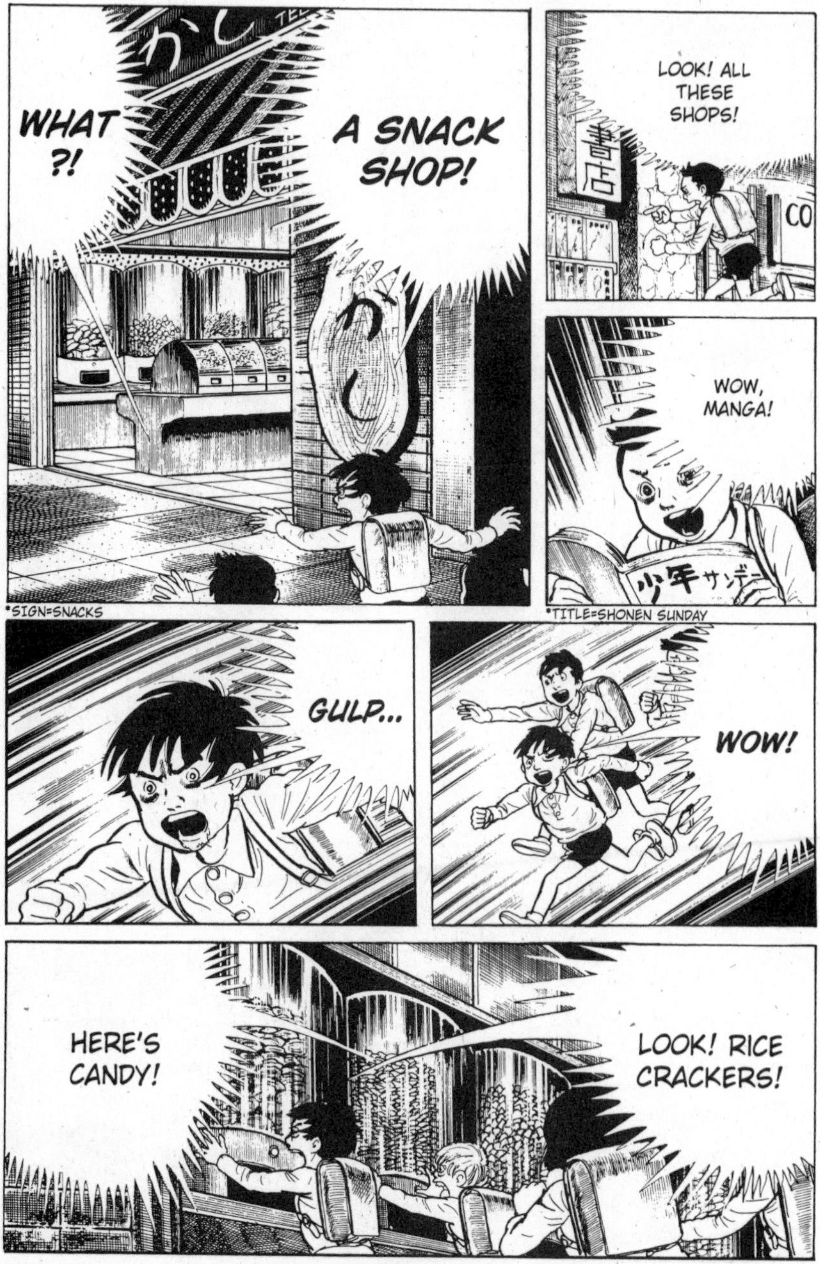
LOOK! ALL THESE SHOPS!
WOW, MANGA!
*TITLE=SHONEN SUNDAY
A SNACK SHOP!
WHAT ?!
*SIGN=SNACKS
WOW!
GULP...
LOOK! RICE CRACKERS!
HERE'S CANDY!

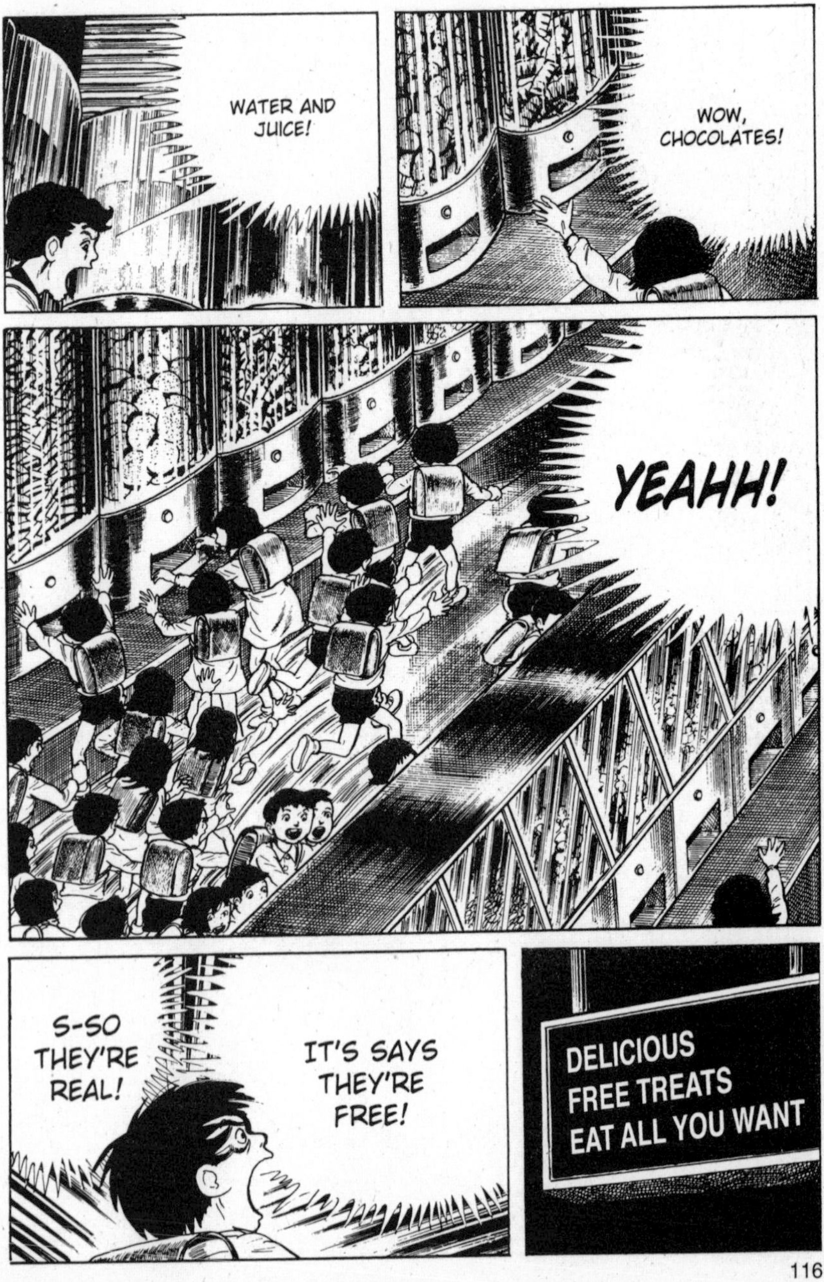
WOW, CHOCOLATES!
WATER AND JUICE!
YEAHH!
DELICIOUS FREE TREATS EAT ALL YOU WANT
IT'S SAYS THEY'RE FREE!
S-SO THEY'RE REAL!

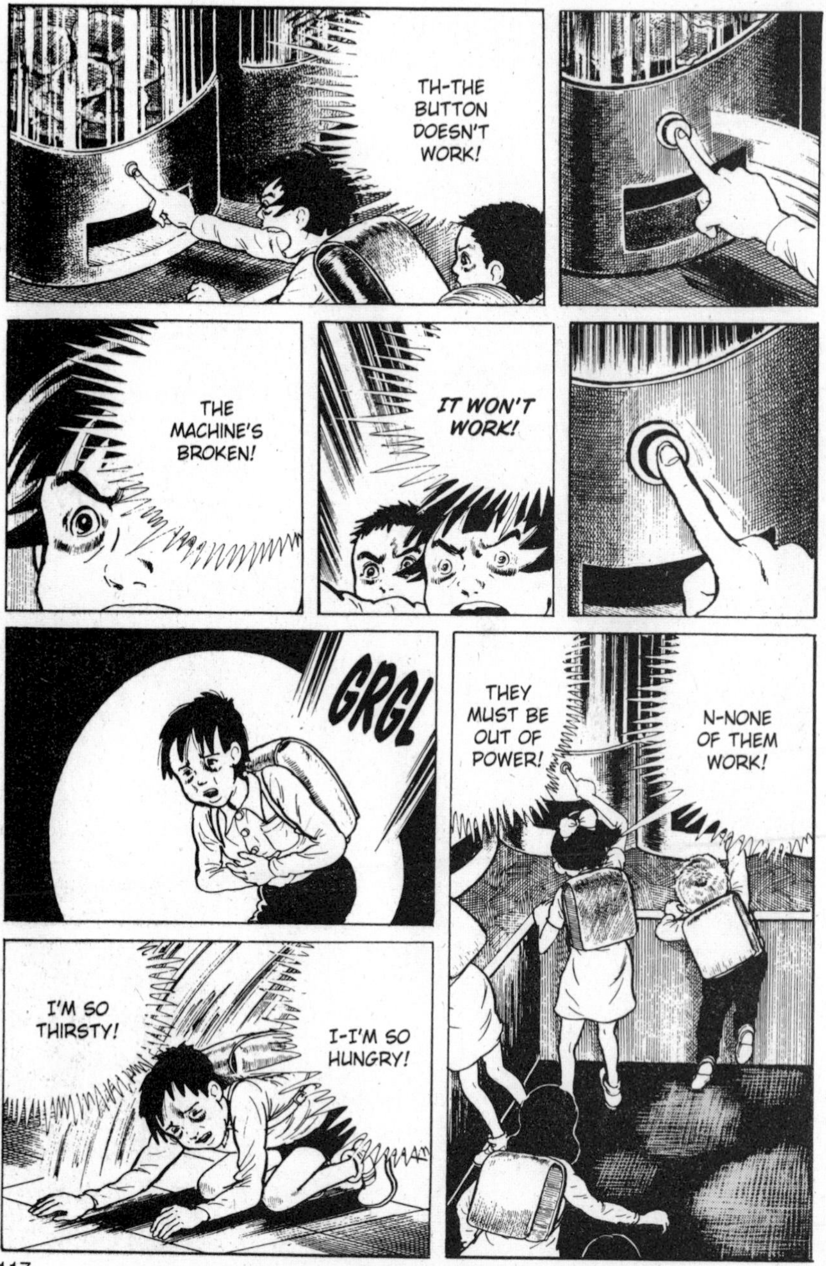
TH-THE BUTTON DOESN'T WORK!
IT WON'T WORK!
THE MACHINE'S BROKEN!
N-NONE OF THEM WORK!
THEY MUST BE OUT OF POWER!
GRGL
I-I'M SO HUNGRY!
I'M SO THIRSTY!

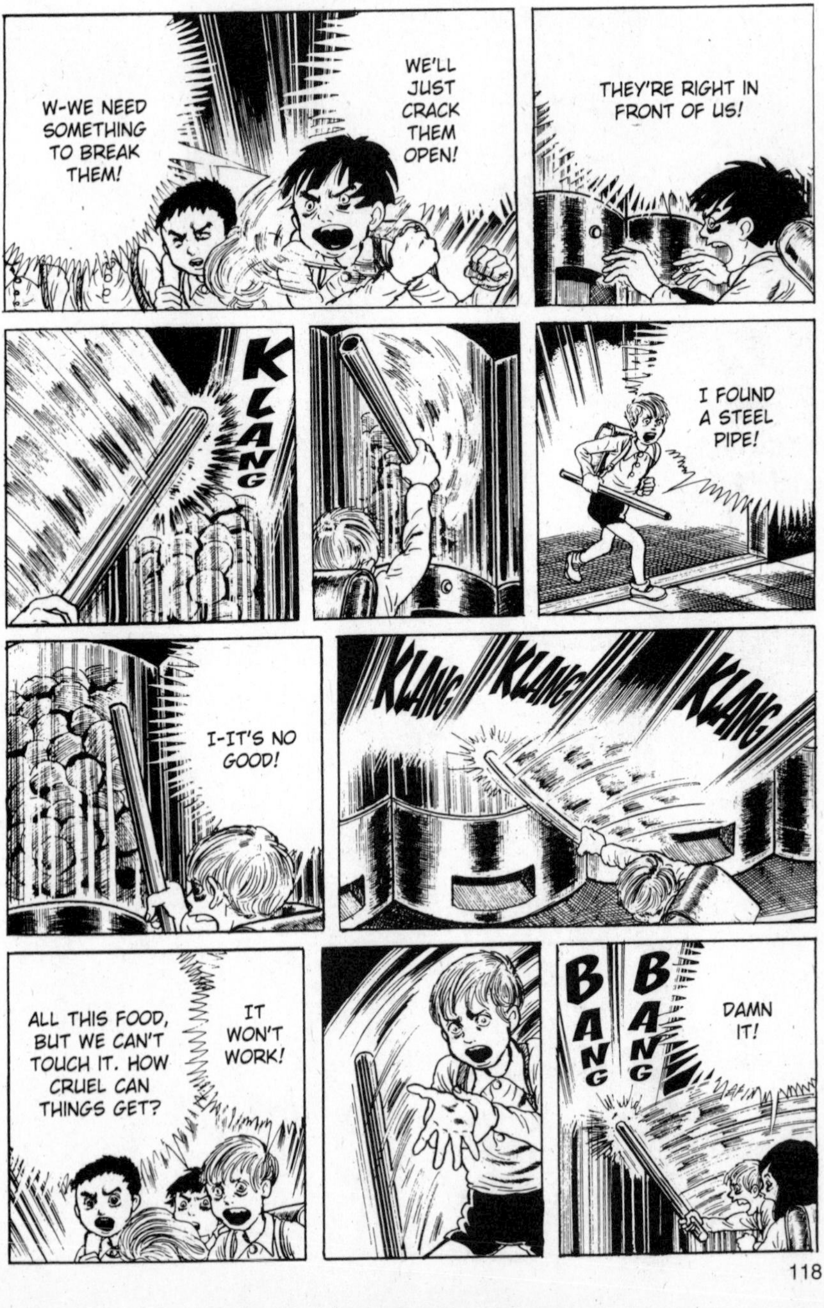
THEY'RE RIGHT IN FRONT OF US!
WE'LL JUST CRACK THEM OPEN!
W-WE NEED SOMETHING TO BREAK THEM!
I FOUND A STEEL PIPE!
KLANG
KLANG KLANG KLANG
I-IT'S NO GOOD!
DAMN IT!
BANG BANG
IT WON'T WORK!
ALL THIS FOOD, BUT WE CAN'T TOUCH IT. HOW CRUEL CAN THINGS GET?

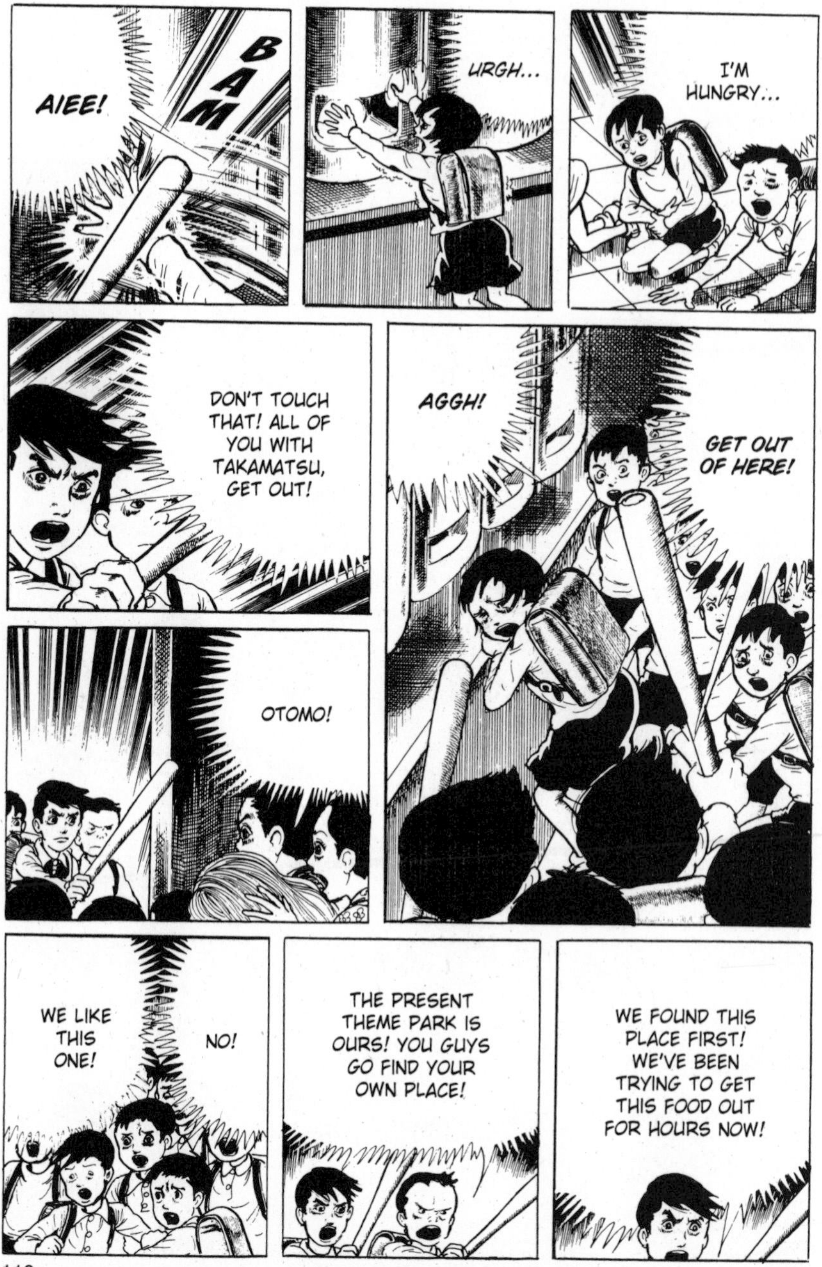

I'M HUNGRY...
URGH...
BAM
AIEE!
GET OUT OF HERE!
AGGH!
DON'T TOUCH THAT! ALL OF YOU WITH TAKAMATSU, GET OUT!
OTOMO!
WE FOUND THIS PLACE FIRST! WE'VE BEEN TRYING TO GET THIS FOOD OUT FOR HOURS NOW!
THE PRESENT THEME PARK IS OURS! YOU GUYS GO FIND YOUR OWN PLACE!
NO!
WE LIKE THIS ONE!

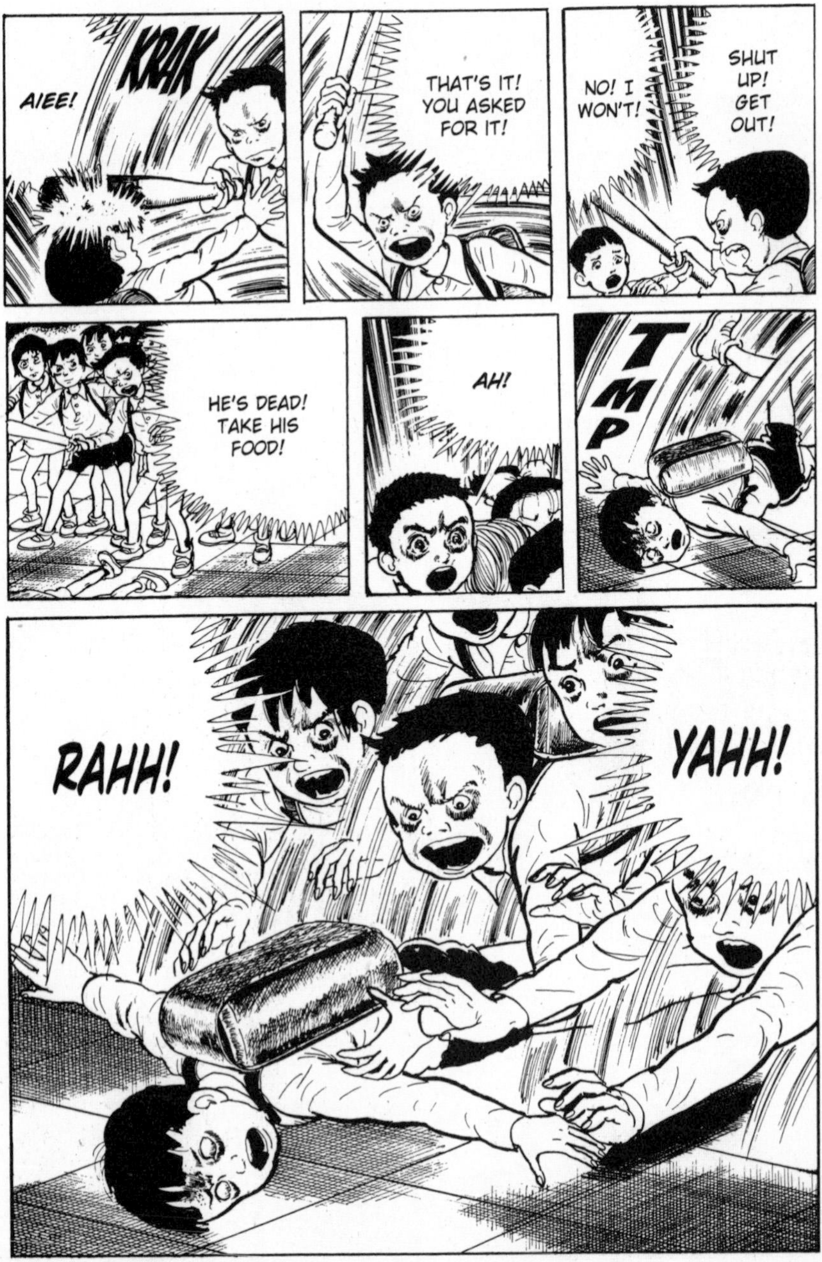
SHUT UP! GET OUT!
NO! I WON'T!
THAT'S IT! YOU ASKED FOR IT!
KRAK
AIEE!
TMP
AH!
HE'S DEAD! TAKE HIS FOOD!
YAHH!
RAHH!

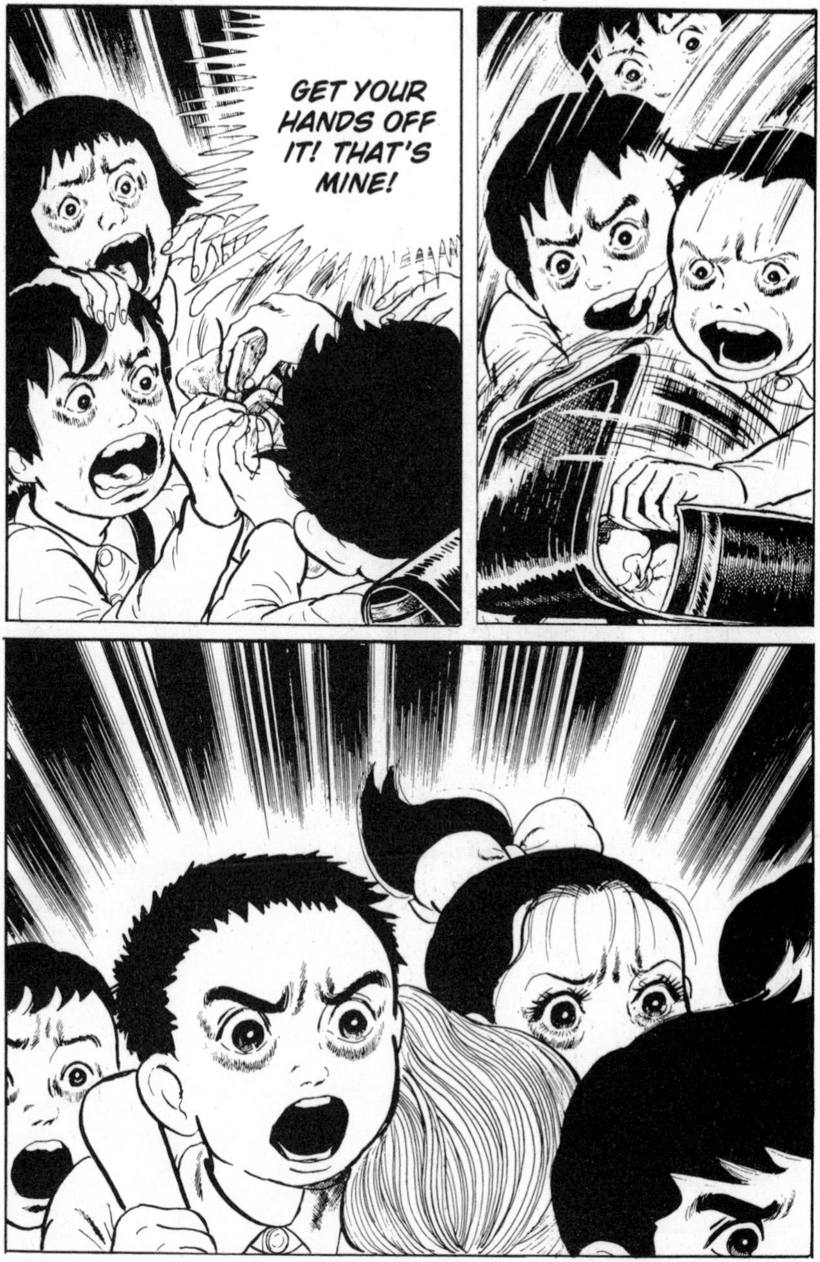
GET YOUR HANDS OFF IT! THAT'S MINE!

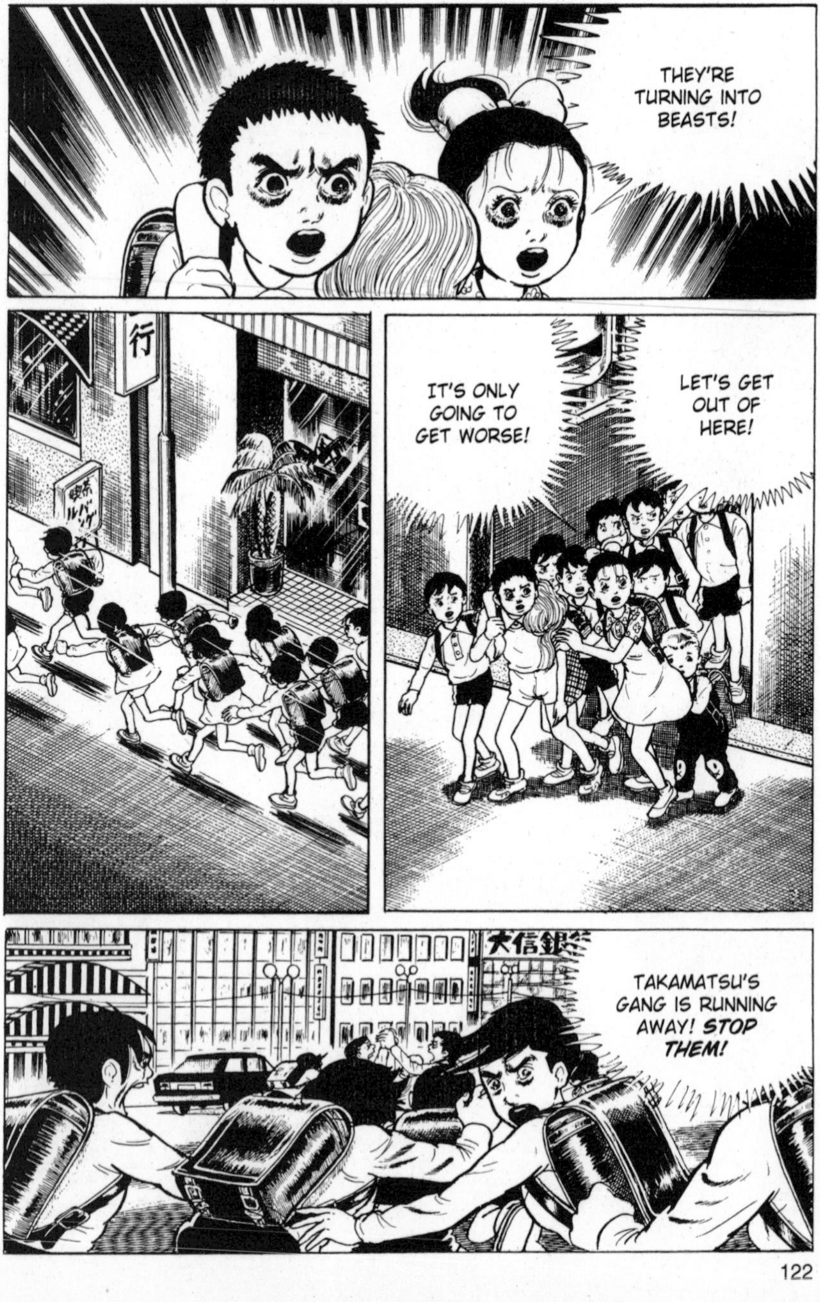
THEY'RE TURNING INTO BEASTS!
LET'S GET OUT OF HERE!
IT'S ONLY GOING TO GET WORSE!
TAKAMATSU'S GANG IS RUNNING AWAY! ***STOP THEM!***

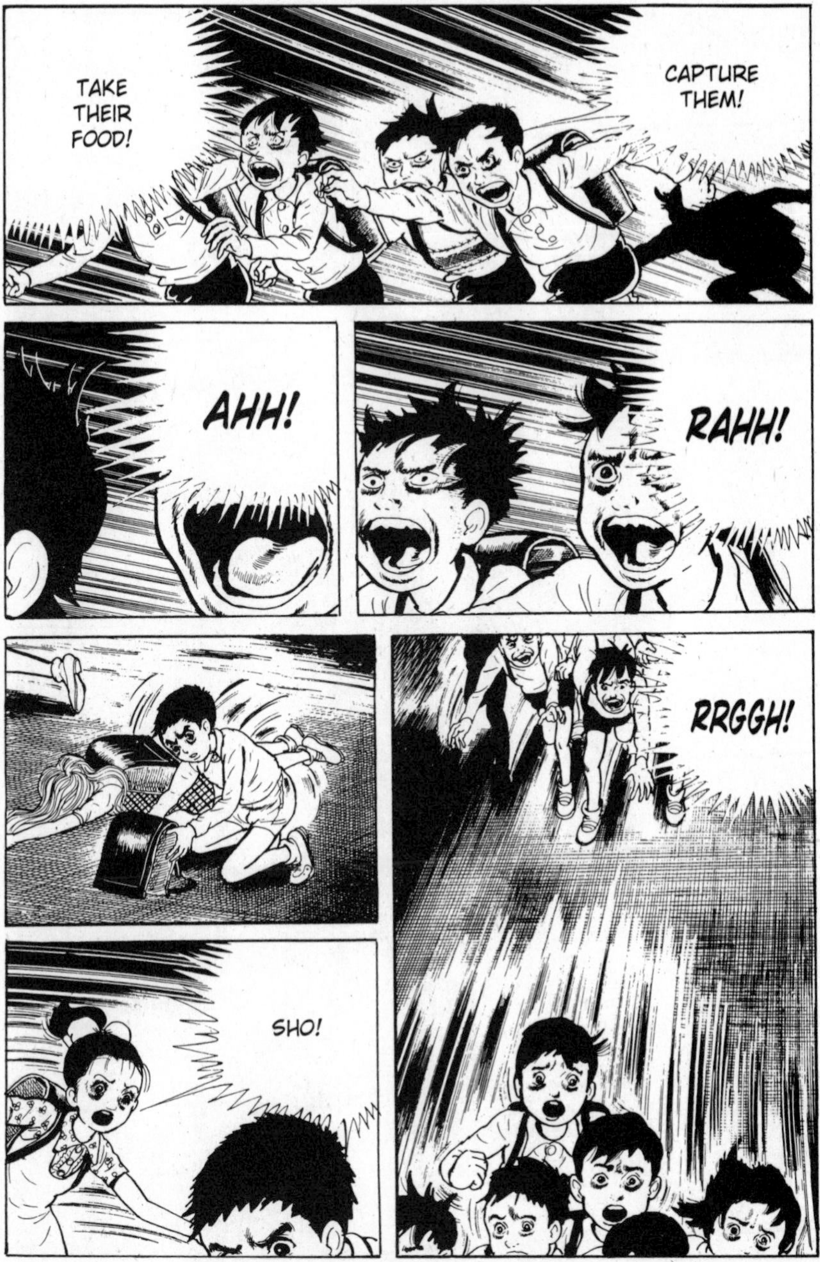
CAPTURE THEM!
TAKE THEIR FOOD!
RAHH!
AHH!
RRGGH!
SHO!

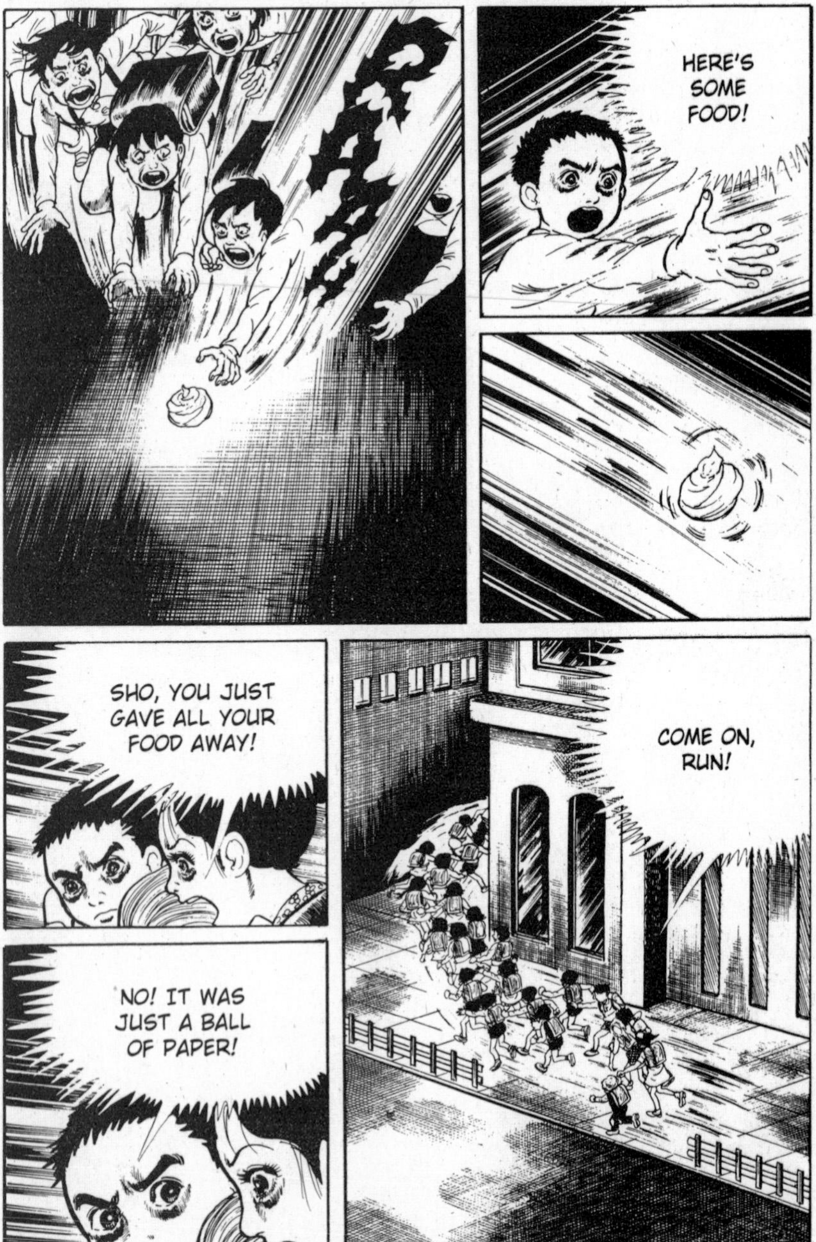
HERE'S SOME FOOD!
COME ON, RUN!
SHO, YOU JUST GAVE ALL YOUR FOOD AWAY!
NO! IT WAS JUST A BALL OF PAPER!

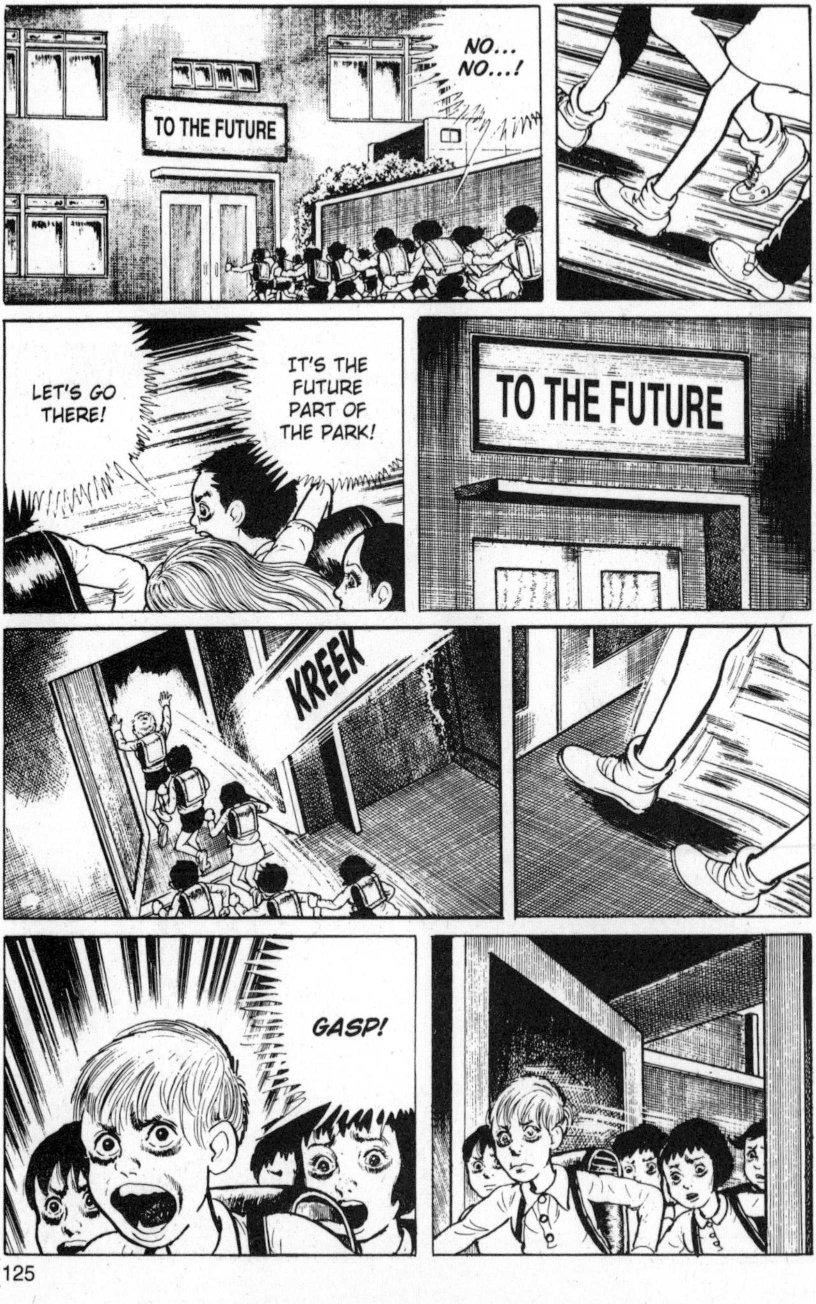
TO THE FUTURE
NO... NO...!
TO THE FUTURE
IT'S THE FUTURE PART OF THE PARK!
LET'S GO THERE!
KREEK
GASP!

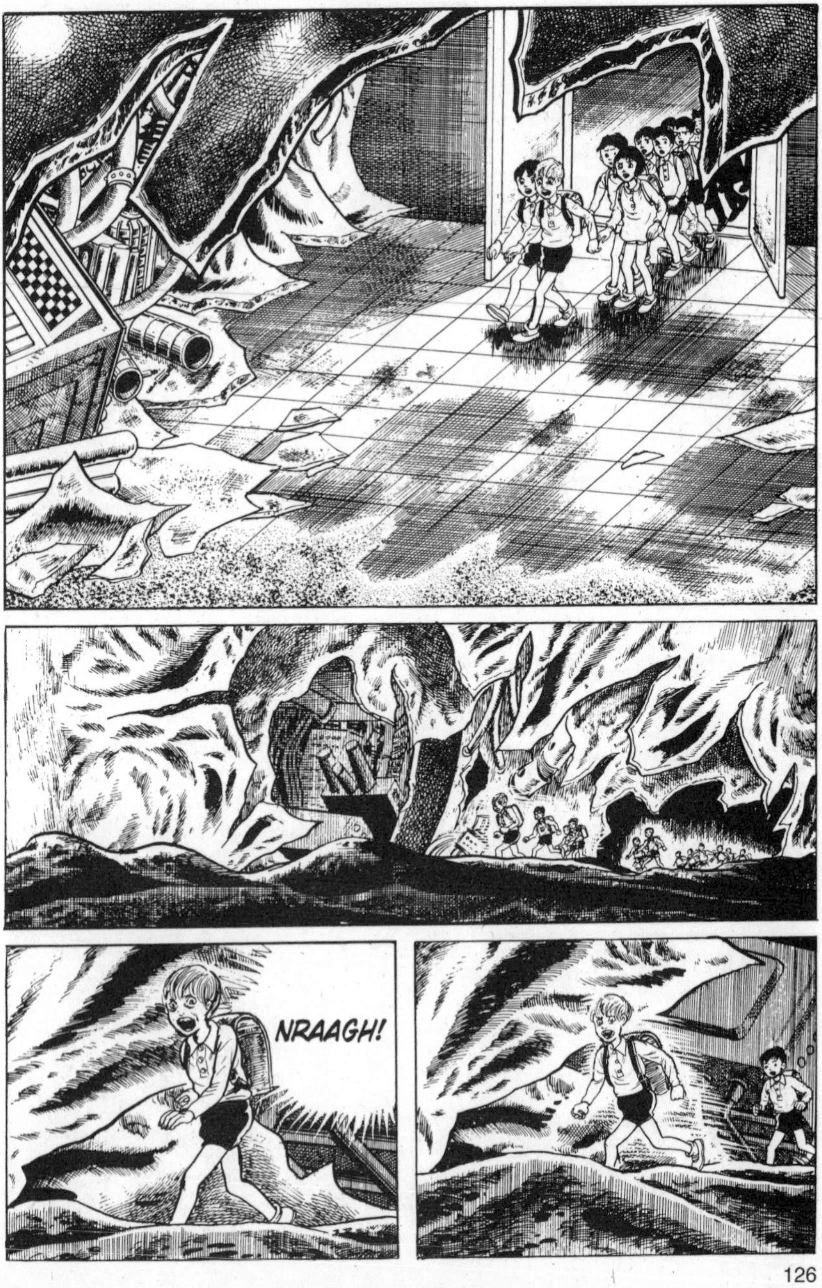
NRAAGH!

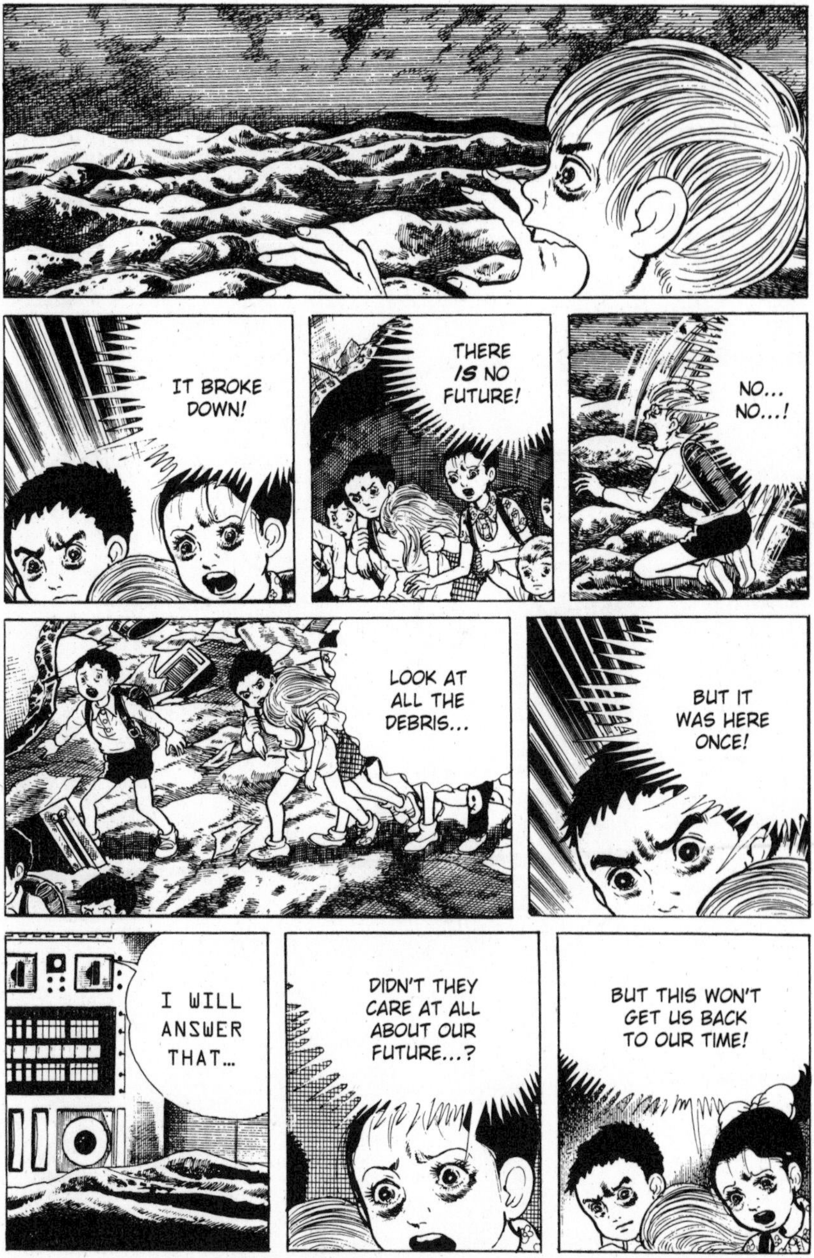
NO... NO...!
THERE *IS* NO FUTURE!
IT BROKE DOWN!
BUT IT WAS HERE ONCE!
LOOK AT ALL THE DEBRIS...
BUT THIS WON'T GET US BACK TO OUR TIME!
DIDN'T THEY CARE AT ALL ABOUT OUR FUTURE...?
I WILL ANSWER THAT...

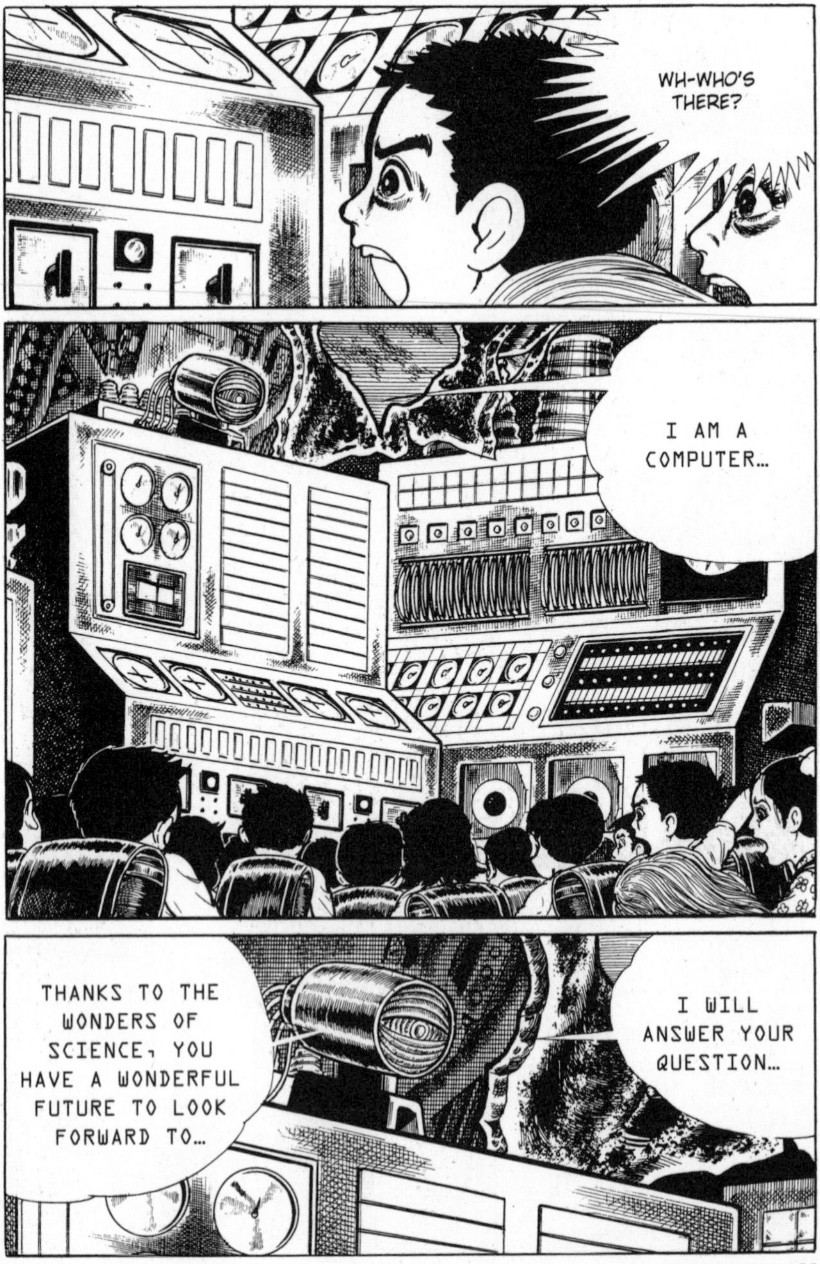
WH-WHO'S THERE?
I AM A COMPUTER...
I WILL ANSWER YOUR QUESTION...
THANKS TO THE WONDERS OF SCIENCE, YOU HAVE A WONDERFUL FUTURE TO LOOK FORWARD TO...

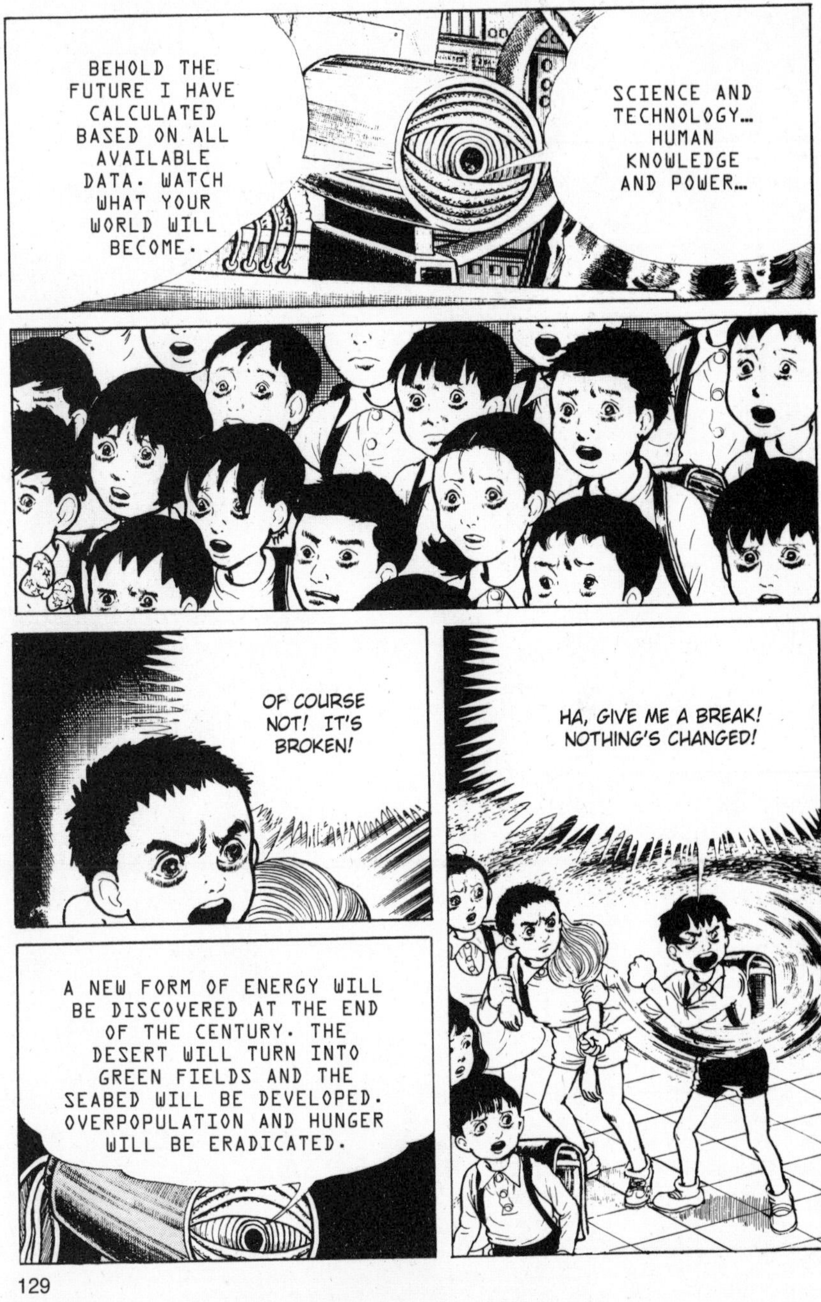
SCIENCE AND TECHNOLOGY... HUMAN KNOWLEDGE AND POWER...
BEHOLD THE FUTURE I HAVE CALCULATED BASED ON ALL AVAILABLE DATA. WATCH WHAT YOUR WORLD WILL BECOME.
HA, GIVE ME A BREAK! NOTHING'S CHANGED!
OF COURSE NOT! IT'S BROKEN!
A NEW FORM OF ENERGY WILL BE DISCOVERED AT THE END OF THE CENTURY. THE DESERT WILL TURN INTO GREEN FIELDS AND THE SEABED WILL BE DEVELOPED. OVERPOPULATION AND HUNGER WILL BE ERADICATED.

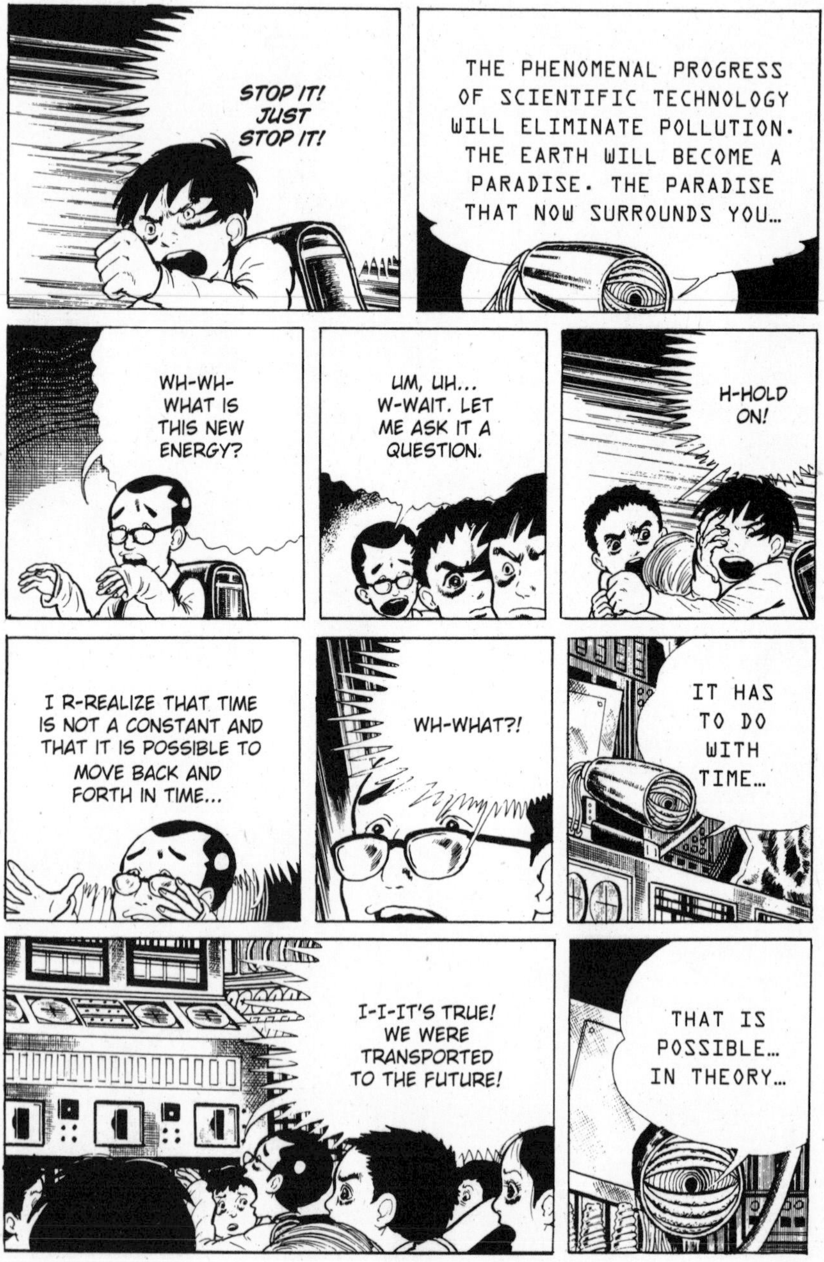
THE PHENOMENAL PROGRESS OF SCIENTIFIC TECHNOLOGY WILL ELIMINATE POLLUTION. THE EARTH WILL BECOME A PARADISE. THE PARADISE THAT NOW SURROUNDS YOU...
STOP IT! JUST STOP IT!
H-HOLD ON!
UM, UH... W-WAIT. LET ME ASK IT A QUESTION.
WH-WH-WHAT IS THIS NEW ENERGY?
IT HAS TO DO WITH TIME...
WH-WHAT?!
I R-REALIZE THAT TIME IS NOT A CONSTANT AND THAT IT IS POSSIBLE TO MOVE BACK AND FORTH IN TIME...
THAT IS POSSIBLE... IN THEORY...
I-I-IT'S TRUE! WE WERE TRANSPORTED TO THE FUTURE!

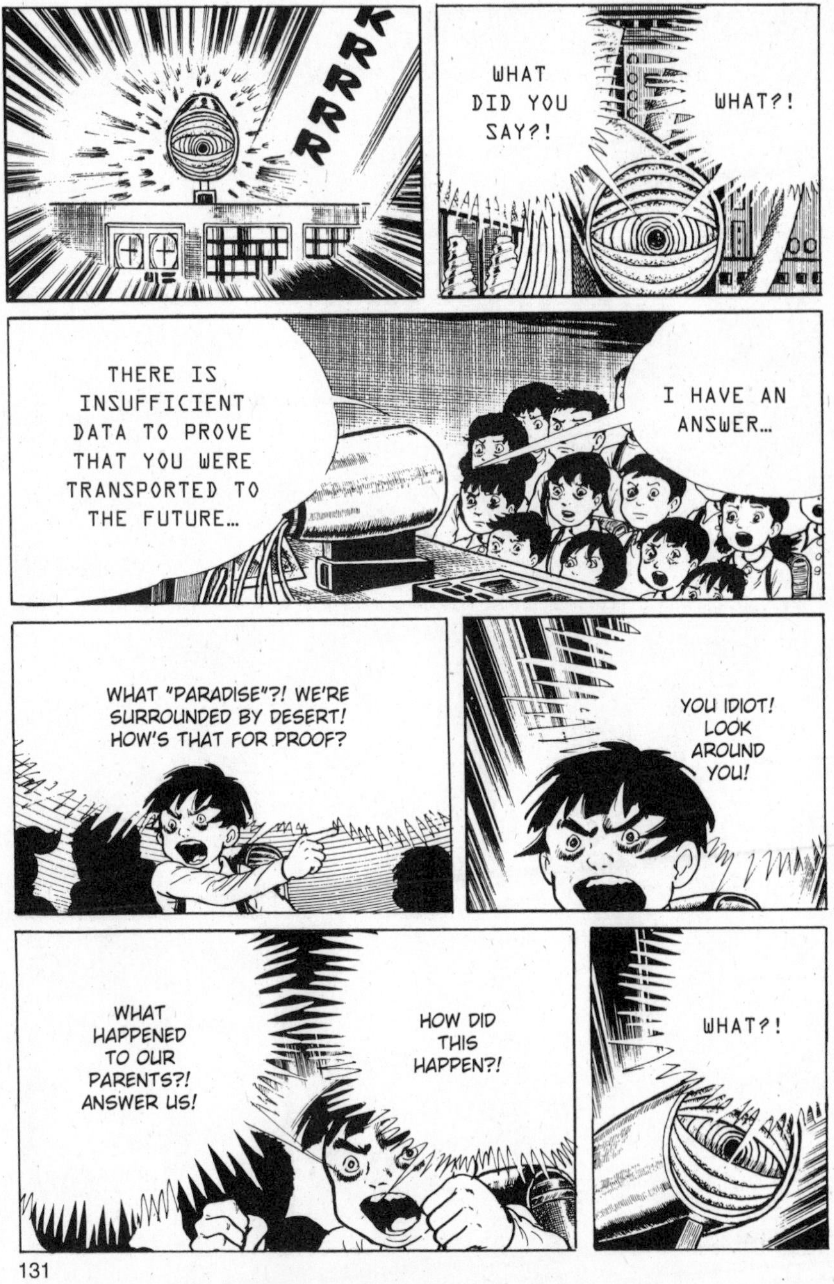
WHAT?!
WHAT DID YOU SAY?!
KRRRR
I HAVE AN ANSWER...
THERE IS INSUFFICIENT DATA TO PROVE THAT YOU WERE TRANSPORTED TO THE FUTURE...
YOU IDIOT! LOOK AROUND YOU!
WHAT "PARADISE"?! WE'RE SURROUNDED BY DESERT! HOW'S THAT FOR PROOF?
WHAT?!
HOW DID THIS HAPPEN?!
WHAT HAPPENED TO OUR PARENTS?! ANSWER US!

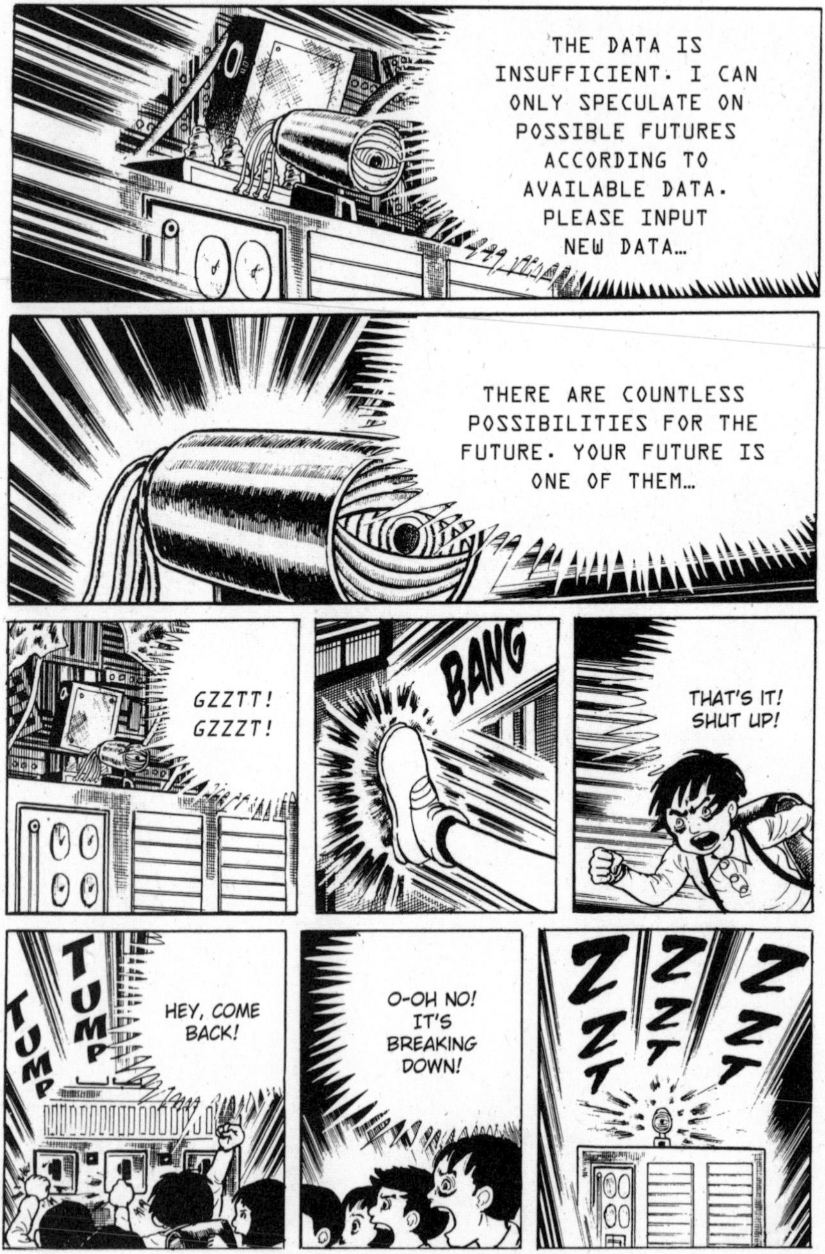
THE DATA IS INSUFFICIENT. I CAN ONLY SPECULATE ON POSSIBLE FUTURES ACCORDING TO AVAILABLE DATA. PLEASE INPUT NEW DATA...
THERE ARE COUNTLESS POSSIBILITIES FOR THE FUTURE. YOUR FUTURE IS ONE OF THEM...
THAT'S IT! SHUT UP!
BANG
GZZTT! GZZZT!
ZZT
ZZT
ZZT
O-OH NO! IT'S BREAKING DOWN!
HEY, COME BACK!
TUMP
TUMP

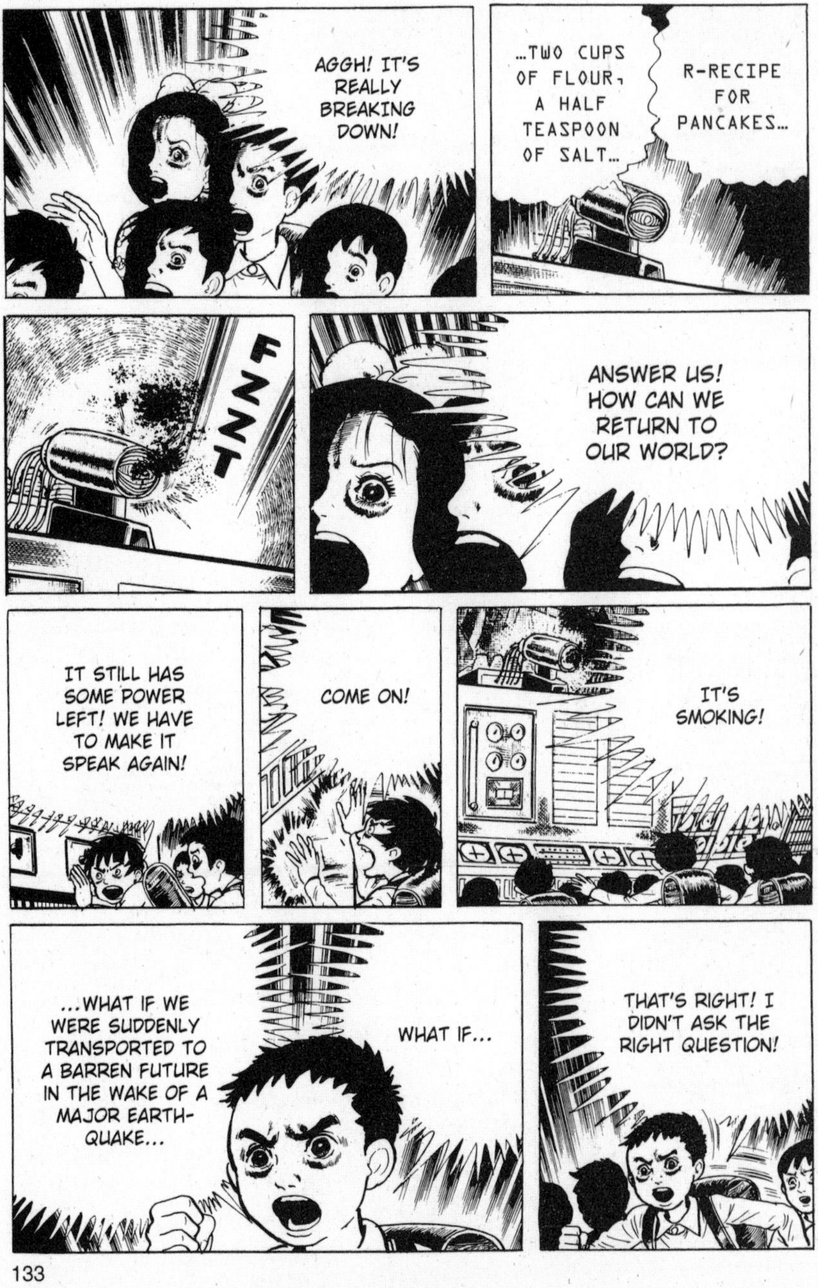
R-RECIPE FOR PANCAKES...
...TWO CUPS OF FLOUR, A HALF TEASPOON OF SALT...
AGGH! IT'S REALLY BREAKING DOWN!
ANSWER US! HOW CAN WE RETURN TO OUR WORLD?
FZZT
IT'S SMOKING!
COME ON!
IT STILL HAS SOME POWER LEFT! WE HAVE TO MAKE IT SPEAK AGAIN!
THAT'S RIGHT! I DIDN'T ASK THE RIGHT QUESTION!
WHAT IF...
...WHAT IF WE WERE SUDDENLY TRANSPORTED TO A BARREN FUTURE IN THE WAKE OF A MAJOR EARTH-QUAKE...

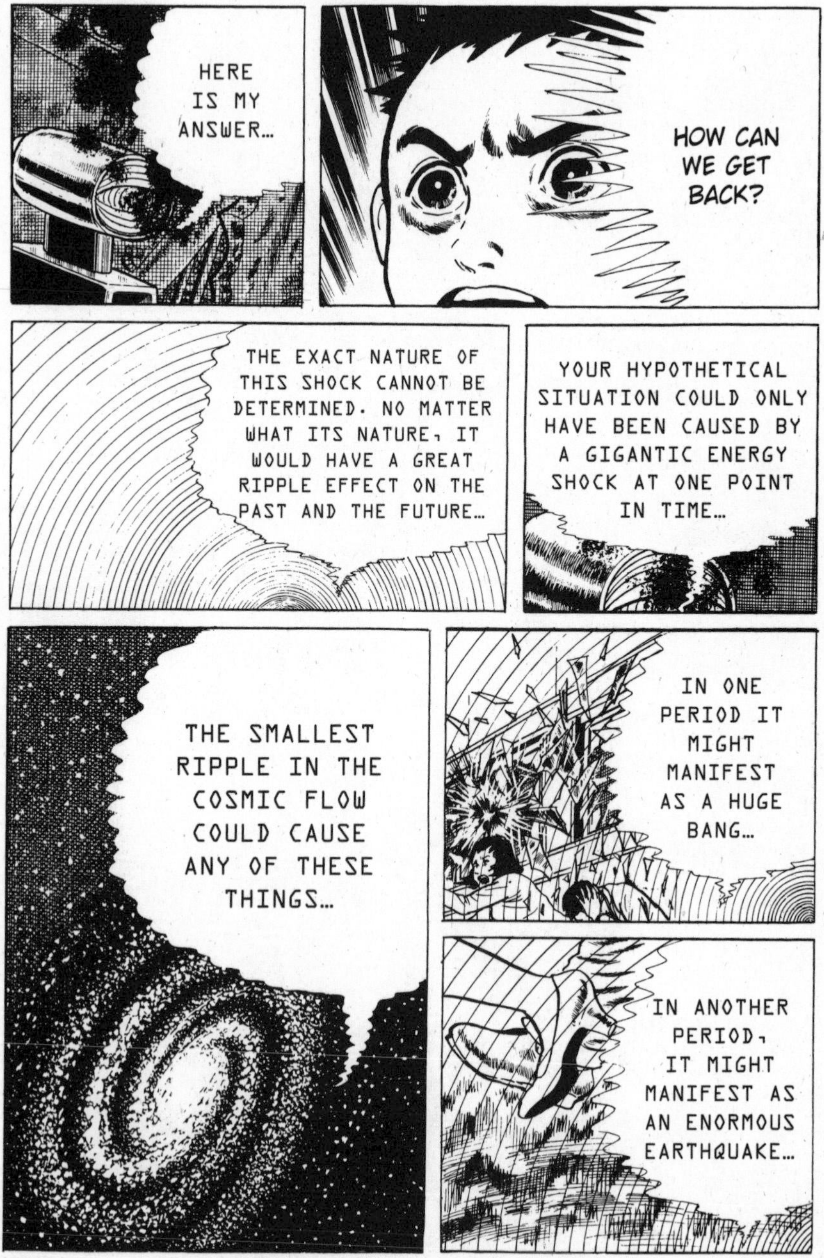
HOW CAN WE GET BACK?
HERE IS MY ANSWER...
YOUR HYPOTHETICAL SITUATION COULD ONLY HAVE BEEN CAUSED BY A GIGANTIC ENERGY SHOCK AT ONE POINT IN TIME...
THE EXACT NATURE OF THIS SHOCK CANNOT BE DETERMINED. NO MATTER WHAT ITS NATURE, IT WOULD HAVE A GREAT RIPPLE EFFECT ON THE PAST AND THE FUTURE...
IN ONE PERIOD IT MIGHT MANIFEST AS A HUGE BANG...
IN ANOTHER PERIOD, IT MIGHT MANIFEST AS AN ENORMOUS EARTHQUAKE...
THE SMALLEST RIPPLE IN THE COSMIC FLOW COULD CAUSE ANY OF THESE THINGS...

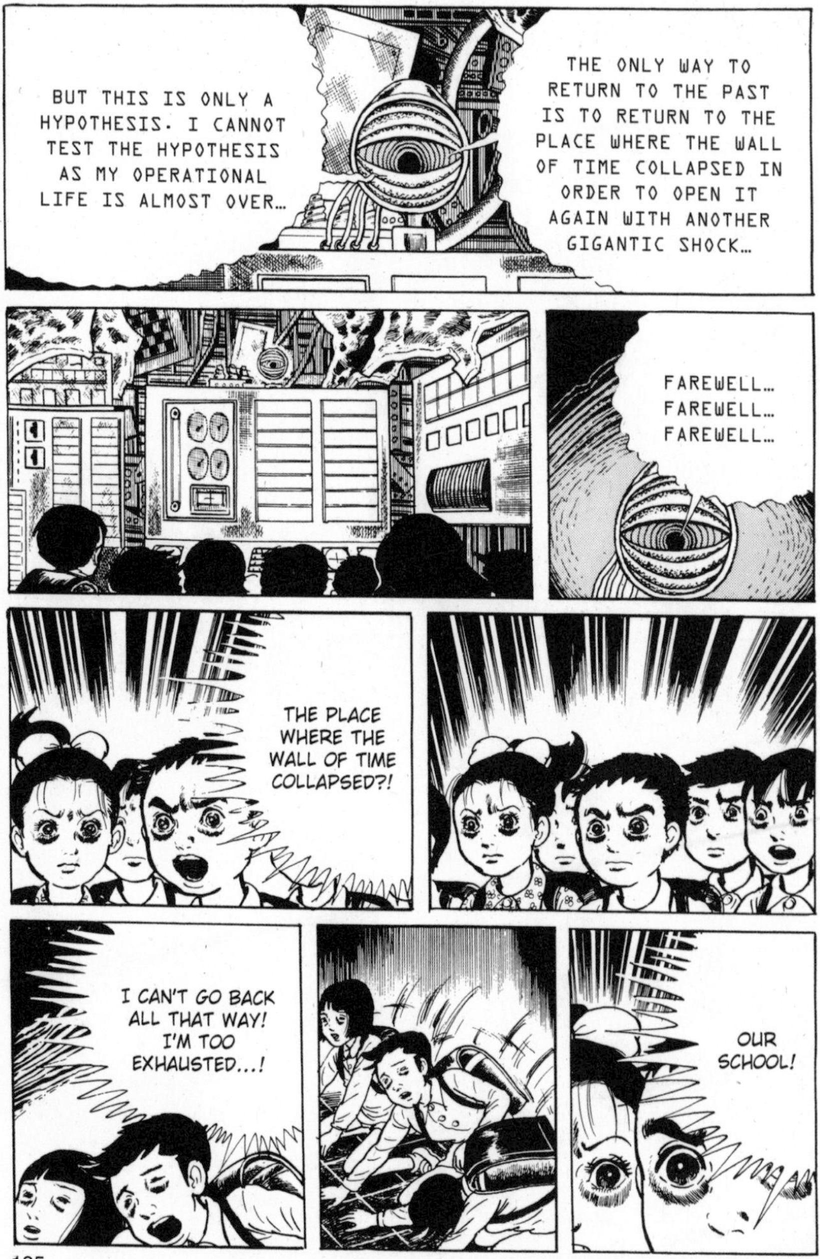
THE ONLY WAY TO RETURN TO THE PAST IS TO RETURN TO THE PLACE WHERE THE WALL OF TIME COLLAPSED IN ORDER TO OPEN IT AGAIN WITH ANOTHER GIGANTIC SHOCK...
BUT THIS IS ONLY A HYPOTHESIS. I CANNOT TEST THE HYPOTHESIS AS MY OPERATIONAL LIFE IS ALMOST OVER...
FAREWELL... FAREWELL... FAREWELL...
THE PLACE WHERE THE WALL OF TIME COLLAPSED?!
OUR SCHOOL!
I CAN'T GO BACK ALL THAT WAY! I'M TOO EXHAUSTED...!

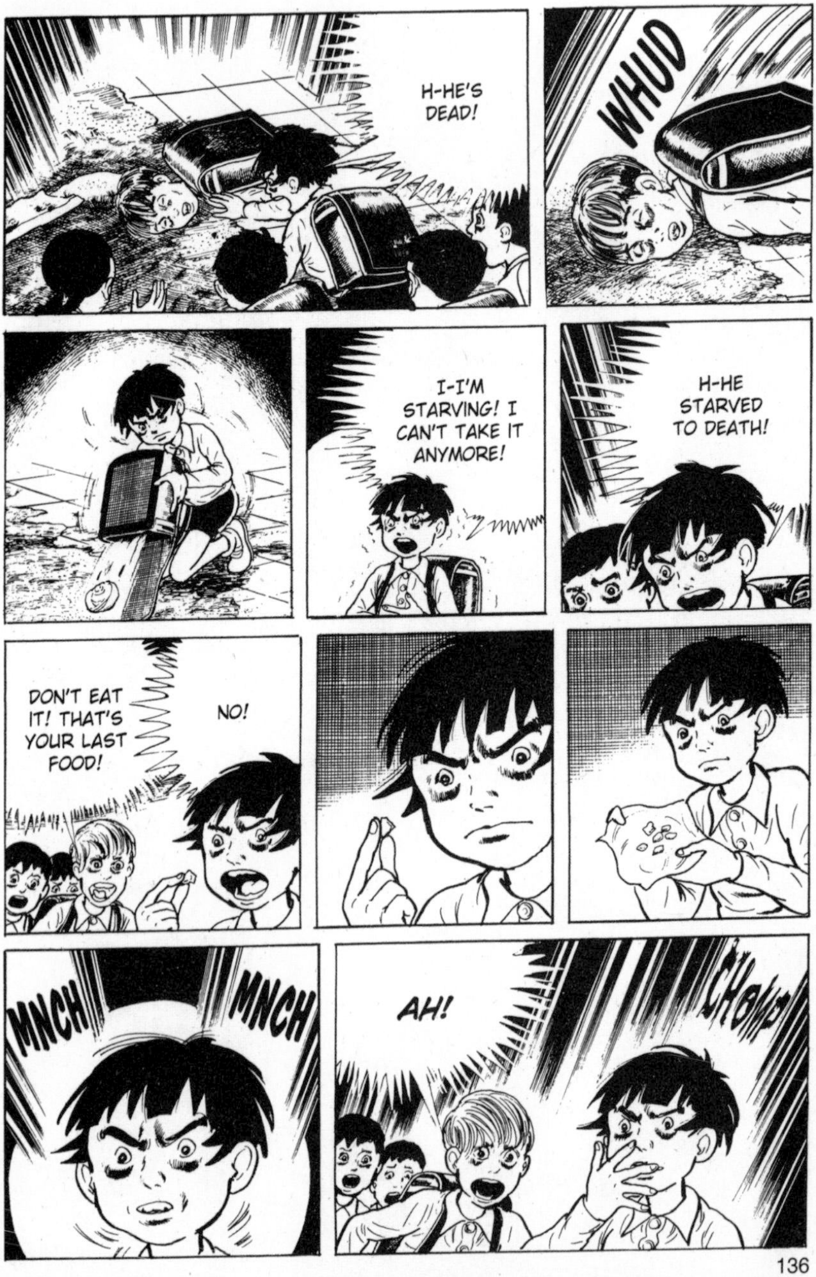
WHUD
H-HE'S DEAD!
H-HE STARVED TO DEATH!
I-I'M STARVING! I CAN'T TAKE IT ANYMORE!
NO!
DON'T EAT IT! THAT'S YOUR LAST FOOD!
CHOMP
AH!
MNCH
MNCH

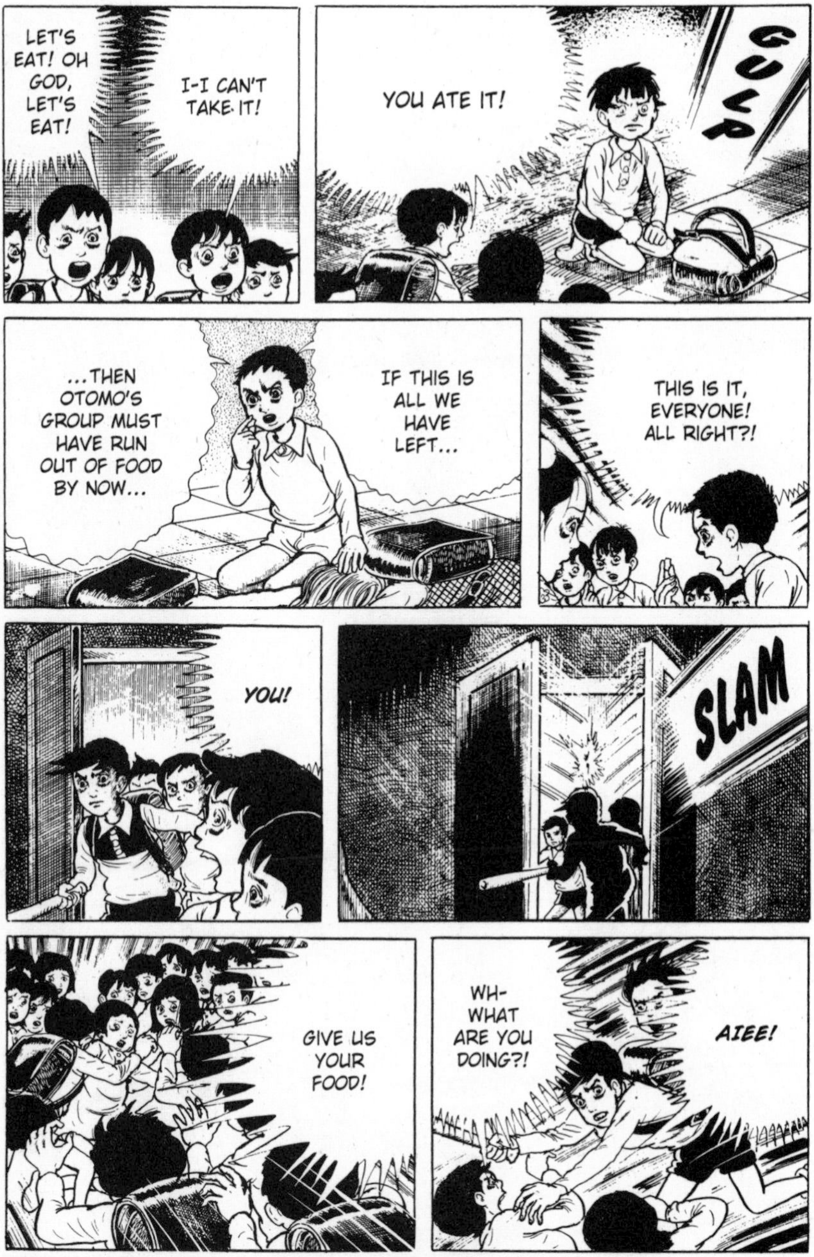
GULP
YOU ATE IT!
I-I CAN'T TAKE IT!
LET'S EAT! OH GOD, LET'S EAT!
THIS IS IT, EVERYONE! ALL RIGHT?!
IF THIS IS ALL WE HAVE LEFT...
...THEN OTOMO'S GROUP MUST HAVE RUN OUT OF FOOD BY NOW...
SLAM
YOU!
AIEE!
WH-WHAT ARE YOU DOING?!
GIVE US YOUR FOOD!

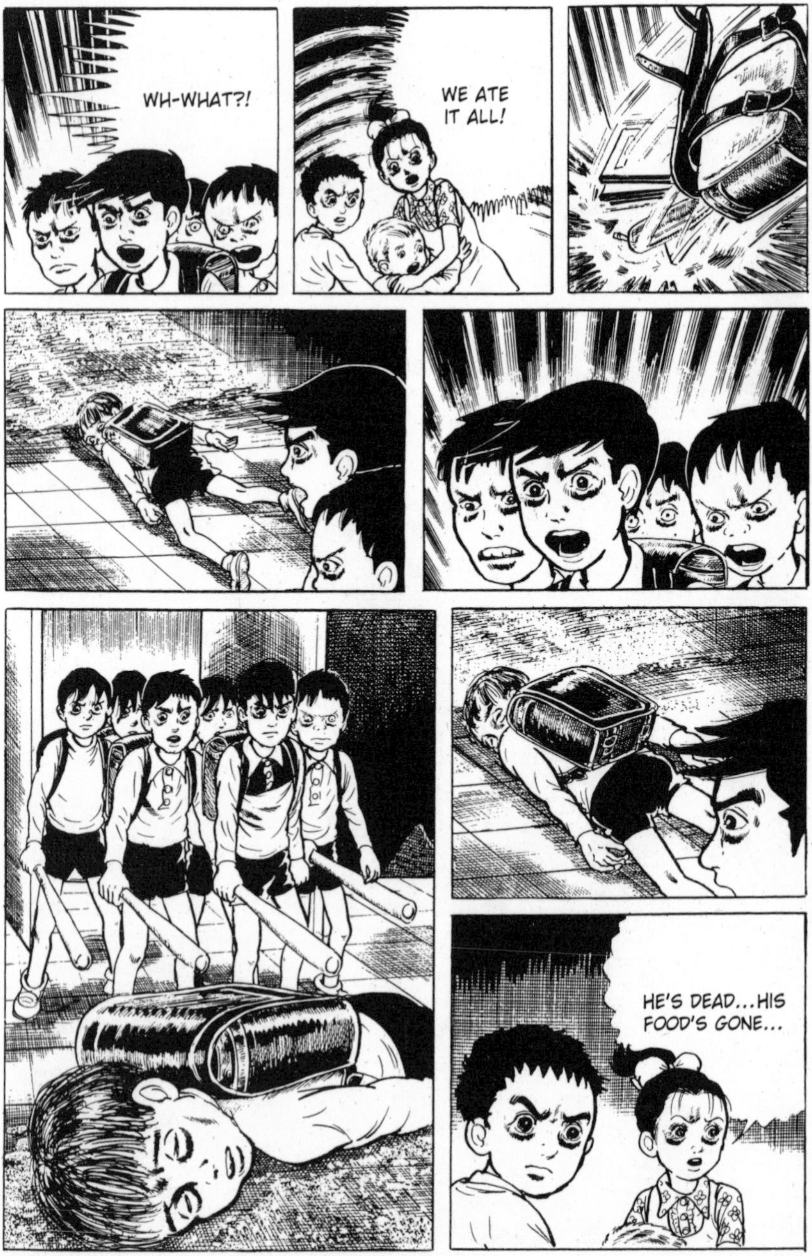
WE ATE IT ALL!
WH-WHAT?!
HE'S DEAD...HIS FOOD'S GONE...

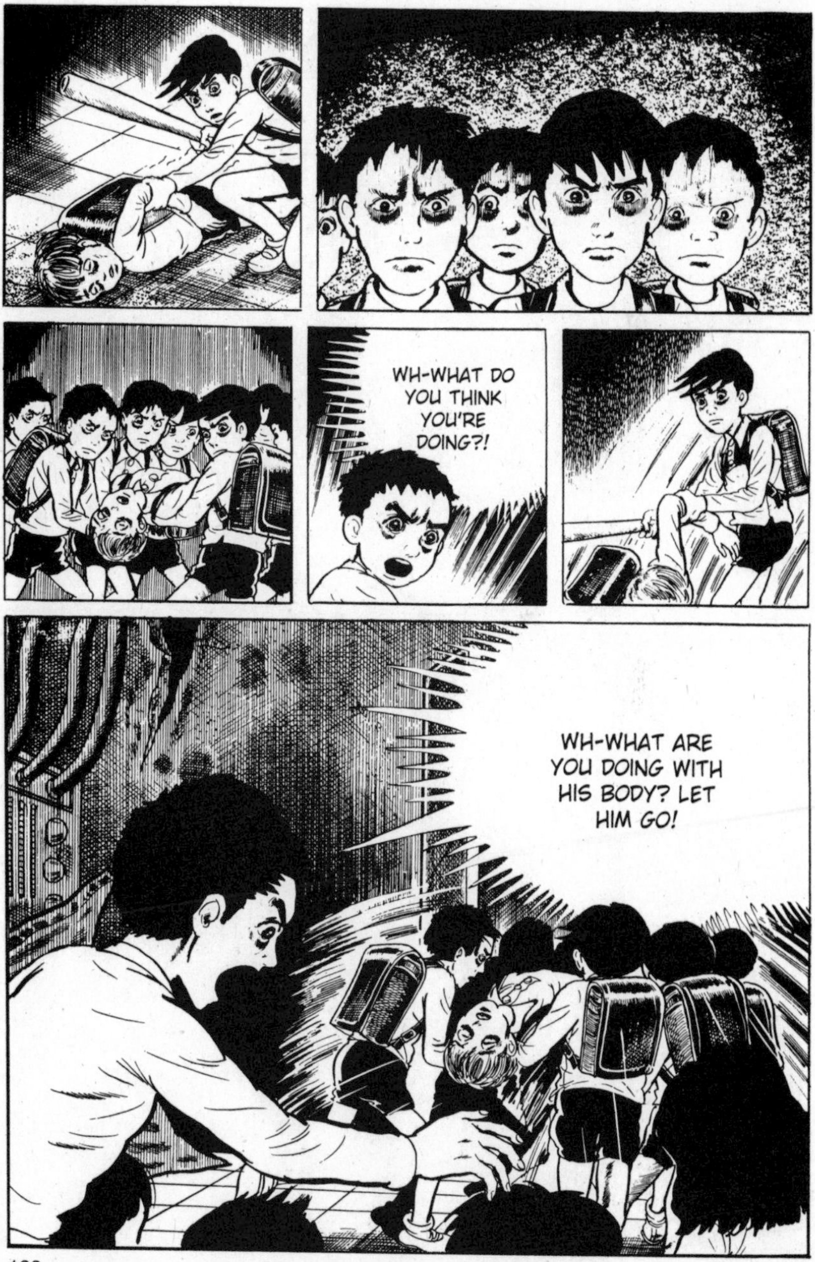
WH-WHAT DO YOU THINK YOU'RE DOING?!
WH-WHAT ARE YOU DOING WITH HIS BODY? LET HIM GO!

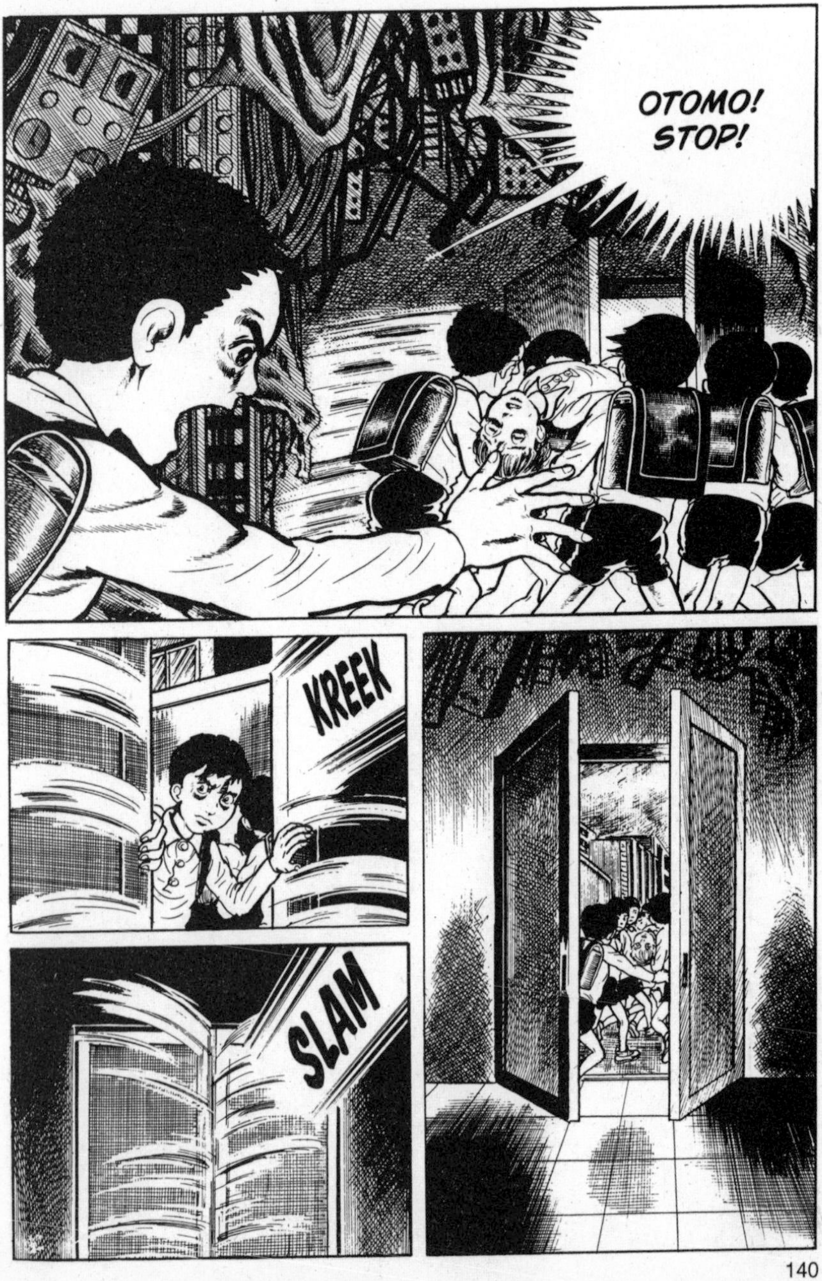
OTOMO! STOP!
KREEK
SLAM

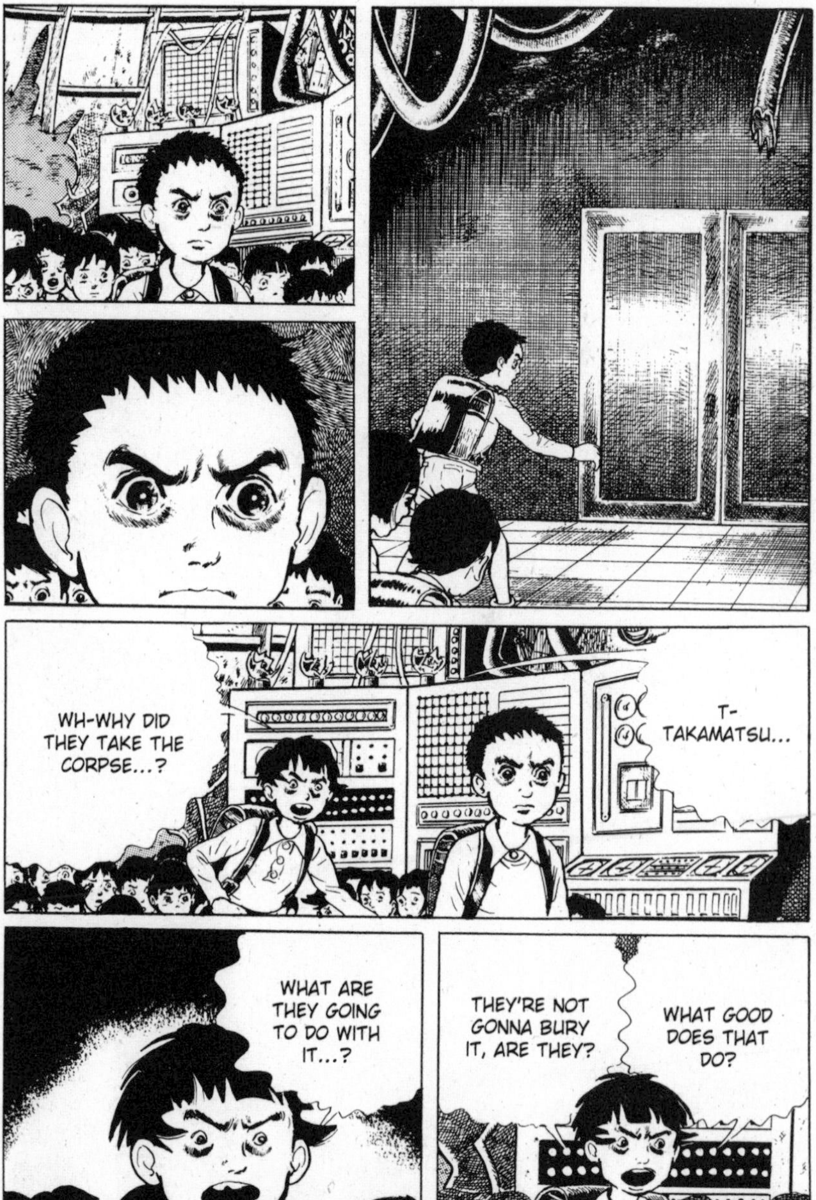
T-
TAKAMATSU...
WH-WHY DID THEY TAKE THE CORPSE...?
WHAT GOOD DOES THAT DO?
THEY'RE NOT GONNA BURY IT, ARE THEY?
WHAT ARE THEY GOING TO DO WITH IT...?

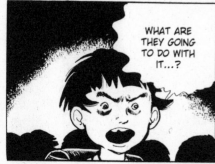

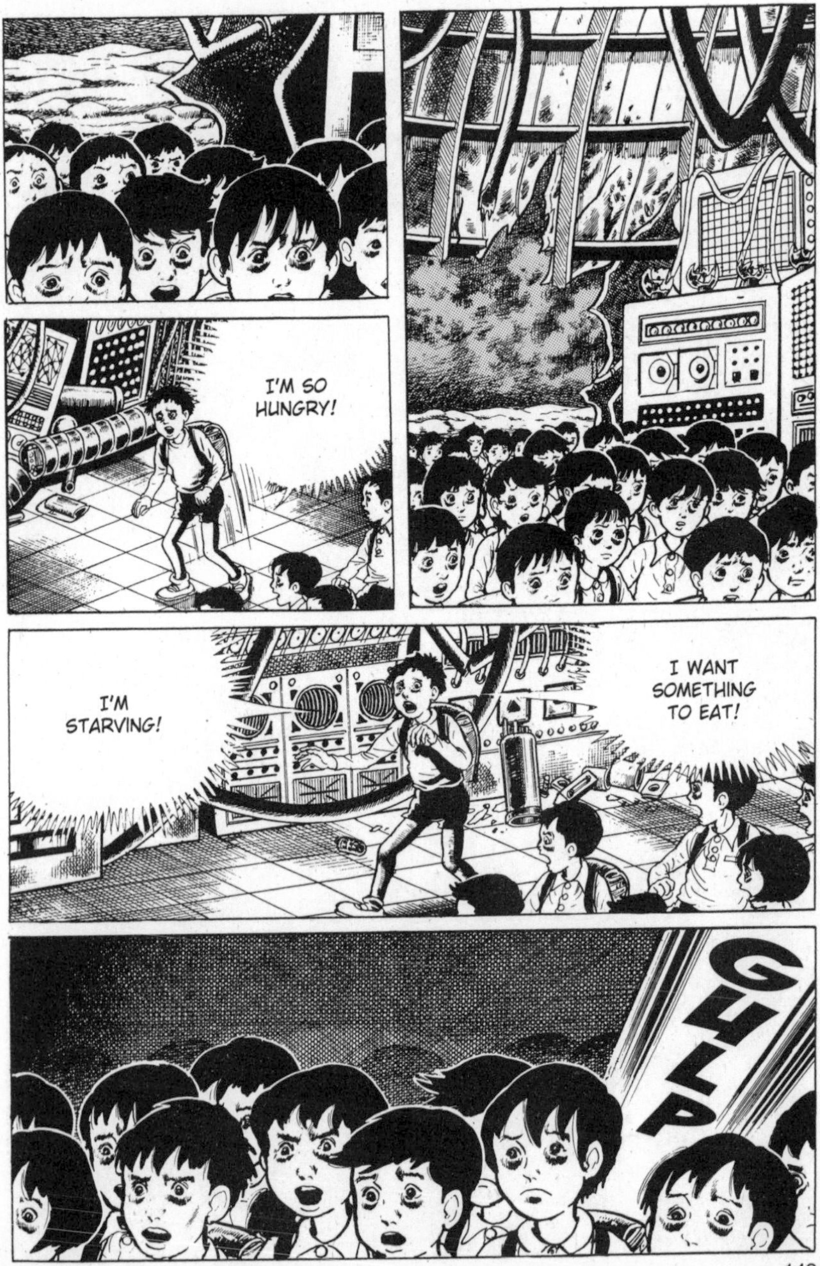
I'M SO HUNGRY!
I WANT SOMETHING TO EAT!
I'M STARVING!
GULP

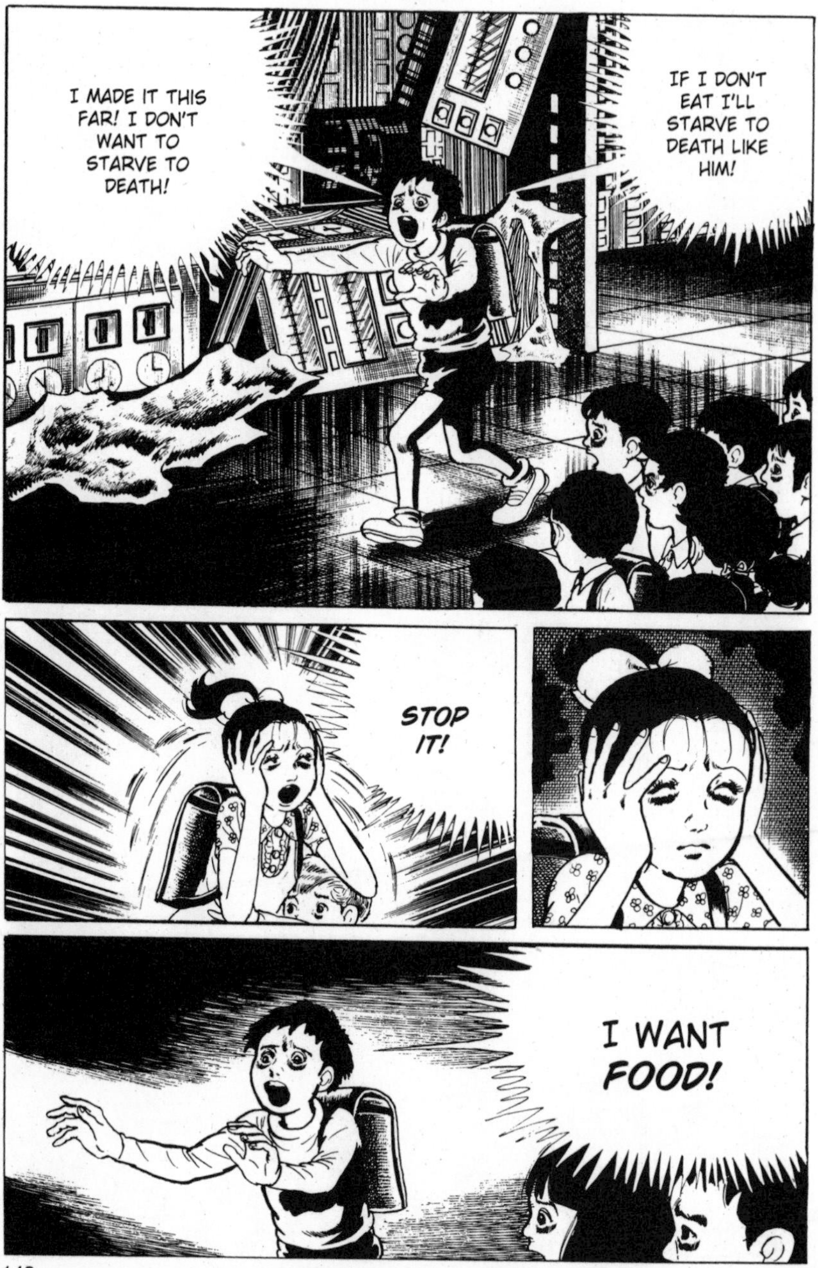
IF I DON'T EAT I'LL STARVE TO DEATH LIKE HIM!
I MADE IT THIS FAR! I DON'T WANT TO STARVE TO DEATH!
STOP IT!
I WANT FOOD!

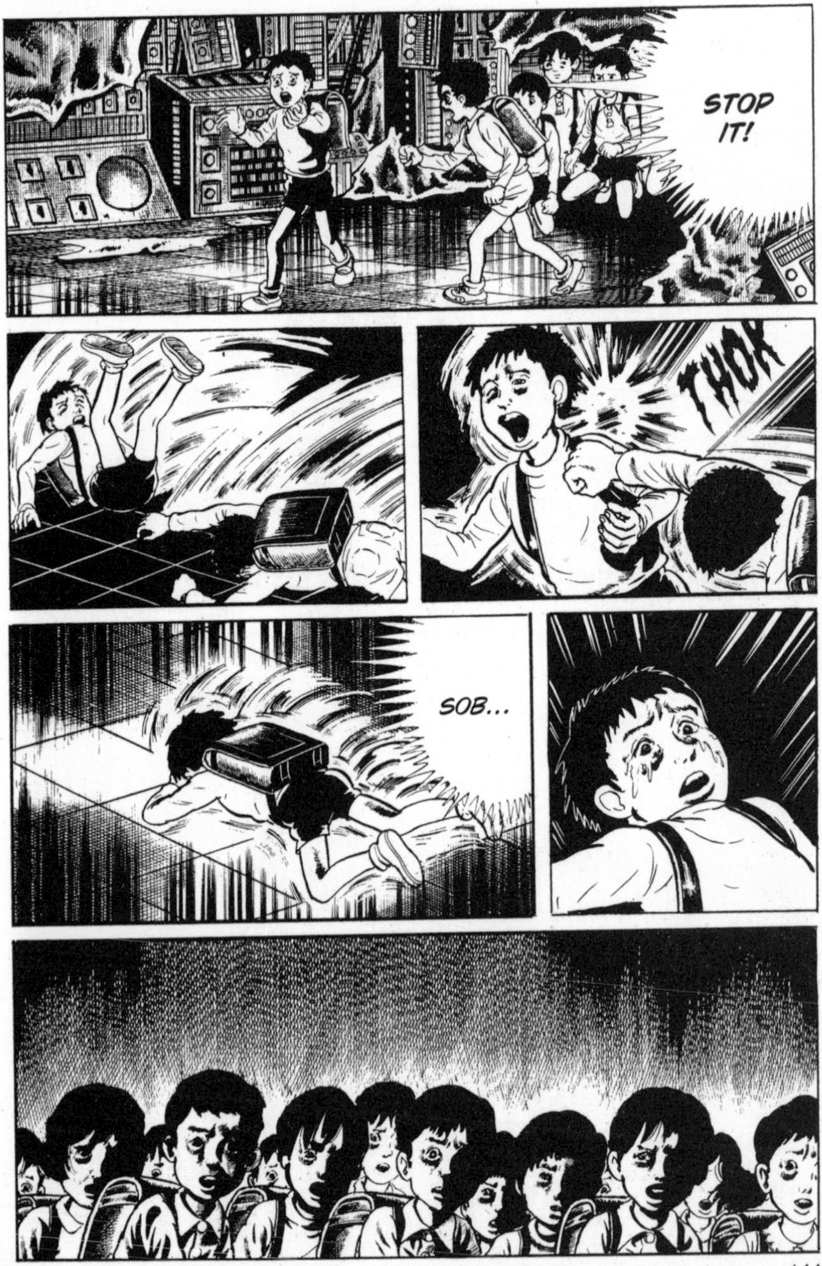
STOP IT!
THOK
SOB...

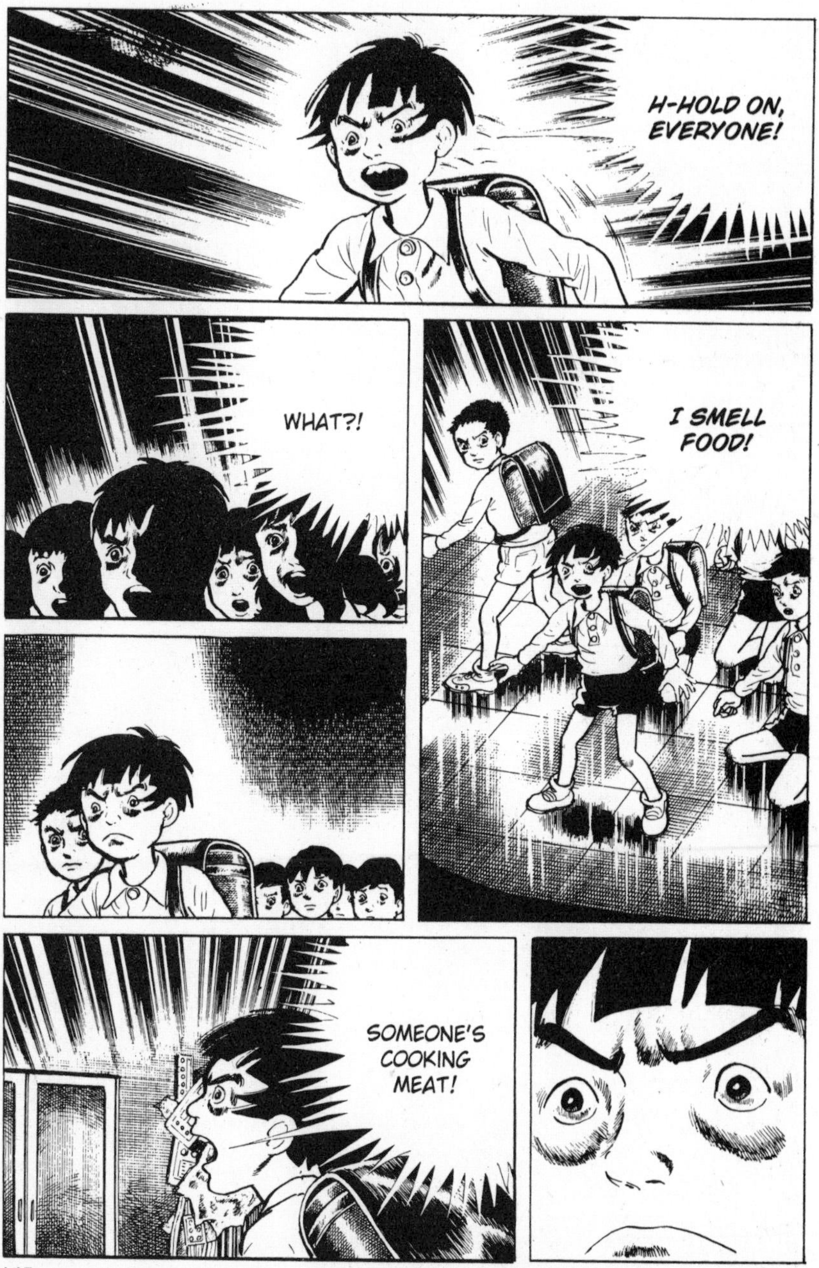
H-HOLD ON, EVERYONE!
I SMELL FOOD!
WHAT?!
SOMEONE'S COOKING MEAT!

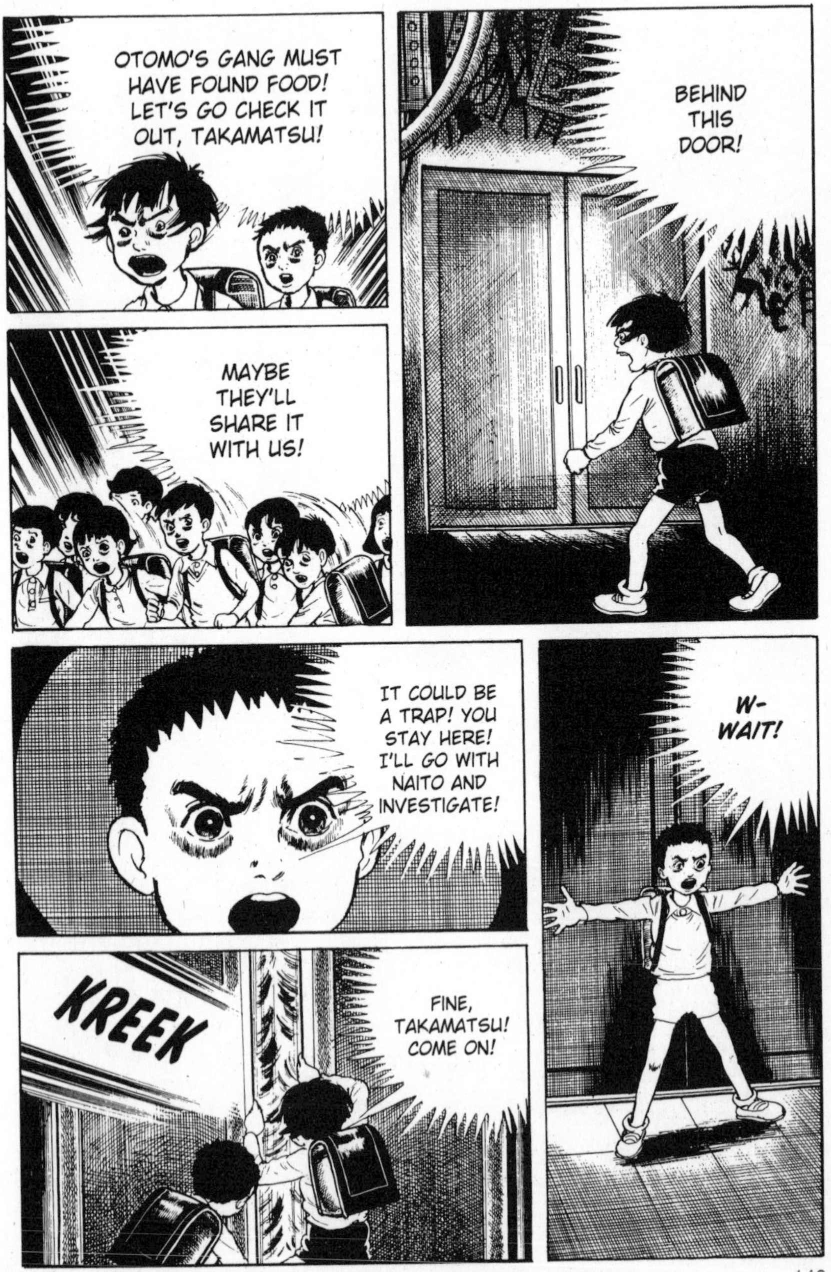
BEHIND THIS DOOR!
OTOMO'S GANG MUST HAVE FOUND FOOD! LET'S GO CHECK IT OUT, TAKAMATSU!
MAYBE THEY'LL SHARE IT WITH US!
W-WAIT!
IT COULD BE A TRAP! YOU STAY HERE! I'LL GO WITH NAITO AND INVESTIGATE!
FINE, TAKAMATSU! COME ON!
KREEK

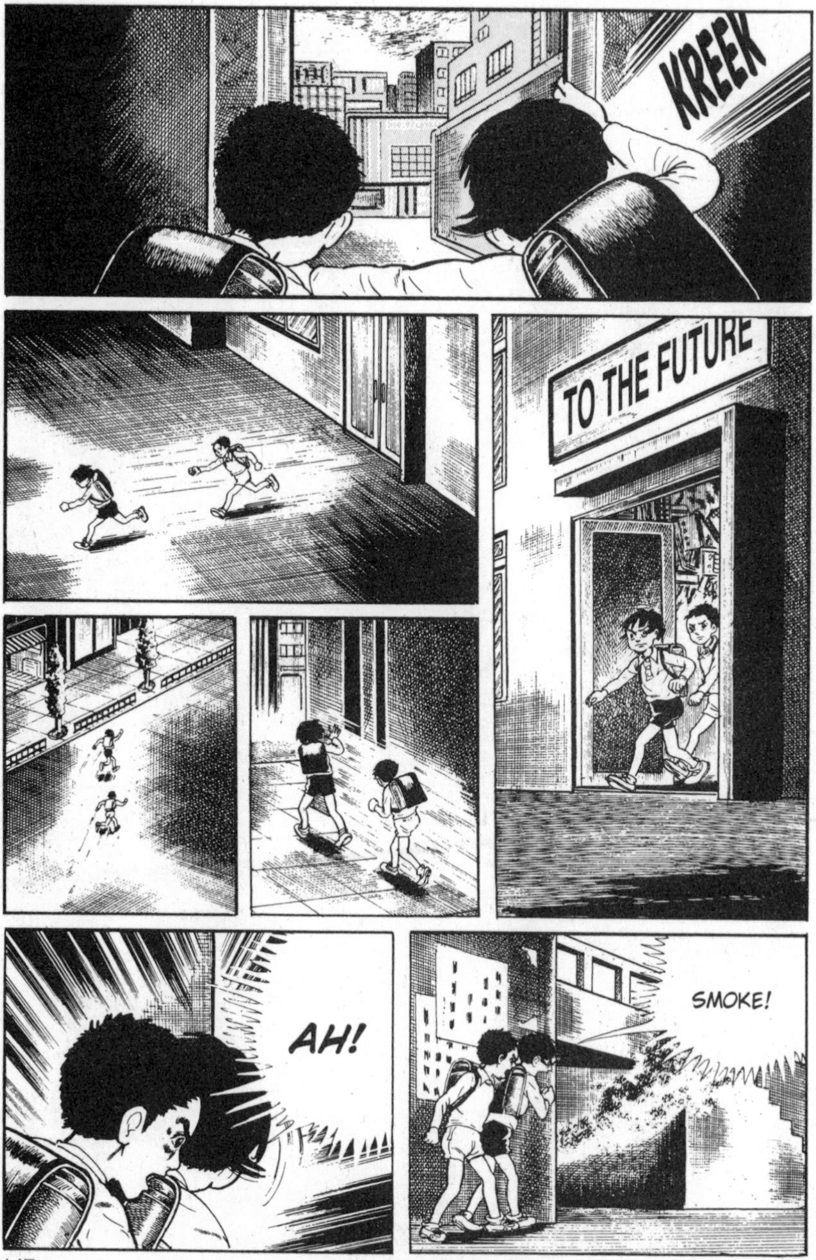
KREEK
TO THE FUTURE
SMOKE!
AH!

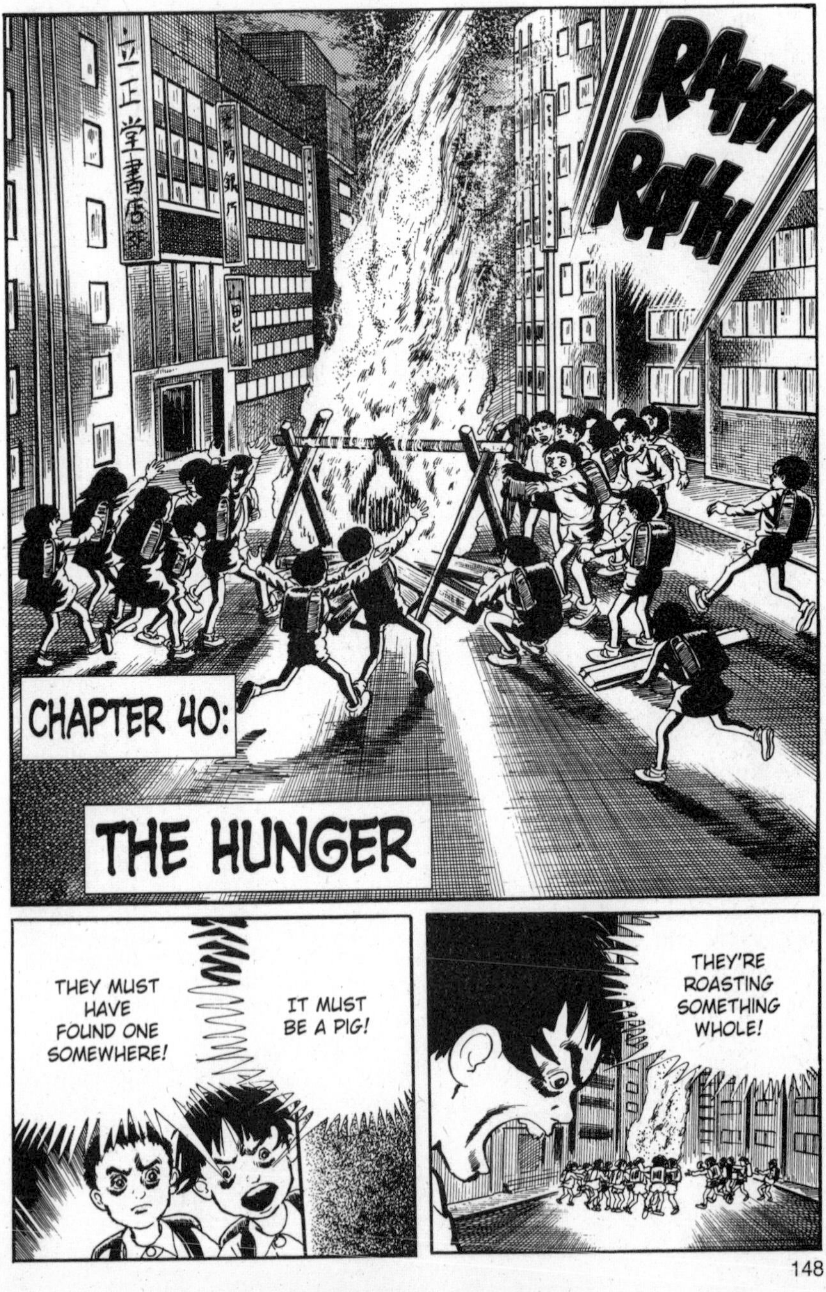
RAHH RAHH
立正堂書店
CHAPTER 40:
THE HUNGER
THEY'RE ROASTING SOMETHING WHOLE!
IT MUST BE A PIG!
THEY MUST HAVE FOUND ONE SOMEWHERE!

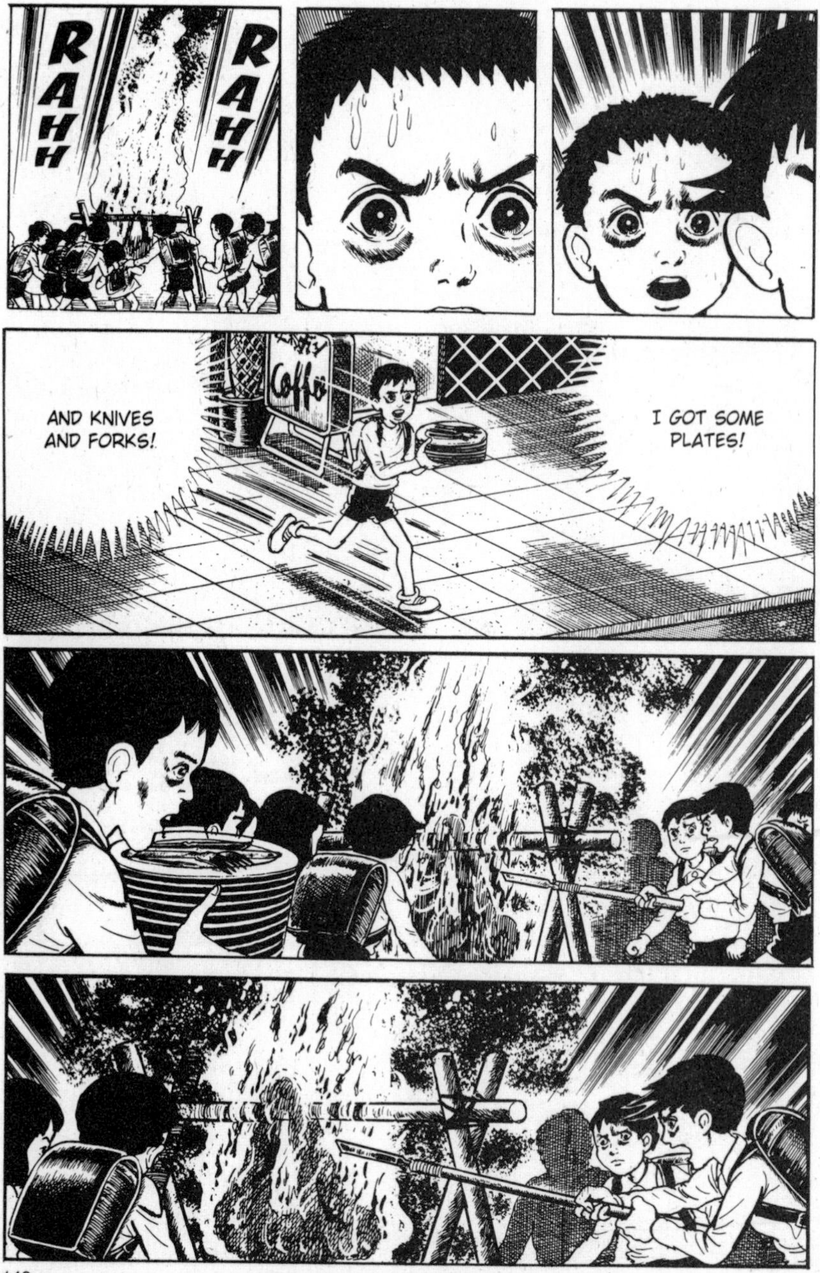
RAHH
RAHH
I GOT SOME PLATES!
AND KNIVES AND FORKS!

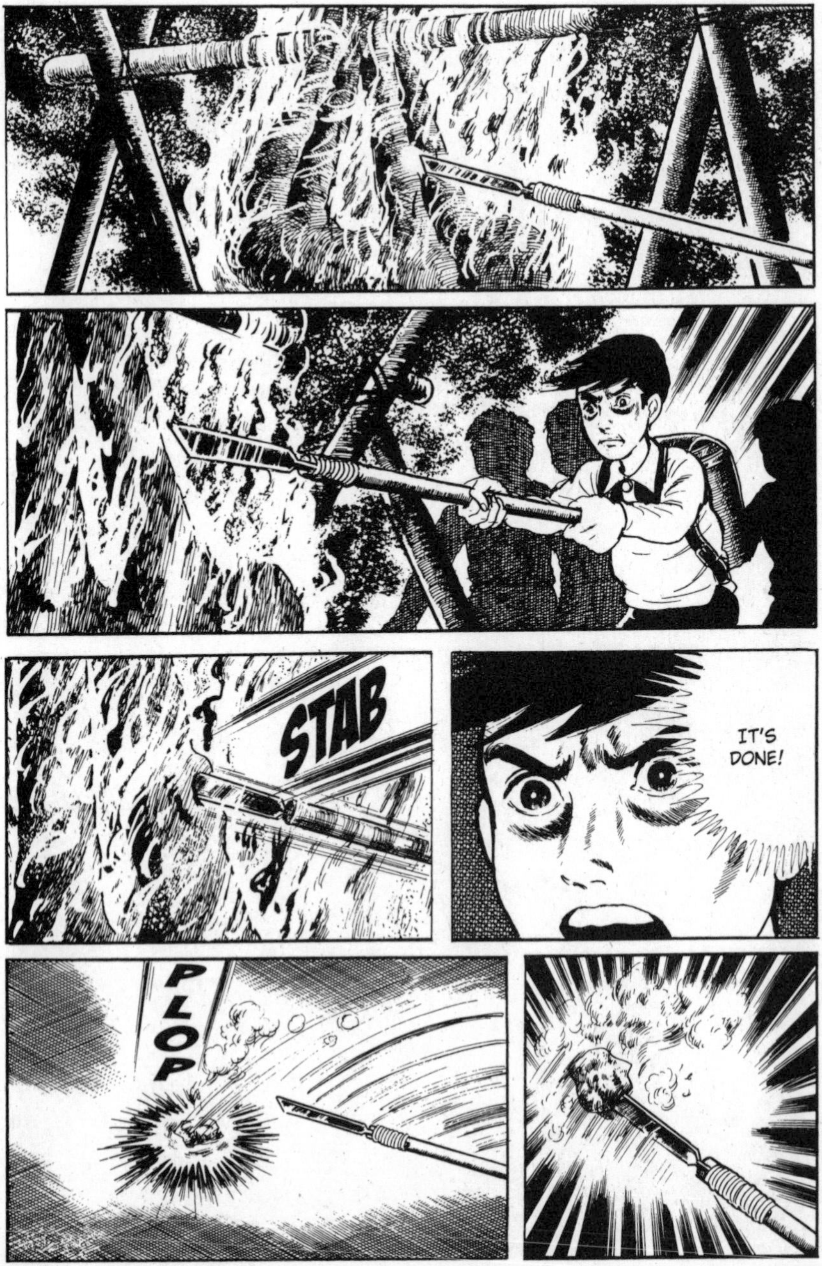
IT'S DONE!
STAB
PLOP

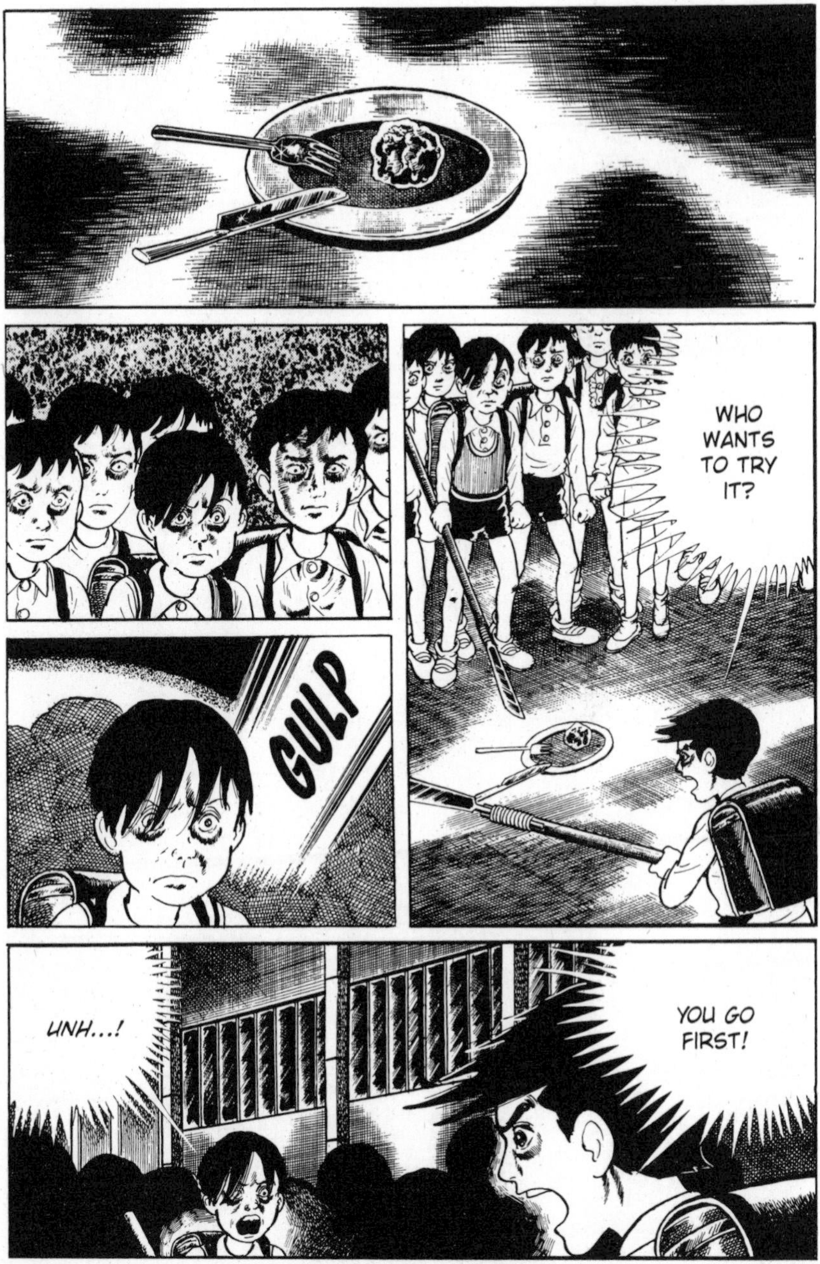
WHO WANTS TO TRY IT?
GULP
YOU GO FIRST!
UNH...!

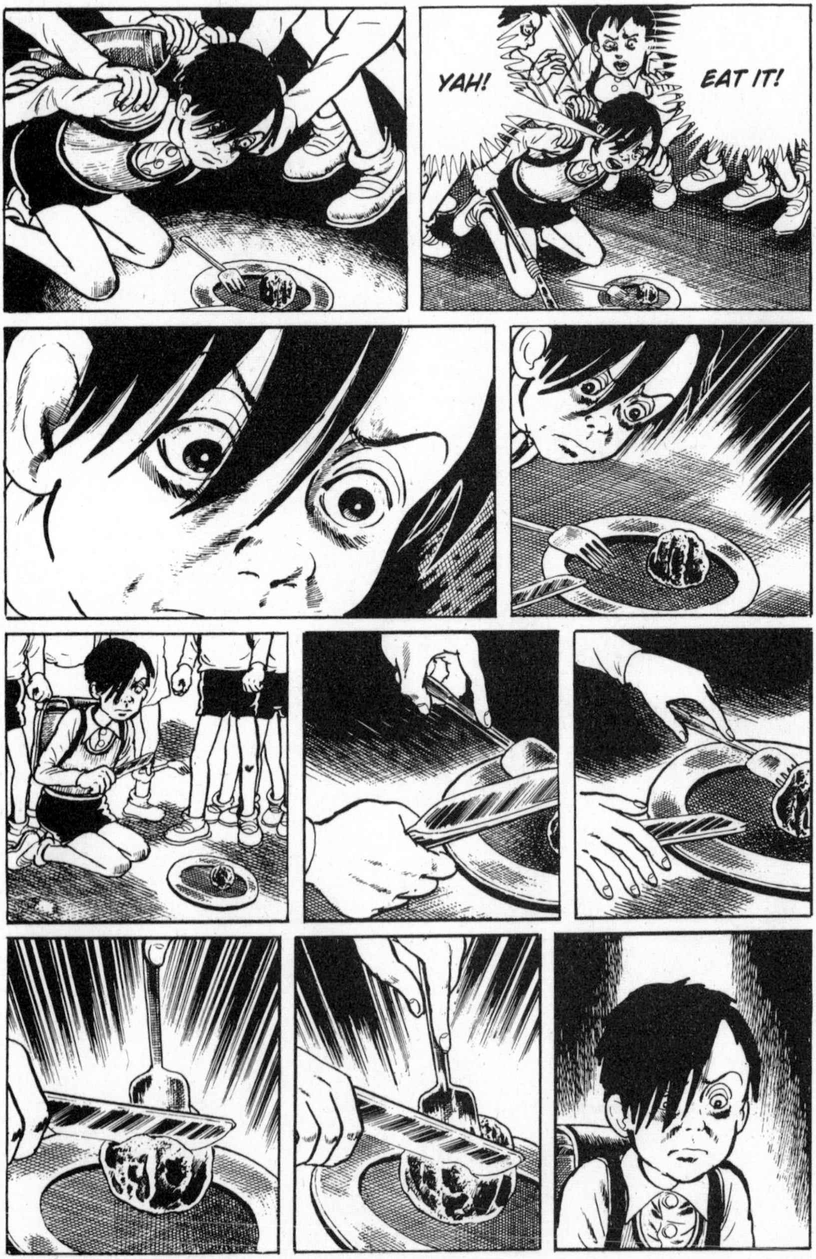
EAT IT!
YAH!

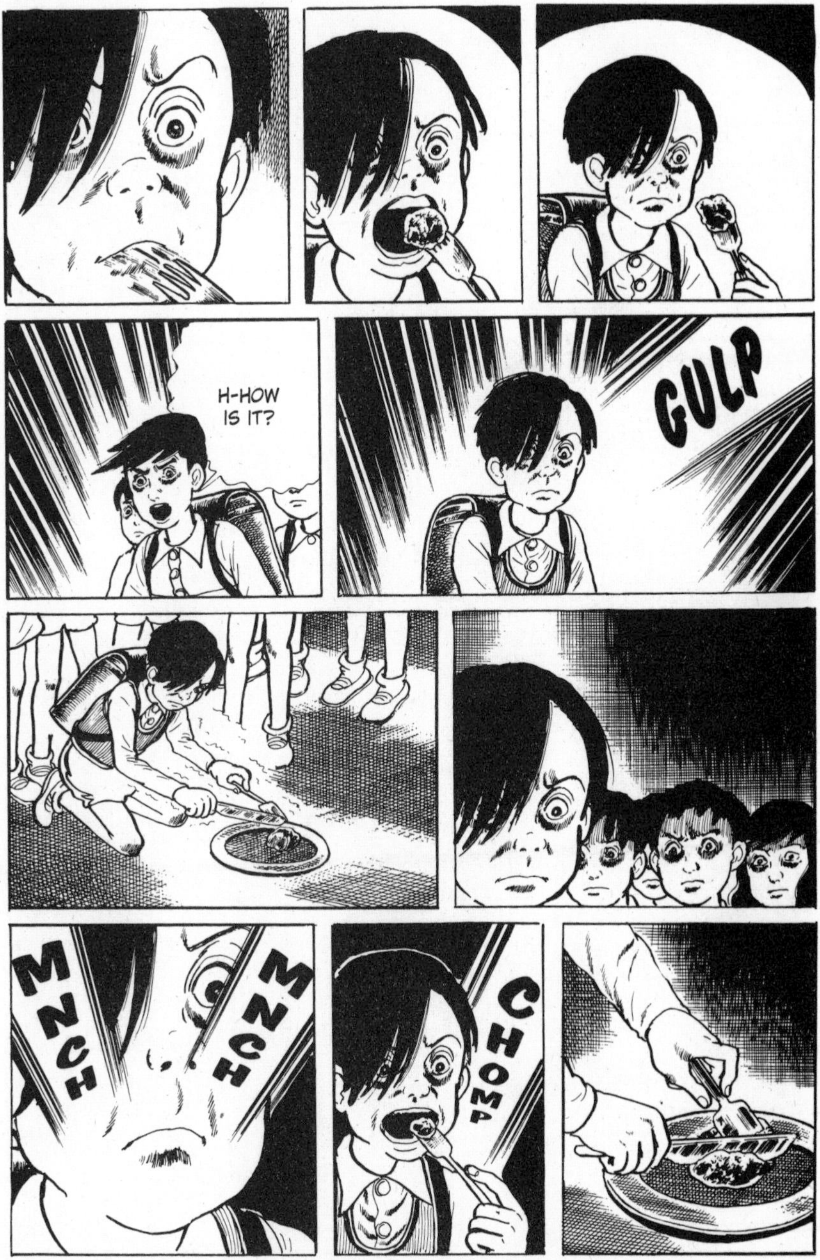
GULP
H-HOW IS IT?
CHOMP
MNCH
MNCH

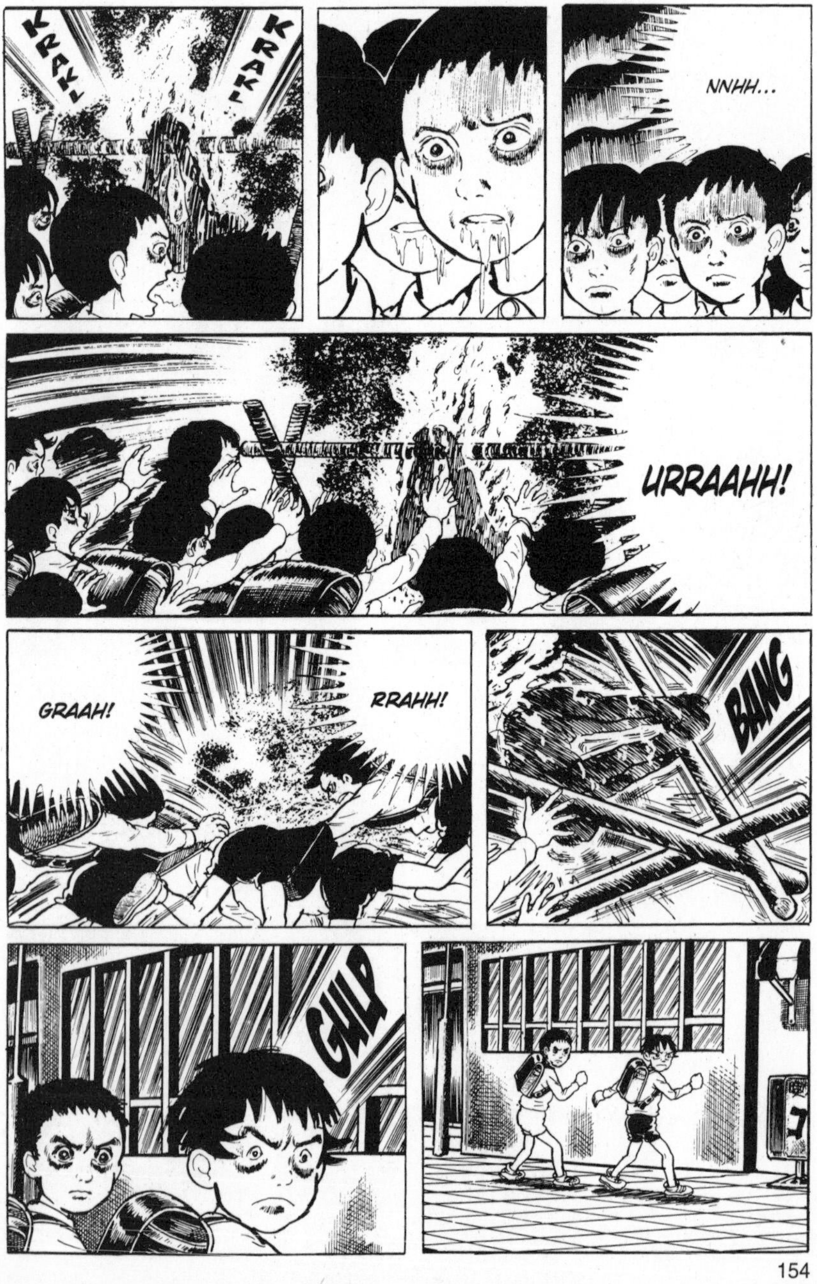
NNHH...
KRAK!
KRAK!
URRAAHH!
BANG
RRAHH!
GRAAH!
GULP

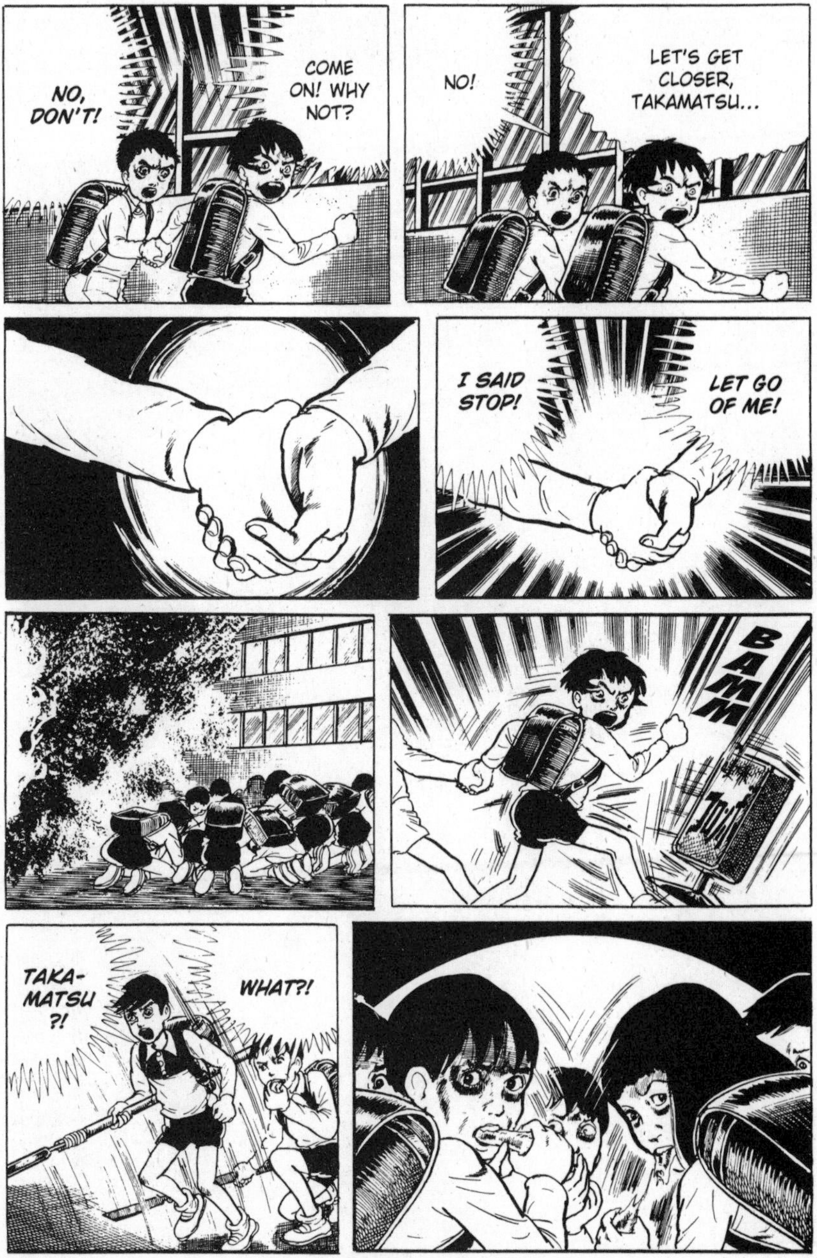
LET'S GET CLOSER, TAKAMATSU...
NO!
COME ON! WHY NOT?
NO, DON'T!
LET GO OF ME!
I SAID STOP!
BAMM
WHAT?!
TAKA-MATSU ?!

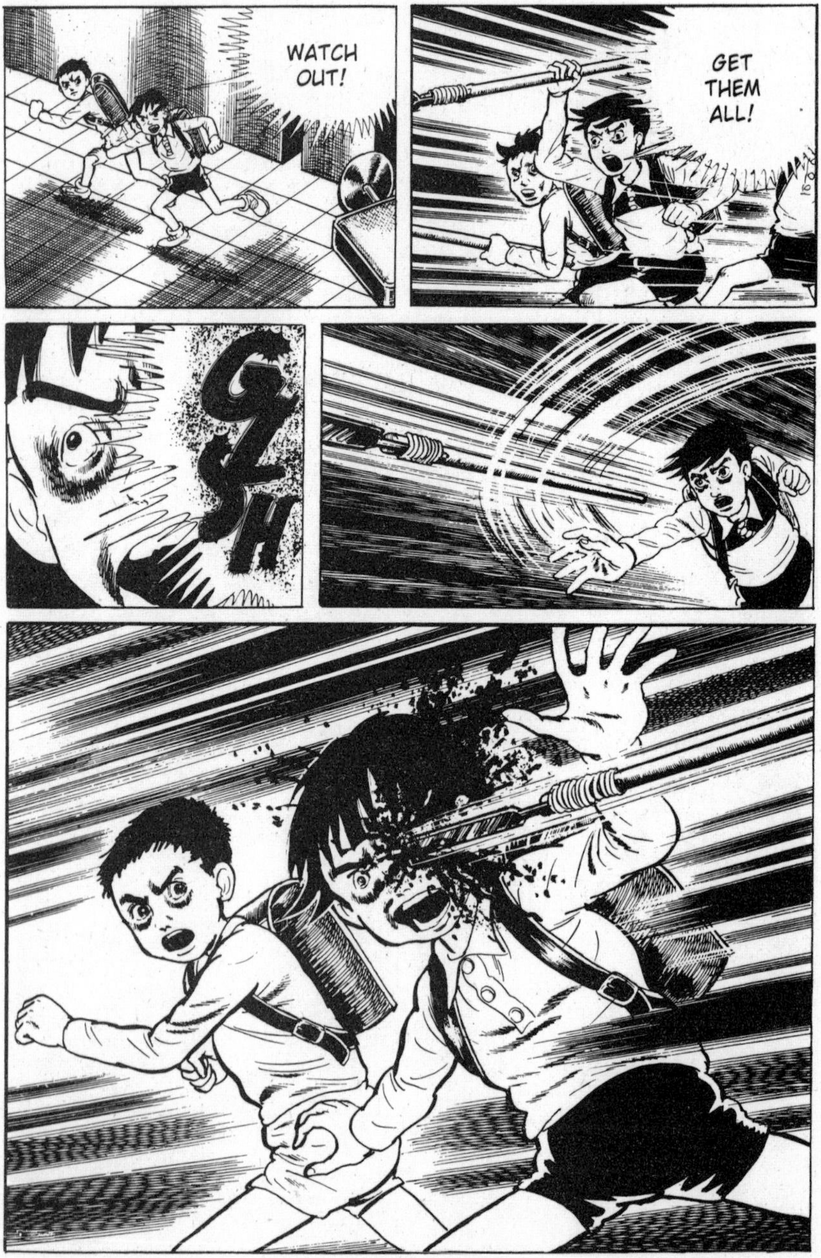
GET THEM ALL!
WATCH OUT!

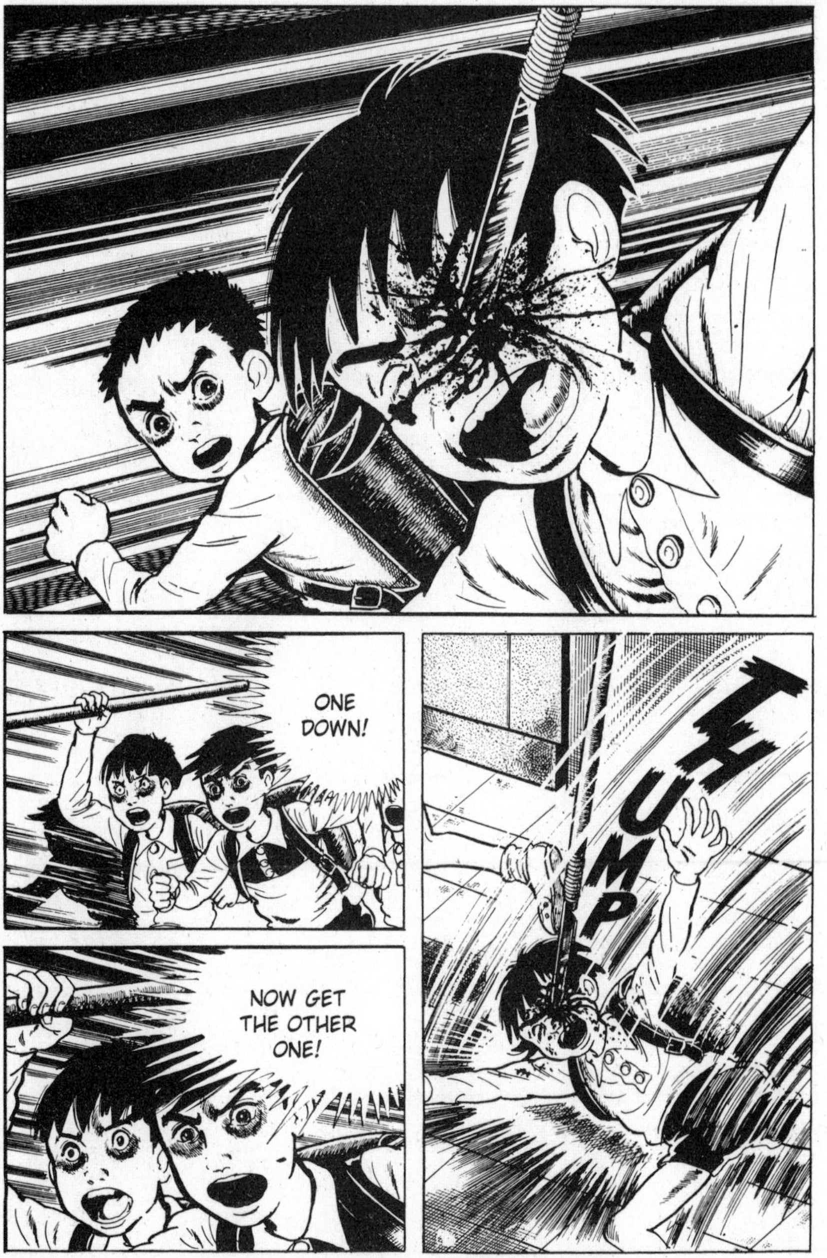
THUMP
ONE DOWN!
NOW GET THE OTHER ONE!

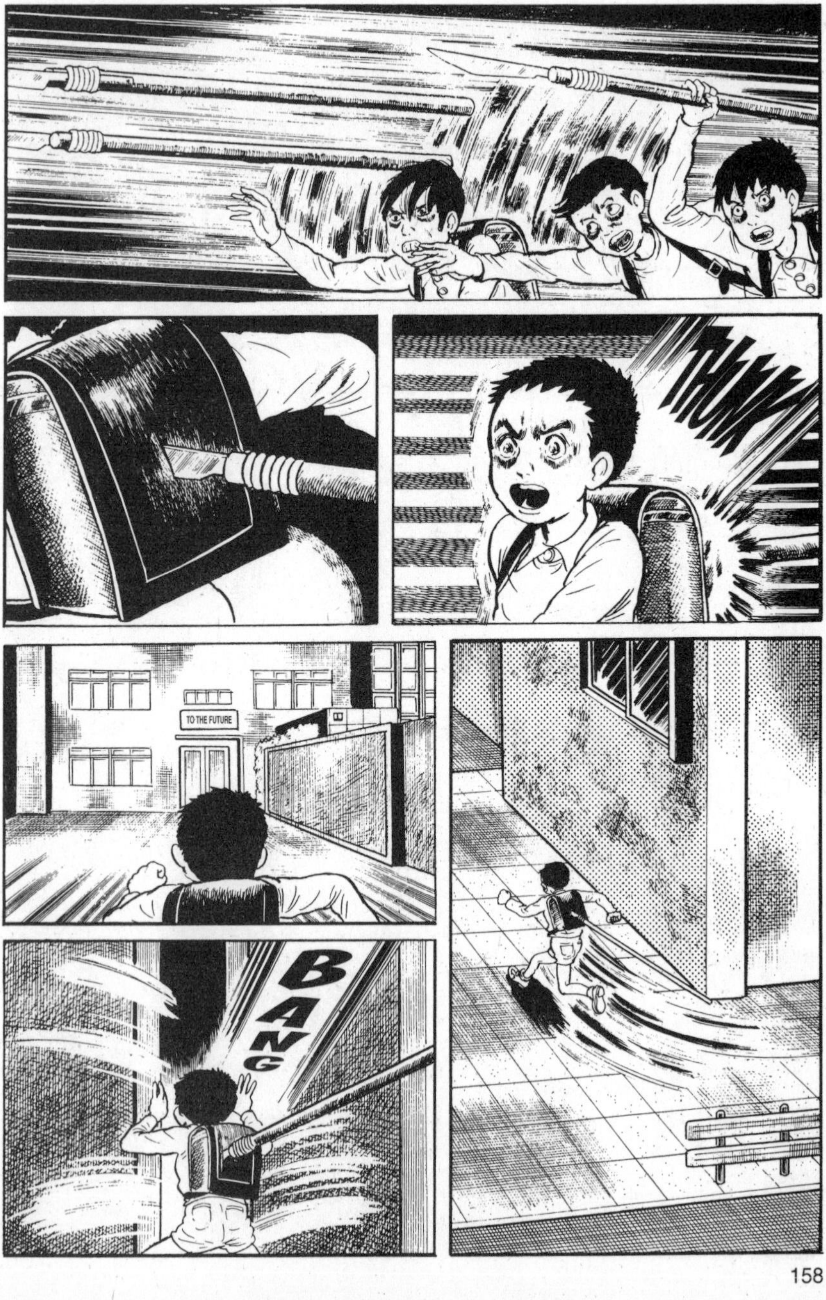
THUNK
TO THE FUTURE
BANG

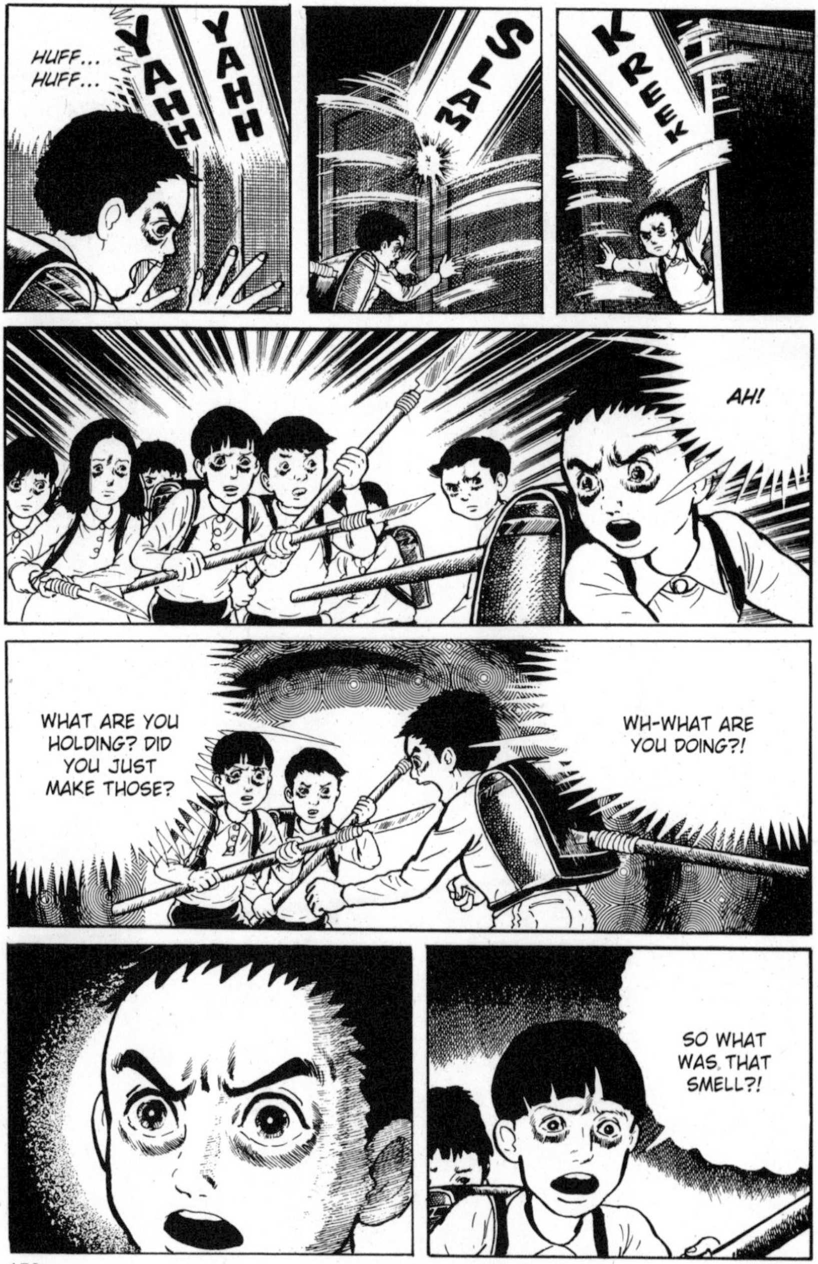
KREEK
SLAM
YAHH
YAHH
HUFF... HUFF...
AH!
WH-WHAT ARE YOU DOING?!
WHAT ARE YOU HOLDING? DID YOU JUST MAKE THOSE?
SO WHAT WAS THAT SMELL?!

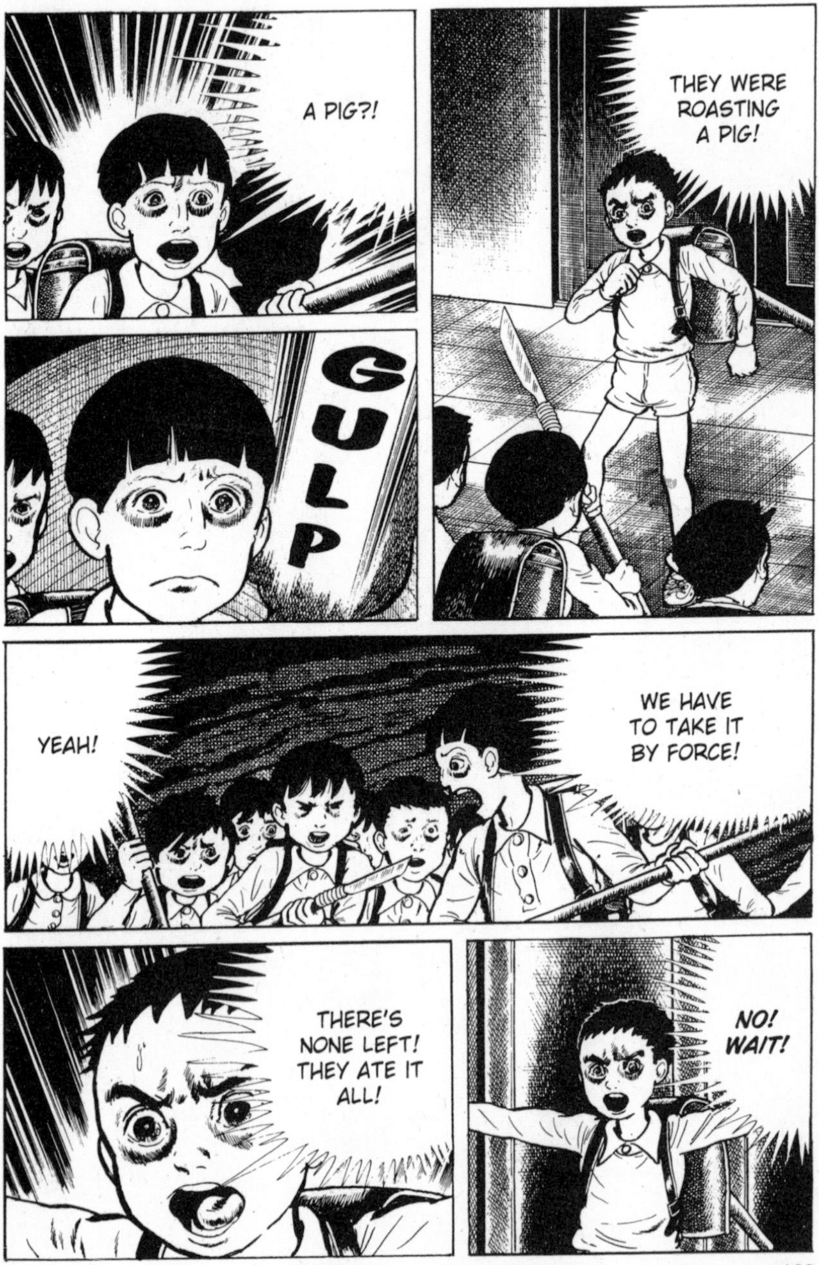
THEY WERE ROASTING A PIG!
A PIG?!
GULP
WE HAVE TO TAKE IT BY FORCE!
YEAH!
NO! WAIT!
THERE'S NONE LEFT! THEY ATE IT ALL!

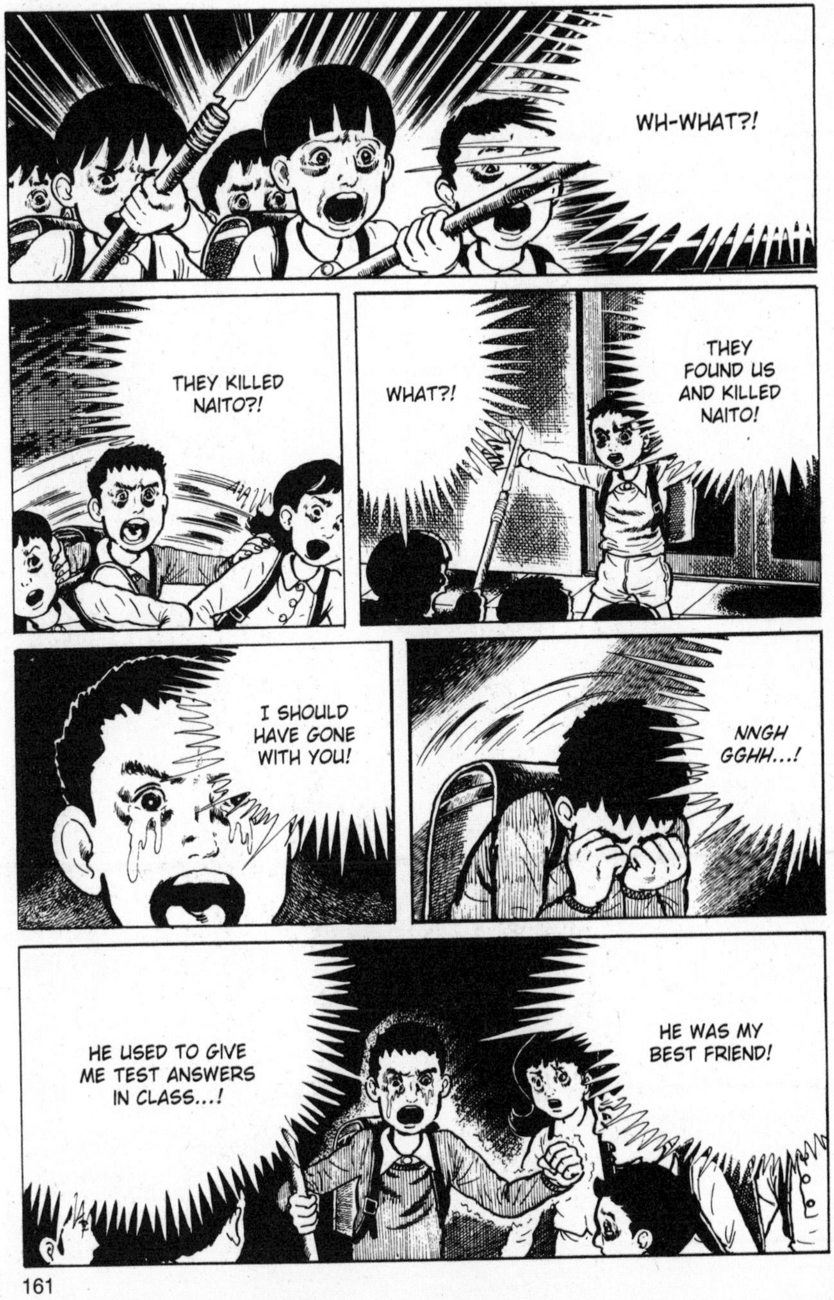
WH-WHAT?!
THEY FOUND US AND KILLED NAITO!
WHAT?!
THEY KILLED NAITO?!
NNGH GGHH...!
I SHOULD HAVE GONE WITH YOU!
HE WAS MY BEST FRIEND!
HE USED TO GIVE ME TEST ANSWERS IN CLASS...!

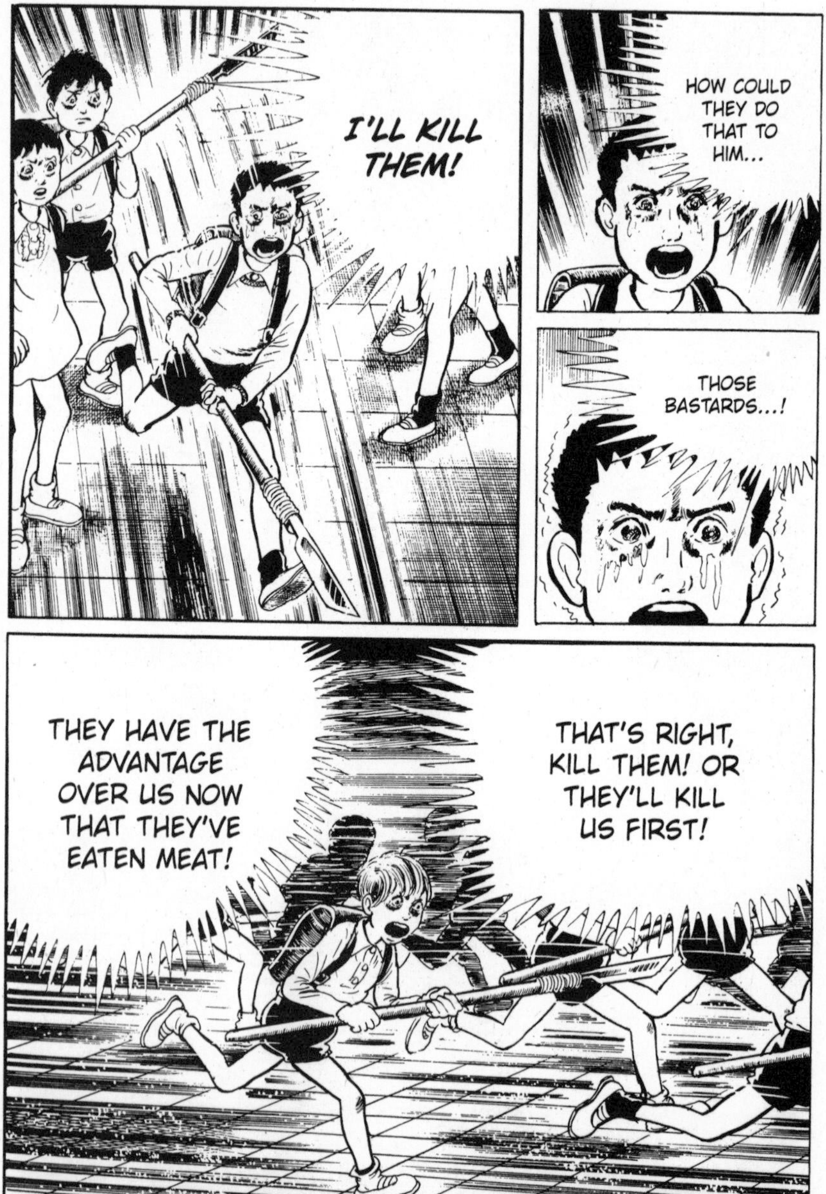
HOW COULD THEY DO THAT TO HIM...
THOSE BASTARDS...!
I'LL KILL THEM!
THAT'S RIGHT, KILL THEM! OR THEY'LL KILL US FIRST!
THEY HAVE THE ADVANTAGE OVER US NOW THAT THEY'VE EATEN MEAT!

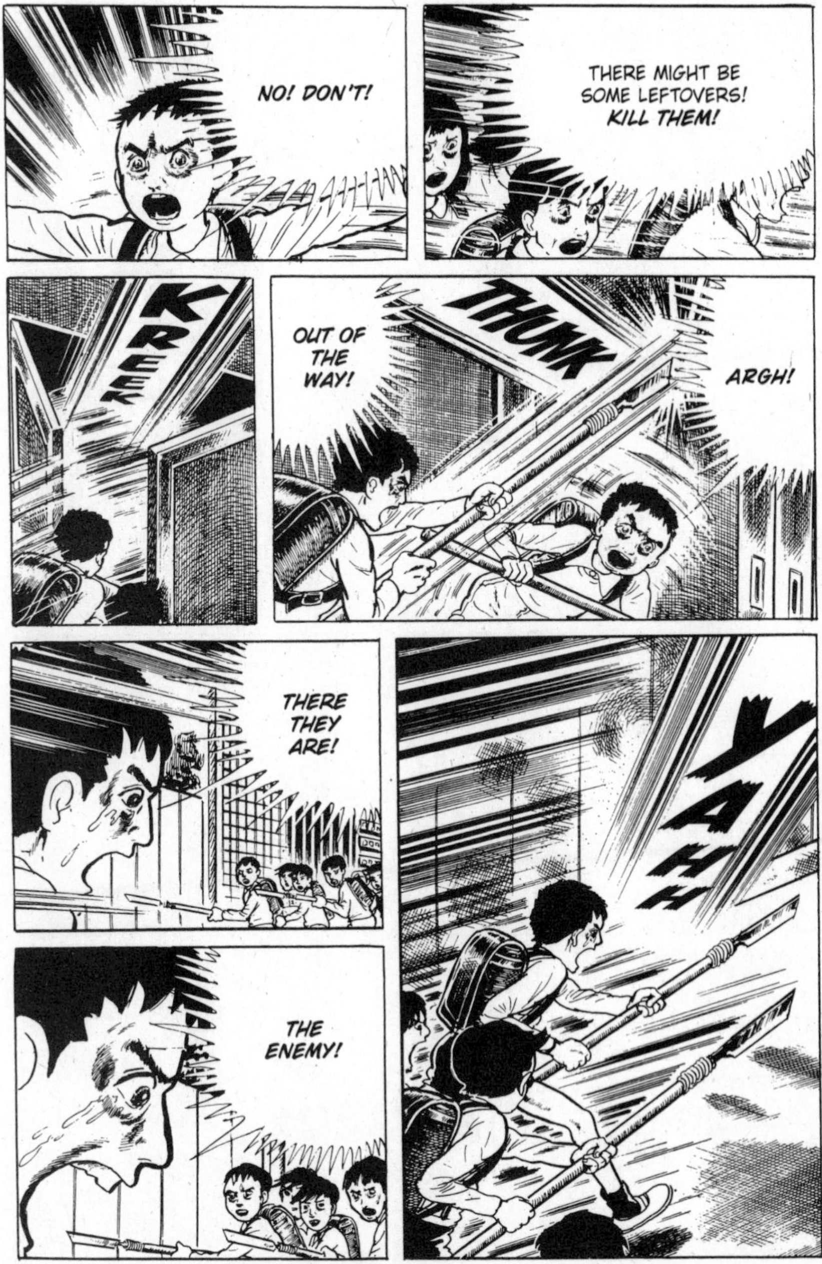
THERE MIGHT BE SOME LEFTOVERS! KILL THEM!
NO! DON'T!
THUNK
ARGH!
OUT OF THE WAY!
KREEK
YAHHH
THERE THEY ARE!
THE ENEMY!

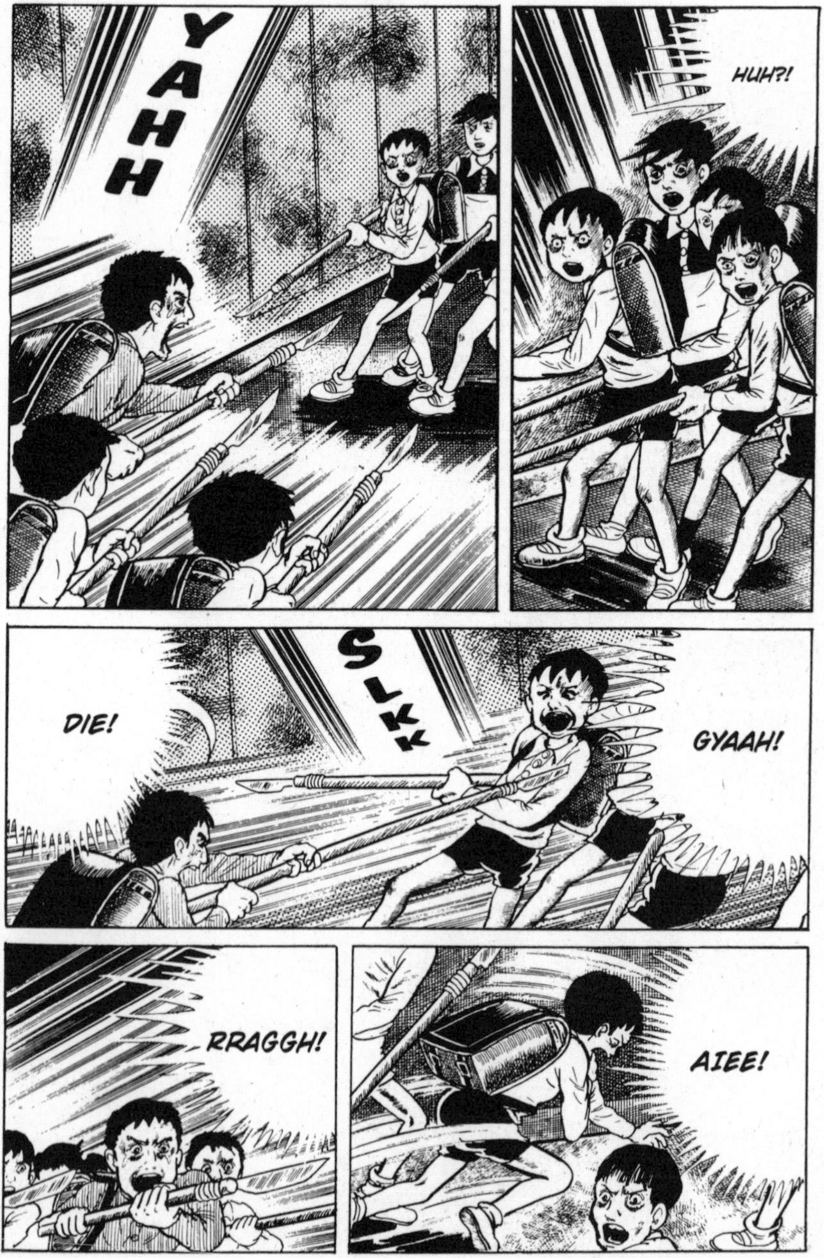
HUH?!
YAHH
SLKK
GYAAH!
DIE!
AIEE!
RRAGGH!

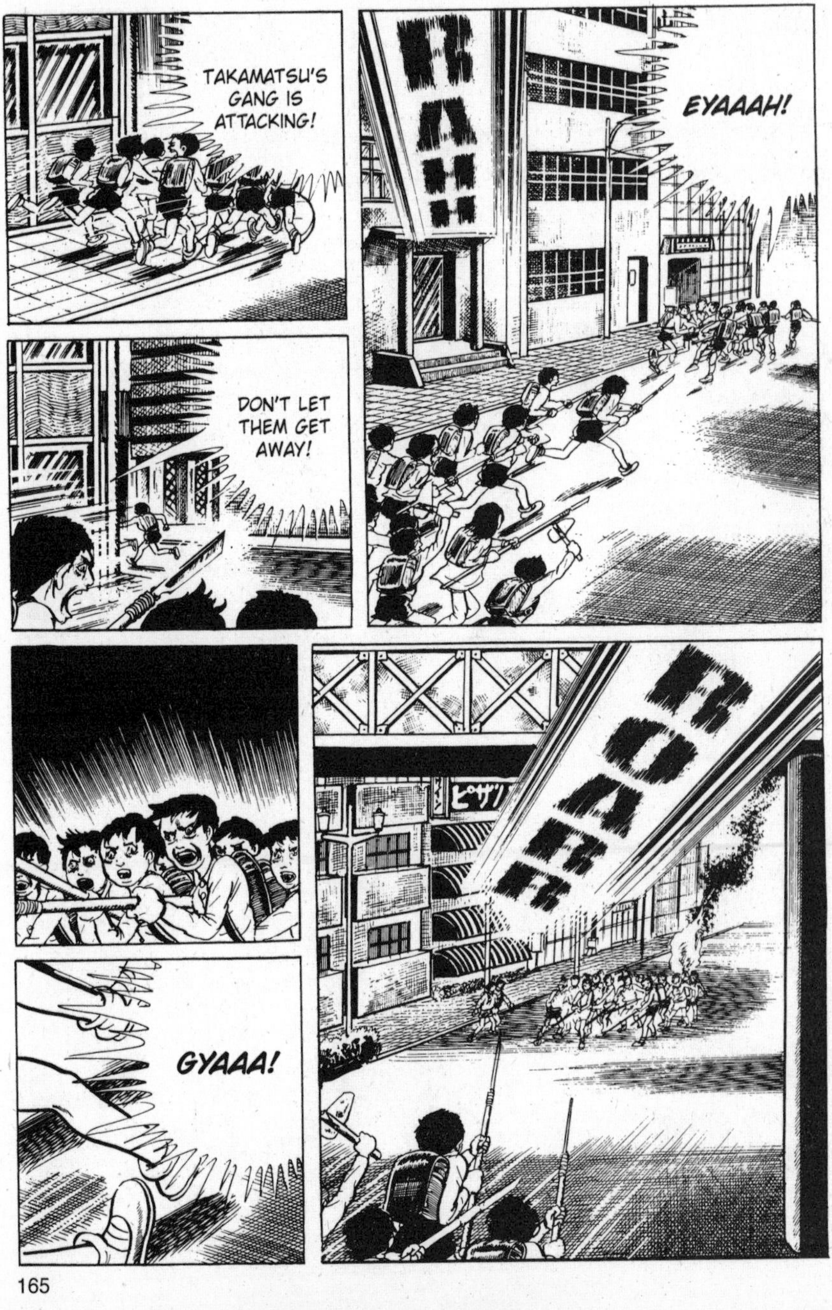
EYAAAH!
RAHH
TAKAMATSU'S GANG IS ATTACKING!
DON'T LET THEM GET AWAY!
ROARR
GYAAA!

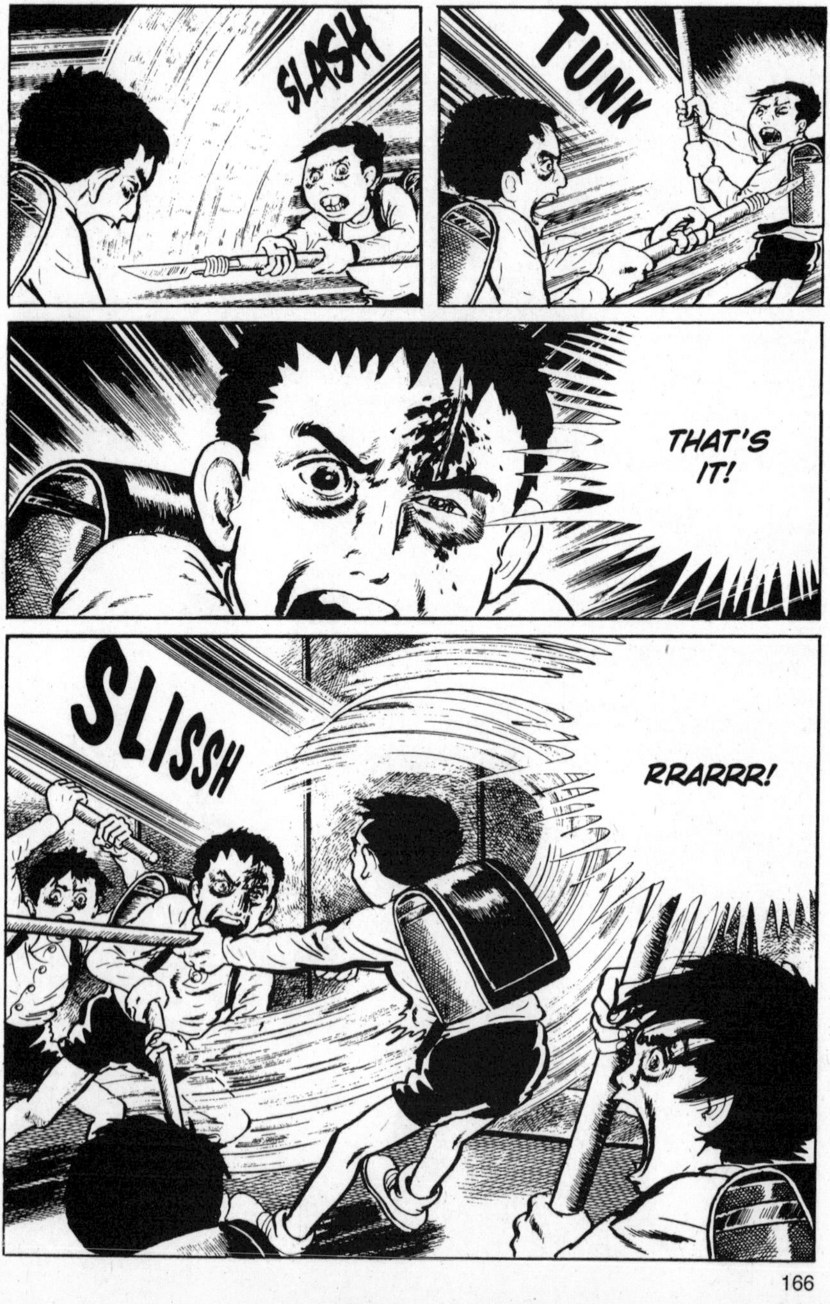
TUNK
SLASH
THAT'S IT!
RRARRR!
SLISSH

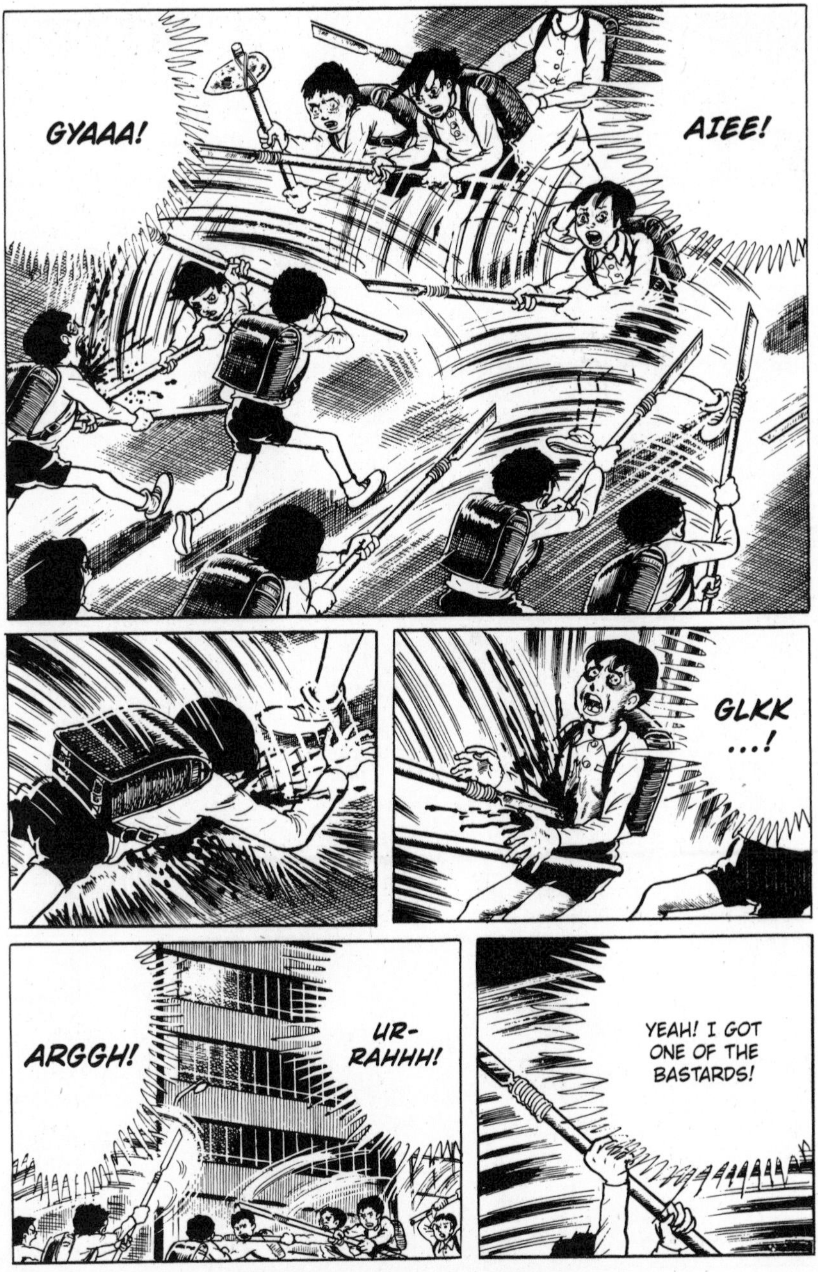
AIEE!
GYAAA!
GLKK ...!
YEAH! I GOT ONE OF THE BASTARDS!
UR-RAHHH!
ARGGH!

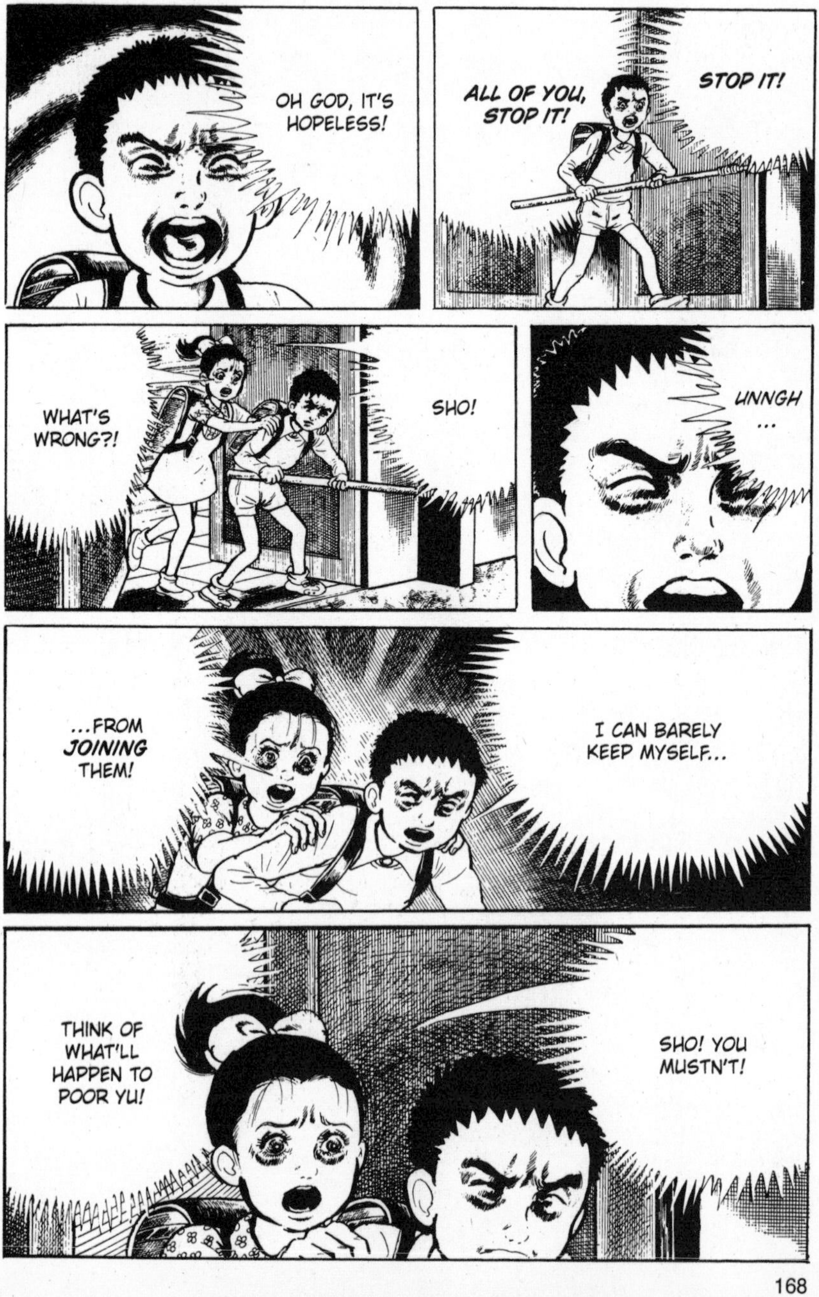
STOP IT!
ALL OF YOU, STOP IT!
OH GOD, IT'S HOPELESS!
UNNGH ...
SHO!
WHAT'S WRONG?!
I CAN BARELY KEEP MYSELF...
...FROM *JOINING* THEM!
SHO! YOU MUSTN'T!
THINK OF WHAT'LL HAPPEN TO POOR YU!

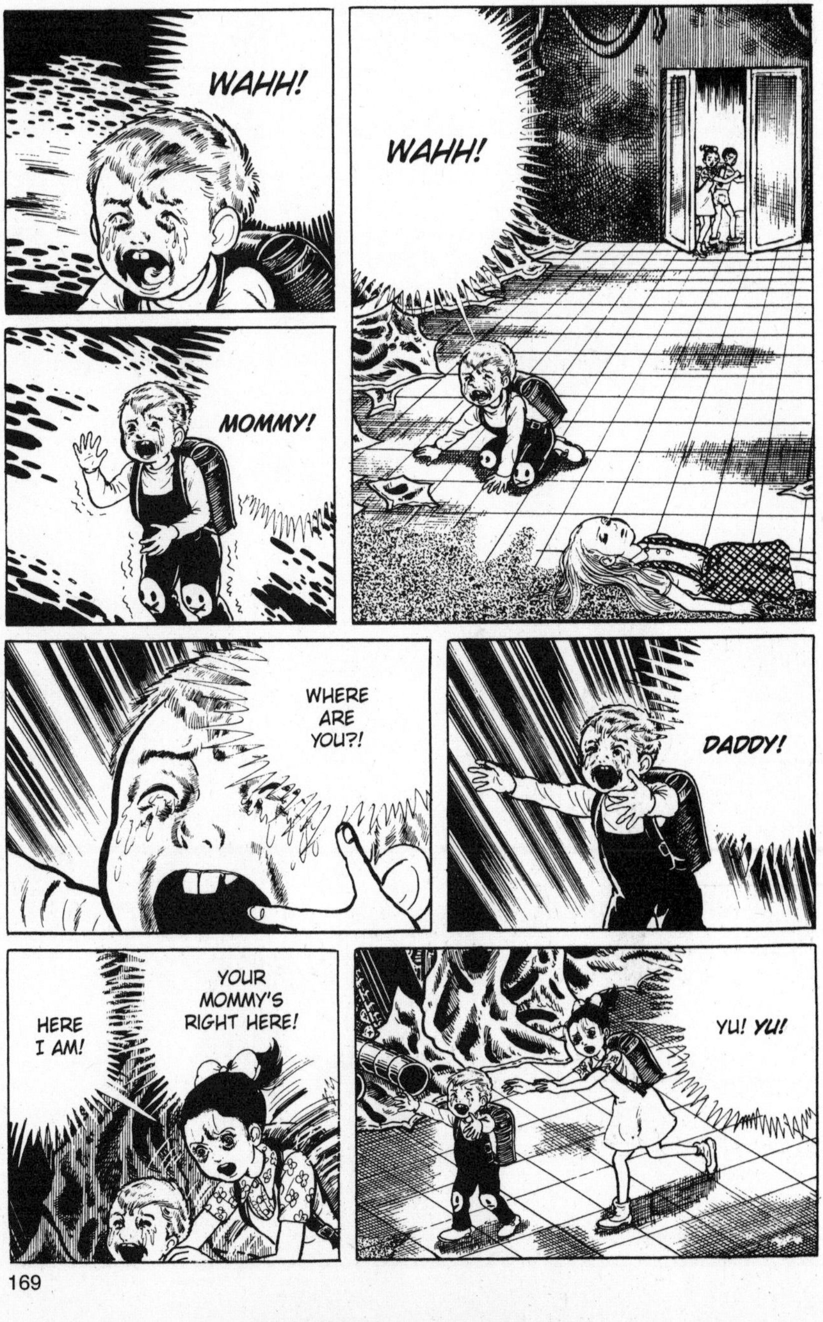
WAHH!
WAHH!
MOMMY!
DADDY!
WHERE ARE YOU?!
YU! YU!
YOUR MOMMY'S RIGHT HERE!
HERE I AM!

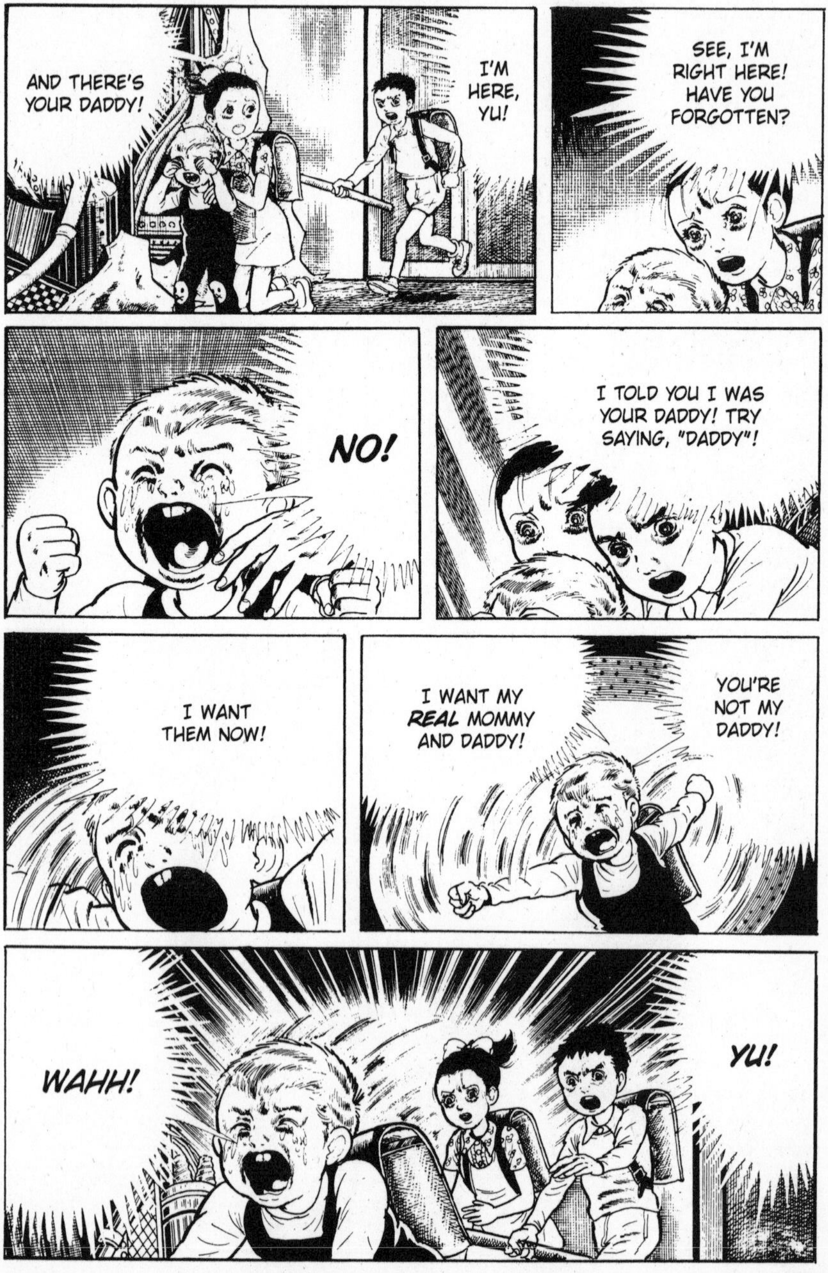

SEE, I'M RIGHT HERE! HAVE YOU FORGOTTEN?
I'M HERE, YU!
AND THERE'S YOUR DADDY!
I TOLD YOU I WAS YOUR DADDY! TRY SAYING, "DADDY"!
NO!
YOU'RE NOT MY DADDY!
I WANT MY *REAL* MOMMY AND DADDY!
I WANT THEM NOW!
YU!
WAHH!

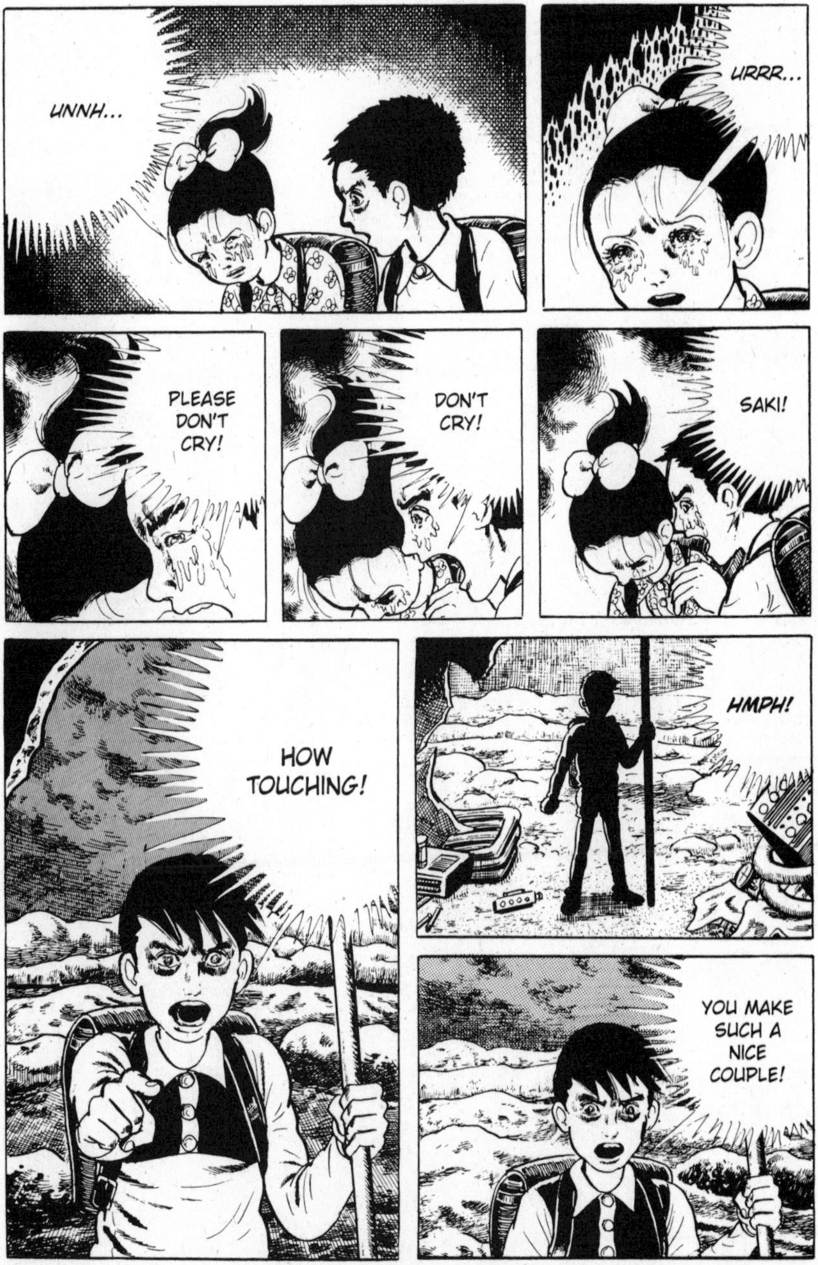
URRR...
UNNH...
SAKI!
DON'T CRY!
PLEASE DON'T CRY!
HMPH!
YOU MAKE SUCH A NICE COUPLE!
HOW TOUCHING!

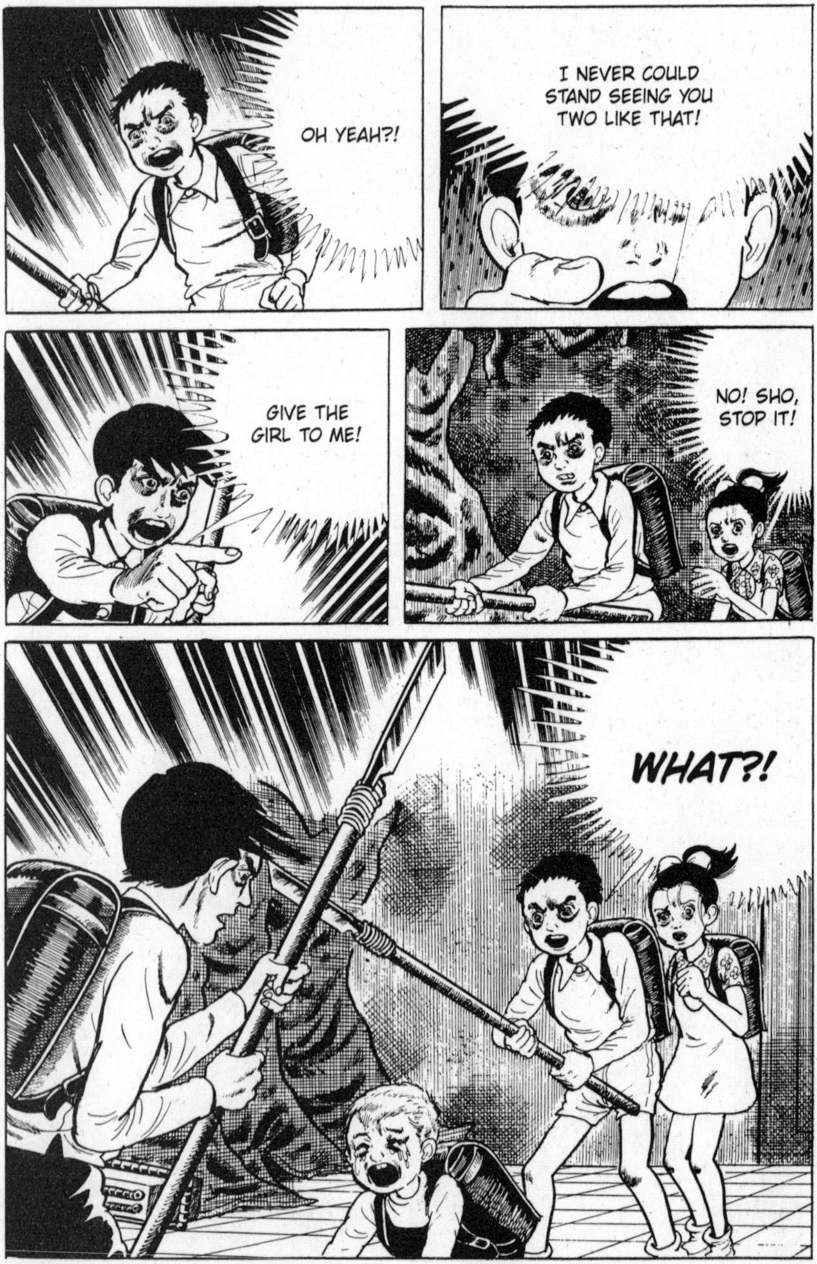
I NEVER COULD STAND SEEING YOU TWO LIKE THAT!
OH YEAH?!
NO! SHO, STOP IT!
GIVE THE GIRL TO ME!
WHAT?!

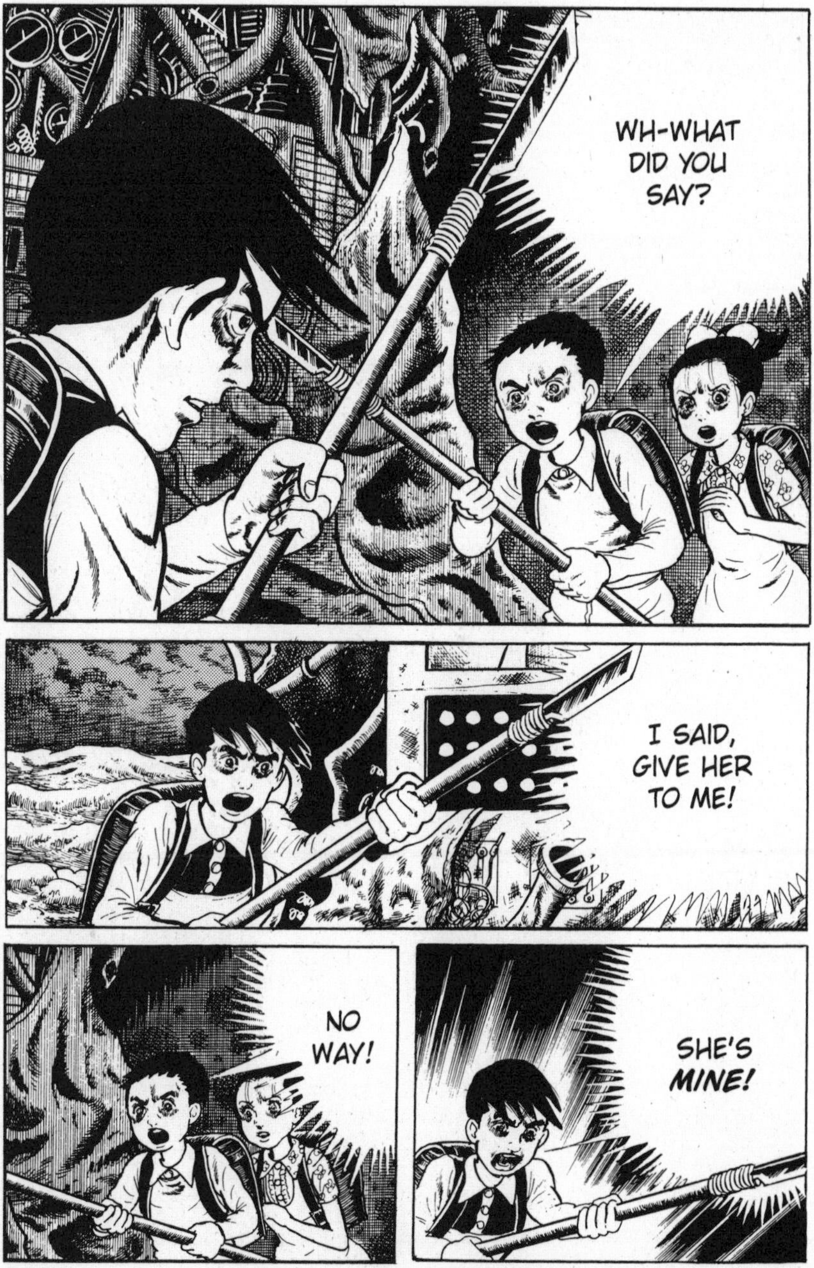
WH-WHAT DID YOU SAY?
I SAID, GIVE HER TO ME!
SHE'S *MINE!*
NO WAY!

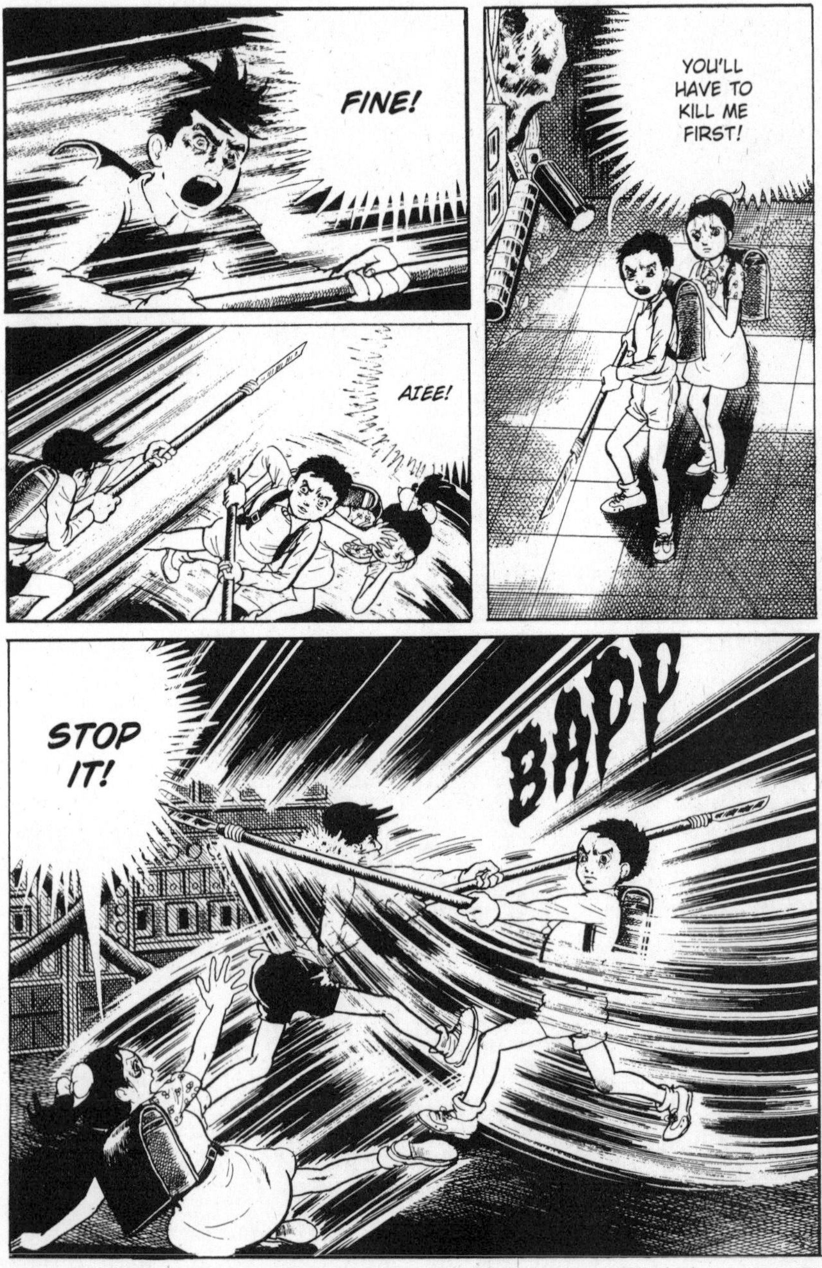
YOU'LL HAVE TO KILL ME FIRST!
FINE!
AIEE!
BAP
STOP IT!

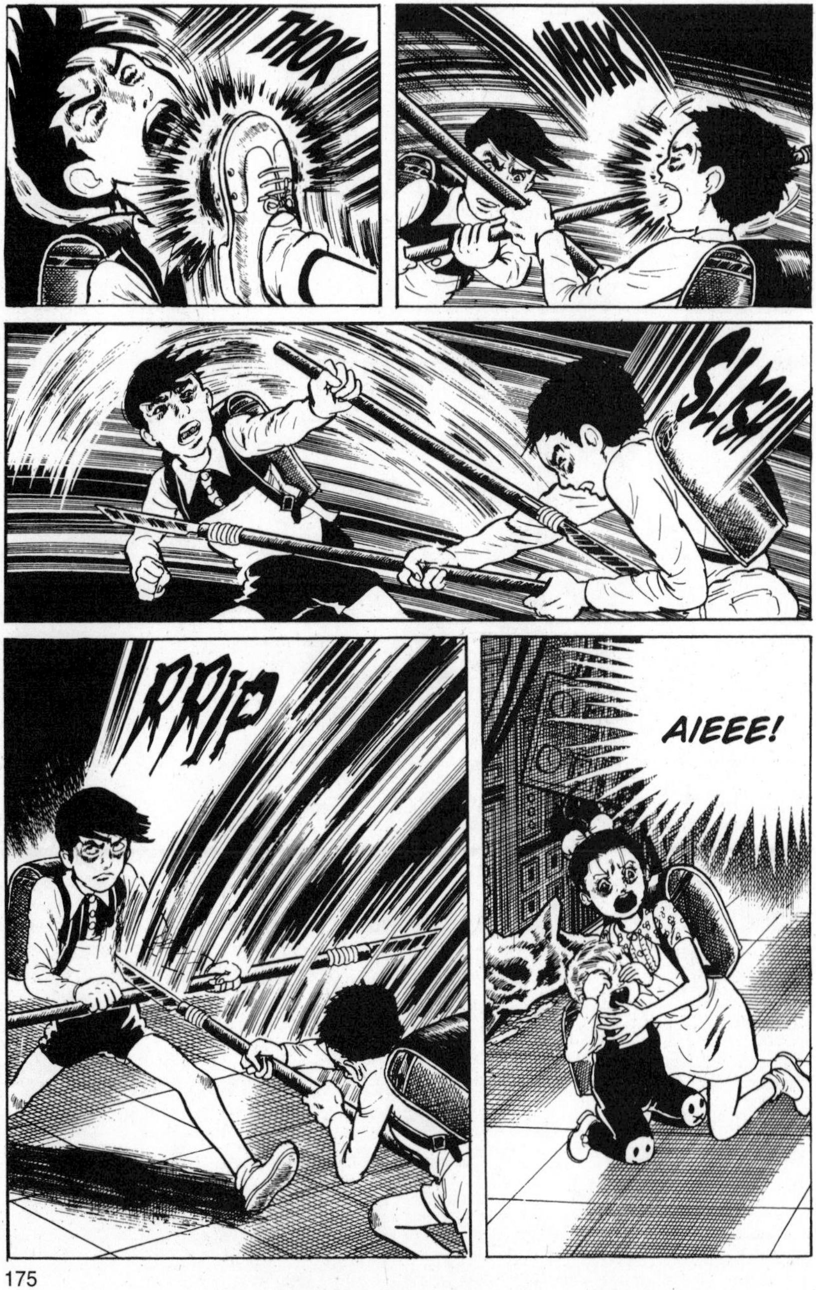
WHAK
THOK
AIEEE!
RRIP

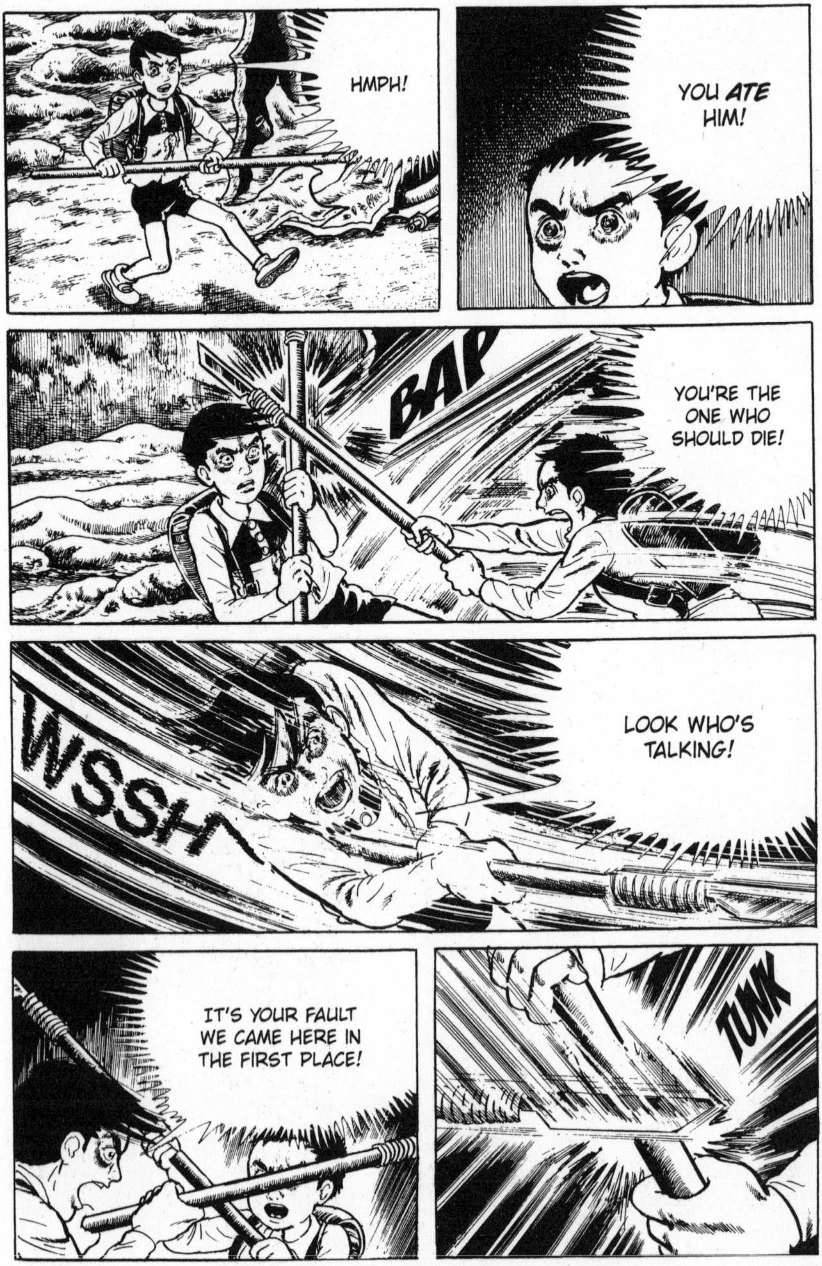
YOU ATE HIM!
HMPH!
BAP
YOU'RE THE ONE WHO SHOULD DIE!
WSSH
LOOK WHO'S TALKING!
TUNK
IT'S YOUR FAULT WE CAME HERE IN THE FIRST PLACE!

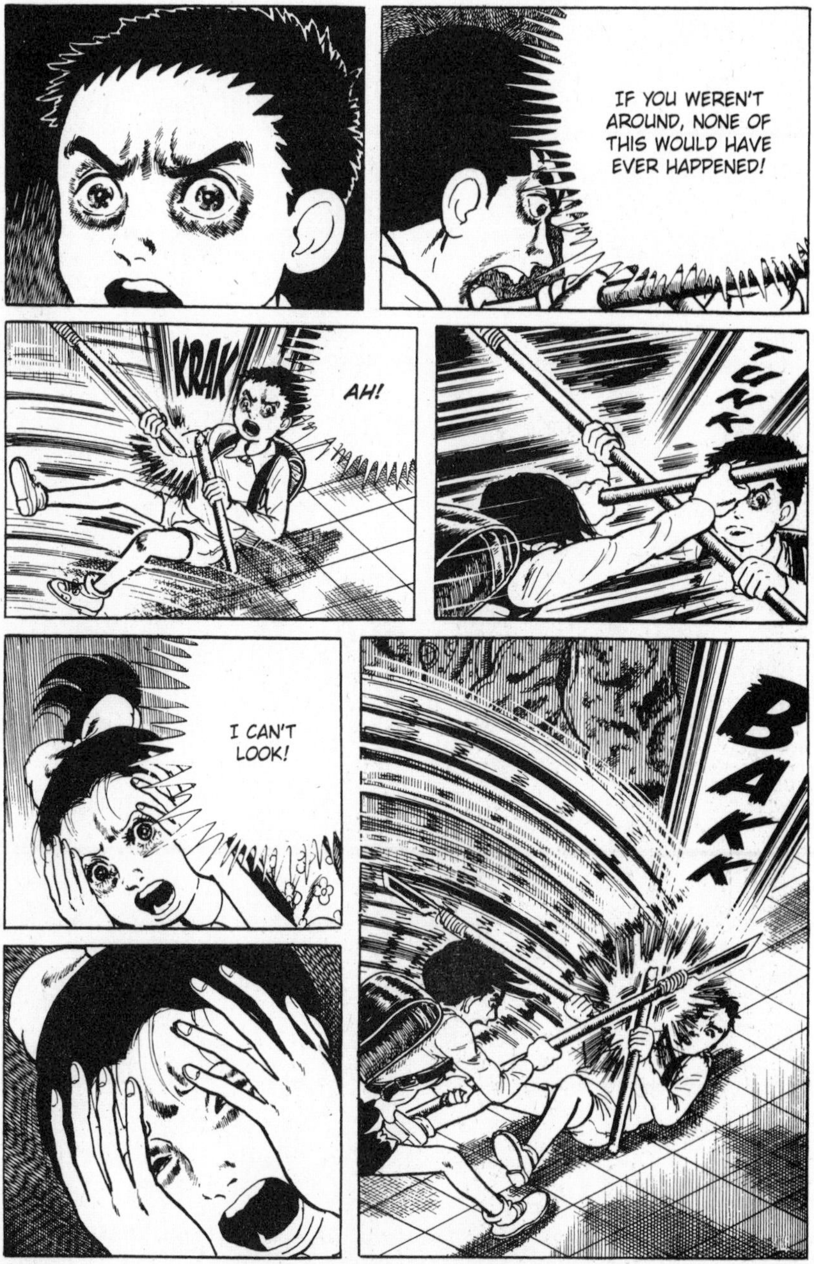
IF YOU WEREN'T AROUND, NONE OF THIS WOULD HAVE EVER HAPPENED!
TUNK
KRAK
AH!
BAKK
I CAN'T LOOK!

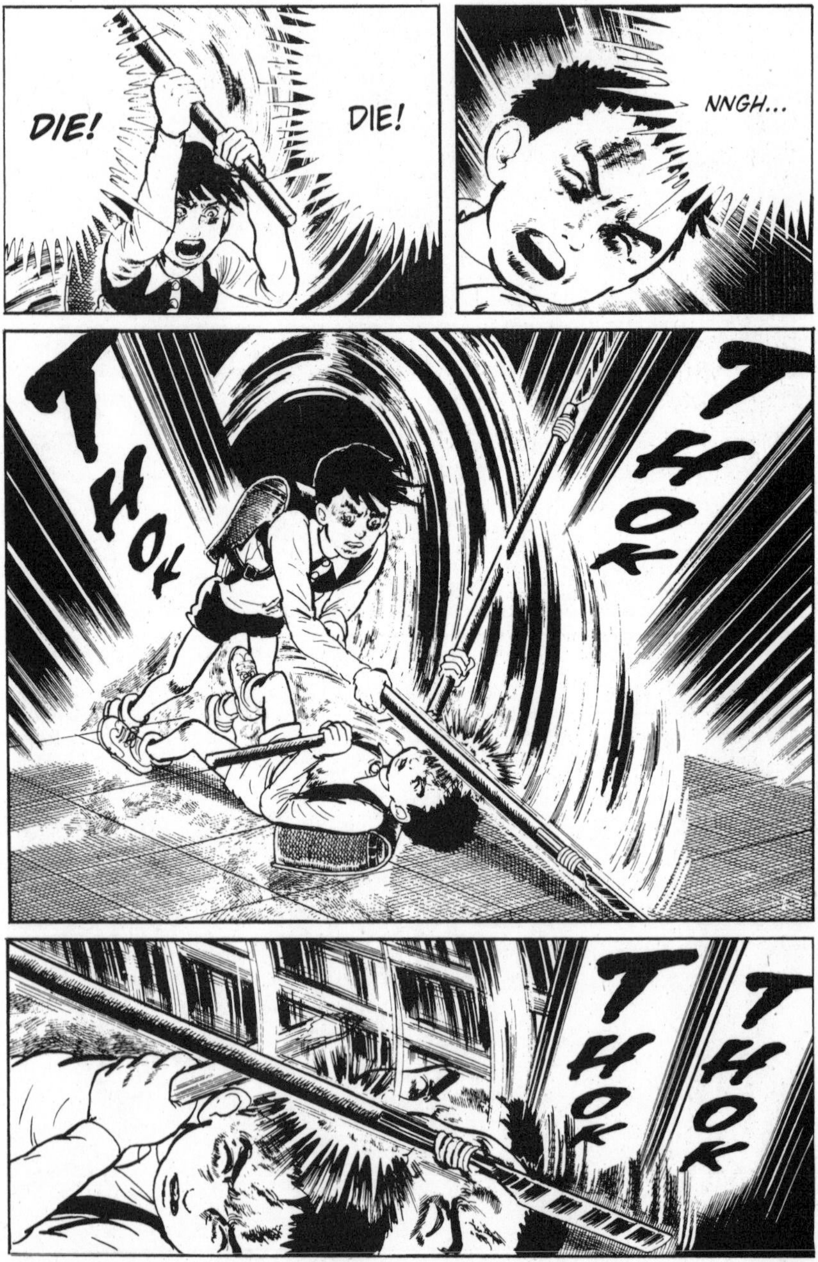

NNGH...
DIE!
DIE!
THOK
THOK
THOK
THOK

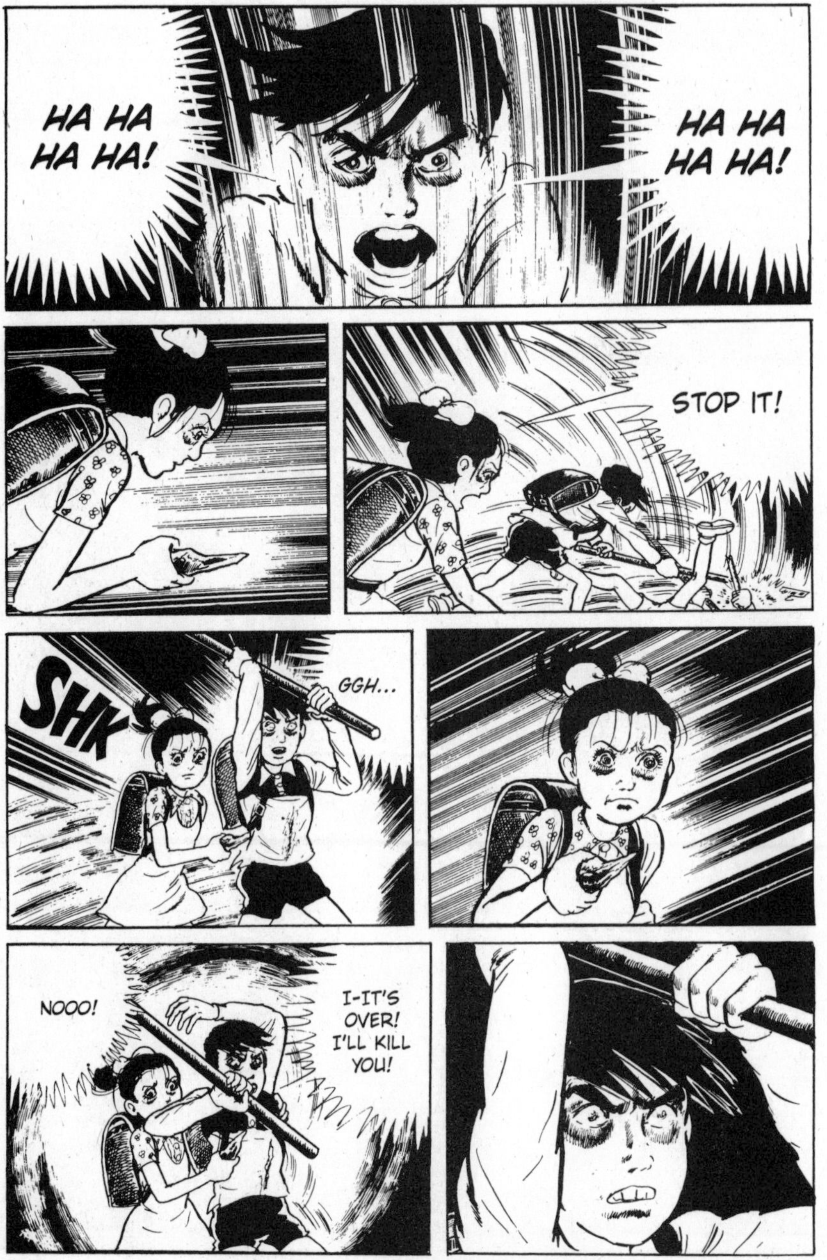
HA HA HA HA!
HA HA HA HA!
STOP IT!
GGH...
SHK
I-IT'S OVER! I'LL KILL YOU!
NOOO!

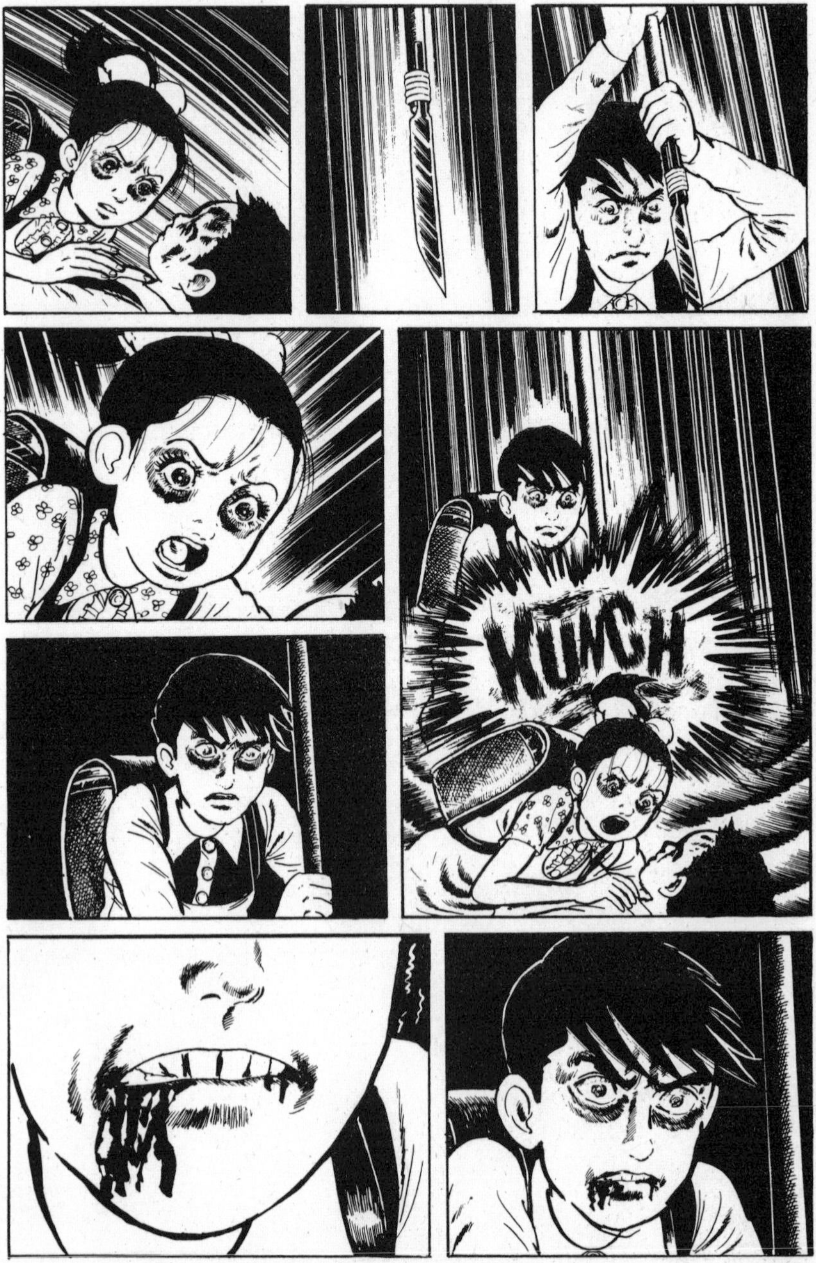
KUNCH

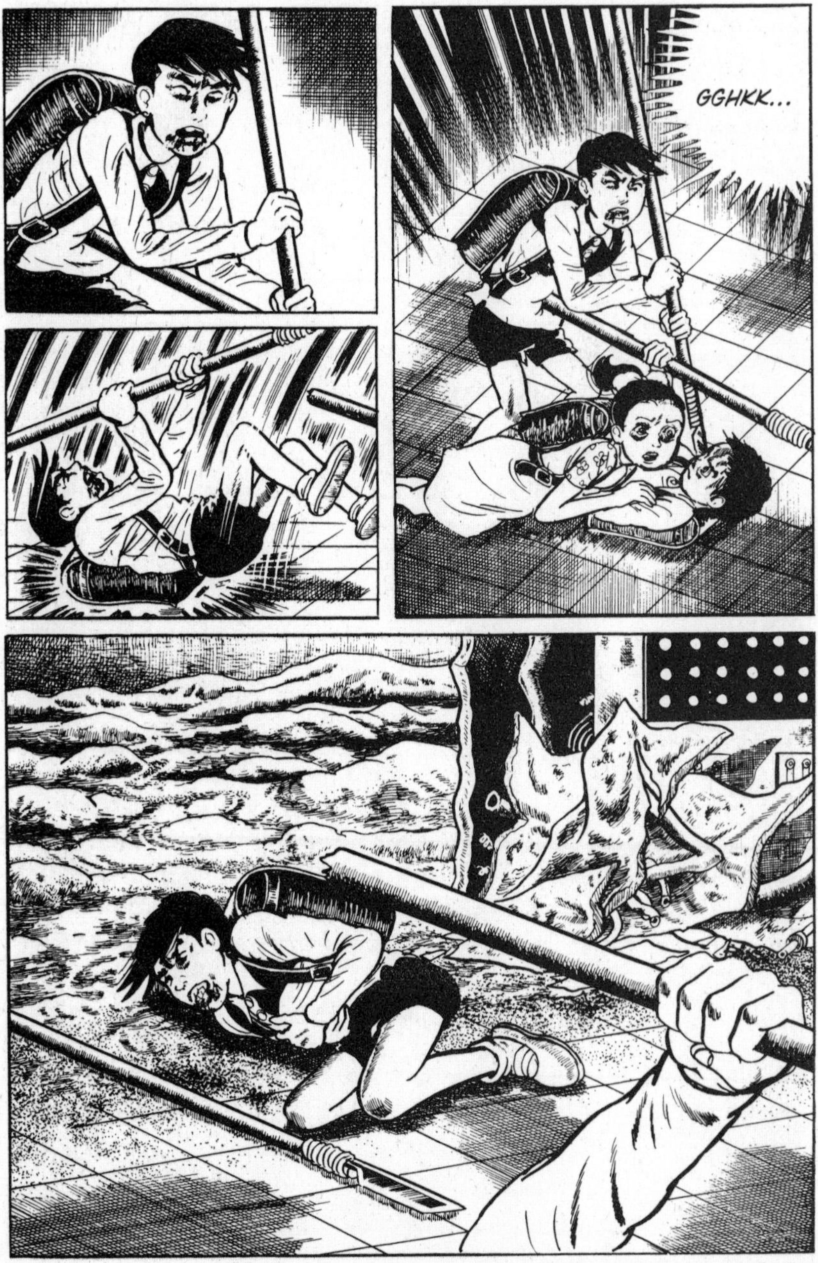
GGHKK...

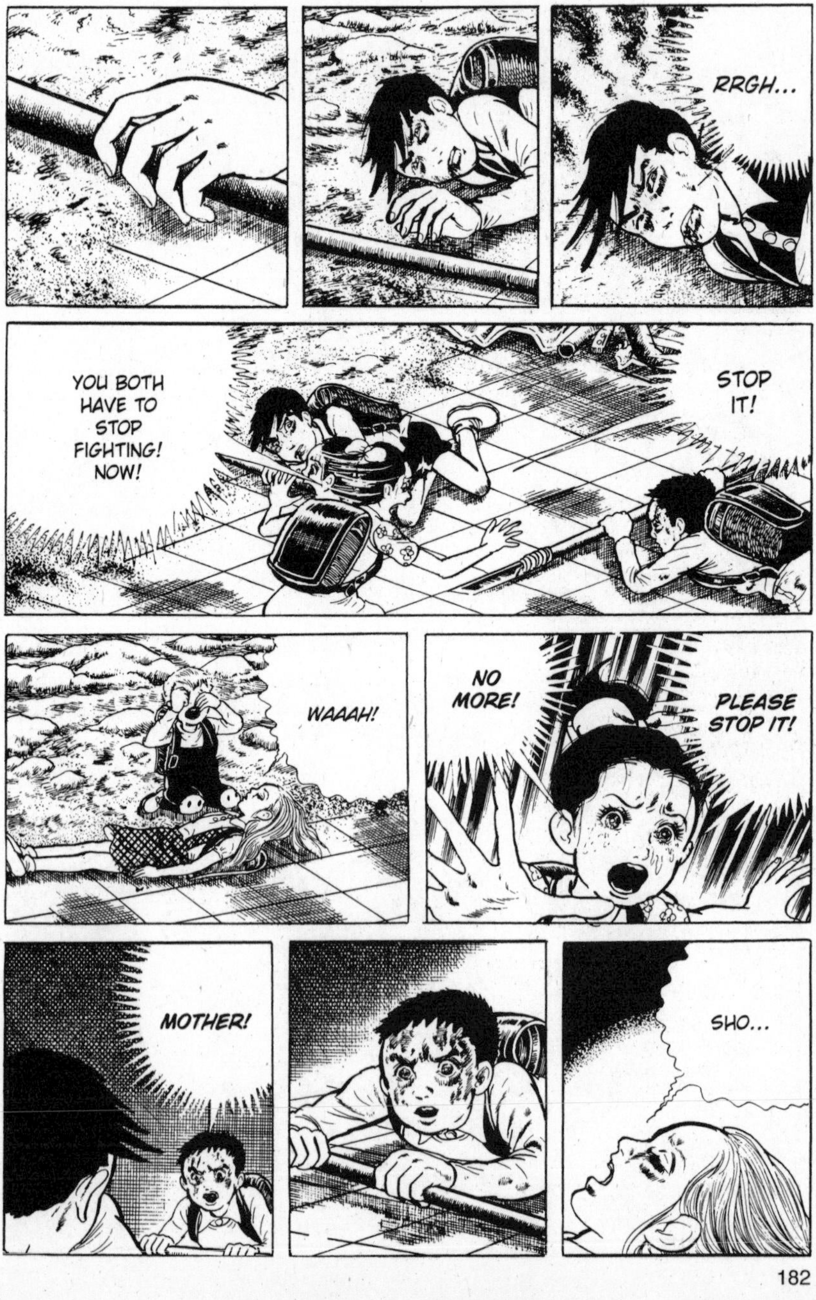
RRGH...
STOP IT!
YOU BOTH HAVE TO STOP FIGHTING! NOW!
PLEASE STOP IT!
NO MORE!
WAAAH!
SHO...
MOTHER!

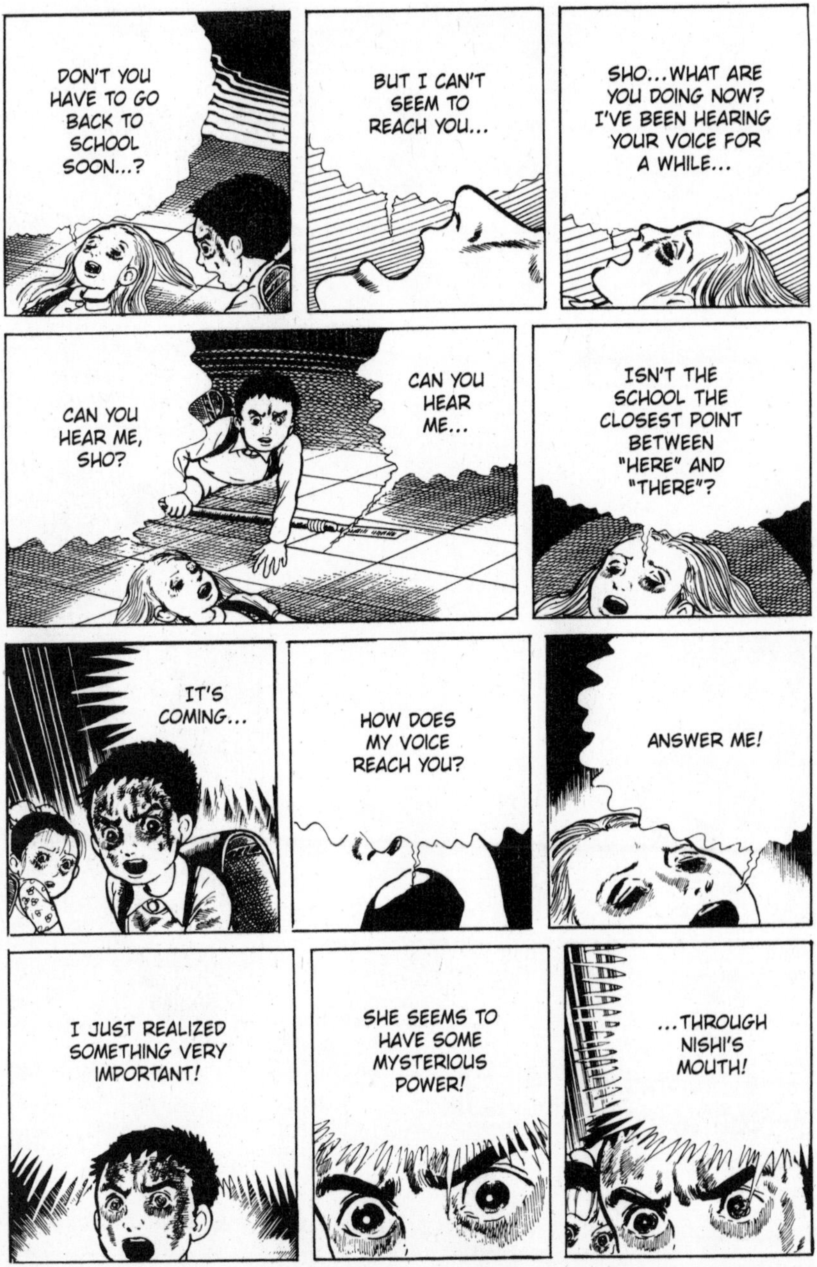
SHO...WHAT ARE YOU DOING NOW? I'VE BEEN HEARING YOUR VOICE FOR A WHILE...
BUT I CAN'T SEEM TO REACH YOU...
DON'T YOU HAVE TO GO BACK TO SCHOOL SOON...?
ISN'T THE SCHOOL THE CLOSEST POINT BETWEEN "HERE" AND "THERE"?
CAN YOU HEAR ME...
CAN YOU HEAR ME, SHO?
ANSWER ME!
HOW DOES MY VOICE REACH YOU?
IT'S COMING...
...THROUGH NISHI'S MOUTH!
SHE SEEMS TO HAVE SOME MYSTERIOUS POWER!
I JUST REALIZED SOMETHING VERY IMPORTANT!

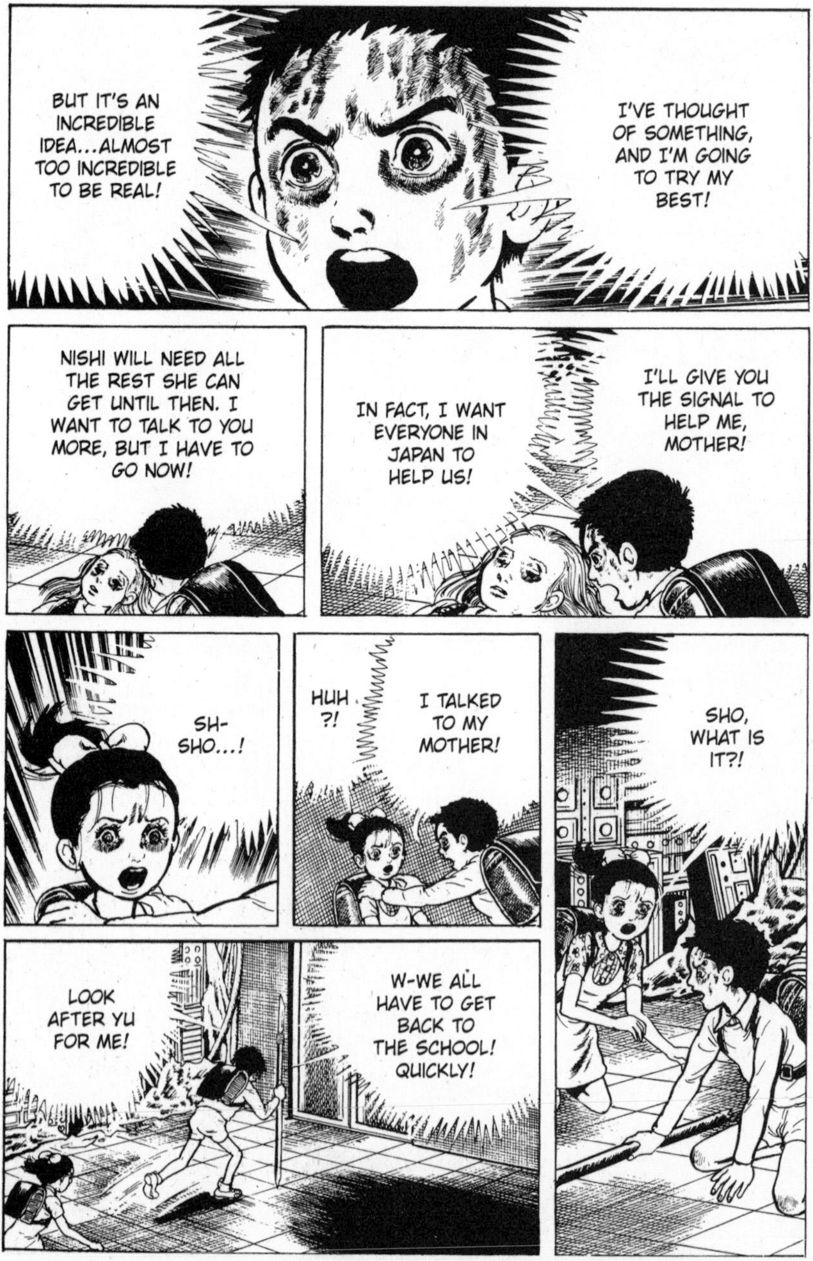
I'VE THOUGHT OF SOMETHING, AND I'M GOING TO TRY MY BEST!
BUT IT'S AN INCREDIBLE IDEA...ALMOST TOO INCREDIBLE TO BE REAL!
I'LL GIVE YOU THE SIGNAL TO HELP ME, MOTHER!
IN FACT, I WANT EVERYONE IN JAPAN TO HELP US!
NISHI WILL NEED ALL THE REST SHE CAN GET UNTIL THEN. I WANT TO TALK TO YOU MORE, BUT I HAVE TO GO NOW!
SHO, WHAT IS IT?!
I TALKED TO MY MOTHER!
HUH?!
SH-SHO...!
W-WE ALL HAVE TO GET BACK TO THE SCHOOL! QUICKLY!
LOOK AFTER YU FOR ME!

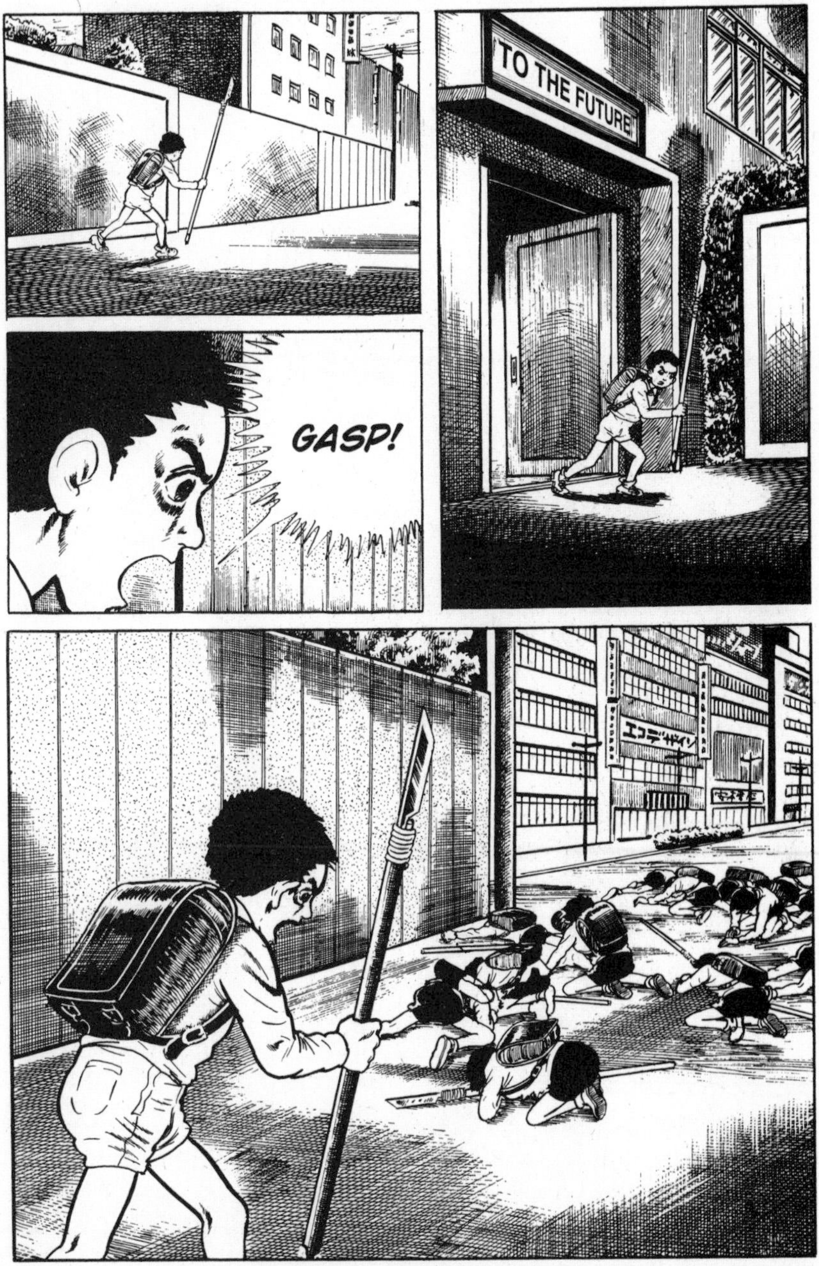
TO THE FUTURE
GASP!
エコデザイン

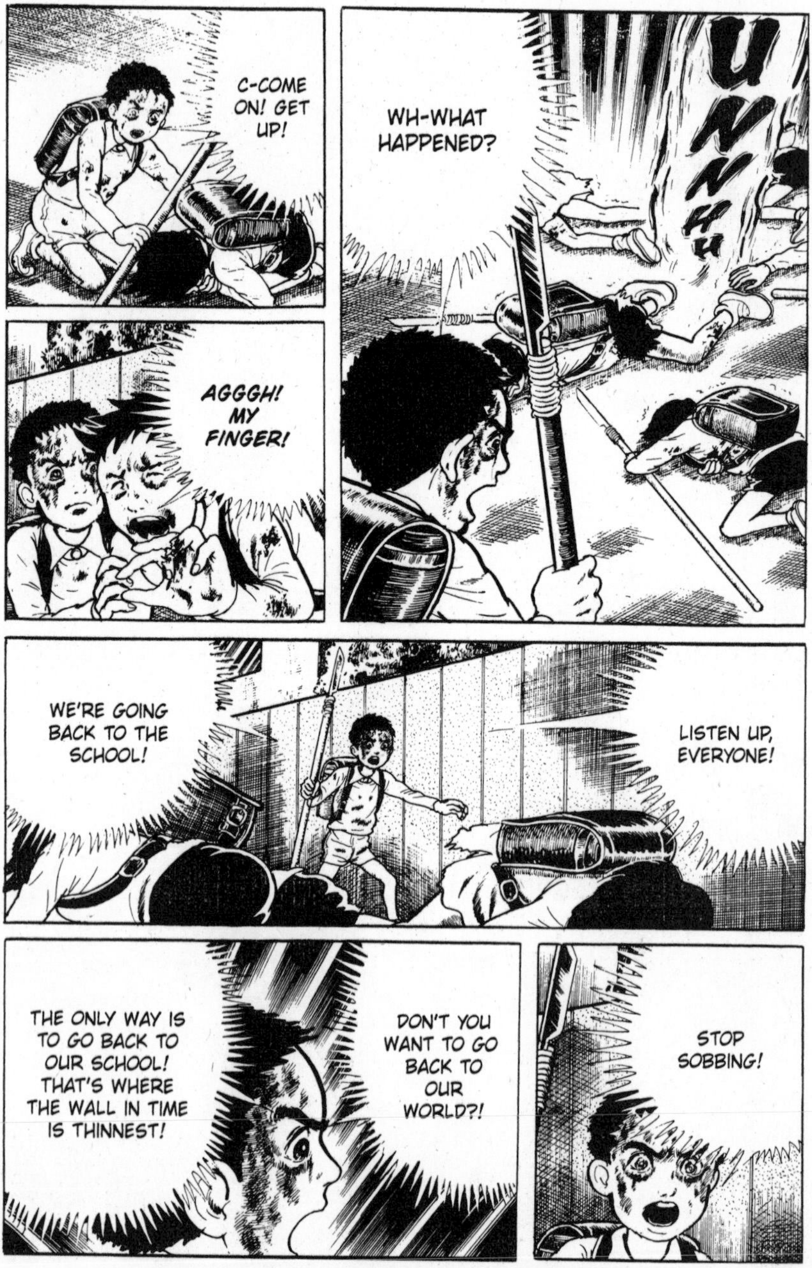
UNNHH
WH-WHAT HAPPENED?
C-COME ON! GET UP!
AGGGH! MY FINGER!
LISTEN UP, EVERYONE!
WE'RE GOING BACK TO THE SCHOOL!
STOP SOBBING!
DON'T YOU WANT TO GO BACK TO OUR WORLD?!
THE ONLY WAY IS TO GO BACK TO OUR SCHOOL! THAT'S WHERE THE WALL IN TIME IS THINNEST!

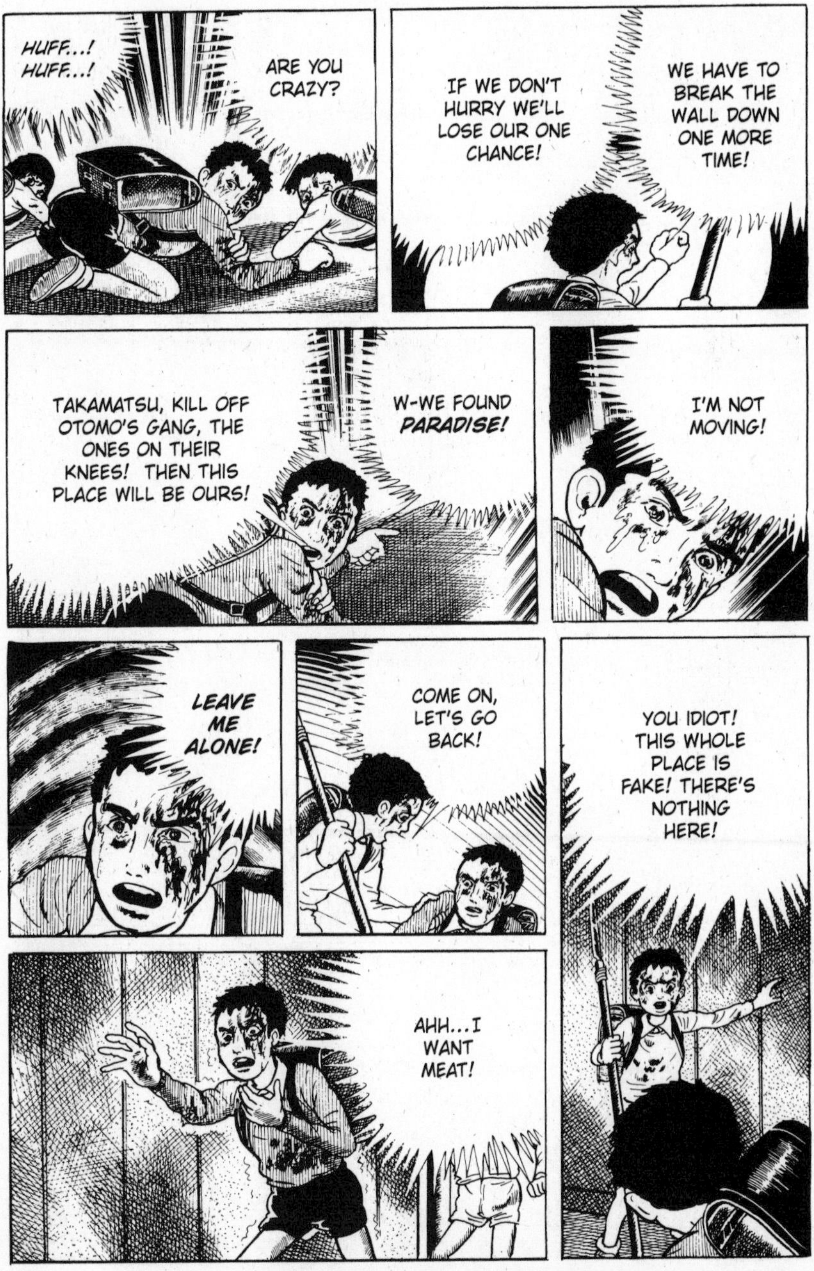
WE HAVE TO BREAK THE WALL DOWN ONE MORE TIME!
IF WE DON'T HURRY WE'LL LOSE OUR ONE CHANCE!
ARE YOU CRAZY?
HUFF...! HUFF...!
I'M NOT MOVING!
W-WE FOUND *PARADISE!*
TAKAMATSU, KILL OFF OTOMO'S GANG, THE ONES ON THEIR KNEES! THEN THIS PLACE WILL BE OURS!
YOU IDIOT! THIS WHOLE PLACE IS FAKE! THERE'S NOTHING HERE!
COME ON, LET'S GO BACK!
LEAVE ME ALONE!
AHH...I WANT MEAT!

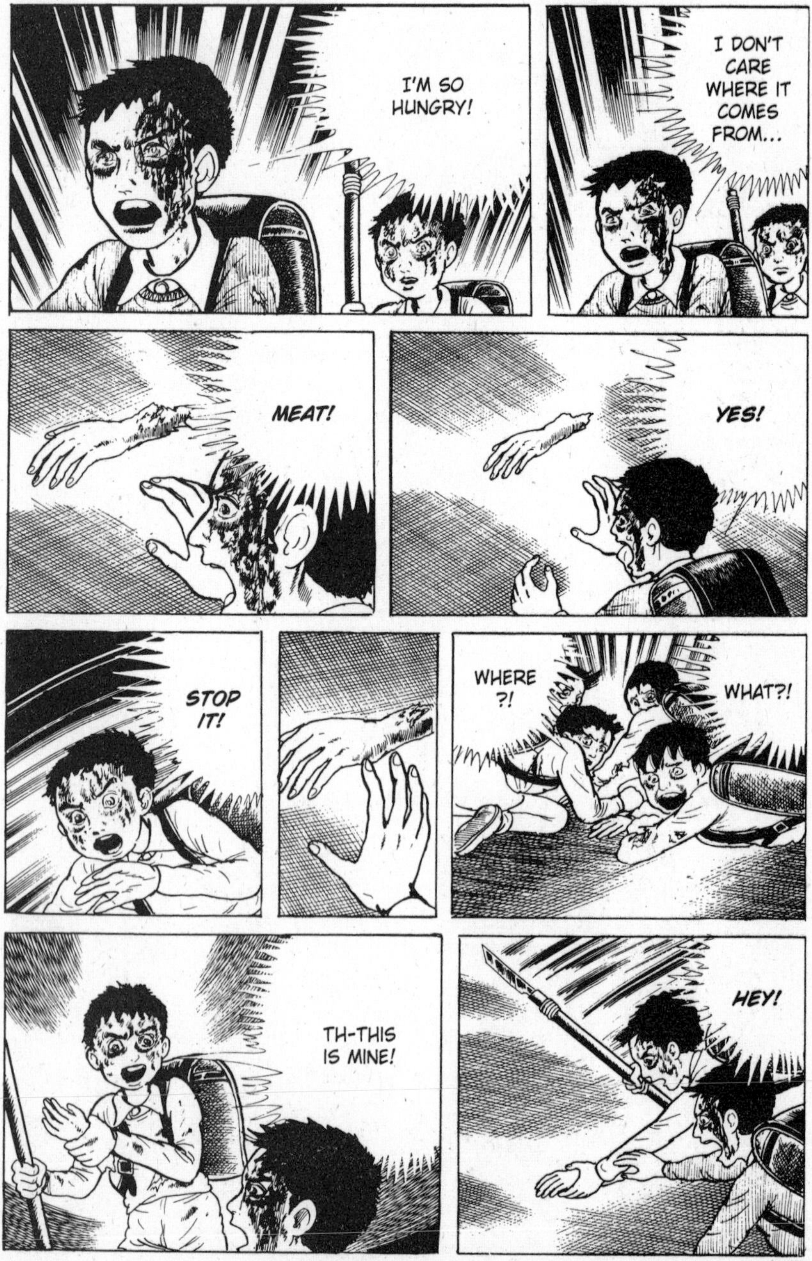
I DON'T CARE WHERE IT COMES FROM...
I'M SO HUNGRY!
YES!
MEAT!
WHAT?!
WHERE ?!
STOP IT!
HEY!
TH-THIS IS MINE!

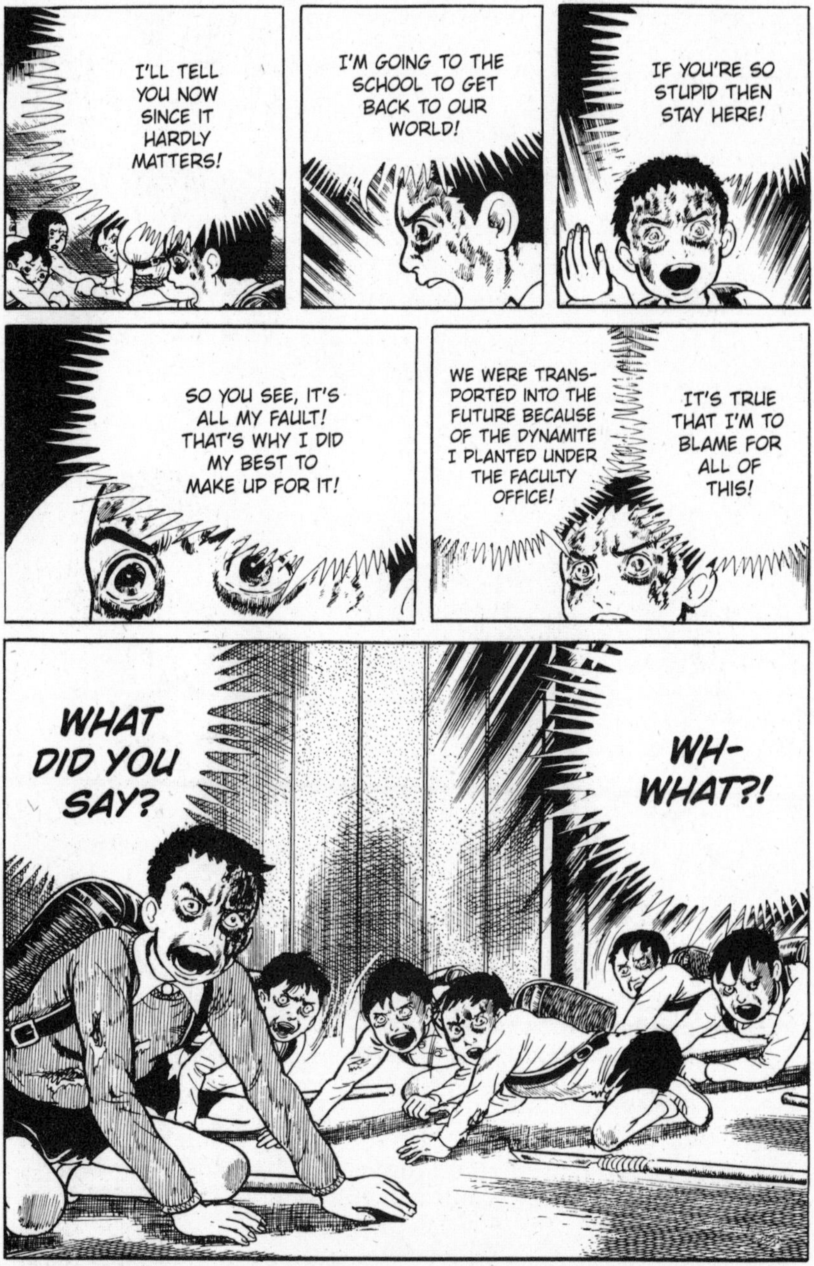
IF YOU'RE SO STUPID THEN STAY HERE!
I'M GOING TO THE SCHOOL TO GET BACK TO OUR WORLD!
I'LL TELL YOU NOW SINCE IT HARDLY MATTERS!
IT'S TRUE THAT I'M TO BLAME FOR ALL OF THIS!
WE WERE TRANSPORTED INTO THE FUTURE BECAUSE OF THE DYNAMITE I PLANTED UNDER THE FACULTY OFFICE!
SO YOU SEE, IT'S ALL MY FAULT! THAT'S WHY I DID MY BEST TO MAKE UP FOR IT!
WH-WHAT?!
WHAT DID YOU SAY?

TO BE CONTINUED...

IN THE NEXT VOLUME...

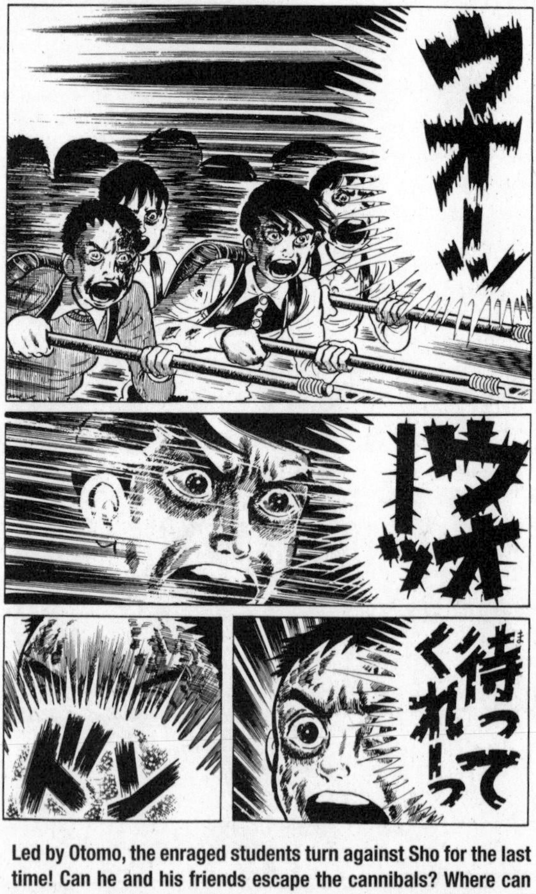

ウオーッ
ウオーッ
待ってくれーっ
ドン

Led by Otomo, the enraged students turn against Sho for the last time! Can he and his friends escape the cannibals? Where can they go...and will any of them survive? Find out in the shocking final volume of *The Drifting Classroom*!

AVAILABLE APRIL 2008!

FINAL VOLUME!!!